'*The New Europeans* seems likely to remain a classic. . . . Ask almost any question about present-day Europe and *The New Europeans* will give you a clear stimulating answer in a highly readable style' – *Wall Street Journal*

'*The New Europeans* reflects with a breadth and completeness it is almost impossible to fault the mood, trends and problems common to western Europe today. A thoroughly European book in every way' – *Times Literary Supplement*

'An excellent guidebook' – *New Statesman*

'Admirable. We do need books like *The New Europeans* badly' – *The Times*

Anthony Sampson, the son of a scientist, was born in 1926. He was a scholar at Westminster school, served in the navy, took a degree at Oxford, and went to South Africa to become editor of *Drum*. He returned to England four years later, worked on the *Observer*, wrote three books about the racial situation in Africa, and in 1962 published his bestselling *Anatomy of Britain*.

Anthony Sampson

The New Europeans

A guide to the workings, institutions and
character of contemporary Western Europe

Panther

A Panther Book

First published in Great Britain by Hodder &
Stoughton Limited 1962. Revised edition
published 1968.

Panther edition with new material published 1971
Copyright © Anthony Sampson 1968, 1971.

for Sally

*Printed in Great Britain by Cox & Wyman Ltd.,
London, Reading and Fakenham and published
by Panther Books,
3 Upper James Street, London, W.1.*

Contents

DIAGRAMS

DESIGNED BY MICHAEL MCGUINNESS

Acknowledgements

My indebtedness is too great to be listed in detail. I have taken advantage of hundreds of people in different parts of Europe who allowed their brains to be picked, who checked drafts and proofs and offered advice. But I must mention with special gratitude the people who saw me through the painful and complicated putting-together of the book; my secretary, Mrs. Bridget Cash, for her patient help and constant encouragement; Virginia Makins, for her inspiration in the original project and her expert assistance in individual sections (particularly on the Ecole Polytechnique); my research assistant, Mrs. Mollie Philipps, for her invaluable fact-finding under the most trying conditions; Dr. Willy Guttman, for his scholarly and perceptive proof-reading; Liz Trow-Smith of Chatham House, for help with checking and research; Robert Urwin for his thorough and rapid indexing and his miraculous handling of my chaotic copy; Michael McGuinness for his imaginative design of the diagrams; and as always my friend Robin Denniston who, even more than in my earlier books, has seen the project through every stage with consistent encouragement and vision, in a collaboration which has been enriching and indispensable. To my wife, who has shared the adventures of the book through all its ups and downs, its travels and blockages, who has translated, researched, read and reread, my debt is incalculable.

For any mistakes, I can only blame myself. I am aware that in covering such a large field so rapidly some errors will have crept in, in spite of precautions. I will be most grateful for any corrections from readers (however angry) which will be rectified in later printings.

A.S.

Thanks are due to the Trustees of the Estate of the late Lord Keynes and Macmillan and Co. Ltd. for permission to quote from *The Economic Consequences of the Peace* by John Maynard Keynes.

Introduction to the Panther edition

This book records the institutions, forces and some of the personalities of the western European scene as they looked at one point in time, late in 1968. Many of those structures have changed very little in the following two years: but the political balances have altered in such a way as to allow some major opportunities in the movement for European unity. In France, General de Gaulle has died. In Germany, for the first time since the war, a Social Democratic government has come to power with Willy Brandt as Chancellor: a fact which, coming twenty-five years after Hitler, is little short of a miracle. In Italy, the prolonged period of political chaos has raised new doubts about the country's stability. In Britain, a Conservative government has come to power with a Prime Minister inclined more strongly than his predecessors to take Britain into Europe. The pattern of European politics has thus shown an odd reversal: with Social Democrats in power in Germany, it is no longer possible for Britain to portray the common market as a solidly right-winged block; while Britain herself has turned to the right. And in the meantime the mounting troubles in the United States, both in Vietnam and within her frontiers, is leading to a very different balance of relationships across the Atlantic.

In this new context, the common market has begun again to move ahead. Already before his departure from the presidency, De Gaulle had come to realize reluctantly that France's progress was dependent on that of the common market, and that he could not indefinitely frustrate the Commission in Brussels. The students' revolt and the general strike of 1968, with the subsequent inflation, left the French much less confident of their ability to go it alone. Moreover, the economic supremacy of Germany was leading towards a political supremacy; Germany could not indefinitely remain, as Franz-Josef Strauss put it, 'an economic giant, and a political pigmy'; and the French, when they become worried about Germany, are always inclined to look towards Britain as a counter-weight. These tendencies became far stronger with the retirement of the General. President Pompidou, though he had no great love for Britain, was surrounded by men (like Giscard d'Estaing and Schumann) who were very sensitive to the pressures and arguments of European big businessmen, who believed that the entry of Britain to the common market was essential to its prosperity and stability. Most people expected that the disappearance of De Gaulle would open the way to the expansion of the common market, but the speed with which Pompidou's government relaxed their opposition was remarkable. The French technocrats and senior civil servants, who had been so loyal to Gaullist policies, began talking in a quite different and more international language. The signals were clear that Paris would welcome the enlargement provided that the structure of the common market, and particularly the sacred agricultural agreement, could remain intact.

In the meantime in Brussels a new Commission of nine men was installed in July 1970, in place of the previous fourteen, younger, more radical, and distinctly more anglophile. The new President, Franco Malfatti, is a left-wing Christian Democrat from Italy of only 43; an ambitious intellectual who, while speaking no English and little French, is an ardent internationalist, and sees a wider community as the means to much greater stability, particularly in Italy. Sicco Mansholt, the veteran Dutch farmer politician, remained in charge of the agricultural policy, increasingly determined both to get Britain in and to cut down the escalating prices of European farm products: if possible, to use the first as a means to the second – a plan which soon aroused the further suspicions of the French. From Germany there came the outspoken young sociologist, Ralf Dahrendorf, a liberal crusader who had been educated at the London School of Economics, and married an English wife. And another new member from Italy was the veteran Federalist Altiero Spinelli, a man with a heroic anti-fascist record who had been dedicated from the early days to a wider community.

Amidst this changed scenery, Britain for the third time moved towards Europe, and opened negotiations, just after the change of government in July 1970. But the British public's attitude to Europe in Britain had become increasingly hostile, so that the subject was carefully avoided by both major parties during the election: a dangerous evasion. The relations between Britain and Europe (and France in particular) have, over the last twenty-five years, come to resemble an immensely long-drawn-out love affair; whenever one side appears keen on matrimony the other side becomes frightened. The contrariness of the relationship has many times come to a head: Churchill pressed for a united Europe after the war, and then when Europe began to unite, backed out of it: after encouraging France and Germany to come together with the European army, the British took fright at the prospect. When Britain was relatively rich and prosperous, the continentals all wanted her in, but Britain was determined to go it alone. When Britain, in the late fifties, began to fall back economically she became much more interested in coming into the common market, but the Europeans then began to lose interest. By the late sixties, when the continentals were becoming again more affectionate towards Britain, the British again became worried about the continent. The swings of the relationship were made more poignant by the traditional emotional tensions between London and Paris and the mutual distrust which had become built in to the two national characters over the previous eight centuries. A psychologist, inspecting the amorous tangle between Britain and the common market, might suspect that the emotion was more connected with fantasy than with a real desire to live together.

But above the level of these emotional waverings, the arguments for Britain entering the common market continued to press on the people in power. It is true that some British pro-marketeers had swung against it, either because the price would be too high, or because the common market itself was in a mess, or because they were now convinced that Britain could survive on her own, like Sweden or Japan; such diverse intellectuals as Enoch Powell, Eric Heffer (the left-wing Labour M.P.) and Samuel Brittan (the Economics Editor of *The Financial Times*) had publicly recanted their faith. But from those at the top of the power structure, in big business, in politics, in the civil service or in technology, the pressure towards Europe was as strong as ever: for so many of the problems they confronted – in defence, industrial technology, international companies, or pollution control – seemed only to be soluble within a European context. The fact that the Conservatives were once again trying to get into Europe, eight years after the first painful fiasco, underlined the apparent inevitability of the pressures, and the lack of any viable alternative foreign policy.

The Conservatives were back with the same Foreign Secretary as in 1962 and with the then Minister for Europe now as Prime Minister. But the impression of *déjà vu* was very misleading, for the world context of the negotiation was now much changed. Most important of all, it was happening without any blessing from Washington, and even with some quiet imprecations. In the early sixties the American enthusiasm for the common market and its extension to Britain seemed unbounded: American foundations and companies poured money into boosting the European Movement; and President Kennedy's 'grand design' implied that the fates of the two continents were bound up together, and that America could only profit, both economically and diplomatically, from a stronger united Europe. But by the end of the sixties the American response to any further unification of Europe was a resounding silence. Partly, of course, this was a result of the extreme preoccupation with Vietnam and the internal American revolt: there were altogether too many other things to worry about. But also, murmuring just above the silence, there were growing worries from American businessmen about the industrial competition from a united Europe, with West Germany in the middle of it. And meanwhile American politicians were increasingly concerned about the cost in men and material of defending Europe and of maintaining her huge stake in NATO. The alliance of two decades was becoming much more fragile in the face of American commitments elsewhere, and the European allies showed no sign of wanting to take over the American burden.

This withdrawal of American political interest in Europe made Britain's application a more far-reaching one: for it could no longer be presented as having no effect on Anglo-American relations. In 1962 it was possible for Macmillan at least to pretend that his Polaris agreement with Kennedy would not affect his relationships with De Gaulle. In 1970, the choice between a European defence commitment and an Anglo-American one was a much more definite one. The new Prime Minister, Ted Heath, had already shown, in his Godkin lectures in 1967, his interest in the possibilites of a European nuclear force, pooling British and French resources; and he had none of the pro-American background – no American mother, no close American relationships, no wartime friendships – that had been characteristics of his predecessors. The choice of a European commitment in economic and defence terms would not be unwelcome to Mr. Heath; but for the British people it was a more extreme choice than they had faced in the previous attempts.

While America has become less interested in Europe, America has also clearly lost much of its fascination and prestige to Europeans as a model for the new shape of their continent. The talk of 'a United States of Europe' which came from Jean Monnet and the Federalists in the fifties and later, was based on a profound admiration for the American system, and a confidence that only large units could have a real influence in the world of the future. Some of those assumptions now seem more questionable in the light of the American troubles. Not only the Vietnam war and the Negro's place inside America, but the whole materialist basis of American prosperity has been challenged: and the continuing anger of the American student generation calls fiercely in question the values and assumptions of corporate business. The wave of enthusiasm for the American way of life in the fifties and early sixties, which deeply affected European Socialists and Conservatives, has now broken.

Europeans, particularly young Europeans, look towards American prosperity with increasing scepticism. Yet at the same time the machinery of the common market as it exists, and the whole nexus of interests concerned with uniting Europe – the bankers, international managers, technologists – are still concerning themselves with just those continental-sized structures and those commercial ambitions which have caused such tension and eruptions across the Atlantic. It is odd to move from a European conference, discussing the need for European companies, for management training, for bridging the technological gap, the managerial gap, the education gap, for closer co-operation between industry, government and universities: to move from these discussions to America itself, where it is just these kind of interlocking commercial-government structures; and their accompanying value-systems which have exasperated and provoked the American students. It has often been the weakness of Europeans to follow American projects ten or twenty years later, without perceiving the difficulties that these projects have caused in the meantime; to embrace mass motoring, mass air travel, mass advertising, mass mutual funds, without foreseeing and planning for their effects and abuses (an important exception is television, where the Europeans *have* avoided the major excesses of the American system, though they have not been able to do without some of the worst American serials). A kind of caricature of the European failing, of not benefiting from American mistakes, is to be found in the phenomenon of Bernard Cornfeld of the Investors' Overseas Service, whose operation at its prime is described in Chapter 9. Cornfeld's mutual funds romped ahead, unfettered by the restrictions of the American stock exchanges; properly controlled, his mobilizing of savings into investments could have made a useful contribution; but Cornfeld was given enough rope to hang himself, which he nearly did; and the near-collapse of the I.O.S. in 1970 contributed to the wave of pessimism that swept through the stock exchanges of western Europe.

Many of the ambitions of the common market were based on the American system as it appeared ten or twenty years ago; the elements of socialism and *dirigisme* which were quite strong in the foundation of the community were subsequently much weakened by the blocks on the political progress, and by the need to compete with the great invasion of American industry. The European Movement has become increasingly a big businessman's movement, preoccupied with reorganizing European industry to hold its own against the Americans, and this commercial interest has found a kind of pseudo-ideology in the preachings of Jean-Jacques Servan-Schreiber, the new secretary of the French Radical Party who has been fiercely challenging the Pompidou government, from a very European platform. The weakness of the propounders of 'the American Challenge', in the school of

Servan-Schreiber, is that, despite their disclaimers, they still see the challenge essentially in American terms and do not really analyse the faults inside the American system (it is characteristic of Servan-Schreiber that he should have assumed in 1968 that the Vietnam war was a very temporary aberration which was about to be concluded). In France, the stubborn, narrow nationalism of De Gaulle had led many people to believe that the internationalism of his critics, like Servan-Schreiber, was necessarily liberal and enlightened. But internationalism, too, can be narrow: and after the stagnation of the last decade, and the waning idealism within its bureaucracy, some sectors of the common market have become little more than businessmen's lobbies. The potential Europe of the Left, of the Socialist Parties or of the trades unions, is incoherent and disorganized in the face of the bankers and businessmen. It is not surprising that among the current student generation on the continent, the idea of the common market now generates very little excitement; as a lecturer over the past two years at the new French university at Vincennes, I have noticed how little the common market is discussed, or even attacked by the new students; for them it is little more than a trading organization, an economic background which is cut off from their own political ideals, if not actually antagonistic to them; their most passionate interests – in the Third World, in 'participation' and workers' control, in the opening to the East – are not the interests of the market, and the community has done little to try to attract them.

In this rather melancholy context, Britain's new attempt to enter Europe raises again every question about the community's character: and some are questions that Britain could help to answer. What kind of Europe? becomes a more urgent and difficult question as the economic motives become more questionable, and the boom years leave their detritus: over-crowding, under-housing, pollution and the ruining of the countryside are all pressing the Europeans to think more clearly about the kind of lives they wish to be leading; and the shortage of space makes the need for decisions and planning much more evident than in the United States. The absurdity of measuring standards of living by purely economic yardsticks soon becomes apparent in a continent where the natural resources of space, scenery and peace are so precious and so rare, and where each country has a different idea of what is most valuable. To compare the British standard of living with the continental is specially difficult. On the one hand Britain's poor economic growth has restricted the kind of developments which can bring fulfilment or reduction of suffering – universities, schools, hospitals, holidays. On the other hand the average Briton still enjoys many advantages over his continental equivalent: his house (for instance) is still likely to be bigger and better equipped, with a bathroom, a garden and his own front door. The conservatism and bloody-mindedness, which shows itself in the unwillingness of British workers to adapt themselves, shows its other side in the insistent privacy and easy-goingness of their home lives. The industrial strikes which have crippled sections of industry over the last two years have helped to diminish still further Britain's economic prospects; but they seem to be a symptom, not so much of a grasping desire for more money, as of a general dis-illusionment with work and production: an attitude which could be described either as sophisticated, or decadent. In terms of useful or enjoyable leisure, the unenthusiasm of British workers is self-defeating, since the British now have to work longer hours and have shorter holidays than other Europeans; but the British workers' attitude may prove less disruptive and politically dangerous than those of French or Italian workers, who submit for most of the time to stricter discipline, but whose anger can erupt very suddenly from the shop floor and spread through a whole industry overnight.

The British contrast continues into the new generation where, in spite of the constant talk of back-lash and reaction, there is less sign of extreme discontent than in most parts of the continent. The comparative quiet in British universities is partly the consequence of the sheer lack of pressure in the education system, and the continuity of the privileged status of students. But it is also certainly linked with the greater tradition of tolerance and the greater flexibility of the British institutions. The troubles of 1968, which rushed so quickly from one continental university to the next, left Britain almost as uninfected or bored as the troubles of 1848.

The stock caricatures of the phlegmatic British and the excitable continentals still, in fact, have some relevance, and the blending of the two is an important part of the

justification of Britain's entry into the common market. This
assumes that the common market must and will change and
develop with Britain inside it; and with a new mood in Brussels, Paris and Bonn, the prospects for political development are better than at any time since its foundation. The
Conservative Party is in many respects more naturally suited
to negotiate with the continental powers, since it accepts
more readily and credibly the benefits of a large capitalist
market: while at the same time the Labour Party in opposition has a great opportunity to mobilize itself in a continental framework (as it signally failed to do in 1966), to
forge stronger links with the other Labour parties and above
all to help build up a European trades union system, to
counter-balance the international corporations. The 1970
elections showed how insular and largely irrelevant the
language of British party politics has become: national elections had become almost as dull and narrow as local elections, concerned above all with accountancy questions.
Neither party dared raise the real international issues for
fear of revealing their own internal divisions, or for fear of
showing how little control Britain had over events: no politicians wished to admit that most crucial decisions lay right
beyond the national government's control; in committee-
rooms somewhere between Washington, Brussels and
Moscow. But the fraud cannot be kept up indefinitely: the
very fact that two weeks after the general election, in which
the common market question was so well hushed-up, Britain
opened negotiations with the common market showed how
petty the election arguments had been.

And whether or not Britain succeeds in entering the
common market, the context and framework for the decisions which most affect Britain will increasingly be on the
continental scale, whether she likes it or not. The expansion
of international companies, the interdependence of currencies and the scale of technology enforces that dependence;
only by making a political entry into the larger community
can Britain be sure of having a proper part in the decisions.
The gross imbalance in the common market between the
powerful interests of big industries and banks and the feeble
uncoordinated interest of trades unions and Socialists is an
imbalance that Britain can rectify more effectively than any
other country; but this rectification can only be ac-

complished inside the community's structure. The community is very far from perfect, but it is still the only community we have got.

December 1970

Preface

My first experience of the mainland of Europe was in Germany in the icy winter of 1946. For the Germans that was the *schlechte Zeiten*, the terrible times, worse for many of them than the war itself. I was in the British Navy at Cuxhaven, at the mouth of the Elbe: the harbour and the whole Baltic Sea was frozen for three months. For Germans there was no fuel, little work, little food; but their obsessive craving was for cigarettes. The country was governed by a cigarette economy, so that anything could be bought for packets of fags – cameras, food, binoculars, girls; girls walked along the sea-front in high white socks, waiting to be picked up, and afterwards went back to their husbands to deliver the cigarettes. When we drove into Hamburg it seemed not a city but a group of camps among the ruins; the rubble was flat, there was no shape. People emerged from the rubble and hung on to the outside of trams and trains. The hub of the city, the centre of all patronage, was the Atlantic Hotel, the British officers' headquarters: inside the central heating was too hot, *The Times* was in the foyer, and the long bar was full of drunk officers. The British and Germans seemed equally corrupted by the chaos. The British occupation added to the confusion, split between two opposite policies – blowing up some things while patching up others. Only a few objects, like Leicas or Volkswagens, mysteriously emerged from the ruins.

The rest of the continent was hardly more hopeful: it seemed finally to have torn itself apart, ruined and exhausted. Italy was caught between an ugly right wing and a massive communist party, and right until 1950 it seemed quite likely to go over to the communist bloc. France was striking, rioting and tottering from government to government. Everywhere the Americans were dominant – welcomed, resented, envied or hated, a rich race apart. They, on their side, seemed to despair of Europe. 'How depraved and macabre the whole continent at the end of the second war,' wrote one of the most pessimistic of them, Edmund Wilson: 'how far gone in decomposition seem so many things one sees there today! How futile to try to save Europe, who does nothing to save herself!'

Then the 'miracles' overturned everyone's picture of Europeans, and seemed to make anything possible. It was not simply that they recovered from the war; they recovered from the pre-war. The stagnation and gloom of the twenties and the thirties which had seemed to be the permanent condition now looked like a mere aberration from the earlier pattern of *La Belle Epoque* – a thirty-year civil war that was now finally over.

The German miracle was astonishing enough, but everyone knew that the Germans could work hard. The Italian miracle was much more amazing, for it seemed to show a revolution in national character. Tourists had been accustomed to the Italians as fat singers and incompetent soldiers – an image encouraged by the Italians themselves. But suddenly after 1950 the Italian streets filled up with pop-popping Vespas, Lambrettas and three-wheeled trucks; then the Vespas gave way to Fiat 500s, then to 600s and 850s. Lean, puritan tycoons emerged instead of joke admirals; Renaissance cities like Parma or Bologna, known for ham, cheese or spaghetti, sprouted huge new industries and began exporting refrigerators or washbasins all over Europe.

Driving through Europe in the course of writing this book, twenty years after my first glimpse of the continent, I found the transformation still scarcely believable. I was travelling with my wife and baby daughter, staying in flats in suburbs, surrounded by sounds of cars and lawnmowers; the cosy society seemed to have no link with the wildness of the early post-war period. In Hamburg white villas and rich shopping centres had sprung out of the rubble; the Atlantic Hotel was the centre for cosmopolitan big business. All over western Europe a shiny and uniform superstructure had grown up, of supermarkets, skyscrapers, television towers, motorways. It was the kind of fantasy that post-war children had dreamt of, or glimpsed in Hollywood films. Yet the dream, having come true, had lost its magic; the things turned out to be no more than things, bringing their own problems – motorways brought traffic jams, travel brought tourism, suburbs brought boredom.

Talking to the politicians, tycoons or trade unionists, I found everyone seemed preoccupied by material growth. The hopes of European integration, dashed on the political rocks, now depended on industry; the Brussels Eurocrats enthusiastically discussed industrial mergers; international corporations had come to be regarded as the benefactors of the new European unity, and bankers were its prophets. Left-wing newspapers devoted themselves to discussing money, cars or holidays. It all seemed out of character with the old continent, like a wild bachelor who had settled down to a domesticated middle-age; but there did not seem much sign of a breakdown. The continent was cut off from the desperate troubles of the world outside – the war in Vietnam, the racial crises in Africa, or the poverty of India. With the retreat from the empires, and the settling of overseas wars, Europe had turned in on itself, content with its new self-sufficiency.

Yet in 1968 a challenge did come, from an unexpected quarter – from the very heart of the future élite. A generation of students, on which so much of the new Europe depended, suddenly opened up as out of a Trojan Horse in the midst of the settled society, refusing to take note of national achievements, insisting on looking at Europe from a quite different perspective. For a month or two the whole smooth apparatus that had emerged in the past twenty years seemed about to overturn. The panic subsided, the students went on holiday licking their wounds: but no one could now be so confident that the structure was unshakeable. The wheel had come full circle since the terrible times: the generation that had thankfully rebuilt the continent was giving way to a generation which had never seen the rubble.

In what follows, I try to build up a picture of the major countries of western Europe by showing some of the common institutions and trends, as they have developed in the past two decades. I approach the continent not with any particular preconceptions, but rather as an inquiring traveller. Ever since finishing *Anatomy of Britain* I wanted to extend the scope of it to European dimensions – because so many of the national problems turn out really to be much larger ones. The question of the common market is only a small part: in nearly every field of British life – whether politics or big business, education or technology, films or transport – the national context is really too small to make sense by itself: not only in the formal political field, but in the whole interchange of ideas, fashions, culture, leisure.

This book is built round the question – How far are the countries of western Europe, including Britain, coming closer together? Of course I cannot hope to cover the whole field. Regrettably, I must use Europeans to mean western Europeans, because I find eastern Europe too obscure and impenetrable to try to analyse. I do not believe that Europe will be permanently divided. I believe, in spite of the events of the past year, that the influence of the two sides on each other will grow. But the complex relationships of the Warsaw Pact countries, their separate institutions and backgrounds, belong to too huge and separate a field to be manageable in the same volume. This book is mainly concerned with the biggest and richest countries – Germany, Britain, France, Italy – which are most likely to influence the future of the rest. In trying to answer the question, I found myself led from one field to another, from technology to defence, to Americans, to education. I believe that the sociological influences are as important as the political ones, and I have wandered into such fields as television, languages and suburban life. This is not just a book about European unity, but a book about European trends and European life, whether uniting, disuniting or just there.

I don't present this book as an authority about European economics or politics; but (as in *Anatomy of Britain*) I offer myself as a guide, travelling round the new centres of Europe, using the licence of the inquiring writer, asking questions, interviewing leaders, speculating and generalizing, not trying to conceal English prejudices.

I begin in Part One by describing some contemporary visions of Europe, through the personalities of three leaders and through the history of the European movement and the 'Eurocrats'. I pass in Part Two to the industrial and economic structures (I do not describe British institutions in detail, having already done so in *Anatomy of Britain*). In Part Three I look at some of the new European habits and communications; and in the last part I deal with political trends, and the new mood of unrest. In each section I try to follow several themes; the integration of Europe as it was envisaged, compared to what actually happened or didn't happen; the contrasting character of America and Europe; the spread of the consumer society, and the reaction to it; the conflicts between growth and stability, and between respectability and revolution, the pressures towards centralization and decentralization; the tension between international technology and local rooted communities. In the last chapter I pull together these threads, and speculate about what kind of Europe may be emerging.

September 1968   ANTHONY SAMPSON

Part One

Chapter One

Three Europeans

The nether sky opens, and Europe is disclosed as a prone and emaciated figure, the Alps shaping like a backbone, and the branching mountain-chains like ribs, the peninsular plateau of Spain forming a head. Broad the lengthy lowlands stretch from the north of France across Russia like a grey-green garment hemmed by the Ural mountains and the glistening Arctic Ocean.

The point of view then sinks downwards through space, and draws near to the surface of the perturbed countries, where the peoples, distressed by events which they did not cause, are seen writhing, crawling, heaving, and vibrating in their various cities and nationalities.

Thomas Hardy, *The Dynasts*, 1910

The basic question 'What *is* Europe?' has always been impossible to answer. From the outside, and particularly to Americans, the continental entity seems clear enough; even to Englishmen, surveying the land-mass across the channel, the continent is very definite. But once inside, the definition soon blurs. It is not just the English that feel that they 'are not really part of Europe'; Italians enjoy the idea that they are quite different from the northerners across the Alps; in Germany there is always talk about looking to the east, not the west; Holland and Denmark have always preferred to stress their links with the sea; Switzerland has kept separate from continental broils. Spain is 'the missing piece in the jigsaw'. Even France likes to regard herself, in De Gaulle's words, as 'the cape of the continent'.

Moreover, the word 'Europe' is used and abused in so many senses that it sometimes seems to have lost all meaning, except in Metternich's phrase as a 'geographical expression'. There is a long history of attempts at European unity, from the Roman Empire through Charlemagne, Napoleon and Hitler; but the most consistent historical fact has been not unity but a process of fragmentation which came near to total self-destruction.

It was the experience of that destruction, after the Second World War, which gave the last big push to unity. In the late forties and early fifties nearly everyone was arguing for some kind of united Europe. No political speech, from right, left or centre, was complete without some reference to it, but the woolliness and contradictions of the terms employed left plenty of room for escape.

These 'Europeans' had very little in common, except the awareness of one basic fact: that Europe had emerged from the second war to find itself destitute, while the two continental powers, America and Russia, were supreme. There were the pre-1914 Europeans, the old bankers, industrialists and aristocrats, who longed for a return to the old days of free trade, free travel and gay capitals. There were the Catholic or 'Carolingian' Europeans, galvanized by the threat of communism from the east, who saw Europe as a beleagured Christian citadel which must unite to fight off the barbarians. There were the socialist Europeans, who saw a new age of planned prosperity on a continental scale. There were American Europeans who saw some kind of federal 'United States of Europe'. There were industrial Europeans who saw the continent as an unbroken market for their goods. To each section Europe was a different dream.

The high point of waffle was reached at the Congress of The Hague in 1948, with delegates from all over Europe. A few quotations from that period recall both the vagueness and the splendour of the notions:

This Europe must be born. And she will, when Spaniards will say 'our Chartres', Englishmen 'our Cracow', Italians 'our Copenhagen'; when Germans say 'our Bruges', and step back horror-stricken at the idea of laying murderous hands upon it. Then will Europe live, for then it will be that the Spirit that leads History will have uttered the creative words: FIAT EUROPA!

Salvador de Madariaga

A hundred and fifty million Europeans have not the right to feel inferior to anyone, do you hear! There is no great country in this world that can look down on a hundred and fifty million Europeans who close their ranks in order to save themselves.

Paul-Henri Spaak

We must proclaim the mission and the design of a United Europe whose moral conception will win the respect and gratitude of mankind and whose physical strength will be such that none will dare molest her tranquil sway ... I hope to see a Europe where men and women of every country will think as much of being European as of belonging to their native land and wherever they go in this wide domain will truly feel 'Here I am at home'.

Winston Churchill

We wish to unite Europe, to raise, by means of a continental market and a stable currency, the standard of living of millions of Europeans from their present state of utter misery. We wish to unite Europe to protect every single European man and woman against murder and deportation by secret police, against torture and concentration camps.

Count Coudenhove-Kalergi

We could say: 'Eternal Europe, now that you take shape, now that muscles come to you, you have still ahead of you so many dreams to realize, such grandeur to reveal on earth, that tomorrow you may well open a new era of humanity.'

Paul Ramadier

This is the light that has been kindled here,
A hope to man through half a hemisphere.
Hope that is brightness in Earth's darkest day
A glorious gift for guests to take away.

John Masefield (after the Congress of The Hague)

Those first hopes of a united continent are still embodied in the Council of Europe which arose from the Congress of The Hague in 1949. It occupies a functional building called the Maison de l'Europe in Strasbourg, the town which more than any other symbolizes past Franco-German battles, and post-war reconciliation. Outside are the eighteen flags of its members, and inside is the austere assembly chamber, with an atmosphere of red lino and faded hopes: a bust of Churchill adorns the lobby, and a relief map of Europe in the entrance hall has the words:

LE CONSEIL DE L'EUROPE CRÉE L'ESPRIT EUROPÉEN
L'ESPRIT EUROPÉEN FAIT TOMBER LES FRONTIÈRES
LA SAGESSE DES PEUPLES LES AURA LIBÉRÉS

The Council of Europe has lost this optimism, but it still does practical work. Representatives of the eighteen countries meet once a month, to thrash out common problems, from blood plasma to air pollution to youth meetings; a secretariat of four hundred produce mountains of reports, studies and even some agreements. At the head of it is the Secretary-General, Peter Smithers, a tall, wealthy English Tory known as Smoothers, who runs it with an autocratic calm: 'We aim to build the fabric of united Europe from the bottom up,' he told me. A curious little parliament, called the Consultative Assembly, meets four times a year, with one hundred and forty-four members chosen by national parliaments, who make their way with some difficulty to Strasbourg. Their debates do not have much effect, but they are a useful sounding board, and an opportunity for well-known European bores.

The chorus in praise of United Europe in the late forties was misleading. Europe not only meant different things; it was often being used as a new kind of camouflage for nationalistic ambitions. Patriotism was denounced, but the machinery of national interests continued as before – in some ways made stronger by the accretions of the welfare state. The protestations about the historical vocation of Europe did little to interrupt those interests. The most eloquent European, Winston Churchill, had not the slightest intention of handing over any part of Britain's sovereignty to anyone else. When the first bold visions faded, the national politicians were sucked back into their own smaller whirlpools.

Yet the ideas of individuals about Europe have had great power, and still have. In this chapter I take three men, each with a different picture of the continent, each with an important following, who have become symbols as much as individuals – Jean Monnet, Charles de Gaulle and Franz-Josef Strauss. Their ideas and viewpoints will recur through the book.

1: JEAN MONNET

> Europe has never existed. It is not the addition of national sovereignties in a conclave which creates an entity. One must genuinely *create* Europe.
>
> *Jean Monnet*

The most consistent of European influences has been Jean Monnet, the 'father of the common market'. For ten years the history of European unity centred on his personality. His private influence is still evident among people all over Europe. His quizzical eyes look out from photographs in offices in Brussels, Paris or Bonn; a network is held together by the common experience of having worked with him. His power comes not so much through his personal spell as through his way of thinking, and the language of 'Monnetiste' Europe – a vocabulary of perspectives, contexts, *engrenage*, dialogue, evolution, and above all of 'making Europe' – the conviction that nationalism can be by-passed and superseded by human effort.

Monnet operates as a private person, with no political party, no real organization. His method has been to avoid being anyone's rival, to convince people not by pressure but by persuasion. He manoeuvres discreetly (like Moral Rearmament) through top people – telephoning, visiting, introducing: he will suddenly fly off to Bonn or to London, to persuade a politician with a new plan. His special influence derives from his detachment from immediate issues, his being *hors de combat*, thinking in larger terms. The detachment has been both his strength and his weakness.

I first met him in 1962, when he seemed really to be 'making Europe', in his quiet, old-fashioned apartment in Paris, where he works every day, among faded furniture and signed portraits of the Great. Each time I have seen him since, once or twice a year, in spite of all his setbacks, he has seemed the same – coming silently into the room, with a questioning smile and a pat on the shoulder, expounding with clipped sentences his current view of the world, prescribing a plan of action, not tolerating any defeatism. He seems always to be looking at the planet from outside, or from some still point in the turning world.

Monnet looks very French. He is short, well-groomed, spruce in spite of his eighty years and takes great care of his health. He has a neat moustache, sits upright, produces from his pocket a pair of patent folding spectacles. He reminds one of Hercule Poirot. Talking precisely and logically, he has a recurring theme: 'It's all quite simple.' But his experience has been overwhelmingly international and ever since he began as a brandy salesman in Canada, before the First World War, he has broken away from the French mould of examinations, *cadres* and hierarchies. He talks excellent American-English, is much influenced by America and devoted to Britain. He has been an American banker and a British civil servant.

He has never held a conventional position: he recalls the advice of an American friend, Dwight Morrow: 'There are two kinds of people in the world: those who want to be something and those who want to do something. There's less competition among the second.'

Monnet began as a businessman, the heir to a prosperous brandy business, and in his approach to politics he has always had something of the far-sighted tycoon – fixing politicians without coming too close to them, and getting experts and technicians to work for him, without becoming bogged down in their particular expertise. He was never an authority on tariffs or economics, and no match for the mandarins; he is not an intellectual, and does not have a good memory. He has always understood how to delegate, to put ideas and administration into different compartments, and the one time when he became most involved – running the Coal and Steel Community – was the time he least enjoyed. His way of life helps him stay aloof: he lives outside Paris, in a thatched country house and commutes into the city – very un-Parisian. Put briefly, he believes that to solve international problems you must *change their context*: once the context is changed, people's attitudes will change. As he put it in a speech in London in 1962: 'Human nature does not change, but when nations and men accept the same rules and the same institutions to make sure that they are applied, their behaviour towards each other changes. This is the process of civilization itself.' Or, to quote a passage which he admires, from the Swiss philosopher Amiel: 'Each man's experience starts again from the beginning. Only institutions grow wiser;

they accumulate collective experience, and owing to this experience and this wisdom, men subject to the same rules will not see their own nature changing, but their behaviour gradually transformed.'

This conviction rose out of his astonishing career. He chose his own tasks – 'I never had a job I didn't ask for' – and from the beginning was concerned with the merging of national interests. The First World War broke out when he was twenty-six. He was working for the French Government and suggested a new approach to Anglo-French buying of American arms: that the two countries should not compete, but jointly plan their allocations. After the war, he became deputy-secretary of the new League of Nations where he perceived more clearly the dangers of nationalisms: 'I saw the power of one country to say No: I realized that good will was not enough – among men or nations.' He left the League disillusioned, and went back to a new range of international operations: banking in America, reorganizing Swedish matches, Polish currency, Chinese railways. In the Second World War he was back again, co-ordinating Anglo-French buying from America. When France fell he came to London, and swiftly proposed the extraordinary plan for an Anglo-French union, actually drafting Churchill's historic offer. In London he kept aloof from De Gaulle, became a British civil servant and went again to America. He pressed Roosevelt to provide war materials without worring about the cost, and said, 'we must become the great arsenal of democracy'. He sowed the seeds for Lend-Lease.

This extraordinary experience gave Monnet new confidence. After the war, back in France he was for a time preoccupied with the economic recovery: he drafted the celebrated Monnet Plan for modernizing the backward industries of France, bringing together committees of businessmen, trade unionists and civil servants. It was a ruthless rebuilding – for the plan with its massive investments created inflation, with corresponding suffering for ordinary people – but it began France's post-war pattern of economic planning and expansion. The plan embraced the favourite Monnet principle (later echoed in Britain's 'Neddy') that when people themselves devise plans, they rise above their own interests, as they could never do if they were imposed from above.

Monnet knew that France could not plan in isolation and he surveyed Europe with apprehension. He was disappointed by Britain's post-war preoccupation with herself while the problem of Germany's ambition was mounting. By 1950 he was convinced that the only solution to the German problem was to change its context: and this led to the key decision in his career. He drafted for the French foreign minister, Robert Schuman, the plan to pool coal and steel in a new Community – thus breaking the national hold on the two crucial commodities. 'It was the simplest and the hardest solution. All the vested interests were against it.' But the six governments, at this time of crisis, accepted it, and Monnet ran it for three years. The new context, as Monnet predicted, began to produce a new way of thinking, and brought French and Germans together in the same problems. The Coal and Steel Community later ran into difficulties of over-production and national protection (*see* Chapter 4). But its political influence at the time was great, and it became the model for Euratom and the common market itself.

In 1955 Monnet resigned from the Coal and Steel Community, and since then his only formal organization has been the 'Action Committee for the United States of Europe', which really means Monnet and his friends. It consists of 'Europeans' from trade unionists and most of the political parties, a roll-call of leaders who would not otherwise speak to each other, Nenni and Malagodi, Barzel and Brenner, Mollet and Pinay. The committee meets about once a year, to produce a statement. For the rest of the time the committee *is* Monnet, with his small secretariat, working from his office in the Avenue Foch in Paris.

When the common market[1] was established in 1957, Monnet watched (he insists, without much surprise) his principles put into practice, change begetting change. The early results (helped by the crest of a boom) were spectacular. He watched industrialists and planners visualizing not nations of fifty million, but a continent of one hundred and eighty million. People not only adjusted themselves, but anticipated changes that actually took place. 'The history of European unification,' he said in 1962, 'shows that when people become convinced a change is taking place that creates a

1. See chapter 2.

new situation, they act on their revised estimate before that situation is established.'

At each stage of his varied career he accumulated more key disciples. During the wars, in London and Washington, he established his Anglo-American bonds. In America his friends have included Eisenhower, Dulles, Felix Frankfurter and George Ball. In Britain he was worked with Churchill, Macmillan, Heath and George Brown. After the last war, in Parts, his team for the plan included some of the best brains in France, notably Robert Marjolin, Pierre Uri and Etienne Hirsch. Marjolin later became head of OEEC, helped to negotiate the Treaty of Rome, and was, until 1967, Vice-President of the Commission in Brussels. Uri, an international economics don, later helped to draft the Coal and Steel treaty and the Treaty of Rome, and is still close to Monnet. Hirsch, an intellectual engineer, took over from Monnet as head of the French Plan and then became President of Euratom until he was deposed by De Gaulle.

Monnet's influence on these kind of men caused him often to be regarded as the chief of the technocrats. But he himself was always pragmatic and sensitive to politics. His driving force has always been an intense interest in growth and the future, a mixture of vague continental socialism (Monnet always regards himself as a socialist) with a fervent belief in the necessity for expansion and change, and a dislike of the past. It is this that distinguished Monnet's activity from the British post-war socialism. While Britain was preoccupied with nationalization, full employment, sharing existing resources, Monnet's group were worried above all about building new systems, a new future. They were baffled by the British Labour Party's lack of interest in growth and in changing world politics.

Nineteen sixty-two was Monnet's peak. He seemed almost the magician of Europe, exorcizing the nationalist demons, conjuring up the new international era. The common market was booming with a higher growth-rate than America's, and looked like embracing Britain and others, developing at last into a real political unity. Monnet insisted that Britain must come in. 'You ask my why I desire so strongly the entry of Britain to the common market?' he said to Jean Daniel in February 1963. 'It's because of the parliamentary and democratic traditions of the English. Beside them, we are not democrats. We are republicans, sometimes revolutionaries, but never as essentially and deeply democratic as them. We are going, whatever happens, towards European political institutions; for that we need the English; it's they who operate the methods of parliamentary control and popular education which they have brought to the whole world.'

He saw the common market developing close ties with America, in a 'partnership of equals', which could lead to a peaceful settlement with Russia. He never hid his admiration for the United States (in an ante-room there hangs a cover of *Time* with his face on it), though his open American-ness has reduced his effectiveness and made him obviously vulnerable to French critics: 'He is not a Frenchman in fee to the Americans,' said De Gaulle, 'he is a great American.' In 1962 Monnet's belief in the partnership was echoed by President Kennedy's speech in July, heralding the 'Grand Design' linking America to an enlarged European Community.

All that seems a long way off now. In January 1963 came De Gaulle's veto of Britain's membership. Monnet rushed to Brussels. He quickly advocated that the Five should continue to negotiate with Britain, leaving an 'empty chair' for France; and pressed Adenauer to press De Gaulle. But Adenauer was set on signing the Franco-German treaty, and De Gaulle won the day. Monnet was baulked, but not defeated. 'We are off the autostrada,' he said to me in February 1963, 'but the process of change will go on: De Gaulle cannot stop it.' He went on working for Britain's admission, and put his faith in the process of *engrenage* or meshing: 'Our countries have begun to delegate part of their national sovereignty to common institutions,' he said to German Social Democrats in February 1964. As the common market crisis of 1965 developed, Monnet clashed more openly with De Gaulle and by the time of the Presidential elections in the Autumn he was – rather rashly – endorsing Jean Lecanuet as the 'European' candidate against De Gaulle.

By the end of 1966 the new nationalism of Europe was much more evident, and the vision of a 'partnership of equals' with America was fast vanishing. In a speech at Bonn in December Monnet warned that 'if we, Europeans, do not unite ourselves and organize to speak with the same voice, we will force the United States to decide for herself, in an attitude of superiority which her resources make possible – to the great detriment of everyone.' He was still hopeful that Britain could get into the common market; but six months later De Gaulle made it clear that he would stop it again. I saw Monnet soon afterwards, when he was watching the impotence of Europe in the face of the Middle East crisis: for the first time he seemed deeply pessimistic: 'In this grave conflict the voice of a United Europe has remained silent,' he said through his Action Committee in June 1967. Speaking in Saarbrücken in January 1968, he summed up his worries about the behaviour of nations:

I am struck by the difference between the principles that we apply within our frontiers and those we apply across them. Within national frontiers, men long ago found and developed civilized ways of dealing with conflicts of interest; they no longer need to defend themselves by force. Rules and institutions have established equality of status. But across their frontiers, nations still behave as individuals would if there were no laws and no institutions. Each, in the last resort, clings to national sovereignty – that is, each reserves the right to be judge in its own cause.

For many of the younger generation who have no memory of the war, Monnet seems now a distant, scarcely relevant figure, belonging to the early cold war: his preoccupation with western Europe seems dated, his optimism about dissolving nations seems hollow. Monnet himself has been visibly discouraged by the outbreak of nationalism, regionalism and demagogy through Europe. His gloom, I believe, is excessive; his influence has not been what he hoped, but has been great in other ways. The young Europeans worry much less about reconciliation and free trade because they take if for granted; but for part, at least, of their casual acceptance of a frontier-less continent, and a new context of living, they have Monnet to thank.

Above all, Monnet bequeathed his confidence in institutions to form new patterns and attitudes. However bitter the arguments at Brussels, the common market remains a new kind of forum, where national rivalries take for granted a common objective. However long the retreat from the first supranational ideals, the state of Europe is not comparable to the desperate non-communication between the

two wars. The new machinery is still working, still
influencing people and bringing them together.

II: DE GAULLE

Europe, the mother of modern civilization, must establish herself all the way from the Atlantic to the Urals, and live in a
state of harmony and co-operation with a view to developing her
immense resources, and so play, together with her daughter
America, her worthy role in relation to the billion people who
so badly need her help.

De Gaulle

For nearly a decade, the boldest show of European diplomacy has been the twice-yearly press conference of General de Gaulle. I went to the one in November 1967, just
after his second veto of Britain's application to join the
common market. The ritual at the Elysée had become fixed.
The thousand guests began arriving an hour beforehand,
walking through the gravelled courtyard and the big glass
doors, past the anterooms and vestibules hung with chandeliers and tapestries, into the great *Salle des Fêtes,* with
rows of little gilt chairs set out in front of the dais. The
damask, the gold and the chandeliers all added to the sense
of great theatre. In the front rows the Gaullist dignitaries
walked up and down, looking carefully to see who was
where. In the back rows were the world's journalists, finger-
ing notebooks, dashing out for smokes. Right at the back was
a recess filled with television cameras and their anxious
crews. The combination of the pomposity of the functionaries and the casualness of the photographers – adjusting
light-meters, focusing, shouting – summed up the artificial
magic, the meeting of traditional splendour with modern
communications. A few minutes before three o'clock there
was a shuffling of curtains on the left and familiar figures of
ministers walked in, and sat down in rows of three, facing
sideways the empty dais; in the front row Pompidou, Debré,
Malraux, then lesser ministers, all waiting like schoolboys on
their cramped chairs. Then at exactly three, the curtains
parted – and in strode, quite briskly, the General. Like other
old men, he seemed to look more like an odd mammal – a

walrus, perhaps a frog, a camel or something more pre-
historic; his beak, his bald, furrowed forehead, his long
under-chin, and his red sunken eyes, all conveyed the look of
some strange creature peering out through the mists of time.
The TV cameras whirred, the arc lights glared, the Leicas
clicked, the necks of the audience strained, and everyone
stood up. The general sat down and, with a generous gesture
of rotating arms, invited others to do so. He operated with
exaggerated vigour, as if inviting his audience to inspect not
only his views but his state of health also; he knew that he
was, above all, an exhibit.

What the ritual of the conference showed, all too clearly,
was how easily Press and television could be lured to come
to terms with a spectacle, and to accept it on its own terms;
to barrack or to boo would have been unthinkable. Questioners popped up in different parts of the hall, asking the pre-
dictable question; the general leant his great head, bowed
slightly at the end of the question, and nodded in understanding; sometimes he smiled or gave a quizzical pout, provoked dutiful laughs which showed still more clearly his
hold over the audience. Then he summed up the main subjects, and asked the questions again. He answered in long,
careful monologues, stating his view of the world in perfect
rounded paragraphs, without notes or reminders; building
up to emotional climaxes, with the hands suddenly falling on
the desk, in time with a sudden word like *même, déplorable*,
or *Francais*; and then briskly moving to a new mood or a
new question. The timing was precise, generating a sudden
silence, then a new wave of camera clicks. As the sentences
marched on, the head rolled, the eyebrows switched up and
down, the mouth opened and shut without rest or refresh-
ment. His ministers watched self-consciously, exposed to a
thousand spectators – occasionally whispering to each other,
but echoing the mood of the master, and knowing that
everyone knew that they did not know what he would say.

It is the privilege of every strong ruler to be able to make
his own scene so powerfully that people forget that other
scenes exist. For ten years De Gaulle stole the limelight so
effectively that his critics found it hard to contest his ideas
except on his own terms. His whole scene was concerned
with the splendour of the nation; the questions of gold,
foreign policy, and industrial growth reverberated from the

press conferences, drowning any worries of the workers or students. The whole of Europe, twice a year, waited to hear what he had to say. Very few people noticed that behind the magnificent front, the whole edifice was in danger. In the six months after that press conference, the assumptions of the show were quite undermined. The students and strikers showed that they, too, could make their own scene, and that there were other things to talk about; for almost a month De Gaulle's leadership seemed to have dissolved. His broadcasts during the crisis showed a bewildering range of roles – the tired disillusioned statesman, then the stern fighting soldier, and finally the man-to-man talk with Michel Droit, interpreting the students' case for them. Yet so close was the identification between him and the state, that he was able to emerge at the end, detached from his politicians, as both the guardian of security against 'totalitarian communism', and as the old revolutionary, the champion of participation, who had 'understood' the students as he had 'understood' the French Algerians ten years before.

The contrast between De Gaulle and Monnet is total for they look at Europe from opposite ends. Both the same age, both brought up in the nineteenth century, both were involved in two world wars, yet remained contemporary prophets. Monnet is short and anonymous, De Gaulle, tall and theatrical. Monnet was brought up as an international businessman; De Gaulle, as a patriotic soldier. On two dramatic occasions they came together, revealing their contrast. The first was in June 1940, just after the defeat of the French Army, when Monnet in London thought up the idea of the Anglo-French Union, and persuaded De Gaulle, who persuaded Churchill, only to have it turned down by the French cabinet. The second was when Monnet went out to Algiers in February 1943, asked by Roosevelt to reconcile – with temporary success – the two rival French leaders, De Gaulle and Giraud. On both occasions Monnet was trying to overcome nationalism; De Gaulle remembers with scorn, and ten years later joked that Monnet had 'tried to integrate King George VI with President Lebrun, and to integrate De Gaulle with Giraud'. De Gaulle kept his suspicion of Monnet, while Monnet's attitude to him veered from patient disapproval to mounting anger: 'It is terrible what that man is doing to Europe,' he said in June 1967.

It is still impossible to disengage the historical accident of one man's character from the tendencies of a nation and a continent. De Gaulle's story is so mixed up with the story of France that it is sometimes hard to distinguish them. When he was once asked what France would do after his departure, De Gaulle characteristically answered: 'You must find another De Gaulle.' He knew they could not: in France as elsewhere, strong leaders have been rare and have always been succeeded by weak ones. French voters may continue to be 'Gaullist' in their desire for strong nationalist leadership, but there is difficulty in being Gaullist without a De Gaulle.

De Gaulle's attitude to Europe has always depended on his faith in the state. He never used the phrase 'Europe des patries': what he said was really stronger – 'Europe des États'. As he described it in February 1953, the state must be 'a political, economic, financial, administrative, and above all, moral entity sufficiently living, established and recognized to obtain the congenital loyalty of its subjects, to have a political policy of its own, and, if it should happen, that millions of men would be willing to die for it'.

Partly, his belief in the state came from his background; and from his father, headmaster of a Jesuit school, who was 'permeated by his feeling for the dignity of France'. De Gaulle's early writings emphasize the need for perpetual struggle between states. Then his experience of the Second World War bore out (as it seemed to him) all of his beliefs: he observed the same processes as Monnet and drew opposite conclusions. After 1940 he believed that 'it was essential to bring back into the war not merely some Frenchmen, but France'. Certainly if De Gaulle had not maintained his aggressive wartime role, the humiliation of France would have been even greater. The prospect of a united Europe might have been easier, but the continuity with the past would (as in Germany) have been dangerously slender. Surrounded by appeasers or pessimists, De Gaulle's own personality was the strong, thin thread seeming to connect France's past and present glory.

De Gaulle's belief in the nation-state underlay, naturally enough, all his attitudes to a united Europe. He has never believed that supranational Europe could inspire people in the same way as a nation. For Germans or Italians, with their discredited dictatorships and their short national histories, Europe might be an escape and some sort of substitute; but France did not need one. With old-fashioned eloquence he has poured scorn from their beginnings on the 'supranational' organizations of Europe, the 'alchemic mixtures, algebraic combinations and cabalistic formulas'. When the idea of a European Army was put foward, he protested in 1951: 'I ask in the name of what, can ardour, confidence and obedience be demanded from French citizens incorporated in an anational organism?' When the common market was formed, he asked in May 1962: 'Would the French people, the German people, the Italian people, the Dutch people, the Belgian people or the Luxembourg people dream of submitting to laws voted by foreign deputies if these laws were to run contrary to their own deep-seated will?' As the common market progressed he came to terms with its achievement, but kept up his attacks on supranationalism: 'It is quite clear,' he said in January 1964, after shutting Britain out of the common market, 'that the peoples, I mean the peoples of Europe, each people of Europe, do not want their destiny handed over to an Areopagus mostly composed of foreigners. It is also clear that England, which is a great nation and a great state, would accept it less than anyone else.' His relations with the 'Areopagus' bumped along in constant friction – culminating in the great crisis over majority voting in 1965, which appears in the next chapter. But he probably never contemplated leaving the common market, and he sometimes likes to appear as its champion, defending it against the 'disruptions' of Britain or America.

Britain has always been the obvious rival, and his relations have swung between his desire for a strong Europe and his belief in the struggle between states. He was often wiser than Churchill. After the war he vainly hoped for a close Franco-British alliance to compete with America and Russia; and when Churchill came to Paris in November 1944, De Gaulle told him: 'Confronting a new world, then our two old nations find themselves simultaneously weakened. If they remain divided as well, how much influence will either of them wield?' Churchill answered (according to De Gaulle) that he remained close to Roosevelt, and that 'in politics as in strategy, it is better to persuade the stronger than to pit yourself against him' – which summed up the difference between them. De Gaulle was soon discouraged by Britain's dependence on American policy; but there remained a large ambivalence in his attitude to Britain. As late as 1961, in a speech at Metz, he said that 'it is necessary that Britain should join the common market, though without laying down any conditions'. During the negotiations in 1962 De Gaulle had good causes for doubting whether Britain had really chosen Europe, borne out by Macmillan's agreement at Nassau, which enabled him to pronounce his veto with conviction.

In the next years De Gaulle still sometimes suggested that Britain might be becoming more European, but he had less and less reason to welcome her. The common market, French-speaking and French-thinking, provided a closed shop for Gallic diplomacy and dominance which Britain would certainly upset; and the main reason for wanting Britain in the fifties – to bring stability into an unstable continent – seemed now (though wrongly) quite inapplicable. In the new mood of Europe it was balances of payments and gold reserves that seemed to matter, and it was Britain, with a shaky pound and weak leadership, which now seemed unstable. By the time of Wilson's application to join the common market in 1967, De Gaulle and his government had no doubts; the whole weight of French diplomacy was devoted to keeping Britain out. It was easy to mistake economic weakness for inherent political instability. De Gaulle himself abetted this confusion, and probably believed it, and some of the British caught doubts.

De Gaulle took full advantage of the glamour of nationalism. After 1960, liberated by the end of the Algerian war and the first signs of *détente*, he embarked on his breathtaking international adventures, exploring new global alliances and balances of power. Unlike Britain, France had divested herself of nearly all her overseas commitments: as Couve de Murville, De Gaulle's foreign minister, explained smugly in April 1964, 'Having settled all the great problems of her past, France has today a freedom of action that no other nation enjoys.' De Gaulle made the most of it, changing direction and alliances with all the ruthlessness of nineteenth-century rulers, but speeded up by the jet age and television. He was determined to break 'with the absurd and outdated conformity of self-effacement'.

Forgetting the traumas of the thirties and forties he first
wooed Germany, with a fulsome courtship culminating in
his triumphal tour in September 1962 (*'Sie sind ein grosses
Volk!'*), and followed by the Franco-German treaty. In 1963
he vetoed Britain from the common market and stepped up
his hostility to America. In 1964 (disproving any view that
he was right-wing in his foreign policy) he recognized Communist China, denounced the Vietnam war, and toured
Mexico and South America. In 1965 he serenaded Russia
and eastern Europe, bringing up his old policy of 'Europe
from the Atlantic to the Urals', thus alarming the Germans.
In 1967 (a gala year) he denounced the Israeli attack on
Egypt, visited Canada to proclaim *'Vive le Québec libre'*,
and toured Poland to encourage their independence and to
urge German recognition of the Oder-Neisse line – thus
alarming both Russia and Germany. In 1968 he made
further attacks on the dollar, using the strength of his gold
reserves; then he toured Rumania, and talked about the
détente – 'the salubrious wind that is blowing through
Europe'.

In his foreign policy he seemed to enjoy complete freedom, unhampered by problems at home, and fortified by a
pile of gold. Hardly anyone was aware that he was on a
razor's edge, that his indifference to domestic complaints and
his high-handed style was building up a head of resentment
that was to undermine the whole operation. De Gaulle and
his ministers had become so intoxicated by the outward
splendours and weapons of the nation-state – the prestige, the
gold, the *force de frappe* – that they had neglected the one
thing that gives it real meaning and strength, the support of
the home population. While he was still in Rumania, the
students were writing their own slogans on the wall of the
Sorbonne, about 'the salubrious wind that is blowing
through Europe'.[1]

In all De Gaulle's peregrinations and shifting alliances the
consistent thread was hostility to America. As the American
industrial machine raced ahead of Russia, and the Vietnam

1. De Gaulle never really recovered his confidence and prestige after
the students' revolt, and when he resigned the following year the students
could claim with justification that they had got rid of him.

war continued, De Gaulle became more alarmed by the American monopoly of power. But the whole character of his breakneck diplomacy, based on the nation-state, prevented his achieving a lasting counterweight. His friendship with Russia was limited by his alliance with Germany: his obstruction of the common market frustrated a strong Europe: his whipping up of Quebec limited the chances of enlisting Canada as an ally against the United States. This always was the contradiction in De Gaulle's nation-state: however effective as an inspirer of people, it could not achieve much in a world dominated by two continents. De Gaulle could play the big powers against each other, with short-term advantages for France: but he was always up against the fact that France had only a fraction of their population. As he once said: 'If only we had a hundred and eighty million people!'

It is difficult to deny De Gaulle's effect on French morale. He reaped a good harvest from the technocrats of the Fourth Republic – the industrial revival, planning, the nuclear bomb, the common market. But he added a sense of purpose, and harnessed the reflected energies of patriotism in a way that other nations came to envy. His outward panache – whether in flamboyant state visits, in emotional outbursts or in cleaning the Louvre – might seem childish, but it could still move grown-up men.[1]

His magic was as powerful outside his country as in it: at his peak, in 1966 and 1967, he had achieved an almost hypnotic influence over diplomacy. In Germany or Italy, however much politicians mocked his tricks and resented his French-ness, he could still appear as a leader, not just of France, but of Europe; when the common market had its tenth anniversary in Rome, it was not Hallstein or Monnet who was the hero of celebrations, but De Gaulle. In Britain, behind the anger and humiliation, there was growing envy for the decisive leadership, untrammelled by parliament and parties, which had seemed to reverse so quickly the standing of England and France. In eastern Europe (like British liberals in the last century) he could present himself as the champion of nations against the hegemony of the east.

1. The extent to which this patriotic zeal depended on De Gaulle became clear soon after his resignation, when the pressures for coming to terms with the common market, and with Britain, soon made themselves felt.

All through Europe, the concept of patriotism slipped back into favour. Ten years ago it could hardly be mentioned; it was so closely associated with war. Nation-states seemed to most Europeans a spent force, an adolescent phase best left to Africa or South America: the cold war, by freezing the alliances and terrifying both sides, helped to keep nations in check. But with the thaw, the fading memories of war, and the sheer dullness of the new Europe, national rivalries became more attractive, as a source of self-respect and excitement. In 1967 we find Helmut Schmidt, the German socialist, saying:

The role of the national states will increase, both in eastern and in western Europe. It is pretty certain that with growing freedom of movement their solidarity towards one another will decrease. It is therefore pretty certain for us Germans that our foreign policy will be much more interesting in the next decade than in this one.

De Gaulle cannot be held responsible for the greater part of this trend, for many other changes, including healthy ones, were pressing the nations towards new self-consciousness. But De Gaulle's greatness (like Churchill's twenty years before, but much more so) had confused people as to what the nation really was, or could be. The extraordinary accidents of his life – the fact that twice he had apparently rescued France from ignominy – gave him such unique authority and outspokenness that he could give to the state his own interpretation, which he never tired of doing. The state may not have been as easy to by-pass or supersede as Monnet and the federalists thought; but it was also something much less certain and solid than De Gaulle so brilliantly made it appear.

III: STRAUSS

Germany needs Europe more than any other country. In its post-war insecurity and solitude, it has been seen in the European idea not only a way of compensating for the immediate past but an honourable outlet for its formidable energies.

Franz-Josef Strauss, 1965

Of all the protagonists of the European idea the most controversial has been Franz-Josef Strauss, the rogue elephant of West Germany, and its present finance minister.[1] Strauss has from the beginning been convinced of the need for a united Europe, but his political attitudes have been so autocratic, so militant and even blood-curdling, that he has frightened away many of his allies. He has sometimes seemed to embody a crude power-lust, and he has probably made more enemies than anyone in Europe. Yet, among the discreet and wavering German politicians he stands out as an authentic voice who can comprehend and guide his country's ambitions.

He has always maintained that only 'a new European architecture' can safely contain Germany's energies; and listening to him talk, bristling, vibrating with energy, seeming about to burst out of his coat and his shirt, I felt that the same might be true of him – that only a bigger unit can contain *his* energies, and that may even be alarmed by his own ambition. He does not, like Monnet or De Gaulle, present any particular philosophy; there is no real 'Straussism'. What he represents is the vague but powerful yearnings of the German people. Since the European problem revolves round the German problem, he cannot be ignored.

I talked to him at length in Bonn just before he went back into the government, in the autumn of 1966. An encounter with him is difficult to forget. He bursts into the room like a missile, propelled by some unseen force, generating waves of energy around him. His entourage are electrified by his presence. He sits down as a leopard might, ready at any moment to spring up. He has (in his reconstructed version which first appeared in 1967) short swept-back hair, a mouth with an extraordinary range of expressions, and piggy eyes which are often bloodshot. He talks, as he describes it, in a mixture of Bavarian and broken American – but also with a sharp vulgarity; when I asked him whether Germany would ever have to choose between France and America he said: 'Do you choose between your shirt and your underpants?' His public performances, especially in Bavaria, are much coarser. On one occasion (which specially shocked *Spiegel*) he was

1. In 1969, with the formation of the Brandt-Scheel coalition, Strauss went into opposition and has since become a fierce critic of Brandt's *rapprochement* with Moscow.

heckled in Bavaria by a left-wing student: he turned on him and said: 'You up there, I'll tell you something. I'd rather have Eisenhower's arse than Stalin's face.' He can play both the bully and the baby, turning from hectoring to disarming charm. It is hard not to be fascinated by his explosive personality, after the measured politeness of the other men in Bonn; but it can be hair-raising.

His background is super-Bavarian, and he enjoys the caricature of the fat extrovert beer-drinker. His political weight comes from his leadership of the Bavarian section of the Christian Democratic Party, the CSU, which is very independent. He was the son of a village butcher, and he married a brewer's daughter. As a young man he was a champion cyclist, and although he is now huge, he was quite recently said to have been seen bicycling dangerously with drop-handlebars through Bavarian lanes.

His career spans two ruins of Germany. He was born in 1915, and brought up under the shambles of the Weimar Republic; he looked back with longing to the Europe before the First World War, 'at the summit of splendour on this earth'. He had a brilliant career at school and university, excelling in Greek, Latin and History. He was called up into the army in 1939, and spent much of the war on the Russian front. Eventually he was captured by the Americans, and was soon in their good books: he became an interpreter, helped with de-nazification, and become a district commissioner. He was already a dynamo, and the Americans loved his anti-communism.

He became a co-founder of the Christian Social Union (CSU), a revival of the old Catholic Bavarian People's Party. His roaring oratory and guilt-free extroversion soon made their impact, and he was elected to the first Federal Parliament. Adenauer made him minister responsible for atomic energy, and then, for six years, minister of defence. He was in his element, building up the new army with auto-cratic enthusiasm, mastering the nuclear chess-game. He was convinced of the importance of a United Europe, and pleaded with British diplomats to bring Britain into it. He seemed to have good chances to succeed Adenauer as Chancellor. He was statesmanlike abroad but at home he showed – as he put it – 'a complete indifference as to whether I manufactured friends or foes'.

Then came the Spiegel Affair.[1] For some years the weekly magazine *Spiegel*, a more radical version of *Time* magazine, had been conducting a vendetta against Strauss; its editor Rudolf Augstein, an ex-admirer of his, had become convinced that he was a menace to democracy, had attacked him for corruption, incompetence and drunkenness, and – most important and justified – a disregard for justice. Finally, in October 1962, *Spiegel* came out with a damning attack on Strauss's defence policy, based on much inside information from military sources. Strauss was furious and lost his head. Three weeks later, in the middle of the night, police raided and occupied the *Spiegel* offices, and arrested Augstein and other members of the staff. The author of the article, Conrad Ahlers, was arrested by the Spanish police while on holiday in Spain.

A national outcry followed. The German Press, overcoming their customary dislike of *Spiegel*, rallied to Augstein's defence; the international Press descended on Germany to report with relish on the Gestapo-like arrests. Students demonstrated outside the *Spiegel* offices, while police stood guard over the *Spiegel* files; the atmosphere in Hamburg was electric. The minister of justice who belonged to the Free Democrat (Liberal) Party, resigned in protest, saying he had not been consulted. The socialists moved into attack, for once with effect. In Parliament, two weeks after the arrests, Fritz Eerler questioned Strauss, who replied with fumbling mendacity: 'I did not know what was going to happen; I did not know when it was going to happen; I did not know against whom it was going to happen ...'; but finally admitted that he had actually been on the telephone to Spain on the night of the arrests. Adenauer doggedly defended his minister, insisted that he himself did not know of the arrests until the last minute, and delivered an extraordinary outburst: 'We have an abyss of high treason in this country.'

In the subsequent inquiry and recriminations it became clear that Strauss had certainly been involved in the arrests, and had told Adenauer about the plans. The Liberal members of the cabinet refused to serve with Strauss. Eventually he had to resign, but without contrition; he even arranged a farewell military parade for himself, attended by

1. See also chapter 15.

Adenauer. Soon afterwards, in the Bavarian elections, he was triumphantly returned as leader of the CSU. He continued to deny that he had made a mistake. 'Perhaps I could have formulated my answers in Parliament rather better,' he said to me; 'but I was fighting against wind-mills.'

The Spiegel Affair seemed at the time to have finished him. It had brought out the old fears of German democracy, and revealed an ugly mendacity and ruthlessness. 'If Strauss in relatively quiet times treats the constitution in this way,' asked the constitutional expert, Professor Eschenburg, 'what will he do with it in a time of emergency?' Sebastian Haffner, the political columnist, wrote in March 1963: 'The thought that in the future Strauss might ever act in the same reckless way as a German Chancellor – perhaps in a matter of war and peace in the atomic age – is indeed appalling.'

But Strauss kept his leadership of the Bavarian Party, and gradually and systematically rehabilitated his reputation and image, with a highly-organized public relations campaign. It was made know that he was analysing his past mistakes, seeking the advice of Catholic priests, and being counselled by his wife. He took up shooting and became much more polite: he seemed able to control his temper. He travelled abroad, tourist class, and took great trouble to impress the British; he produced a book, *The Grand Design*, to persuade them of his seriousness, and wrote an article in *International Affairs*. He took a course in economics, and convinced some businessmen of the weakness of Dr. Erhard. He even looked different – with short hair and two stones lighter. He took flying lessons. It was a remarkable refurbishing.

Four years after the Spiegel Affair, Erhard fell, and a Grand Coalition with the Socialists was formed which, ironically enough, gave Strauss his new opportunity. The Socialists tried to stop him, but the Bavarian Party insisted. He got the job he wanted, minister of finance (though working alongside the Socialist minister of economics, Dr. Schiller). He was now on his best behaviour. His political position was not as strong as had been expected, since Dr. Kiesinger proved more than a stop-gap Chancellor, holding the ring between powerful rivals. But Strauss had a more solid following than Kiesinger, and he was once again being tipped as the next Chancellor.

On his new eminence, Strauss was soon again an important European influence. He maintained a wary relationship with the new wave of German nationalism; he at first pooh-poohed the nationalist party, the NDP, but insisted that 'people abroad make a great mistake if they think they can deprive us of the right to have a healthy nationalist party in Germany again today'. When the non-proliferation treaty came up in 1967, he denounced it as 'a new Treaty of Versailles' (admitting later that that was an oversimplification). At the same time he maintains: 'I have always been, and still am, a sworn enemy of nationalism. I regard it as having dug Europe's grave.'

His attitude to European unity is simple and fairly consistent. He believes (as he put it to me), that 'it's not natural for three hundred million Europeans to be dependent on either one hundred and ninety million Americans or two hundred million Russians'. He denies being anti-American, but insists that 'we want to be a partner of America, not a nuclear protectorate'. He believes that Europe must have its own nuclear force (ENF) and that a united Europe without it would not make much sense. With a strong nuclear Europe and an integrated European army he believes that the Atlantic alliance can be much healthier and stronger, and that the Atlantic can become the equivalent of the Mediterranean of ancient times. He denies that he is rigidly anti-communist and supports the opening-up to the east. But he hates the word *'détente'*. ('What do you mean? let the Russians walk into West Berlin?') He believes that the European nations must give up some of their sovereignty to survive: 'For the outdated conception of a Europe of the nations we must substitute a Europe of its peoples. Not a melting pot, but a continent in which differences of character and temperament in the individual are preserved in a community which raises their standard of living without standardizing their lives and guarantees their security. In order to remain German, or British, or French, or Italian, we must become Europeans.'

Strauss is often described as a German Gaullist: but the word does not mean much. He wants to be independent of America, but in a more European way than De Gaulle. He likes to mock De Gaulle's international cavortings: 'A mixture between Joan of Arc and a political cosmonaut.' He has often stressed that the Paris-Bonn axis is the key to

European unity, but likes to remind Englishmen that it was Churchill who first urged it. And he insists that the axis must become a triangle between Paris, Bonn and London; and that only Britain's entry to the common market will make Europe strong enough industrially to hold its own with the super-powers. In the past he has shared De Gaulle's suspicions that Britain would not break away from her links with America, and would not bring her nuclear expertise to Europe. But after De Gaulle's press conference in May 1966, Strauss came out with an unexpected outburst: he said that De Gaulle was incapable of interpreting the signs of the times, and that 'it would be a tragedy if Britain were to be severed by force from the continent of Europe. ... The British are as tough a people as ever. They could certainly have held out against the common market, but they have decided that their future lies with Europe'.

Strauss's vision of Europe is more aggressive, less idealistic, than Monnet's; more straightforward and less nationalistic than De Gaulle's. Some of his political attitudes are still pretty appalling – for instance his attitude to Africa. He went out to South Africa, where he has business interests, in April 1966, and made speeches ecstatic in its praise. I asked him about it, and he delivered an emotional and unstoppable tirade against the sentimentality of British colonial psychology, the primitiveness of South African natives, the hypocrisy of the Kennedy family, the communist agitators, the black men going 'back to the trees' – repeating familiar clichés. Strauss is insensitive to the feelings of the third world and the horrors of *apartheid*. But that is a common German failing. What is more serious is that he is not a natural democrat; all his instincts are authoritarian.

The strongest reason for uniting Europe has always been to absorb the danger of Germany – the reason which Monnet has never lost sight of; and the most important reverberations of De Gaulle were not in France, but across the Rhine. The blocking of the common market and the humiliations of West Germany helped to push German ambitions further into a nationalistic context, and to give encouragement to the new right; the Franco-German alliance could be no substitute for an integrated Europe. The German problem remains more obvious than ever, twenty years after the Congress of The Hague; after the interim of prosperity and apparent stability, western Europe faces again the same prospect of upheaval and violent questioning. But the building of Europe, as I hope to show, cannot make sense without Britain's inclusion, for Britain is the only major country with a long tradition of stable government. Her economic weakness, which De Gaulle made his argument against Britain's entry, was closely linked with this very stability: in a time of crisis, the very conservatism and pigheadedness of its institutions, most of all the trade unions, become the ultimate political safeguards. This solid British bloody-mindedness remains the key piece in the European jigsaw – for only Britain can be a real counterweight to Germany; it may be to the credit of Strauss that he has realized it.

Chapter Two

Eurocrats

The common market is a process, not a product.
Jean Monnet

Brussels is not the city that most Europeans would choose as their capital. It shows the mean materialist side of the continent, boring and bourgeois; it seems appropriate that the Revolution of 1830, which brought Belgium into being, first broke out in the opera house. The hub of the city is the stock exchange which looks like a cathedral, with a great baroque portico surmounted by a heavy frieze showing Belgium protecting Commerce and Industry. The most imposing street is made up, not of government offices, but of the banks which dominate Belgium's industry. The centre of the city is a memorial to *laissez-faire*: old trams still rattle by along bumpy cobble streets, and rude taxi drivers extort huge tips. The shops have the faded look of shops in the thirties, and prefer exorbitant profit margins to bigger turnover. The social structure is similarly antique, more suited to the thirties than the sixties. A closed circle of bankers and barons, carefully intermarried, dominate the high social life, cultivating evening dress and gloomy formality: servants are in easy supply. The cultural life is bleak and self-conscious; most cultural heroes, like Simenon or Jacques Brel, have long since left.

Yet Brussels is now the nearest thing to a capital of Europe. The trend began with the setting up of the common market and Euratom, when the parliamentarians of Europe couldn't decide between Strasbourg and Paris, and had to settle for Brussels; the common market headquarters attracted armies of diplomats, delegations, pressure groups, trade associations, trade unionists, supplicants, intriguers. In the sixties more and more big companies, particularly Am-

erican, moved their headquarters to Brussels, often from
Geneva or London: their names stare out from the new parts
of the cities. Then in 1967 a whole new contingent arrived
when NATO and SHAPE were chucked out of France by
De Gaulle, bringing another army of hangers-on.

Alongside the complacent old Belgian society there has
grown up a quite separate one, unrooted, un-Belgian. The
Brussels burghers, with a passion for property investments,
have zealously prepared for any kind of expansion. Brussels
is the only capital with a surplus of building, and in spite of
the waves of invasions, it still has brand-new blocks proclaiming *appartements à louer*. A *Quartier d'Europe* with
neat white villas and flats, is much favoured by diplomats
and Eurocrats. A Hilton and a Westbury, twin temples of
international commerce, allow Americans to forget they are
abroad, with the help of English-speaking waiters, English
papers, and magazines devoted to English-speaking Brussels.
There are two main worlds of expatriates in Brussels, the
common market Eurocrats on the one hand, and the international businessmen on the other: the first speak French as
their common language, the second English. A hint of the
international business can be gained from looking up
'Euro . . .' in the telephone directory, which conjures up a
bleak Europicture, including:

Eurocomfort	Euromatic
Eurodesign	Eurolabor
Euroffice	Euromusic
Eurofoam	Europe-Union marriages
Eurogreeting	

The materialism which makes Brussels culturally depressing, makes it welcoming to business visitors. It is a city
of car-parks, air-conditioned offices, bilingual secretaries,
telephones which work and new office equipment: there is a
whole street of typewriter shops. The Belgian government
goes out of its way to lure foreign companies, particularly
American ones, with tax benefits and large loans: the banks,
which are not eager to invest in Belgian industry, always
have capital to spare for Americans. And Brussels, above all,
is central. You can drive into France, Holland, or Germany
or to Ostend in two hours; it is the nearest capital to London,
and the Trans-Europe Express glides to Paris in three hours.
It is in the middle of the map of capitalist Europe.

EUROPEAN COMMUNITY

On the east side of Brussels is a new star-shaped glass palace, which contains the headquarters of the European Community, usually known as the 'common market'. Here, in their natural habitat, can be seen the 'Eurocrats', the three thousand international civil servants whose careers are dedicated to making a new kind of unified Europe. It is this central bureaucracy which embodies Jean Monnet's basic faith, that new institutions, becoming wiser than people, can change men's behaviour. In spite of all their setbacks, they are still the focus of hopes and ideas, and the nucleus for any further progress. The bleak name 'the common market' is misleading and not strictly correct; it is properly the 'European Community' – which conveys much more clearly what it is; not just a customs union, but the starting-point for a much broader unity.

It is important to recapitulate the short history of this unique institution, to realize how much of its achievement is now taken for granted, and how many ups and downs it has already survived. Its foundation was one of the great accidents of history. The movement for European unity, which had begun after the war with those high but vague intentions, soon ran into troubles: Britain kept aloof and, without Britain, the French were scared of Germany. The first serious step forward was the Coal and Steel Community, the original of the 'Community idea', whose preamble briskly set out the characteristics of Monnet's Europe: 'Thus will be realized, simply and rapidly, the fusion of interests which is indispensable to the establishment of an economic community.'

In the alarmed state of Europe at the time, still more alarmed by the Korean War, the plan took shape quickly, embracing 'the Six' – France, Germany, Italy, Holland, Belgium and Luxembourg. The prime movers in the first three countries – Schuman, Adenauer, De Gasperi – were all men who had seen the two world wars, all passionate believers in reconciliation, all German-speaking, all Catholics. Behind the plan, and the subsequent treaty, were a group of enthusiasts in all six countries, much influenced by Monnet, who visualized a supranational Europe emerging from the wreckage of war. The British were asked to join, but were too worried by the supranationalism and by Germany. The treaty was signed in April 1951, and ratified the next year; the Community was set up in Luxembourg, with Monnet as president.

The new Community prospered, and schemes were prepared for extending the idea to agriculture, transport and health. Under the growing menace of the Korean War, a bolder plan was put forward, encouraged by the Americans and Churchill, to extend the system to a 'European Army'; the treaty for a European Defence Community (EDC) between the same six countries was actually signed (with Britain, as before, backing out) and a still further extension was planned, in the form of a 'European Political Community' (EPC). The optimism did not last. The French became increasingly alarmed at rearming the Germans – particularly without Britain as a counterweight. In August 1954 the French assembly, encouraged by Mendès-France, refused to ratify the European defence treaty. The unity broke, and the European movement seemed already to have struck the rocks.

Then, in June 1955, came the extraordinary 'relaunch'. The foreign ministers of the Six (Britain was again invited, but sent only a junior observer from the Board of Trade, Mr. Bretherton, who was shortly afterwards recalled) met at Messina to consider new proposals and appointed a committee to study methods of integration, under Paul-Henri Spaak, the Belgian foreign minister. The committee, not much noticed, got to work with extraordinary speed, meeting for intense sessions at the Château de Val Duchesse outside Brussels. Behind the scenes was Monnet himself, who had just resigned from the Coal and Steel Community to set up his own 'Action Committee'.

The first preoccupation of the Europeans, on which they pinned much hope, was the idea of Euratom, a pooling of nuclear energy: odd as it seems now the broader idea of a general common market was seen (as Pierre Uri has put it) as 'a kind of by-product of Euratom', insisted on by the Germans. In eight months at the Val Duchesse, the Spaak committee put together a report of unusual lucidity and imagination, which laid the basis of both Euratom and the common market. 'The object of a European common market,' it said, 'should be to create a vast area with a common political economy which will form a powerful productive unit and permit a steady expansion, an increase in stability, a more rapid rise in the standard of living, and the development of harmonious relations between the member states.' The report was accepted by the foreign ministers in May 1956, and the same committee was asked to prepare a formal treaty. It was an amazing victory for a tiny élite. As Hallstein described it to me: 'The genius of the method was that it took a group of people who became committed to general ideas, and then transformed the human beings into delegations; they then resisted national pressures to preserve their international conceptions.'

Spaak and his experts set about drafting the treaty, still at the Château. The British government were convinced by their embassy in Paris that the French government would not ratify it – as they had turned down the EDC. Their scepticism was not surprising. But the French prime minister, Guy Mollet, after his calamitous role in the Suez affair, was determined at least to push through the common market and was in a strong position to do so. The two disasters of November 1956, Suez and Hungary, played a crucial role in persuading the continent of Europe, and particularly France, of the fatal weakness of Europe. The British at the time, and for years later, were too obsessed with the Eden failure at Suez to notice that his more important blunder was his refusal to join Europe.

In March 1957, less than two years after the Messina meeting, the Treaty of Rome was signed on the Capitoline Hill in four languages by six countries. It is a dry document of 248 articles, the length of a short novel; it begins with the words: 'By the present Treaty, the High Contracting Parties establish among themselves a EUROPEAN ECONOMIC COMMUNITY', and it ends with a long list of tariffs, from acid oils to raw hemp. It was, in Hallstein's words, 'like one of the Dutch old masters, where parts are painted in great detail and other bits left blurred'. Behind the dry text lay all kind of hopes, ideas and theories, and it marked the convergence of several different schools of thought. In the first place, it was based on the belief that free trade in a larger market would increase not only prosperity but political stability – as in the United States or (a more doubtful precedent) the old German *Zollverein*. To achieve this, the treaty prescribed not only a customs union, but rules for fair competition, free movement of labour and capital, and common policies in transport. But the drafters were also determined to restrain a free-for-all, and the treaty gave large powers to the central authority to maintain a balanced expansion, to prohibit cartels, to offset hardships through a special Social Fund and an Investment Bank. In agriculture it called, in very vague terms, for a common policy to sta-bilize markets and ensure 'reasonable prices' – objectives which, as we will see, were to prove impossible to combine. Behind the trading arrangements was a political purpose, to provide 'close relations between its member states' and to prepare for a closer union.

Many hopes were to be dashed. But after all the vague idealism about 'Europe' of the post-war years, the Treaty of Rome marked the first major practical achievement. From this point onwards, people in the six countries and even in Britain were apt to use the word 'Europe' to mean the common market – to the fury of everyone else.

EFTA AND COMECON

The common market in Brussels is not the only one, as the map over the page shows. There is COMECON, the Soviet-based customs union or 'council for economic aid', made up of ten countries, including all eastern Europe, with Mongolia, Albania and Russia; it has rather petered out since Khrushchev's day. And there is EFTA, the rival group in western Europe, run very modestly from Geneva. EFTA's history is chequered; it was set up in 1960, after a convention in Stockholm, signed by an odd collection of countries: Britain, Austria, Denmark, Norway, Portugal, Sweden and Switzerland. Their only common characteristic was that they were all outside the other common market, and the con-vention was signed after Britain had tried to make a free-trade area out of all western Europe – which was foiled by France. They do not have much else in common; two of them, Switzerland and Sweden, are long-standing neutrals; two others, Denmark and Austria, are heavily dependent on Germany; Portugal is out on a limb. But they all have tra-ditional trading relations with Britain, the centre-piece; apart

from Austria and Portugal, they are predominantly Protestant; and the links between Britain and the 'Scans' are very
friendly. EFTA began with high hopes – a Swedish diplomat
even called his daughter Efta – and it achieved its main
purpose of a customs union (with some big exceptions, including agriculture) ahead of time, in December 1966. It
makes up a formidable trading group, with two-thirds of the
purchasing power of the common market, and without its
political complications. But it will not develop into anything
more than a trading arrangement, and it has no common
political ideals. If a new political structure is to emerge, it is
far more likely to come from Brussels than Geneva.

COUNCIL V. COMMISSION

A new kind of political animal.
Professor Hallstein

The administration of the common market was set up on a
delicate balance between two bodies – the Council of Ministers and the Commission. The 'dialogue' (the key word of
the Community) between these two represents in miniature
the battleground between the conflicting forces of Europe,
between internationalism and nationalism; and however dull
and disguised their arguments may seem, they are the
embryo workings of a federal Europe: as Hallstein has put
it: 'In this system we can clearly recognize the features of a
federal constitution; a structure that depends on co-operation between the higher entity and the constituent
states.'[1]

The Council of Ministers is made up of the foreign ministers or their deputies from the six countries. They consider
proposals from the Commission, and if necessary vote on
them, according to a weighted system of majority voting, in
which the big countries (France, Germany, Italy) have four
votes, Belgium and Holland have two votes, and Luxembourg has one. The Council is meant to represent the
national interests: 'If federation is unity in diversity,' explains Hallstein, 'the Commission represents the unity and
the Council the diversity. The balancing of individual

1. Walter Hallstein: 'Some of our *faux problèmes*', EEC, 1964, p. 4.

Three Common Markets

interests and Community interests is accomplished by discussions between these institutions, culminating in the meetings of the Council of Ministers.'[1]

The foreign ministers take turns to be chairman, for spells
of six months, and they meet in Brussels, Luxembourg or
Strasbourg. Behind the ministers is a large organization to
represent their interests, a 'committee of permanent representatives' in Brussels, and a huge secretariat of about five
hundred people, with their own information services, statistics and diplomats, in a big office-building in Brussels. The
Council, and the permanent representatives, meet in secrecy
and only reveal their final decisions; and the secrecy helps to
camouflage the real power of the Council.

On the other side of the dialogue, in a more public and
publicized situation, is the Commission, the permanent
bureaucracy which represents the 'supranational' element.
The Commission proposes, and the Council disposes; if the
Council cannot agree, the Commission comes back with
another proposal. As Pierre Uri has described it: 'A group of
men – the Commission – have been appointed to think out
and propose new formulae, to create a balanced approach
and to provide a concrete idea of the common interest. Supranationalism and co-operation between countries are therefore not contradictory terms in the Community system. It is
based on co-operation, but co-operation better organized
and made more effective because a body of men can stimulate the parties involved into joint action.'[2]

From the beginning of the common market the balance
between the Commission and the Council of Ministers has
constantly shifted. The Commission for its first ten years was
headed by Professor Walter Hallstein, a tireless and sometimes tactless lawyer who was determined to assert the full
power of his position, and who summed it up: 'We are not in
business; we are in politics.' In the first years Hallstein's
strong position was reinforced by the economic success of
western Europe and the new Franco-German alliance; although De Gaulle was openly critical of the Commission, he
evidently had no wish to break it up. There were successive
crises between Commission and Council, but a breakdown

1. Hallstein: 'Faux problèmes,' p. 9.
2. Pierre Uri: From Economic Union to Political Union. From Western
Europe, A Handbook, Blore, 1967, p. 598.

was averted. A special 'Community method' evolved, in which the Commission and the Council wore each other down with negotiating in 'marathon' sessions going late into the night, and eventually making bargains from sheer exhaustion. The end of each year, when new regulations came into force, marked the climax of negotiations, and at the new year the Council and the Commission retired exhausted, to prepare for the beginning of the next cycle. It was an exciting and nerve-racking system, but it worked.

'POPE' AND 'EMPEROR'

In the middle of 1962 the prestige of the Commission, and of Hallstein, was probably at its peak. The first serious set-back came soon afterwards when De Gaulle vetoed the British application to join the common market. Hallstein was not himself an ardent advocate of Britain's entry, and many members of the Commission had doubts; but De Gaulle's veto pointed the conflict between his conception of Europe – a kind of glorified Council of Ministers, with great scope for France – and the federalist conception of the Commission. De Gaulle's veto seemed for a time to threaten the whole continuation of the common market; but it held together for mutual self-interest, with diminished enthusiasm.

The real showdown followed in 1965; and this clash brought into the open all the underlying conflicts of the common market, and the real power-struggle between the Commission and the Council.[1] At the beginning of 1965 the Commission seemed confident. Cereal prices for the year had been fixed; and although De Gaulle was obstructive, there seemed to be an understanding between 'the Pope' and 'the Emperor' – between Hallstein and De Gaulle. The Council of Ministers was due to settle the question of farm finance, which specially concerned the French, by the end of June. Early in the year Hallstein put forward to the Council of Ministers some bold proposals, linking together the date for the Common Agricultural Policy (1st July, 1967), the financing of the agricultural fund through the Commission

1. For a detailed account of this crisis see Miriam Camps, *European Unification in the Sixties*, 1966 – to which I am indebted.

rather than through the governments, and the strengthening
of the European parliament to give it power to debate and
reject the Community's budget. The link between the three
proposals was logical, but it was clearly likely to anger De
Gaulle by involving a stronger Community. Hallstein, however, seemed determined to show that he could be independent of 'the Emperor'; he was supported by one
vice-president, Sicco Mansholt, and advised against it by
another, Robert Marjolin; but the Commission was publicly
unanimous. In March, before the Council of Ministers had
seen the proposals, Hallstein described them to the European
parliament in Strasbourg, which delighted the parliament but
infuriated the French. And in the next three months the proposals were further welcomed by the European parliament,
the European socialist parties and by Monnet's Action Committee.

In the meantime the Council of Ministers was discussing
the proposals. Couve de Murville, representing France,
wanted the farm finance settled without any strengthening
of the Community, and insisted that it must still be settled by
the end of June. After a series of meetings, with complex
technicalities, the Ministers held their Council meeting at the
end of June, to thrash out an agreement. The other five still
wanted all proposals to be settled together; Couve de Murville rapidly became more obdurate and then, as the dead-
line approached, gave a mysterious warning that if the
financial regulations were not settled by 30th June, serious
consequences would follow. Relations became tense, but the
other five were convinced that an agreement could be
reached. Then at two o'clock on the morning 1st July,
Couve abruptly broke up the meeting. He gave a short press
conference, saying that solemn undertakings had not been
fulfilled and that 'each government must draw the consequences'. The same afternoon Hallstein gave *his* press conference, insisting that agreement could be reached. But the
next week French delegates withdrew from all meetings in
Brussels, and the French permanent representative returned
to Paris. The boycott was on. The whole common market
seemed in danger of collapsing.

Hallstein continued as calmly as possible, and the Commission prepared new proposals much more conciliatory to
the French; but everyone now knew that the real quarrel

would not emerge until De Gaulle's press conference in September. When De Gaulle spoke, he soon brushed aside the technicalities and obfuscations, and emerged as the mastermind in the mystery: 'What happened in Brussels on 30th June in connection with the agricultural financing regulation, highlighted not only the persistent reluctance of the majority of our partners to bring agriculture within the scope of the common market, but also certain mistakes or ambiguities in the treaties setting up the economic union of the Six. That is why the crisis was, sooner or later, inevitable.' He went on to explain how the Treaty of Rome had taken advantage of France's weakness at that time, and angrily attacked the Commission – 'this embryonic technocracy, for the most part foreign' – for its attempt to increase its power by introducing majority voting. He mocked once again the idea of a European federation, and insisted that the proper course was 'organized co-operation between the states'.

De Gaulle's outburst at least cleared the air: it was now apparent that the General had become alarmed that French sovereignty would be threatened by the next phase of the common market, and was personally intervening. The boycott continued, and De Gaulle's speech was echoed by Couve, in a speech to the French Assembly in October; he further attacked the Commission for trying to step up its powers, and even asked for a 'general revision' of the Treaty of Rome, to eliminate among other things the system of majority voting: 'The conclusion forced upon us by the lamentable experience which we have just undergone is that French interests have no other defender than the French government . . .'

But if Couve was weeping crocodile tears, the French soon appeared to be overplaying their hand; the other five ministers met by themselves, inviting the French to join them, but were united in their determination to defend the Treaty against revision; and within France itself, where the presidential elections were brewing up, there was much concern at the thought of destroying the common market; the farmers' organizations and industrialists protested, and all De Gaulle's opponents in the election rallied to the support of the European Community.

By November, De Gaulle appeared to be willing to talk again with the five, and after the elections a meeting of foreign ministers was fixed for January, in Luxembourg, Couve put forward ten points, demanding among other things the curbing of the Commission's powers and the right of veto on all major decisions. But the five still held firm, led by the German foreign minister, Dr. Schroeder; and there was now even talk of the five inviting Britain to join them, and to occupy the 'empty chair' left by the French. Ten days later the foreign ministers met again, and this time the French were ready for compromise. The six governments agreed that the Commission should consult member states before making major proposals, prepared a new timetable for farm finance, and left the vexed question of majority voting in a very ambiguous state, agreeing to disagree, and recording that 'the French delegation considers that, when very important interests are at stake, the discussions must be continued until unanimous agreement is reached'. The crisis was over, the French rejoined the Brussels committees, and the bumpy journey towards a full common market went on.

Brussels, and particularly the Commission, was never as rash again. It was true that the French had had to climb down, and that the five had stood solidly against them: and in the following months the French often, in fact, accepted majority voting. But in the trial of strength the Commission had been chastened and the whole Community spirit had been diluted. The hope behind the Treaty of Rome, that the supranational body would gradually accumulate more power, and that the economic 'meshing' of the member countries would draw their interests close together, had been dashed. The Commission had tried to force the pace too quickly. De Gaulle, for the time being, had won.

The residue was bitter. The next year, in March 1967, the six countries celebrated the tenth anniversary of the Treaty of Rome: in spite of all his obstructions, De Gaulle was the hero of the meeting, and was received with awe and enthusiasm by the Italians and Germans. But Hallstein, who had made the treaty workable, was kept in the background; De Gaulle refused even to shake his hand. Paul-Henri Spaak, who had helped to draft the treaty, was invited to the celebrations, but refused to come. In an article in *Le Monde*, called 'Why I did not go to Rome', he passionately attacked De Gaulle's brutal treatment of Hallstein, and said: 'I do not want to spoil one of the best memories of my life by making it appear credible that it is the same ideal that we celebrate today, and that there is no difference between the egoist and introverted Europe that is now offered, and the open and generous Europe for which we fought ten years ago.'

EUROPEAN PARLIAMENT

At the point in the triangle of common market institutions, opposite the Commission and the Council of Ministers, is the assembly of the common market – the 'European Parliament' as it grandly renamed itself in March 1962. It is entrusted with the democratic control of the Community. It has 142 members chosen by the parliaments of the six countries – 36 from the big ones, 14 from the small. It has its own 12 standing committees, and its own secretariat of about 300 people in a skyscraper in Luxembourg: in their first nine years they had 2,204 committee meetings, 563 committee reports, and 281 plenary sessions. The parliament itself meets once a month in Strasbourg, when it borrows the chamber of the Council of Europe. It is a curious spectacle. The deputies sit in their semicircle, facing the president of the assembly; on his right, as if in dock, sit some members of the Commission from Brussels, waiting to answer questions. Behind the president, in glass boxes, are batteries of interpreters, translating in five languages; in the galleries are a few journalists, some diplomats and Strasbourg schoolboys.

The unique feature of the European parliament is that the members are grouped, not by nations, but by parties. Liberals and Christian Democrats sit on the right, Socialists on the left, and each political group meets beforehand to thrash out their line. The Gaullists used to sit with the Liberals, but now have their own group, called the Group for the Democratic Unity of Europe (UDE), consisting only of Frenchmen. The Christian Democrats are by far the biggest group, with 44 per cent of the seats, followed by Socialists (25 per cent), Liberals (18 per cent) and Gaullists (11 per cent). There is a blatant omission – the communists; and their absence gives a certain absurdity to the gathering. It happened because when the common market was established (and before it the Coal and Steel Community) the founders insisted that political groups which were aginst the whole idea should be excluded – i.e. the communists. Since then, in fact, the Italian communists have accepted the principles of the common market, but the Italian parliament could not elect communists to Strasbourg without producing a major split in the government; so that the same Italian members remain – some of them by now no longer members of the parliament in Rome, some of them actually dead. It is a farcical and dangerous situation, which helps to perpetuate the earlier cold-war character of the Assembly; but the Italian government has now promised that the communists will be admitted.

The members of the European parliament go through the motions, and have the trappings of power. They make a lot of reports on proposals from the Commission, about labour or non-proliferation or animal foodstuffs. They can even report on the common market budget; when I watched a debate one member was actually accusing the Commission of *manipulating* the accounts. The appropriate Commissioner from Brussels politely replies and explains. Before the Commission makes a proposal, it consults the parliament's standing committee and exchanges ideas. In theory they can sack the entire Commission by a two-thirds majority: but since they cannot appoint a new one this power is meaningless. They cannot confront the government of the common market, because it does not have a government; their real opponents are the Council of Ministers, to whom the Commission ultimately make their proposals; but the Council of Ministers are responsible not to the European parliament, but to their own national parliaments. Like advisory directors in a business, the parliament is constantly confronted by people who are responsible to someone else. On the crucial question of the budget, the source of all real parliaments' powers, they have no control; in the 1965 crisis, De Gaulle insisted that the budget must remain under the control of the Council of Ministers; and it has. There was an indication of the impotence of the parliament in December 1967, at the time of De Gaulle's press conference; the president discovered that they no longer had a quorum, because the members were all watching De Gaulle on TV.

In this ineffectual condition, the parliament might still be able to enjoy fiery political debates, to publicize issues and stir up opinion; but its topics reflect those of the Commission, and it is hard to be passionately political about animal foodstuffs. As Elena Bubba, the director of parliamentary documentation, put it on the tenth anniversary[1]: 'A sense of accomplishment, vague dissatisfaction and deep concern about the future of the communities permeates the European parliament.... As the communities grow, they offer more and more details and less subject matter for great political debates.'

So long as the Council of Ministers, responsible to national parliaments, remains the arbiter of common market decisions, the European parliament can be no more than an interrupter, a heckler with words-in-edgeways, in the main dialogue between Commission and common market. Only a rebuilding of the Community would achieve a stronger parliament; and this is only likely if the common market were to be joined by the one country with a continuous parliamentary tradition, which is Britain.

COMMISSION

We are not only the clergy, we are also the prophets of Europe.

Jean Rey, 1967

Though the Commission has come through its first ten years scathed and chastened, it is still the essential instrument, the 'motor', not just of the customs union, but of the whole process of integration. Unlike the other polyglot bureaucracies – OECD, FAO, NATO, UNESCO – where national governments have a direct influence, the Commission is meant to be the engine of supranational interests: national concerns are supposed to merge into the international idea. The word Eurocrat is often used for this sequestered bureaucracy, and the word sums up the fears which surround them – the fears of an international technocracy, cut off from political pressures and public hearing. It is an image which the Eurocrats greatly resent, with some reason. In the first place their actual power is severely limited by the Council of Ministers. In the second place they go to great trouble to appear in public arguments, to receive visiting delegations, politicians, journalists, dons, to explain

1. *Form and Function of the Opposition in the European Communities: Government and Opposition*, April 1967.

their policies in pamphlets or lectures: most of them would genuinely welcome a strengthening of the European parliament. But their unhappy conflicts with the Council of Ministers, with De Gaulle in the background, has forced them into a cautious, depoliticized approach which makes it all the easier to attack them as bloodless bureaucrats. With the rising temper of nationalism, they are increasingly forced back on legalistic attitudes, regarding the Treaty of Rome as the Ark of the Covenant.

In July 1967 the three European communities, the common market, Euratom and the Coal and Steel Community, were formally merged into a single body: the nine men at the head of the common market Commission were increased to fourteen, to take charge of the two extra communities.[1] It is those fourteen commissioners who are the custodians of the supranational ideal; when they took office in July, they decided by seven votes to six (the president abstaining and the three French members voting against) to pledge their complete independence from national control, and they went to Luxembourg to take the oath in front of the Community's Court of Justice. Their commitment was soon to be made clear; when the British application came up a few months later the French members, though critical, were noticeably independent of De Gaulle's line.

The new fourteen-man commission may have less political weight than its predecessor; of the fourteen, only Mansholt and Jean Rey, the president, have much political following in their home country. Some commissioners give the impression of having been kicked upstairs by their national governments; some seem to have just floated into their jobs; but others are men who represent the authentic spirit of the European movement. Sicco Mansholt, who has been a vice-president since the beginning,[2] was dedicated to European unity when he was a Socialist minister in the Dutch government; Jean Deniau, the youngest commissioner, is one of the ablest of the French technocrats who has written a standard work on the common market.

The 'fusion' of the three communities was an agonizing process. Jobs had to be cut out, departments rationalized, and the national pressures became much more evident;

1. Later reduced to nine again – see introduction.
2. See chapter 3.

bureaucrats threatened with demotion appealed to their national governments. In the upshot, jobs were more carefully balanced between nationalities at all levels; an able Frenchman might be succeeded by a second-rate German, to satisfy Bonn. 'The supranational idea is giving way before the inter-governmental structure,' as one commissioner said; or as another Eurocrat put it: "We're all being OECD-ized." Both in personnel and in budgets, the ominous principle of 'the fair return' began to show itself – that each country should get back what it put in – the exact opposite of the 'Community Spirit'.

For any Eurocrats who have been in it since the beginning, the change is saddening. Some of the officials have been in Brussels now for eleven years, and have developed into a new species of man. They remain separate from Belgian society but are also cut off from their own countries. They may go home for weekends and for holidays (in August the whole common market shuts down completely); but many of them – Germans particularly – feel detached. There is quite a lot of intermarriage, though not just between common market countries: EFTA people and even Americans get involved and there are signs that English is becoming more, not less, of a *lingua franca*. The secretaries are a special sub-species: many of them come to Brussels to escape their home countries, and they are often quite *déraciné*. With the accumulation of international secretaries, much enlarged by NATO, this non-Belgian Brussels is becoming more and more a province of its own. You get a glimpse of the Eurocrat's life from the notice boards: posters for national festivities, film societies, Alfa Romeos or Triumphs for sale, villas in Spain or Italy to be let, spare seats in a car driving to Rome, flats to let in the *Quartier d'Europe*. The situation of the Eurocrats has been compared to the young 'New Dealers' who came to Washington in the Roosevelt era, building a new detached community. Brussels already has something of the rarefied diplomatic atmosphere of Washington (or Canberra), the same lack of roots. The smaller countries, Belgium, Holland or Luxembourg, not surprisingly, produce the most internationalized people. Of the Six, the Italians seem the most obviously homesick and clannish – partly no doubt because Italy is the farthest away. To the French, Brussels is still a kind of province of Paris.

Many Eurocrats have been emotionally deeply involved in the Community idea, and saw it both in political and personal terms as an escape from the trammels of nationalism; the Germans who joined the Community in the fifties were part of a generation who desperately wanted to become part of a larger unity and to escape from their national past. For them the Community was more than an idea; it was a new kind of nationality. For them and others the splitting-apart of the supranational loyalty is a personal tragedy.

JEAN REY

Building Europe is like building a gothic cathedral. The first generation knows that they will never see the work completed, but they go on working.

Jean Rey

At first sight Jean Rey, president of the European Community, might be taken for the kind of 'stateless technocrat' whom De Gaulle likes to talk about. He does not have obvious political sex-appeal. He is a short Belgian with thick-rimmed glasses and a huge mouth, which flaps up and down. He can talk four languages, equally fast. He wears dark suits, does not drink or smoke, and is said to be able to read dossiers all night. He presents an almost opposite impression to his predecessor, Hallstein – who worked equally hard, but had a certain flamboyance, loved to venture into politics, and liked to drive very fast in an open Mercedes. But Rey's patience and unobtrusiveness may make him a more effective politician than his predecessor.

Rey's background lends some support to the theory that the European Community is a collection of outsiders, of odd-men-out. He looks, and is, very Protestant, and is very conscious of it. Belgian Protestants are a beleaguered minority – only two per cent – and this certainly helps to give Rey detachment and toughness. Rey has been very critical of the arrogance of his native Wallonia: recently at a speech in Liège he said: 'There are some people who speak three languages – we call them trilingual; some speak two languages – they are bilingual. Some speak one language – we call them Walloons.' (He himself speaks French, Flemish, English and German.) Not surprisingly he is not regarded as being very Belgian.

He was always internationally-minded. He was a refugee in the First World War, at the age of twelve. When the Germans came into Belgium, he crossed with his mother to England for a year, and went to school in Croydon: there he learnt English and some English history ('I only got up to Edward III,' he told me: 'I still don't know what happened between then and Churchill.') After the war he studied law at Liège university and became a successful advocate. His mother was a prominent pacifist, a disciple of Norman Angell of *The Great Illusion*; and in the thirties Rey became active in the League of Nations. He remembers Aristide Briand, the premier of France, saying in 1930: 'As long as I am where I am, there will be no war.' Before the war he became a deputy in Brussels, and attacked the ill-fated government policy, advocated by Paul-Henri Spaak, of Belgian neutrality. Rey was already a European before the second war; but the war strengthened his determination. He spent four years as a prisoner-of-war in Germany, partly in the top people's prison camp, Schloss Colditz; and his prison time gave him a new sense of solidarity with other countries, and (as he put it to me) 'the ability to distinguish between what is important and unimportant'.

After the war he was soon struck by the realization that the great world decisions were no longer being taken in Paris, Berlin or London, but in Washington and Moscow: as for so many Europeans, the desire for peace was mixed with a desire for power. He went back into Belgian politics, and soon became a minister, first of reconstruction, then of economics; but he was increasingly involved in international politics – first at the United Nations, then at the Council of Europe, then in 1958 as one of the original nine members of the common market Commission, acting as a kind of foreign minister to the Community. He impressed his colleagues and diplomats by his obvious integrity, his mixture of idealism and realism. His real rise to fame came when he pulled off the 'Kennedy Round' of tariff cuts in 1967, arguing as a single spokesman for the Six, facing the Americans as equals. He explained afterwards: 'We see that in the only domain where Europeans are integrated, where they speak with a single voice, they find themselves on an equal footing with the great American power.'

Hallstein was ousted by De Gaulle in 1967, and there was

a period of intense politicking over his successor. The Six
wanted the job to go to an Italian, and at least two men were
asked, Emilio Colombo (Minister of the treasury) and Guido
Carli (governor of the Bank of Italy); but they both preferred to remain in Italian politics: that might be a sad
reflection on the fallen prestige of the Community, or on the
Italians' shortage of first-class brains. Eventually Rey
emerged as the most acceptable candidate, and took over the
job in July 1967. He was immediately in the midst of every
kind of problem. The Commission itself was in turmoil, with
the three Communities being merged into one. De Gaulle's
tactics were increasingly ruthless. European defence was at
odds. And the British had again applied for entry. Rey, when
he took over, soon surprised people. He insisted that the
Commission had a 'political temperament' and that it must
act independently of the Six governments, and he made no
secret of his support for British entry, which (unlike Hallstein) he regards as indispensable to genuine European
unity. In the following months, as the British application was
discussed and rejected, Rey played his cards coolly against
De Gaulle. His job required that he must above all keep the
Six together; and he insisted that their differences over
Britain must be ironed out between themselves. But he made
sure that there was no doubt about the fundamental division
between the Commission's policy and France's, and he managed to bring his thirteen colleagues to a unanimous (if
qualified) view of the need for Britain to come in.

Like some other European federalists, Rey has been much
influenced by American history; and the success of American unity gives him encouragement. 'We are in the same
process you Americans went through two hundred years
ago,' he has said. 'We may have our quarrels between federalists and nationalists, but everyone knows very well we are
moving toward unity.'[1] He is more patient than Hallstein; he
sees the difficulties with De Gaulle as only one of a series of
troubles that will face the Community; but he shows no
doubt about the eventual outcome, even if he does not live
to see it.

1. *Business Week*, 16th September, 1967.

RICH MAN'S CLUB

An unnatural marriage – of men only.

Khrushchev

Listening to conferences and reports of the Eurocrats, it is hard not to feel oppressed by the exclusiveness and introversion of their business. Being blocked from political progress, their hopes of unity are caught up in the detailed machinery of material trade. To many visitors it comes as a shock, after all the idealistic manifestos of the common market. It is as if having expected to go to a meeting on world government one was shown into the accounts department of Harrods.

The Eurocrats are sensitive to the charge of insulation, particularly from the developing countries that ask their aid. The post-war developments in Europe have cut it off from Asia and Africa. At the end of the war six countries of Europe still had large empires. In the following years most of them were abandoned, with varying speed and reluctance: their loss made the European powers, as it turned out, not poorer but richer. They were relieved of the costs of administration and armies: capital and brains could be diverted back to commercial advancement at home: and, most important, the terms of trade between the ex-colonial countries and Europe shifted rapidly in favour of Europe. Keynes predicted in the thirties that the Afro-Asian countries would become rapidly industrialized, making raw materials more expensive and manufactured products cheaper – so that Europe would pay more for its imports and get less for its exports. Many Eurocrats at the beginning took the same view.

But the move was in the opposite direction. The price of raw materials went down and the dependence of Afro-Asian countries on Europe became greater. The Europeans could pick and choose between the developing countries for their primary products – taking iron ore, copper or cocoa from wherever it was cheapest. New synthetic products, particularly plastics, took the place of some materials; whose industries (like sisal) collapsed. In Africa one cannot help but notice how the economy of whole countries can depend on the whims of European housewives. The trade in cashew nuts, a crucial industry of Tanzania, depends on fashions in cocktail parties: the income of Ghana depends on the sweet tooth of European children. For all the exaggerations about the 'neo-colonialism' the bitter fact remains that for ex-colonial countries the economic dependence on Europe and America has taken the place of colonial dependence.

In the meantime, the European countries trade more and more with each other. As they produce more sophisticated goods – tape-recorders, machine tools, cars – so they find that their best customers are next-door; like rich men everywhere they discover that the best people to deal with are other rich men. Even the poorer countries of Europe – Iberia and eastern Europe – are left out of much of the trade. The proportion of trade with ex-colonial countries has steadily diminished. In 1953 the developing countries had 27 per cent of the world exports, in 1966 it was only 19.3 per cent.[1] This is a fact which the British are most bitterly aware of: having stuck to the Commonwealth as a trading alternative to the common market, they found the Commonwealth less and less able to afford her goods, while the common market increasingly could.

This change of trade would have happened anyhow; but the new institutions of Europe have spurred on the process by measuring one rich country against another, and encouraging the European rat-race. The common market, OECD, GATT and EFTA have all enhanced the sense of solidarity of the rich countries; their bleakly materialist statements are apt to assume that no other countries exist. The loss of empires, the sense of relief that followed, and the maddening behaviour of the new countries, have all made Africa and Asia seem farther away. The Kennedy Round was hailed as a triumph for free trade between America and Europe but it did nothing to resolve the trade disadvantage of the third world.

The attempts to increase financial aid to the developing world have been desperately disappointing; in theory, with such a rapidly rising standard of living, to allocate one per cent of the national income to aid should be easy enough. The case for it is constantly argued, both from human decency and from fear of a coming racial explosion. But the

1. *The Observer*, 28th January, 1968.

internal pressures are too strong, and in the last decade the proportion of national budgets devoted to aid has not risen but fallen. In 1967 the *Economist* reckoned that aid to developing countries amounted to no more than an average of four dollars per head of their population.

The developing countries have organized two big conferences called UNCTAD (United Nations Conference on Trade and Development), sometimes known as 'the poor man's club'; and a permanent UNCTAD organization has been set up in the old Palace of Nations in Geneva, under an Argentinian, Dr. Prebisch. But the hundred countries – each with its own interests and links with rich countries – cannot make a common front, and their last meeting, at New Delhi in 1968, ended in tragic disorder.

Many members of the Commission (notably Rey and Mansholt) are genuinely concerned; but the common market, at present, has the worst of both worlds. It has developed far enough to stimulate much greater competitiveness between countries: but it has not gone as far as to achieve a strong federal centre which could in turn acquire a corporate conscience.

For the new generation of rebels, this gilded European cage offers a special nightmare. They feel both guilty and bored by the self-enclosement, and strive to escape. But the withdrawal of Europe from both trading and military commitments gives less opportunity for involvement with Afro-Asia; and what the new countries most want from Europe is just that technology and consumer society from which European rebels most want to escape.

INTEGRATION

Watching the declining morale of the Eurocrats in the past five years, and looking back at their past hopes, it is easy to write them off altogether as a force for unifying Europe. With the politics denied to them, they had turned their minds to the mechanical side of the business and have pursued means rather than ends. They have won some important victories – such as the introduction of a common tax system, the added-value tax (TVA), and the common bargaining with America over the Kennedy Round; but their efforts to create a common European industry and technology, as we will see, have been frustrated by the tensions between countries and the dominance of America.

The free trade among the Six has gone ahead, but no one knows how much is a result of the lowering of tariffs, how much would have happened anyway. As the tariffs have come down, other obstacles become more apparent – local taxes, retailers' agreements, secret cartels, or sheer prejudice; local regulations for safety or food hygiene are more and more invoked to keep foreign goods out. Looking at European shops, it is surprising to see how little difference the common market has made to them; prices vary between countries, for no apparent reason; TV sets (for instance) still cost almost twice as much in France as in Germany. The most spectacular 'common market industry' has been the refrigerators, where the big Italian firms, led by Ignis have swamped Europe, undercutting everyone and specially taxed by the French; but they are not restricted to the common market, and now Britain too has raised duties against them. It is the newest industries which can most easily cross frontiers, unhampered by old agreements and prejudices; but they are very likely to be American. Most traditional industries, including cars, remain deeply involved in national networks and habits.

Behind the free trade and free movement, the actual development of integration between the countries is impossible to gauge. A formidable study was made by Professor Karl Deutsch of Yale University, who spent two years with a team of researchers analysing the relations between France and Germany, with special reference to the prospects of arms control.[1] He interviewed the élites, examined public opinion polls and disarmament proposals, analysed editorials and collected statistics about Franco-German exchanges. From all this evidence, Professor Deutsch insisted, the results were the same; that in 1957 Europe attained a level of integration greater than at any time since 1890; but that since 1957 the rhythm of integration had slowed down, with no further progress – except in so far that the people were becoming more prosperous, and so more mobile.

This gloomy result created a minor furore; and Jacques-René Rabier, director of the common market's information service, complained that Deutsch was preoccupied with ex-

1. *American Political Science Review*, No. 2, 1966.

changes, not with the real influences of integration, and that France and Germany were not necessarily the decisive powers. A year later another American researcher, Ronald Inglehart of Michigan, came out with an investigation based on the opinions of five thousand selected students in France, Holland, West Germany and England.[1] His results showed that in all these countries (though opinions fluctuated from month to month) the 'Europeanness' of young people was greater than that of their elders; and that over seventy per cent of people under twenty in Holland, Germany and France, believed in a common foreign policy, and even in using national taxes to help poorer European countries. 'Far from finding a stagnation of integrative processes since 1958,' said Inglehart, 'I would argue that, in some respects, European integration may have moved into full gear only *since* 1958.'

I believe that both Deutsch and Inglehart are right – depending on what is meant by integration. In the sense of common interests in defence, common fears and common allies, it is obviously true that France and Germany were much closer in 1957 – the heyday of NATO – than they are now; the *détente* has allowed each country to have its own limited foreign policy. But in the sense of a common consciousness, the forgetting of frontiers, the awareness that social and industrial situations are the same – in these senses the younger generation is becoming truly European. The following chapters will show some of the social and economic influences which are changing the assumptions about what 'Europe' actually is.

In their broad hopes to 'make Europe' most of the hopes of Monnet and the Eurocrats have been dashed. The final achievement of the customs union in July 1968 proved to be a point of new despondency; for the French economic crisis had led France to impose import crontrols which, though temporary, raised great doubts as to how irreversible the union was to be. Even the opening of frontiers was something of an anti-climax. The customs posts remained. Lorries still had to wait at the borders for their goods to be checked. There were still local taxes, duties on goods coming from outside the common market, health and security checks. The

1. 'An End to European Integration?' *American Political Science Review*, No. 1, March 1967.

customs union only served to underline how much else had
to be achieved, and how misplaced were the hopes that free
trade would necessarily push forward political integration.
As the Commission itself proclaimed in a statement on 1st
July: 'Europe is not only a matter of customs tariffs. It does
not belong just to the manufacturers, the farmers or the
technocrats. It is not only the Europe of 180 million Europeans living in the Community. It is not just the Europe of the
governments, parliaments and administrations. It must also
be the Europe of the peoples, of the workers, of youth. All –
or nearly all – still remains to be done.'

Some of these other Europes will be the concern of the
rest of this book. In the last ten years many people, particularly in Britain, have tended to confuse Europe with the
Common Market, and to set too much store on the effects of
economic union. The hopes that economic union could in
itself press forward political union have – as we will see –
been frustrated in most fields. And many of the most important trends in integration – international companies, international trade unions, defence, student movements – are
happening in a much larger context than the Six. Moreover
the common market in its present state is inherently unstable; as Hallstein has said, 'integration is like a bicycle;
you either move on, or you fall off'. If the Six cannot move
towards political unity, if they cannot bring together the
countries into the same system of welfare, security and
benefits, the separate interests of the citizens will constantly
be threatening to pull them apart – for it is for security,
above all, that people look to their nation. Each new economic crisis, like the French one, will wobble the bicycle.

Yet for all its limitations, its despondency and consequent
materialism, the common market remains the most important of all European institutions. The element of supranationalism still marks it out from the other bodies –
NATO, EFTA, OECD, or the Council of Europe – as the
one place where people are expected no longer to represent
just their own country: however bitter the arguments in
Brussels, it is better that they should be thus than hurled
from capital to capital. The common market still has a
unique concentration of international brains who can see
above the forest of facts and statistics; in their eleven years,
the Eurocrats have become used to working with each other

and seeing other viewpoints. The common market may be a dry and circumscribed kind of Europe, but it is so far the only really concrete step towards a unified Europe that we have.

Part Two

Chapter Three

Land

Eh! mes amis, peut-on mieux faire
Quand on a dépeuplé la terre
Que de la repeupler après?
Marquis de Boufflers, 1738–1815

At the bottom of Europe, in the middle of the instep of Italy, is the region of Basilicata, which seems barely connected with the North. Its bright white houses, its dry earth and bare villages are more like those of Greece, or even of Arab Africa, than of Italy. This is one way of coming on Europe, where it merges lazily into the sea, the sun and the coast of Africa. You can reach it in a long day's drive down from Rome, past Naples, across the empty country to Foggia, and Bari. You pass through the country of the Trulli, the little round stone houses with steep roofs and bobbles on the top, whose pattern (it is thought) originated in Ancient Greece and has hardly been changed since medieval times, which grow out of the landscape so naturally that they might be giant white mushrooms.

At the end you come to the ancient port of Taranto, originally a Spartan colony, then the first city of Magna Graecia, and later a naval dockyard and port of the new state of Italy. Since the fall of Mussolini's navy, the city's fortunes have fallen, and Taranto now has a forlorn but beautiful peace. Along the waterfront of the old harbour there are piles of mussels which for centuries have been the staple foods of Tarantines; in the narrow back streets, between high white houses, the markets are laid out on the cobbles, with cheap shoes and food being gazed at by the women. The oldest part of the town, round the eleventh-century cathedral founded by an Irish bishop, still has rough crowded streets which a car only navigates with difficulty. The whole town is on an island, joined by a single bridge to the mainland, so that Taranto is cut off both by time and place.

No town seems more effectively insulated from the pressures of the modern world. Yet across the bridge, and two miles further north, there rises the most unmistakable shape – the vast rectangular shed of a steelworks, with tall red-and-white chimneys puffing smoke over the clear blue sky. There is a cement works next door and a brewery up the road; but otherwise, the works stand alone, in the middle of an ancient grove of gnarled olive trees. Outside the main entrance is a milestone saying 645 kilometres: and the official address of the steelworks is Via Appia 645 Km – measured along the old Roman road from the capital.

Looking round it inside, the contrast is still more strange. The steelworks is the pride of Italian nationalized industry, built in a bold attempt to bring employment to the south, and completed in 1964, on a site bigger than Taranto itself. It has all the Italian flair for picking the rest of the world's brains, with equipment and inventions from America, Sweden, Austria, Britain. The site on the sea was chosen so that iron ore could be brought in by ship from anywhere in the world, and carried directly by overhead conveyor into the factory. In front of the steelworks is a block of clean new air-conditioned offices, full of diagrams and eager young executives; and behind is the great red shed of the steel mills, with, in the midst of it, a hanging cauldron of white-hot iron ore controlled from a glass cabin. The workers themselves are hard to find, dwarfed by the machines which have taken over. Most of them are local men, who have worked in the naval arsenal or in car repair shops in the town; they have been sent to Northern Italy, or even to Utah, for their training, and have come back to their home country as skilled workers, to disprove the prophecies that the south would never catch up.

The Taranto steelworks is an extreme case of the sudden industrialization of Europe. It is a deliberate attempt by the Italian government to bring industry to the south, to establish a pole to attract manufacturing industries on the plain. Arguments still rage as to whether the works are a white elephant or a courageous beginning. The factory was opened in the midst of a recession, and the very bareness of it proclaims its lack of success, so far, in attracting other industries. The plant employs less than 5,000 people, making scarcely a dent on the unemployment in Taranto. (Automation brings its own problems: a similar steelworks in Czechoslovakia, I was told, employs 20,000 people.) The obstacles to change in the south are proverbial; the way of life comes from some of the most conservative people in Europe. The Tarantines talk proudly about the steelworks: 'the biggest in the world', we were told. But so far it has not apparently made much impact on the life of the city, except to push up food prices, to provide a luxury hotel, and to cause a perpetual traffic jam on the bridge. The most obvious political change has been a huge increase in the communist vote in Taranto in the 1968 elections.

The enthusiasts of the nationalized steel industry believe that Taranto may yet become the centre of a miniature Ruhr, extending in a triangle to Bari and Brindisi, providing an industrial complex to serve a new Mediterranean market, and to relieve the poverty of this desolate corner. The critics of the scheme, including most northern industrialists, believe that the steel would be far better made in the industrial north. The steelworks may yet be the centre of a new Ruhr; but for the time being it sticks out like a sore thumb from the hot grey plain.

Taranto, with its chimney above the olive-groves, might be taken as a metaphor of the tensions and problems of industrial Europe. For many visionaries of a united Europe over the last hundred and fifty years industrialization has been the great hope, the agent of reason and unity, bringing not only prosperity but international enlightenment to the local peasantries. The railway tycoons, the steelmasters and roadbuilders have seen themselves opening up a great international age, boldly transplanting and grafting their organs from one body to another. Yet the operation has never worked quite as expected; the new body is always liable to reject the organism, or react against it, in some obscure way that defies diagnosis. The universal industrial man never quite takes shape, the old local patterns and politics reassert themselves inside the factories; the obstinate peasant is still there.

In the next eight chapters I will try to follow some of the trails of this physical Europe, to see how far the underlying structures are changing. The trail begins with the oldest industry, agriculture, where each way of life has its roots; then follows to coal-mining and the sources of energy; then to mass-producing industries, in the shape of the giant corporations; and from there to the new technologies and the network of defence. I will ask how far each new development is bringing greater unity to the continent; in each case, the answer is not simple.

PEASANTS

Agriculture is still by far the biggest industry in Western Europe, with 31 million people working on the land. Over most of its area, the typical figure is still the peasant, circumscribed by his own farm, fields and family. But in the rich countries in the next thirty years he will become almost as rare as the English farm labourer is today. No traveller can miss the most visible sign of Europe's industrial boom, the flight from the land. On the steep hills of Tuscany, the turreted farmhouses are deserted and crumbling; the sloping fields run wild, for the first time for centuries, and some vineyards are being uprooted for lack of workers to tend them. The countryside, which ten years ago had a steady life of its own, is now a decaying museum-land inhabited by old Tuscans or smart Kensington visitors with swimming pools. In Umbria land is even being given away to expatriates who will build on it. In France, along the Dordogne, the rough stone farmers' mansions, which seem so permanent, so much part of the untamed country, are shuttered and windowless, or have suddenly been tarted up with bright paint and coach lamps by holidaymakers from Paris or Rotterdam. In some parts of Europe, farmers have quite painlessly switched to tourism as an alternative industry; in mountain villages in the Alps small communities of poor farmers have turned to working ski-lifts or supplying hotels, with less work and more money. But elsewhere there has been wholesale uprooting. In southern Italy, in the wilder corners of Calabria, whole villages have been evacuated, leaving only old men and women, in the great rush to the rich north. The imagined dignity of the Italian farm-workers has disappeared in the scramble for wages, and they would rather clean windscreens than pick grapes.

In all the unhappy history of European agriculture, with
its migrations, famines, pests and wars, there has never been
– on the continental scale – such a sudden evacuation as in
the last twenty years. The total agricultural labour force of
the six common market countries in 1950 was 16 million; in
1963 it was 10 million – an average loss to the land of half-a-
million a year; and this rate is still being maintained today.[1]
These were the percentages of some populations working on
the land between 1960 and 1966.[2]

	1960–61	1966
France	20%	17.6%
W. Germany	14%	10.8%
Italy	29%	24.9%
Holland	10%	8.5%
Belgium	9%	6.0%
Switzerland	12%	8.8%
Spain	42%	32.6%
UK	4%	3.4%
USA	8%	5.5%
Denmark	18%	16.6%

What is happening is not just a straight change of occupation; it is an upheaval in the whole way of life. After the
war, a large part of France and Italy and even of Germany
(though cut off from its agricultural east) was predominantly
peasant country. The earlier industrial revolutions had not
emptied the land as drastically as in England, which alone of
the countries of Europe, had a relatively tiny farming population. While the English had been uprooted and disinherited
first by the enclosures and then by sudden industrialization,
the peasant on the continent was able to survive, usually
with a farm just big enough to keep him. There are still
many parts of Germany, particularly in Swabia, where fac-
tory-workers have small family farms which help to support
them. In France and Italy industry affected mainly the
northern regions, and the railways left much of the country
untouched.

The big peasant families split up the land into parcels
which to English or American eyes seem ridiculous. In England, the smallest economic size is reckoned as 200 acres, and
the average size is 120 acres. In the common market in 1965,

1. *Basic Statistics of the Community 1966*, EEC, p. 54.
2. Sources: 'Low Incomes in Agriculture', OECD 1964; *OECD
Observer*, Feb. 1968.

out of the total area of farming land of about 69 million
acres, 52 million was made up of farms of less than 125
acres. The typical continental farm consists of one man and
his son, with only 40 acres; there are less than 2 million paid
workers in the whole common market, compared to 4
million heads of farms, and 33 million unpaid family
workers.[1] A large proportion of the farm workers (40 per
cent in France, 50 per cent in Germany) are women – wives,
daughters or sisters of the farmers.[2]

French farmers, with nearly half the agricultural land of
the common market, are the key to its success or failure.
Certainly there have been great movements of reform. Some
of the big farms in the north have become highly mechanized, and the group of young farmers emanating after the
war from the Jeunes Agriculteurs Chrétiens (JAC), have
campaigned for more efficient methods and co-operatives.
But the small peasant, unprepared or unable to co-operate
with neighbours, is still the fundamental problem: he has
been left behind by the great movement ot the towns and
nowadays he finds it difficult to find a wife, the most indispensable piece of equipment, in the migration swing away
from the farms. The pattern of small farming in Europe is
perpetuated even on new land, like the Dutch *polders* re-
claimed from the sea: in the newest *polder*, East Flevoland,
the average-sized farm is only 90 acres (though the acres are
very fertile).

Given this small family set-up it is not surprising that
European farmers have concentrated on their own self-
sufficiency, with a few vines, fruit-trees, cows and chickens,
and not much interest in markets. It is the simple heart of the
common market's agricultural problem, to convert millions
of tiny farms, with ageing owners and unprofitable methods,
into a competitive agricultural industry.

In the past the land has lain at the bottom of many of
Europe's wars and revolutions, and the changes in farming
have radically affected politics. One agricultural economist,
Professor Rossi-Doria of Naples, has argued that the break-
up of feudalism in the nineteenth century, and the spread of

1. *Basic Statistics of the Community 1966*, pp. 52–4.
2. *L'Emploi agricole dans les pays de la CEE*, vol. 1, p. 15, Brussels,
1964.

agricultural technology, gave the continent a new self-awareness and similarity, and a kind of European consciousness: national movements were linked with peasants' freedom, and the 'green risings' had a strong supranational element.[1] But this common bond of the land was broken by the First World War and its aftermath. The depression, protection and the crudely national policies for farmers isolated the countries from each other. Each nation thought in terms of defending its own agriculture against international competition and the possibility of war. By 1939 most European countries (except Britain) were self-supporting in most farm products. To reverse this system – to bring back a continental scale – has been the chief aim of the framers of the common market for farmers.

MANSHOLT'S COMMON MARKET

At the storm centre of Europe's agricultural problem stands Dr. Sicco Mansholt, vice-president of the Commission of the common market in Brussels, and originator of the ambitious agricultural policy. He is one of the boldest and more convincing of the Eurocrats, an outspoken politician among discreet technocrats, a master of the common touch, and a real farmer. He is a big Dutchman, with thick hands, pale blue eyes and eyebrows which curl up at the ends; he talks about his complex problems with a jolly simplicity. Now sixty, he has watched the transformation of agriculture at first hand. He was brought up on the family farm, went to a school for tropical agriculture, and learnt his business on Dutch farms; he worked for a time on a tea plantation in Indonesia, then came back to Holland, to farming and socialist politics. In the war he was in the Dutch resistance, and afterwards became Minister of Agriculture in successive socialist governments. He was in the thick of the planning of Benelux and the common market, and in the fifties planned a 'Green Pool', an ambitious forerunner of the common market policy. He describes problems by referring to his own family: 'My grandfather ran the family farm – 200 acres – with eighteen men; my brother now runs it with his son and one other worker, and one animal – a dog. He makes enough money to go skiing in the winter, and to the

1. *Daedalus*, Winter, 1964, p. 336.

Mediterranean in the summer; and he can pay his worker more than the steelworks near by.'

Mansholt is not worried about the exodus from the land which I have described. For proper productivity, there are still too many farm workers and agricultural wages have never been higher. He told me: 'In 1958 I said that within a generation, eight million people in the common market would leave the land. The Germans were furious. But in fact the rate has been much faster than that. The farms in Tuscany are lovely to look at, but they were misery to work on – bad land without water. Tourists are taking the place of farmers: that's fine for people like us, the Dutch and the English, who like to get away from crowds. I'm much more worried about the population of the towns than the de-populations of the country. So many farm workers find that living in the towns is like a prison.'

'Our real problem,' Mansholt went on, 'is the farms with about 50 acres and 35 cows, which are too much for one man to look after, but which can't support two men. The sons don't want to stay on the farms, and the old men can't look after the cows every day. The smallest farms, under 25 acres, are going down in number; but the ones of 50 or 100 acres are still increasing in number. That's my biggest problem. Eventually Europe will have farms with 500 cows, run by three men – but that will take a very long time.'

Mansholt's seat in Brussels has been hotter than any, for agricultural policy was the most awkward and the vaguest part of the Treaty of Rome. Since 1st July, 1967, when the fixing of farm prices passed to Brussels, Mansholt has virtually become European minister of agriculture. Appropriately enough, the occasion was marked by the first delegation of angry farmers to Brussels – a group of Breton pig-farmers.

To integrate the farmers of the common market was bound to be difficult, because European farmers had all grown up under protection. Each country had its own subsidies, which distorted the pattern of farm trade and competition. But the common market agricultural policy was much more than a letting down of barriers between countries, and it was not at all *laissez faire*: it amounted to a system of price-fixing on a continental scale, regulating the market in a deliberate plan. Andrew Shonfield wrote: 'Some of the argument about the EEC in Britain still fails to recognize that in agriculture the community is engaged in a uniquely ambitious piece of interventionism, using a combination of price-fixing and subsidy to secure long-term structural change.'[1]

Agriculture was one of the corner-stones of the common market which was partly designed as 'a bargain between German industry and French agriculture': gradually the French farmers' leaders were converted to the idea that, with greater productivity, they could find a great new market in Germany. The subsequent bargaining was infinitely painful and complex; and Mansholt had to endure massive 'marathon meetings', each ending with delegates exhausted in the middle of the night, and discussions verging on total breakdown, before agreements were finally reached on the regulations of the major components – cereals, pork, eggs, chicken, fruit, vegetables, wine, milk, beef, rice.

But breaking down the barriers inside Europe meant building up a high barrier against the world outside. National protection was diminished, but continental protection was maintained and increased. Wheat and beef pay a high tariff to get in, while exports from the common market are subsidized by the 'agricultural fund'. This has been an object of persistent criticism from outside – that while agriculture should be becoming more and more a world trade, Europe has shut out the world, particularly to the disadvantage of the 'third world' of Africa and Asia. Mansholt is sensitive to the charge, but he insists that Europe must organize herself first. 'We do not want to be misjudged for restricting production when there is a chance of raising nutritional levels elsewhere in the world – yet we also know that we are still not able to solve the problem. To do so we must, in the first place, organize ourselves at the European level.'[2] Mansholt was specially indignant about the outcome of the Kennedy Round of tariff cuts in 1967. 'I talked with Kennedy, and I know that what he wanted was a real liberalizing of world trade, in favour of the developing countries. What we got was hard-boiled negotiations between rich countries.'

1. Andrew Shonfield: 'The Rome Treaty as an instrument of International Relations', *European Community*, 1967.
2. Speech at FAO in 1962.

Like so much else the agricultural policy has not worked out quite as expected – particularly in France. French farmers were too confident that their produce would quickly over-run Germany; but they have been very slow to modernize their farms to prepare for the new competition, and national patterns of trade still pull the countries in very different directions. As *Le Monde* described the position, after the first lifting of wheat barriers in July 1967:

Up till the present, Europe was broadly divided into two zones separated by a membrane, still very hermetic. On the west, France exports cereals; on the east, Germany, Holland and Italy import them. The paradox was that the surplus from the first was exported to distant destinations, and the supplies for the second were imported from places equally distant, without any connection being made between the two movements. The paradox, moreover, is easily explicable when one realizes that the Germans and Italians tend to give priority to food which comes from countries which are clients of their industry, and when one knows that in terms of commerce, Rotterdam is closer to America than to Bordeaux . . .

THE EUROPEAN COW

The common market was very soon faced with an embarrassing problem – it was producing far too much food.

In spite of the exodus, the actual production from the European land has steadily increased; between 1950 and 1960, although the workers on the land went down by an average of 2.5 per cent a year, production went up by 2 per cent – making an increase in productivity of 4.5 per cent each year. Part of this was due to the invasion of tractors and fertilizers. The number of tractors in the common market countries was 370,000 in 1950 and had multiplied by over six times by 1962 to make 2,330,000.

At the same time farming had become much more profitable, thanks to very high prices. The governments of the common market have always been worried about their agricultural voters, who still have a much lower standard of living than town-dwellers – a discrepancy made more obvious by television in the farmhouses. To appease farmers they fixed exorbitant prices for their food, higher than any other industrialized countries in the world; and they guaranteed to buy up their production. So the farmers produced

more and more. The common market countries now produce 85 per cent of their own cereals, and 94 per cent of their
own meat. But the cows have got quite out of hand. There
are about 24 million cows in the common market, and many
of them are scraggy and not very efficient: the 11 million
French ones, for instance, produce a quarter less milk than
the Dutch. But they produce much more than they used to,
and now the continent is awash with milk and butter, all of it
very expensive. By 1st April, 1968, the Community had had
to buy 150,000 tons of butter and whole warehouses in
Brussels and the ports are stacked up with the stuff. In one
year they expected to spend 800 million dollars to support the
price of milk. It is a comic symbol of its self-contained
affluence that the common market should literally be overflowing with milk and butter.

The glut is something of a nightmare, and over-production has produced absurd situations. France, for instance, has begun exporting subsidized powdered milk to
Mexico, wresting the market away from the United States,
and selling butter to Japan, while the whole of Europe has
become more and more dependent on beef imports; half a
million tons of beef are imported to the common market in a
year. The obvious solution would appear to be for France to
increase her beef production, to become the 'ranch of
Europe'. France has already vastly increased her beef production, doubling it in seven years; but the prospect of the
small French farmers merging and standardizing their herds
is still distant and hardly credible.

In vain Mansholt has tried to stem the flood of milk, by
proposing to lower the price and by suggesting 'a structural
intervention', to give a subsidy for farmers who switch from
milk to meat. He knows that the only real solution to the low
agricultural wages is to reduce prices and to encourage
bigger, more efficient farms, with fewer workers. But the
governments could not go against the farmers. Twenty per
cent of the common market voters are still on the land, and
no one dares ignore them. Since common prices came into
force in 1967, farmers' demonstrations have continually protested against them. In Brittany huge marches have led to
riots, with a hundred wounded in one day. In Liège, Walloon
farmers have paraded with white-painted pitchforks as their
bayonets. When the dairy farmers of France, Germany and

Belgium got wind of Mansholt's plan to reduce the milk price, 150 of them came to Brussels to protest to the Council of Ministers.

All this has provoked a unity of a kind among the farmers of the Six. As Mansholt described it: 'I remember in 1958, when we first started, everyone was talking a different agricultural language – it was a Babel. Now there really is a sense of a single market. When I stay with my brother in Holland he aks me questions about wheat prices; and when I stay in my house in the south of Sardinia, the farmers there ask me the same questions.'

It is an expensive unity. The high prices remove the incentive to greater efficiency, so that effective industrialization of agriculture, which alone could provide a sensible European market, proceeds very slowly. For the rest of the world it is not an attractive sight, this community of incompetent and pampered peasants, blocking the import of other countries' foods, far more efficiently produced. If Britain eventually joins the common market, the agricultural policy would be maddening. Britain imports more food than any other country in the world, with almost free entry. The British grain farmers, bigger and more efficient than the other Europeans, long for the chance to invade the common market. But the cheap and desirable butter and lamb of New Zealand or Denmark would have to be cut off in favour of the high-priced food from the continent.

Yet the protection of peasants is more than political pandering; for it has to do with the basic character of the continent. As peasants become scarcer, the problem becomes clearer. Should the continent become one industrialized megalopolis, with a few outcrops of suburbia or tourist centres, leaving the poorer farming areas to become deserted, importing cheap food from outside? Or should the old communities and villages be kept alive? In Italy, where the exodus is fastest, the problem has been greatest. What worries some planners is that, once the communities have died, they will be hard to revive. In twenty years' time the cities may have taken their fill. With growing leisure, decentralization and new industries, a new generation may give up city life and wiping windscreens, and could begin a counter-movement back to the country. But by then village life will have stopped and no one will know how to restart it.

It is not surprising that European politicians have a soft spot for their peasants, for so much of the richness and variety of the continent, so many of its roots, are embedded in the soil. An Englishman might well reflect that if the English industrial revolution had been less abrupt and less drastic in its emptying of the countryside a hundred and fifty years ago, the quality of its subsequent city life – its food, housing or leisure – could have been much less bleak: the sudden uprooting from country to town can and did break the whole rhythm and taste of life. As it is, the overcrowded cities of France and Italy show the strain of this great migration. The recurring character in Italian films, of the bewildered and corrupted country boy sucked into the city, has his original in a Victorian Manchester back street.

It is absurd to mourn the passing of the peasant way of life; however attractive it may seem to tourists, it is a mean and miserable existence which no one, once liberated, wants to go back to. But to break the pattern of the land too drastically, to force the migration and industrialization still faster, could bring about a tragic instability to Europe; and this, I believe, is the unanswerable case for maintaining protection. The land does not only represent poverty; that it also represents a kind of security, psychological or actual, is the origin of diversity. In the bewildering and dehumanized new pattern of industry, which we will see in the next chapters, the need for the anchor of land may become greater; the more urbanized Europeans become, the more (like the English) they are likely to look back longingly to the land for their roots and identity. In the words of one of the advocates of European regionalism, Jean Fourastié; 'in our time, the profound wish is to keep a small remainder of that originality and local personality without which the world will become a fundamental ennui, stretching from Paris to San Francisco'.[1]

1. Colloquy on departmental and communal organization, Paris, October 1966.

Chapter Four

Power

> The German Empire was built more truly on coal and
> iron than on blood and iron.
>
> *John Maynard Keynes*

This is not the first time that visionaries have tried to plan an
integrated continent. Europe is full of the ghosts of an earlier international age. The great baroque railway stations of
the mid-nineteenth century – Hamburg of Frankfurt Haupt-
bahnhof – were monuments not only to the new technology but to a pan-European aspiration; the massive
façades of the German termini were the gateways, not just
to the rest of Germany, but to the whole of Europe. The
magnificent Gare du Nord in Paris is crowned with eight
statues of the eight great foreign cities linked to Paris by the
Ligne du Nord. Blackfriars station in London, which used to
be the starting place for travellers to the continent, is still
adorned with the carved names of St. Petersburg and Baden-
Baden. And long before the railways, the hectic spread of
new industries in the earliest years of the industrial revolution brought a spectacular mobility; the English, like the
Americans today, regarded all Europe as their back-yard,
and companies and even names survive as the memorials to
the industrial pioneers. The great Belgian steelworks of
Cockerill-Ougreé was first established by the son of an illiter-
ate Lancashire mechanic, John Cockerill, in 1817. The biggest French steelworks at Le Creusot was for many years
run by an English company, Manby and Wilson. In the mid-
eighteenth century, an Englishman, John Holker, was in-
spector-general of factories in France, helping to modernize
textile machinery. Many of the continental railways were
built with the help of English capital and expertise; the first
railway in France, from Paris to Rouen, opened in 1843, was
built by an Anglo-French company with an English engineer
and contractors and 5,000 English and Irish navvies; soon
afterwards half the shares of French railways were in

English hands.[1] As the western continent became more developed, British and other tycoons moved eastwards; the town where Khrushchev first worked, Yuzovka in the Donetz Basin, was named after a Welsh mechanic, John Hughes, who set up the New Russia Company in 1869 and built an ironworks in the Donetz Basin which later became a centre for international industry. Khrushchev boasted later: 'I worked at a factory owned by Germans, at pits owned by Frenchmen; and at a chemical plant owned by Belgians'.

The development of new communications in the late nineteenth century brought with it a new internationalism of outlook. Werner von Siemens, the founder of the great Siemens company, who developed the electric telegraph and the dynamo, had one brother in London and one in St. Petersburg with whom (through the telegraph) he was constantly in touch. An Anglo-German Siemens company laid the telegraph line from London to India in 1869. The tunnel below the English Channel, which was begun in 1876, was jointly financed by English and French companies.[2] The French Metro was financed by a Belgian tycoon, Baron Empain; the English deep-level underground was begun by an American financier, Charles Yerkes. Wireless itself was opened up by international capital.

That was the commercial unity to which older men, of the generation of Monnet, can look back; the memory of it helped to inspire the common market. Then the protectionism, the slump and the economic nationalism of the inter-war years, followed by the Second World War, left Europe crippled, divided and dismembered, and the earlier pan-Europe seemed a distant dream. Gradually the continent has moved forward again. But the obstacles and enclaves remain stubborn – greater in many respects than in 1914. And however much Europe may place its hopes in industrial unity and interdependence, she will not easily forget that all the free trade and travel in that earlier golden age did not prevent Europe twice tearing itself to pieces. The great technologies and new communications of the nineteenth century – railways, steelmills, telegraphs, motor-cars – reached their climax not in Utopia but in a new age of total destructiveness.

1. W. O. Henderson: *The Industrial Revolution on the Continent*, p. 101.
2. See chapter 13.

COAL AND STEEL

Although the age of coal is beginning to fade into history, it has deeply marked the face and character of Europe. The sentimental traveller can follow the early history of industrialization through the dour grey landscapes and towns that it has left behind. In spite of their history of squalor, misery and exploitation, I find these landscapes mysteriously moving – more moving than Roman amphitheatres, Napoleonic battlefields or the wind-swept cemeteries of the first war soldiers. They summon up the extraordinary hopes and daring of the nineteenth century, and the upheaval of people into a new alien world. Count Harry Kesler wrote of the journey from Manchester to Bradford in the twenties: 'There is a power about it as of an antique world, grey and sombre, a soul made of coal-dust . . .' At Stockton-on-Tees, where the first railway line brought coal from the inland Durham mines around Darlington to the river, you can see the old warehouses and shipyards now crumbling and deserted. The thin river itself is forlorn and empty; the rows of mean houses above the river are shuttered, and a new generation has departed inland, up the hills, or across the river to the chemical plants of Wilton or Billingham. The early history of the great smoky cities of northern England can be followed to Belgium, the first country to follow English methods, where the dark hilly landscape round Liège is hardly distinguishable from Yorkshire; or from there to the long line of coalfields and textile towns between Belgium and northern France. In small mining towns, rows of severe houses, patterned with blue-and-red bricks, stare at each other across the treeless streets. From there the coal can be traced to Lorraine and the Saar, where open country changes suddenly into smoky bowls, filled with factory chimneys and black slag heaps. The old world of coal, with its tribal loyalties, its gospel of work and its drastic landscape, had a loyalty and a unity of its own. And to the modern train traveller most of Europe seems pitted with coalfields – so closely are railways linked to coal.

Of all the coal-bearing areas of Europe, the most concentrated and spectacular is the Ruhr. It is hard for an Englishman to visit the place without feeling awe at the very

sound of the names: Dortmund, Essen, Duisburg, Krupp,
Thyssen, the marshalling yards at Hamm, the Ruhr – they all
carry grim echoes of the war. In the subsequent plans for
European reconstruction, and above all in the concept of the
common market, the Ruhr was the centre-piece. It is difficult
to get used to the fact that the Rhur is now, above all, a
problem – a decaying area in the heart of Germany.

The Ruhr itself is a dull and muddy river which rises in
the mountains near Marburg and zigzags through small villages until it comes into a wide plain and flows into the
Rhine above Düsseldorf. Here, in a triangle bounded by
three autobahns, barely thirty miles across, is the dense area
of cities, steelworks and mines that is known as 'the Ruhr'. It
has still, like the Tees in the north of England, an odd alter-
nation of pretty countryside and Satanic mills. You can pass
one moment through a hilly village, and then suddenly face
a landscape of factories, pit-heads, chimneys. But, unlike the
north of England, it is not a haphazard-looking place, with
factories from different periods growing, almost like farms,
out of the earth. The Ruhr mills and mines are on a huge
integrated scale. The factory walls stretch for miles along the
roadside, the gates lead into small cities of steel and the
slagheaps stretch like black foothills into the distance.

The development of the Ruhr was the most sudden industrialization that Europe has known. While Britain's industrial revolution straddled a century, happening all over the
place, Germany was transformed in two decades from 1870
to 1890. The basis of the boom was the huge deposits of coal
in the Ruhr, on top of which were built the steel mills and
engineering works. The lateness and speed of this industrialization gave the advantage to the big battalions. As the
Ruhr developed, a few huge companies emerged from the
confusion, whose names still dominate the area: Thyssen at
Duisberg, Gelsenkirchener at Gelsenkirchen, Krupp at
Essen. The Ruhr was the birthplace in Europe of the giant
industrial corporation, and the giants make no secret of their
size. The towns, too, are not accidental, smoky places between the pitheads, but proud, clean municipalities, with
opera-houses and theatres. Essen has nearly a million people,
and a wide city centre as prim and tidy as a spa. One of the
most modern and daring opera-houses in the world is in the
mining town of Gelsenkirchen.

The concentration of industries, selling coal, steel, girders or plates to one another on such a vast scale, gave the Ruhr a unique network of railways, roads, harbours. Above all there were the rivers themselves, the Ruhr and the Rhine, which carried iron ore up from the coast and steel products down again. It was this infrastructure which enabled the Ruhr companies to rebuild themselves so rapidly after the last war. 'The factories were wrecked,' one steelmaster said, 'but the communications and the skills were still there; and so were the rivers. That was why we could rebuild much more cheaply than other countries.'

In the boom days of the German post-war miracle the Ruhr was the centre of the wonder. Steel production went on climbing. Skyscrapers shot up in the Ruhr towns, and Düsseldorf, the commercial headquarters, became the glossiest wonder-city of Germany. But as far back as 1960 there were signs of trouble ahead, when the first coal mines ran into trouble. Since then productivity has improved spectacularly, but demand for coal has slumped. In 1957 400,000 workers produced 149 million tons of coal; in 1966 200,000 workers produced 126 million tons – a drop of 15 per cent. In spite of high productivity, German coal cannot compete with its rivals – oil, gas, cheap American coal and now nuclear energy. At the same time the steel industry, faced with over-production and recession, has had serious setbacks. It took a long time in Germany for the facts to sink in. It seemed inconceivable that coal was no longer supreme: the whole Ruhr complex had been built around, and on top of, the mines. Only during 1967, as more mines have closed and unemployment has risen, did the 'Ruhr crisis' come out into the open. In November 1967 15,000 mine workers marched into Dortmund carrying red flags and singing the 'Internationale', to protest against the closing of pits.

For over a century the central symbol of the Ruhr has been the House of Krupp, the legendary empire of coal and steel – permanent, indestructible, patriarchal. The mythology of Krupp can be sampled in their bizarre family mansion, the Villa Hügel, a Neo-Renaissance pile of magnificent ugliness which looks down on the Ruhr just outside Essen. In a high, panelled hall hangs a collection of life-sized portraits which show the unfolding of the family story in receding episodes: Big Bertha, the family matriarch (who died only ten years ago), presiding in a long purple dress in the 1930s over a brood of shy children; then Bertha as a young bride, with big soulful eyes, thirty years before; then the great bearded Krupp, the founder of the empire, staring sternly down over the house that he built. The portraits and the mansion convey, more strongly even than the mansions of Victorian mill-owners, the belief in the immortality of industry. Now Krupps is a public corporation, supervised by a banker, and ruthlessly rationalized. The Villa Hügel is a European monument to a vanished age, and a forgotten self-confidence.

Coal and the Ruhr for a hundred years, have been inseparable. Now the great age of coal is over. For Germany, it has been a harder realization even than for Britain. For the Germans have only a small national stake in other fuels – not much gas, and a short coastline. They have their own oilfields, but they have no giant oil company abroad. All over Europe energy is still regarded as a national question, and the German government feels bound to support the coal industry, however uneconomic it may become.

The Ruhr has another problem: it is, quite literally, sinking. It has been so heavily mined that the ground is constantly giving way. Houses acquire cracks through the middle, railway lines sag, and a railway that fifty years ago was on an embankment is now in a cutting. When mines are shut down and fill with water, the ground above is almost unusable. Some of the real estate which fifty years ago was so precious now has a negative value. Few industries are anxious to move into the Ruhr. The chemical companies up the Rhine, which are still expanding, and whose plastics have replaced some of the uses of steel, cannot move there because, among other reasons, they depend on pipes which would be wrecked by the subsidence.

The Ruhr will not be allowed to die. In 1967 the German government pressed the coal companies to merge, without actually nationalizing them, with massive subsidies. And the concentration of industry and population along the rivers is so great that it makes its own market: with Mannesmann, for instance, the great pipeline company, three-quarters of its products are sold to other companies within sixty miles of its works. The Ruhr still has the best communications in

Europe; and it still has the oldest and most effective transport system of all – the Rhine. With the help of new giant barges, which can be pushed up the river, carrying a thousand tons each, six in line, the steel companies can carry their materials more cheaply than ever through the middle of Europe.

The Ruhr will surely survive, but in the next twenty years it will be a looming liability for Germany, and never again will it have its old supremacy. The New Europe is growing up in cleaner cities – near the sea for easy import and export, or for gas; near the east for available labour. Few people outside the Ruhr will much regret the diminishing of this joyless region; and the British will find it difficult to restrain their *schadenfreude* in watching their old rivals in trouble with *their* industrial legacy.

Perhaps there is another, less tangible, effect of the decline of coal. As a French diplomat put it to me: 'We've always in France had the feeling that rich coalfields had been denied to the Latins – that they were a natural advantage that God gave to the English and Germans. Now that coal doesn't matter any more, we feel much more confident; we think we can do anything.' Or, as the Italian steel company Finsider describes it: 'The lack of coal gave Italy a Freudian complex, providing a smokescreen to conceal mistakes.'

Yet it is surprising to see how reluctant Europeans are, all over the continent, to move on from the age of coal, which has given so much misery, disease and disaster. 'Why must you worry so much about that filthy and barbarous fuel?' complained a Belgian economist to a group of common market enthusiasts. 'Why aren't you glad to get rid of it?' In its 150 years of dominance, coal-mining in Europe has become, like agriculture, a rooted way of life and a psychological support. Its workers are reared in the mines – in the Ruhr almost as much as in Durham or South Wales – and it's difficult to move them away. It is a big jump into the new world of gas pipelines and nuclear power.

THE SEA

While the sentimental traveller may follow the coalfields and railway lines, the more forward-looking tourist can take a less melancholy route, to survey the new centres of power:

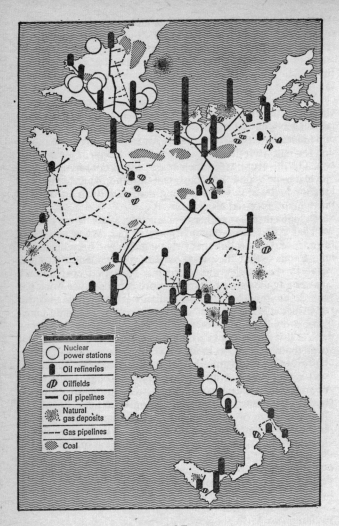

Sources of Energy

the map opposite shows the changing geography of energy supplies. He might visit the boom cities of Europe, where new industries have grown up far away from coal mines or iron ore – like Munich, Birmingham, Grenoble, or Bologna, But much of his journey would follow the coast, for it is on the sea that the new sources of energy depend. The first nuclear power stations, which need their huge consumption of water for cooling, loom up with their bleak concrete rectangles along the coastline of Britain. Natural gas, which has done more for the economy of Holland than Indonesia ever did, rises up from the land of North Holland from the North Sea. Oil, in ever vaster tankers, arrives from all over the world to the refineries along the coastline, where at night tongues of flame shoot out, and the weird tall shapes of the pipes stand like skeleton cities above the harbours. Coal itself comes in from the sea, for in the last few years it has been a new humiliation for European industries that they have to import cheap coal from America. With these growing trades, in spite of the loss of old empires, and of trade with eastern Europe, the seaports of western Europe have become still more important. Rotterdam and Antwerp, already the two biggest before the war, have spread still faster in the last ten years, so that the two ports, only fifty miles apart, may soon make up a single twin-city: Rotterdam, which has overtaken London as the busiest port in the world, handles twice as much cargo as any other port on the continent – over one hundred million tons a year. Many of the big ports in Europe, including Rotterdam, Le Havre, Antwerp and Marseilles, are now reclaiming land from the sea to make room for more factories and giant docks.

Round the new sources of industrial energy, factories and plants have grown up since the war, to rival the old inland centres. Chemical plants, which need the sea to unload their detritus, have appeared along every coastline, and now deface southern Italy. All kinds of industries have moved to the coast: Hamburg has now more people employed in manufacturing than in the port. And even steel, which used to be inseparable from the inland coalfields and iron ore, is beginning to go to the sea. The Taranto steelworks, which can bring in iron ore by ship from Mauretania and can send pipelines by ship across the Mediterranean, looks to the sea for its whole existence.

ENERGY AND UNITY

It has been a central hope of the unifiers that by pooling the resources of industrial power, the old political rivalries of Europe would begin to fall away. The coalmines and ironfields of the Saar and Lorraine have been at the centre of three wars, and since their beginnings the fortunes of the great steelworks of the Ruhr and of northern England have been linked with those of battleships and guns. When Jean Monnet proposed the Coal and Steel Community in 1950, his aim was to remove this basic battleground. In the confident words of the Schuman Plan, 'The pooling of coal and steel production will immediately provide for the establishment of common bases for economic development as a first step in the federation of Europe, and will change the destinies of those regions which have long been devoted to the manufacture of munitions of war, of which they have been the most constant victims.' Once the Coal and Steel Community was established, Monnet and others turned their minds to the new source of power, nuclear energy; and we have seen how for some of the federalists the proposal of Euratom in 1955 was thought more important than the common market itself.

But of all the prophecies made about Europe's future, the forecasts about her energy supplies were among the most wrong. In the first years it was assumed that all kinds of energy, and particularly coal, would be in short supply for decades to come. The Hartley report of OEEC in 1956 recommended that indigenous fuel should be developed almost regardless of cost, and the assumption of fuel shortages was part of the impetus for setting up Euratom. Very soon afterwards the whole pattern began to change, and after the Suez crisis of 1956, in the words of the Community, 'the underlying trend which remained latent so long suddenly emerged into full view'.[1] The oil companies found huge new reserves of oil, speeded up their production, and made transport cheaper with giant tankers and pipelines across Europe: between 1950 and 1965 the share of oil in the energy of the Six shot up from 10 per cent to 45 per cent.[2] Natural gas was discovered off Holland, in the south of France and in Algeria, and piped into factories and homes: experts now

1. *Europe and Energy*, ECSC, Luxemburg, 1967.   2. ibid.

reckon that 15 per cent of Europe's energy will come from gas, following the pattern of America. Coal-mining became much more efficient in its desperate attempts to compete with the other fuels. In most fields, however, coal could not hold its own, and between 1950 and 1965 its share of common market energy slumped from 74 per cent to 38 per cent.[1]

Euratom soon fell into disarray. The immediate necessity of providing new fuel diminished, and Euratom devoted itself less to supplying immediate commercial energy and more to long-term research. France, the only developed nuclear power on the continent was preoccupied with her own nuclear policy. The first president of Euratom, Étienne Hirsch, was sacked by De Gaulle in 1961 for neglecting France's national interests, and replaced by a more obedient Frenchman, Pierre Chatenet. In the following years the 'community spirit' of Euratom steadily evaporated, as each country insisted on having its 'fair return' on the money it had put in. In the meantime, by 1967, it had become clear that the giant America corporations would be supplying the bulk of Europe's nuclear power stations of the future.

The new competition between fuels had left the plans for a 'common energy policy' in chaos. Energy policy in the common market comes under three different organizations – the Coal and Steel Community for coal, Euratom for nuclear energy, the common market for oil. But oil comes from right outside the common market, and generates highly political reactions, at both its source and destination. The big 'international' oil companies, mostly American, have always hoped that a new area of liberal trade would give them free competition; but in the last few years the trend has been the opposite, and each government feels it must safeguard its 'security of supply' in the threat of crisis and war. Italy has built up its own maverick company, ENI; the French government has set up a new company, ERAP, to find new sources of oil; and Germany, which saw its biggest oil company, DEA, bought up by the American Texaco, is now much more sensitive to its dependence on foreign supplies. From having led Europe in coal supplies, Germany finds herself without much of her own oil or gas – which gives her a new and worrying sense of deprivation.

1. *Europe and Energy*, ECSC, Luxemburg, 1967.

So far from being a basis of European unity, energy has become 'a pocket of resistance to integration'.[1] The hopes that energy could be removed from national politics have been dashed: as in agriculture, each government believes, quite naturally, that it must defend the interest of its own workers and consumers, by making its own contracts and restrictions (that is what governments are for); and the threat of war, cutting off supplies from outside, remains in the background. Both oil and gas are in their way, just as political fuels as coal was, and both are more likely to divide countries than unite them. The choice between sources of gas rests on very political calculations. Italy, for instance, has been faced with a choice of bringing gas by pipeline from Russia, or from Holland, or by tanker from Algeria – two of them right outside the common market. Each choice is full of trade implications (the Russian gas, for instance, would mean big orders for pipelines for Taranto), and the arguments about which gas Italy should use rocked her Centre-Left government. To think of Europe, let alone the common market, as being a single entity for fuel is impossible.

But the real energy revolution has only just begun: in the next decades the spread of nuclear energy is likely to change the problem much more drastically. America has now invested massively in nuclear power, continually increasing her targets; and as America turns, so Europe turns later. Nuclear power stations will inevitably rapidly overtake coal and oil for the production of electricity. Europe will be heavily dependent on American companies for her research and her power stations; but at least nuclear energy will be available to any country, whatever their natural resources, without the frictions and resentments between haves and have-nots. It now seems likely that by the 1980s the coal-mines will be no more than quaint and costly reminders of Europe's past battles. But few people would dare predict the consequences of the new nuclear age, after all the outdated forecasts, the ups-and-downs of research and production. If there is one lesson of the last decade, it is that no one can plan Europe's industrial future: and that Europe is, more than ever, at the mercy of events and discoveries outside her frontiers.

1. M. Lapie, Chairman of the common market special committee on Energy Policy: *Europe and Energy*, EEC, p. 10.

Chapter Five

Corporations

Tout par l'Industrie et tout pour elle.
Saint-Simon

The early industries which grew out of the land – agriculture, coal-mining, steel, transport – still look to the nations to defend them, and it is hard to be sanguine about their ability to unify Europe. But in the last twenty years new kinds of industries have grown up, with such speed that economists are only beginning to study their implications, which cross frontiers with far greater ease; for what they purvey is not raw materials (which can always be nationalized or expropriated) but managements, skills and technologies, based on massive capital wealth, with dimensions that make nations look small. The progress of the 'multi-national corporation', the 'international corporation' or the 'trans-national corporation' – the multiplicity of names reveals embarrassments about their real identity – is one of the phenomena of the last two decades. The emergence of these mysterious giants, without visible owners and sometimes without visible headquarters, armed with the keys to the mechanized high-speed world of the future – automation, computers, aircraft, nuclear energy – is of central importance to the European structures; for they have grown up outside the framework of the nation itself.

The international company is nothing new; the British slave-companies, the East India Company, or the eighteenth-century Rothschilds, could all have claimed that title; the oil giants which grew up in the early twentieth century have battled across frontiers for decades. But most of these were essentially trading companies, with no doubts about their home base. What is new is the growth of companies which have internationalized not only their trade but their factories and managers, which have bought up other companies in other countries, and which have thus begun to acquire a global character, not knowing quite where they belong. It only began in earnest around 1950, when the big American companies began spreading their wings abroad, and European companies, more slowly, followed. In the fifties, the American external direct investment went up from 20 billion dollars to 60 billion – with results that anyone can see, in the shape of the factories and offices, with the same names all over Europe.

It has happened often haphazardly. Professor Raymond Vernon of Harvard – one of the authorities on this new business diplomacy – has described how an American company, finding its international business suddenly growing, might abolish its separate international division and absorb it into the main company, which thus becomes gradually internationalized; the directors begin to talk of themselves, with a large element of humbug, as an international company; but the next generation begin to take them literally, thus making the company actually international. There have been all kinds of motives for spreading abroad; sometimes to escape from the American Government and its anti-trust restrictions; sometimes to make quick profits abroad with cheaper labour; sometimes to keep up with rivals. Sometimes the very barriers of nationalism force the big companies (particularly mining companies) to build factories abroad, to look more international to adapt themselves to each country's laws and local demands. Jet-planes and computers can now enable a company to keep control of its satrapies, and while delegating boldly, to hold them together as a single entity. It is this one-ness which distinguishes these giants from the old holding companies which collected properties all over the world but controlled them only through balance sheets. As Professor Vernon defines it, the multinational enterprise is 'a cluster of corporations of diverse nationality joined together by ties of common ownership and responsive to a common management strategy'.

The significance of these clusters in Europe is obvious; in the first place, since most of them still have a strongly American character, they constitute the most obvious sign of the 'American challenge', showing up the weakness and smallness of the European response. In the second place – perhaps more important – they put the nations into a new kind of perspective. Professor Perlmutter of Geneva is another of the prophets of these new leviathans; his theories have now become part of the new language of management. He has reckoned that by 1988 there will be around 300 international giants dominating world business, gobbling up small companies and waging their wars across frontiers and oceans. He classifies them into three different types – the 'ethnocentric' companies (like airlines, Pechiney, Krupp) firmly run from their home country, staffing their overseas subsidiaries with their own countrymen, and thus apt to be very inflexible and unadaptable to world movements; secondly, the 'polycentric' companies (like Philips or Alcan) which have very strong subsidiaries run by local managers, but still with a firm national headquarters. Thirdly, the 'geocentric' companies (like Shell or IBM) which can ignore frontiers, find managers in any country, and move them round the world, and whose headquarters could be anywhere: it is these companies, Professor Perlmutter believes, which will have the flexibility and mobility to give them the dominant role in the future.

The classification is difficult. Big companies are falling over themselves to prove that they are more geocentric than their rivals; while behind their international façade most of them remain very national and mostly American. But Perlmutter's thesis points to the basic phenomenon with which most experts I had spoken to seem to agree; that the international giants, being able to operate more and more freely across frontiers, will provide an increasing amount of the sophisticated goods and services for industrial countries; their usefulness has become acknowledged to the extent (as Andrew Shonfield puts it) that 'one has the impression nowadays that the dialogue between the corporation and the state consists largely of a simple assertion by the former: "anything you can do, I can do better" '.[1] Their power and social influence will rapidly grow; they will be the advance guard of new technological structures, new consumer habits, new environments and hence new social relationships; yet, being everywhere and nowhere, being stateless and headless, they will be increasingly difficult to control. There is already discussion of a new supranational law, a *lex mercatoria*,

1. Andrew Shonfield: 'Big Business in the late 20th century', *Daedalus*, Winter 1968.

which will give the international companies greater freedom: 'the essence of this suggestion', said the American diplomat George Ball, 'is that world corporations should become quite literally citizens of the world'. What then will be their relationship to the old arbiter of welfare and business behaviour, the nation-state?

The conflict between the international corporation and the state has only just begun to be studied; but it has the greatest relevance to the integration of Europe. Already the nations have lost some of their control over this new pattern of industry. Most people whom I have heard discuss the problem, being either businessmen or 'Europeans', assume that these new forces are to be wholly welcome because they break down the old barriers. But the nation may not always be cast in the role of villain; for in the vision of two or three hundred world corporations there is an element of nightmare. Their freedom in Europe – a greater freedom than they enjoy in America – may allow them to ride roughshod over local communities, traditions and balances; the mass-production of a uniform consumer society, with uniform advertising, pressures and incentives all over the continent, may produce a major political reaction. It is possible that in this context the nation – or perhaps (as I will suggest) the region – will emerge not so much as an archaic and bellicose enemy, but as a necessary counterweight to the mechanistic new world, and as the guardian of the welfare state and the public services against the resourceful but ruthless innovators.

The great majority of the multinational corporations are based in America – a fact which itself makes the vocabulary of multi-nationalism somewhat suspect to others. A handful of familiar names – IBM, General Motors, General Electric, TWA, Procter and Gamble, Lockheed, Boeing, Pan-American – will recur through this book, as an inescapable part of the European way of life (Boeing-Boeing is a French farce; 'up up and away' is sung through the continent). But what is important here is to look at the European giants, and to see how far they too are beginning to acquire a global character, breaking through frontiers.

PATERNALISM

Travelling between the industrial centres of Europe, it is

easy to get the impression that corporations have become more important than countries. In the 'city-states' of the giant companies the workers and managers owe their livelihood, their pensions, their sports-grounds and often their holidays to the firm. A man will join a company as a boy and stay until he retires, and it may well have a continuity more reassuring than that of his country. In its 150 years the firm of Krupp has survived Bismarck, the Kaiser, Hitler and the Allies, and is now surviving without its founding family. The oldest corporation in the world, Stora Kopperberg in Sweden, can trace its history back to 1288, when a bishop bought a share in its copper-mine. The original mine is still being worked: but the company now also has the largest paper mills and steelworks in Sweden, and ranks as one of the eight biggest companies in the country.

The frontiers between corporations and their rivals are just as distinct as national frontiers. 'When I deal with industrial corporations,' a Hamburg banker told me, 'their differences seem to me greater than between nationalities.' In Europe most companies are not so vast as in America, but they loom larger in relation to the countries; and in the smaller countries the giants have long ago overflowed the frontier. In Holland, four great corporations (Royal Dutch/Shell, Unilever, Philips, AKU) have international ramifications which dwarf Holland's own diplomacy. In Luxembourg, with a population of 300,000, the steel company of ARBED employs 25,000.

Moreover the sense of identification with a company – particularly for the managers – is much more developed in Europe than in America. The American habit of zig-zagging to the top from one company to the next, each time at a higher salary, is not much approved of on the continent: the Big Four in Holland, for instance, have an agreement not to compete with salaries, and in most big companies a man who leaves for a rival is regarded as some kind of defector. Paternalism can be all-enveloping, and all over the continent – in contrast to Britain and America – a high proportion of earnings are paid in terms of pensions and benefits. German and Italian managers will show off their magnificent welfare services without any doubts as to the rightness of their exclusivity. Where the government itself is remote and inefficient – as in Italy – the company's welfare becomes all the more munificent. Those who are safely employed inside, living in company flats, recovering in company hospitals, sending their children to company crèches and company schools, are bound by ties which are like a continuation or a resurgence of the old feudal ties: those who are outside are nowhere.

It is in Italy that this company benevolence is most striking. Along the northern plain, below the foothills of the Alps, a whole row of company towns grew up in the late nineteenth century or later, attracting poor peasant families away from the hills, in the earlier flight from the land, and building havens of industry and security, with very little contact with the government in Rome. The authoritarianism of Fascist times, with the unquestioned supremacy of the boss, increased the fealty, and in spite of the post-war reaction, the tradition of authority and dependence has survived fairly unscathed.

Perhaps the most interesting paternalist company is Olivetti at Ivrea, near Turin, which has taken the idea of the industrial community to an extreme. The traveller cannot mistake its idealism. Bright-coloured houses are built up the hillside, and in the main street stands a big pink marble headquarters surrounded by lawns. Further on are rows of glass buildings with bold, simple façades, presenting a kind of miniature history of industrial architecture. The letters OLIVETTI seem to be everywhere. For the last sixty years the history of Ivrea has been bound up with the typewriters and the sudden Italian industrial revolution. The company was founded by Camillo Olivetti, a farmer's son who took a degree in the new science of electrical engineering, who came back from a trip to America in 1907 determined that Italy could make her own typewriters. He built up both a community and a company, combining precise engineering with elegant design. 'The Olivetti products,' said Le Corbusier, 'seem to be illuminated by the exact proportions of the love with which every object should be made.' Camillo's son Adriano, who became President in 1938, was a practical visionary; he revelled in industrial relations, and decided 'that man and machine were two hostile elements that needed to be reconciled'. He set up the company's own health service, infirmary, schools and scholarships, and carefully put them under joint control of the workers and the management, so that they should not be regarded as charity: 'I had enormous difficulty in keeping these institutions from becoming instruments of paternalism and privilege.' He instituted the five-day week – the first company in Italy to do so. He was determined to 'make work humane', and evolved his own philosophy and his own concept of the community, which amounted to a kind of return to a medieval scale of living: 'A community neither too large nor too small, geographically well defined, armed with authority, which would provide in all its activities the indispensable co-operation, efficiency, respect for human personality, culture and art, that by chance had been achieved in a part of a given region, in a single industry.'[1]

Adriano went on to involve the company with artists and intellectuals, to enliven the community: he brought superb design into everything – typewriters, architecture, offices, and posters. He employed writers to work at Ivrea; two well-known Italian novelists, Paolo Volponi and Ottiero Ottieri, are still employed by Olivetti. Adriano wanted 'a new kind of enterprise going beyond socialism and capitalism'; he even founded a Community Party, financed by Olivetti, which had one member of parliament (he later joined the socialists). Adriano saw the company expand through the post-war boom. He extended into electronics, and – his boldest, rashest coup – bought up American Underwood typewriters, to challenge America on the home ground.

Adriano died in a train in 1960, and the success story soon faded. His son Roberto took over, but the family were divided; an old family retainer, Giuseppe Pero, became chairman, who (it was said) was accustomed to stand up when talking on the telephone to one of the family. The company still expanded rapidly, shares shot up in value, and then came the 1964 Italian recession. Olivetti was over-extended, and a short panic ensued. A group of banks and companies, including Fiat and Pirelli, stepped in with new capital and new men, and Roberto stood down as managing director. The paternal peace of Ivrea was abruptly disturbed. A man from Fiat, Aurelio Peccei, moved in as chief executive; he was impatient of consultation, ruthlessly reorganized the structure, cut the top salaries. The new syndicate decided to

1. Adriano Olivetti: *Notes Towards the History of a Factory*, 1958.

sell the computer side of the business to the American General Electric. The image of Olivetti's seemed shattered; far from reconquering the new world, they seemed to be conquered by it.[1]

But the battle was not lost. The company painfully recovered; exports moved ahead, and after many troubles Underwoods turned to a profit: the unloading of the computer business turned out to be no great loss. Now Roberto is back as managing director, and the family back in control. The social services are still there, the machines are still beautiful, the workers still loyal. But the paternalist confidence (they say) will never be the same again. The outside world, for better or worse, has broken the spell of Ivrea.

Paternalism, long- or short-sighted, still prevails in Italian industry. As in some earlier British communities – Bournville or Port Sunlight – the welfare company has preceded the welfare state; but the efficiency of modern welfare, and incompetence of the Italian state, makes the contrast more striking. The first upheavals of post-war Italy, the unemployment and migrations from the south, may in some ways have strengthened these paternal citadels, protecting their workers from the chaos and dangers outside. With fuller employment and more attractive jobs, their power may wane; but the psychological need remains. The envelopment of patronage and power alarms many people: one recent much-acclaimed Italian novel, *Il Padrone* (The Boss), by Goffredo Parise, depicts a young man from the provinces, helplessly dependent on and grateful to a dominating boss, who insists that all emotional relations should be devoted to the company.

Is the industrial company a serious substitute in people's loyalties for the nation-state? Can Ivrea, Valdagno or the motor-cities, Wolfsburg, Turin or Leyland, foster a new kind of patriotism – to the company more than the country? In the immediate post-war years in Italy and Germany, where nationalism was totally discredited, it might well have seemed so; the export enthusiasm seemed less for the glory of the country than for the firm. But as objects of total loyalty, companies are, in the end, unsatisfying and boring. However much they may be enriched with culture, sports

1. For a detailed and entertaining description of the Olivetti crisis, see *Fortune*, July 1967.

and pensions, the factories, in the end, do no more than make things; men and machines are still two hostile elements. No play or novel, so far as I know, has really overcome the ultimate dullness of industry. For their real sense of community, their adventure and their final loyalty, Europeans still look outside the company gates, to their country or their tribe.

BIG TWENTY

There has been much generalization about the industrial giants, but their characters and bones are as different as an elephant's from a giraffe's, and it is important to look at the individual examples, their history and background to see how far they are moving towards an international pattern. Here are the twenty biggest companies based on Europe, the list published in 1967 by *Fortune* magazine, classified by total sales:[1] the map overleaf indicates their headquarters and concentration.

1. *Royal Dutch/Shell*

By far the biggest of the European oil companies, it is the only one on the same scale as the American giants. It has long ago outgrown any single country: its annual income is bigger than Switzerland's. It was formed in 1906 by an Anglo-Dutch merger between Henri Deterding, the notorious Dutch financier, and Marcus Samuel, a trader from the East End of London. It is controlled by two parent companies – one Dutch, with 60 per cent of the shares, one English, with 40 per cent; it is run by five managing directors two Dutch, two British and one American; and its shareholding is predominantly British (30 per cent), American (20 per cent) and Dutch (20 per cent). It operates in nearly every country in the world, with largely autonomous marketing companies in each country in Europe – Shell Italiana, Deutsche Shell, Belgian Shell, etc. Shell is one of the companies that claims to be the most 'geocentric' in Europe and it certainly has very international managers; but the problems of Anglo-Dutch co-operation are not easy. Two

1. In the case of three companies merged since that list (British Steel, GEC/AEI and Leyland/BMC) I have added together their total sales at that time. The list is Copyright 1964 Time Inc. All rights reserved.

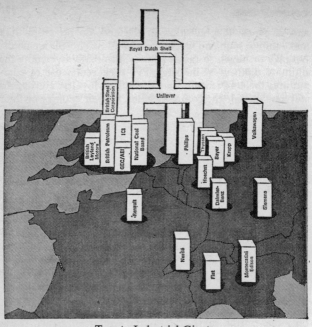

Twenty Industrial Giants

Rank	Company	Sales ($ 000)	Employees
1	Royal Dutch/Shell (Netherlands-Britain)	7,711,432	174,000
2	Unilever (Britain-Netherlands)	5,300,733	300,000
3	British Steel Corporation (Britain)	2,800,000	270,000
4	British Petroleum (Britain)	2,543,240	60,000
5	Volkswagenwerk (Germany)	2,499,500	124,581
6	ICI (Britain)	2,478,560	171,700
7	National Coal Board (Britain)	2,338,095	436,238
8	Philips' Gloeilampenfabrieken (Netherlands)	2,228,959	244,000
9	Montecatini Edison (Italy)	1,998,400	118,906
10	Siemens (Germany)	1,957,750	257,000
11	Nestlé (Switzerland)	1,702,950	86,371
12	Thyssen-Hütte (Germany)	1,694,581	91,763
13	Fiat (Italy)	1,678,710	134,592
14	Daimler-Benz (Germany)	1,475,000	101,569
15	British Leyland Motors (Britain)	1,472,674	120,000
16	Farbwerke Hoechst (Germany)	1,456,750	79,416
17	Renault (France)	1,427,721	94,900
18	Farbenfabriken Bayer (Germany)	1,385,075	71,900
19	GEC/AEI (Britain)	1,245,000	158,514
20	Krupp (Germany)	1,243,750	102,415

drastic reorganizations in ten years have tried to cut out overlapping and muddle between the twin centres, London and The Hague. The Dutch remain touchy about their national interests, but they have admitted an American to the board. One of their directors said, 'The great thing about the Dutch is that they put one thing above everything – making money. I wish I could say the same of the British.'

2. *Unilever* (see pp. 125–30)

3. *British Steel Corporation*

The second biggest steel group in the western world – second only to United States Steel in America. A merger of fourteen separate steel companies, nationalized in 1967; but now much less politically contentious, and run by a smooth merchant banker, Lord Melchett, grandson of one of the founders of ICI, who is pledged to drastic rationalization of the scattered plants.

The emergence of this nationalized colossus has been much criticized on the continent, as a bar to free competition; but whether private or nationalized, the European steel industry is increasingly involved with national governments, particularly since the crisis of over-production. Each country feels the need to have and protect its own steelworks, and Italy likewise has a nationalized steel industry (Finsider). The earlier hopes of European steel companies have vanished.

4. *British Petroleum*

An all-British company, half-owned by the British government but completely independent of it: it takes oil, mainly from the Middle East, and sells it in every country of western Europe, with its green shield competing with the Shell super-girl, the Esso tiger, and the six-legged dragon of AGIP. BP have been less agile than Shell in adapting themselves and they are now busily trying to acquire a more international image; they are sensitive, above all, about their name, and in their subsidiary companies they call themselves simply 'BP': they are run by a Frenchman in France, a German in Germany, a Belgian in Belgium, but they keep a discreet eye through a 'shareholders' representative'.

5. *Volkswagenwerk*

The most famous and astonishing post-war success-story of Europe. It sells cars in most countries in the world, and makes most of them in Wolfsburg, and it is run by an all-German board. (See Chapter 6, pp. 146–50.)

6. *Imperial Chemical Industries*

The biggest chemical company in Europe, it was originally formed by a merger in 1926, partly to counter the cartel of the German chemical companies. It is run firmly from London by an all-British board, but has rapidly expanded its continental factories, to make sure of its access, including two big new plants, one near Rotterdam and one near Heidelberg. ICI has been in the vanguard of the British common market campaign. Its ambition is said to be to link with a continental partner to become a genuinely European company, but it is still relatively small on the continent: it accounts for only 1 per cent of the spending on chemical plant in the common market.

7. *National Coal Board*

The second biggest of Europe's nationalized corporations, and the biggest company to make a loss. It operates entirely inside Britain, and like all European coal industries faces the problems I have already discussed of growing competition from oil, gas and nuclear energy.

8. *Philips' Gloeilampenfabrieken*

A world-wide complex extending from a single small country. Because of its English-sounding name, most consumers are quite unaware (as with C & A) that it is Dutch. It is based on the city of Eindhoven, where a symbolic shape called the Evoluon, like a huge flying saucer, commemorates its 75th anniversary. It was set up by two authoritarian brothers, Anton and Gerard, making electric lamps, and was selling lamps all through Europe by 1900, first undercutting and then beating their German competitors, AEG and Siemens. Since then radio, gramophone and television have caused rapid growth, but also growing competition. It accounts for one-eighth of Dutch exports.

The company still has a family character; its chairman, Frits Philips, is Anton's son, who has been a keen Moral Rearmer and a fervent anti-communist, embarrassed by the fact that his grandfather was a cousin of Karl Marx: the company is still shy of eastern Europe. Philips, sometimes

known as 'the sleeping giant', has been slow to move into the
next stage of electronics, particularly computers; but it must
be a key figure in any European computer industry.

Philips has always been sensitive to the charge of being a
'state within a state', and has stressed that Philips 'lay within
the boundaries of Eindhoven and not vice-versa'.[1] The
group calls itself a world federation, and emphasized the
autonomy of its subsidiaries in forty countries – which includes Mullard valves and Pye radio in Britain, and a half-
share in Deutsche Grammophon. But it is a very national-
minded company, with a pyramid leading up to an all-Dutch
board, and (as with Unilever) competition has made it cen-
tralize more firmly.

9. *Montecatini Edison*

The Italian chemical giant, formed in 1966 by a take-over
of Montecatini by the Edison company, after Edison's electricity interests were nationalized; Montedison (with Fiat
and the state holding company, IRI) make up one of the 'tre
grandi' of Italian industry. The combined group is supposedly run by the Edison chairman, Giorgio Valerio, a
long-time opponent of the Centre-Left government, but the
merger is a very uneasy one, with big private empires: their
organogram was called a 'baronagram'. It produces three-
quarters of Italian chemicals and has many off-shoots, including the chain of 'Standa' shops, the Marks and Spencer
of Italy. Their chemical plants are changing the face of
Italy: five of them are on the coastline. They have already
invested £300 million in the South.

10. *Siemens*

The historic German company, originally contained in a
suburb of Berlin called 'Siemensstadt', now centred on
Erlangen and Munich, which it has helped to make a boom-
city: 10 per cent of Munich's population is dependent on
Siemens. There is a whole network of offices and factories,
with a skyscraper at one end, all in the same pale grey – grey
doorways, grey desks, grey computers, grey telex machines,
and rather grey people. Siemens are proud of their electronic
power; an exhibition room is full of menacing gadgets, including a pfennig that is guarded with a Siemens electronic

1. P. F. S. Otten: *Our Industrial Philosophy*, Philips, 1961.

device which automatically says 'Hands off', and a toy-train system to demonstrate Siemens signals. In the company cinema you press a button and the curtains are automatically pulled back, the screen comes down, and a film starts, showing Siemens achievements accompanied by Siemens electronic music.

Siemens' beginnings are of special interest, with their mixture of brave international adventure, and intense patriotism. The great new electrical discoveries, like the dynamo, came at the same time as the discovery of the nation, and industrial and political power seemed closely allied. Werner von Siemens, with his brothers in London and St. Petersburg, was in the midst of the communications explosion of the late nineteenth century. But the brothers' companies split off, and Werner's enterprises were firmly linked with the Prussian state; he built the first long telegraph line in Europe for Bismarck, to link Frankfurt to Berlin, and he took fervent pride in the victory over France in 1870.

Siemens still have three Siemenses on their boards, including the chairman, though without voting control. They have factories and subsidiaries all over Europe, but their real strength is with the German market and German government contracts. Like Philips they have been backward in computers; they have licences from the American RCA, but they are late in developing their own research.

11. *Nestlé*

The Swiss company founded by Henri Nestlé, who invented 'milk food' for babies in 1865, has grown to absorb a vast range of European products, including Maggi soups, Findus frozen foods in Sweden, Crosse and Blackwell's foods and Keiller's marmalade in England, Locatelli cheese in Italy and a 40 per cent share in Libby's in America. Like Unilever, Nestlé has become increasingly involved in mass-producing European food; and one single invention, Nescafé introduced in 1938 to solve the coffee-glut in Brazil, has revolutionized bourgeos habits. Nestlé claims that a complete and varied meal can be prepared from the output of Nestlé's factories alone'.

Nestlé has been called (by *The Economist*) 'the most international company'; it sells less than 3 per cent of its output in Switzerland. It takes pride in allowing all its subsidiaries a free rein, to be run by their own nationals; the headquarters, in a curved glass palace at Vevey, on Lake Geneva, are compact and full of foreigners. It likes to cultivate 'Nestlé citizenship'; they founded their own management school, IMEDE, at Lausanne; their self-profile insists that 'a great corporation has as distinct a personality and character as any determined, dynamic young human being who strives to accomplish the things he believes in'. Nestlé's have foreigners on the board, including an Englishman (they tried to get an American, but could not lure him to Vevey). Of their two vice-chairmen one, Enrico Bignami, is Italian and the other, Jean Cothésy, is French. But in its ownership and character the company is emphatically Swiss. Only Swiss nationals can buy voting shares, so that control cannot pass to a foreign company, and Nestlé is interlocked with Swiss national life. Their chairman, Max Petitpierre, is a Swiss lawyer who has been President of Switzerland and President of the Swiss Watchmakers; former deputy director, Edwin Stopper, is now governor of the Swiss central bank; and the company have old links with the Swiss Red Cross. It is also Swiss in its passionate secrecy; when it was first revealed by *Fortune* as one of the giants, there was astonishment at Vevey. The paradox of Nestlé is that this international company rests on a strictly national base: the more confident it is of being Swiss, the more it can appear to be English, Swedish or Italian.

12. *Thyssen-Hütte*

Thyssen is the largest steel group on the continent, based on Duisburg, where the Ruhr meets the Rhine. Its founder, August Thyssen, built one of the first integrated steelworks in Europe: his son Fritz introduced Hitler into big-business circles, then repented, publicly denounced the Führer, and was put in a concentration camp. Thirty per cent of Thyssen shares still belong to the Thyssen family and ten per cent to a Thyssen foundation; but the family is in Argentina, and the company is headed by a veteran steelmaster, Hans Günther Sohl, with an army of modern managers: Sohl runs the group from a rustic office at the top of the sharp steel sky-scraper in Dusseldorf – glittering over the city like a giant razor-blade.

In the early post-war years, Thyssen's might have made

links with other European steel companies; but it is now, like all steel companies, closely involved with national problems – and with the problem of the Ruhr. Sohl himself deplores the growth of steel nationalism, and insists that steel is no longer one of the 'commanding heights'. But the industry's troubles link it more closely with the state.

13. *Fiat*

The most spectactular of the Italian private empires, still controlled by the Agnelli family. (See pp. 142–6.)

14. *Daimler-Benz*

The legacy of the two German motoring pioneers, Gottlieb Daimler and Karl Benz, who invented automobiles in the 1880s, it now produces Mercedes cars near Stuttgart: its symbol of the three-pointed star stares out from the skyline of most German cities.

The most astonishing fact about Daimler-Benz is that forty per cent of the capital is owned by one family, headed by an old man of eighty-four, Friedrich Flick, probably the richest man in Germany, reckoned to be worth £200 million. Flick is one of the most enduring figures in the German industrial landscape. The son of a poor farmer, he built up huge steel and coal interests before the war, much of it in East Germany, which he lost to the Russians. After the war, like Krupp, he went to prison for using slave labour. When he got out in 1950 he had the sense, unlike Krupp, to obey the Allies' demands to break up his remaining steel and coal empire, and with the proceeds he moved into a much more lucrative field – cars, chemicals, plastics. His share in Daimler-Benz, which is only half his empire, is worth around £100 million. He and his younger son, Friedrich Karl (he quarrelled bitterly with his elder son, Otto), are both on the supervisory board and keep a close eye on policy. The chief executive, Joachim Zahn, belongs to another, more modest, family of Ruhr industrialists.

Daimler-Benz has grown spectacularly since the war, even through 1967 when Volkswagen slipped back; but they have worries about size, and in 1966 they made a rather mysterious link for research with Volkswagen. There are periodic rumours of alliances with foreign companies, but it is hard to imagine Daimler-Benz being anything but

German: apart from Flick's share, another 25 per cent is owned by the Deutsche Bank.[1]

15. *British Leyland Motors*

The awkward merger, in 1968, between buses and cars made all over Britain. (See pp. 152–5.)

16. *Farbwerke Hoechst*

The pre-war German chemical combine, I. G. Farben, which dominated the European industry, was broken up by the Allies, and split into its three components – Hoechst, Bayer and BASF. There are periodic rumours that they will again coalesce, but in fact their competition is fairly genuine. Anyway, I. G. Farben was never a very efficient merger, and each of the three components is now bigger than the combine was.

Like so many other German giants, Hoechst was founded in the 1860s, developing dyes from coal-tar, when Germany led the world in chemical research. It now has factories in 35 countries including a big plant in Antwerp, and regards itself as very multi-national, but there is no doubt where its home is. It is in the big suburb of Frankfurt, called Hoechst, a smelly city where a dome made of Hoechst plastics commemorates its centenary. Like all German chemical companies it is firmly ruled by a scientist, Professor Winnacker. The paternalism is overpowering – Hoechst houses, Hoechst concrete, Hoechst hotel, Hoechst technical school – but recently some Hoechst workers have begun to kick against it.

17. *Renault*

The only nationalized car company in western Europe, but not noticeably different in its commercial behaviour from its rivals. (See pp. 150–2.)

18. *Farbenfabriken Bayer*

Bayer is the most famous of the German chemical firms, with an amazing record of inventions. They began in 1863 making the fashionable new dyes; in 1892 they invented aspirin; in 1909 synthetic rubber. In 1935 they discovered the sulphonamides; in 1941 they invented Agfacolor. The pace

1. See p. 163.

of invention, as with all chemicals companies, has constantly quickened; 60 per cent of the products they now make were invented in the last twenty years.

Bayer, like Hoechst, is largely concentrated on a single company town – the great rectangle of Leverkusen, on the Rhine above Cologne, crowned by the tallest chimney in Germany and by a lit-up circle with Bayer inside it. The whole town was laid out as far back as 1890 by Bayer's chemical patriarch, Karl Duisberg. The present head of Bayer, Professor Hansen, is one of the most internationalized tycoons, a relaxed manager-scientist. He was even born in Yokohama, and built up post-war exports in America. He is convinced that Europe's chemical companies must combine across the frontiers to compete with America's, and he is responsible for virtually the only European merger – between Agfa (a subsidiary of Bayer) and the Belgian photographic company, Gevaert. The Agfa-Gevaert company, with a double holding like Unilever and Shell, has a historic importance as the first 'common market company'; but its difficulties have been great, and it is still only a tenth of the size of its American rival, Kodak. Hansen hopes that bigger mergers can follow: 'If industry can co-operate across the frontiers,' he said to me in 1967, 'then governments will follow.' (The truth or otherwise of this view is one of the main themes of this book.)

GEC / AEI

The British electrical giant, making everything from railway engines to lamp bulbs, formed in 1967 by a historic take-over of AEI by GEC. The new company is dominated, perhaps more firmly than any other European giant, by one man – Arnold Weinstock. He is still only forty-four, and his career seems to belong to an earlier age. He is the son of Jewish tailor, and married the daughter of an electrical tycoon, Sobell, whose company was soon afterwards taken over by GEC. Weinstock joined the board, became chairman, and reorganized GEC with unheard-of ruthlessness. In four years the profits rose from £4 million to £17 million. With this reputation for profits, he was able to persuade shareholders of his stately rival, AEI, to sell out to him. He is now moving into AEI with similar ruthlessness, closing factories, firing managers, retiring directorial peers and selling off the directors' claret and portraits. Weinstock is a genuine tycoon. He abhors management consultants, committees and divided responsibilities, and concentrates on one thing – profits. The merged company is now on the scale of the continental giants, Siemens and Philips (France is without any comparable electronics company). The further merger now planned, with English Electric, will make this the biggest electrical company in Europe.

20. *Krupp*

The most famous family firm in Europe, which rose to vaster proportions in each of the three wars. Abroad its name conjures up slave labour and big guns, but inside Germany it conveys a benign paternalism. It was founded in 1812 in Essen by Friedrich Krupp, whose son Alfred became the 'Big Gun King', designed mortars to bombard Paris in 1870, but died in pawn to the bankers. His son Friedrich regained control, became the richest man in Germany, but retired in his forties, a homosexual, to live in Capri, where he died. His daughter Bertha married a meticulous Prussian diplomat, Von Bohlen, and gave her name to the gun 'Big Bertha' which shelled Paris in the First World War. Her husband rebuilt the Krupp empire under Hitler and had a stroke just before the Americans entered Essen in 1945. His son Alfried was sentenced at Nuremberg to twelve years for using slave labour; while the Krupp works were dismantled.

Three years later he was let out and took over the company again, with the help of a young tycoon, Berthold Beitz; he defied Allied orders to break up the company and insisted (disastrously as it turned out) on maintaining the old coal-and-steel complex. Krupps expanded too rapidly, making a vast range of products, ranging from false teeth to orchids, and exporting heavily to eastern Europe, which was Beitz's special interest. But they had to borrow, more and more heavily, from the banks.

Finally in 1967 the banks foreclosed and insisted that Krupps, after 155 years, should become a public corporation.[1] Soon afterwards Alfried Krupp died; and his son Arndt gave up his share in the business in return for £100,000 a year. A new chief executive, Günter Vogelsang,

1. See p. 164.

moved in, sold off unprofitable bits including lorries, and set about pushing Krupps into new industries – space, aircraft, nuclear reactors.

SIZE

This jumble of giants have obvious features in common. Nearly all of them were born in the second half of the nineteenth century (centenaries have come thick and fast), but many of them have only reached outsize proportions since the last war. Compared to the Americans, they are obsessively secretive, and uncommunicative to shareholders. Most of them deal with newer commodities: two industries, cars and chemicals, account for nine of them. Two countries, Britain and Germany, account for thirteen. The size of countries has no relationship with the size of companies; Switzerland and Holland each have one giant, and France has only one (Renault). Britain, which used to regard Germany as the country of sinister giants, is now well in the lead, with a new wave of mergers. Taking *Fortune*'s 1967 list of the two hundred biggest corporations outside America, Britain has more of them (56) than France (23) and Germany (26) combined.

The companies look vast enough in the European framework; but in the last decade they have all become much more aware that they are competing in the world market. Beside the American giants, most of them look puny; only two of them, Shell and Unilever, rank with the world's top ten; the rest of them are well down the list.

It is in the shape of the big corporations that the American impact on Europe has shown itself most boldly. However much American dynamism may depend on other factors, and smaller companies, what the Europeans see is only the giants. The coming of the common market, at the same time as a new expansiveness in American industry, brought a new kind of invasion. A host of American corporations were attracted both by the European boom and by the promise of an integrated market. They no longer saw Europe just as a market for exports, but as a manufacturing centre. They bought up European companies and established big subsidiaries. They took the idea of the common market more literally than any of the Europeans. They swept into Europe as if it were another America. They set up headquarters in cosmopolitan cities – Brussels, Geneva or Luxembourg – and planned their strategy on a continental scale. They disregarded warnings about national differences, language or frontiers. They set up their own English-speaking network with the help of American advertising agencies, American bankers and American management consultants. If they needed capital they could raise it in Europe through that extraordinary invention, the Euro-dollar.[1] They established a separate kind of continent of their own, neither Europe nor America, but America-in-Europe.

The impact has been bewildering and traumatic. It has, in the first place, made the European corporations obsessed by the question of size. Having worried about being too big, they became much more worried about being too small. By the mid-sixties bigness of 'gigantism' had become a kind of continental fetish, and left-wing economists, who ten years before had been distressed at the danger of giant cartels, were now rejoicing at such mergers as Renault with Peugeot and Leyland with BMC. Bigness became regarded as a panacea for all kinds of inefficiencies: though mergers could make more troubles than they solved.

Faced with the American giants – with their huge resources for research, development and risk-taking – most of the European ones found themselves with the wrong scale, and the wrong perspective. The very simplicity of the American attack gave a shock to companies accustomed to continental complexities. I can describe this new confrontation by the experience of Unilever – the biggest company in its European operation and a kind of universal provider for the consumer society.

UNILEVER – A EUROPEAN COMPANY

Unilever, like Shell, has internationalism written into its constitution. Two boards, Unilever Ltd. in London and Unilever NV in Rotterdam, maintain the Anglo-Dutch balance, and they operate over five hundred separate companies in sixty countries. Its split headquarters, between London and Rotterdam, has some advantages, and some snags. Having two bases is often wasteful and cumbersome; it slows up

1. See p. 168.

decisions and it may sometimes give scope for mis-
understanding. The more Unilever needs to move quickly
and boldly, the more difficult it becomes. Communication
can be awkward and barbed, in spite of the ease with which
Dutchmen speak English. But the double nationality does –
like a mixed marriage – give Unilever a broader and more
tolerant attitude to the world. It enables it to see Britain with
Dutch eyes and Holland with British eyes. If Britain is unpopular in one part of the world, then Unilever can send in
Dutchmen. If Britain feels emotionally involved, Holland
can be detached and rational.

The fortunes of Unilever were made when its two staples,
soap and margarine, were spreading through Europe, as
people washed more and ate more. Now these two products,
in Europe at least, are hardly expanding; and it has to look
ahead all the time to new habits and desires. Will housewives
take jobs? Will men prefer beer to wine? Will Australian
children like ice-cream with 'Yeah Yeah Yeah' wrapped
round it? There are times when Unilever reports seem less
like business studies than like a broad sociological survey
on the state of the world – featuring a whole pageant of
consumers from English kipper-eaters to Indian buffalo-milk
drinkers. The range of taste presents perpetual problems:
Belgians, for some reason, eat less ice-cream; French
housewives are slow to take to frozen food.

It is not easy to generalize about the 'Unilever men', between the different European nationalities. Commonwealth
men are more prepared to travel abroad than Frenchmen or
Englishmen. Dutchmen – like other continentals – usually
leave university three or four years later than Englishmen,
and this gives them a more highly specialized training, but
can also make them less adaptable. The Dutch, with their
small country and their mastery of languages, are also
specially sensitive to European neighbours. Germans are
most organized in their selection and promotion of a management élite (they even use the study of handwriting as part
of their selection system, though the directors have different
opinions about its usefulness). All through Europe the friction between different nationalities helps to avoid any fixed
idea of what managers should be.

Britain remains by far Unilever's single biggest market; it
accounts for a third of its total sales. And it is in Britain that

Unilever's involvement with the consumer is most thorough. Unilever makes perhaps two-thirds of the margarine in Britain, about half of the soaps and detergents, and an even higher proportion of frozen foods. A properly Unilever-minded English bachelor could begin his day shaving with an Erasmic shaving stick or Erasmic shaving cream, washing with Lux toilet soap, cleaning his teeth with Pepsodent, cooking Wall's sausages in Spry fat, buying Birds Eye Frozen Food at a MacFisheries supermarket, opening a tin of Batchelor's peas, washing up with Squezy, and washing his shirt with Omo. His girl-friend in the meantime can be washing her hair with Sunsilk, colouring it with Harmony, and having a Twink home perm, while she puts on her Astral face cream. Many of the names have long social histories: Vim dates back to 1904; 'Lux' was invented by William Lever in 1899.

Unilever's two head offices, in London and Rotterdam, divide the world's markets between them. Rotterdam is responsible for the continent of Europe – the fourteen countries west of the Iron Curtain. London runs the British business, and the subsidiaries in other continents (though with the United States subsidiaries, Unilever is careful to confine its relationship to one of stockholder control). If you travel between the two headquarters you soon sense in Rotterdam the greater pressure of neighbouring countries. The Rotterdam building itself has a deliberately international look; it is full of polyglot people, and on each floor is a painting or sculpture from one of the fourteen countries. In the Netherlands Unilever, like the other Dutch giants, has grown accustomed to looking across frontiers. The different perspectives of London and Rotterdam have complementary advantages: London is both geographically and psychologically more detached – perhaps more patient, more prepared to leave people alone: Rotterdam is more immediately involved, more quickly aware of change and pressure, and its managers are more international and more mobile. Roughly a third of Unilever's operations (whether calculated by turnover, profits or capital invested) are in Britain. Another third are on the continent of Europe. The rest are in America, Africa, Asia and Australasia. Germany is Unilever's biggest continental market with a scope and complexity almost as great as in Britain.

Unilever in Europe has grown up in national compartments, and this separation has been increased both by past policy and by the recent history of Europe. Germany's pre-war financial policies, under Dr. Schacht, isolated Unilever in Germany behind the tariff wall, and forced it to diversify in its own way. During the war all national managements were isolated from each other, and cut off from Britain and America. Afterwards the loose structure largely remained. As a result, although they all deal in soaps and detergents, their products look, and are, very different: Omo is white in one country, blue in another. Astra, which used to be a soap in the Netherlands, is now a margarine in France. Most confusing of all, Persil, which in France or in Britain is Unilever's biggest single product, in Germany is one of her biggest rivals – owned by Henkel, the original inventors, who licensed it to Crosfield (now a subsidiary of Unilever) before the first war. Under the Treaty of Versailles, Germany lost its patents: the expropriation of Persil is one of the bitter reminders of the cost of the war.

Until a few years ago, this variety, though muddling, did not much matter: the competition was essentially national, and the local managements understood national problems and tastes better than anyone. In the Latin countries they knew that people liked stronger perfumes in Lux; in France they knew that the Frenchmen were sceptical of margarine; in the Netherlands they knew that Dutchmen normally have butter only at weekends. On one side of the frontier people liked salt in margarine; on the other side they could not stand it.

But then, around 1960, several things happened at once. First, the common market had brought the prospect of a far greater mobility of products, and a far bigger market; for the new products at least, a single factory might be able to supply all six countries. Secondly, with the new prosperity, Europeans began travelling much more, and the confusion of products became much more obvious. Thirdly, television and picture magazines overlapped across frontiers: German television was picked up in Austria, Switzerland and the Netherlands, and national advertising managers were bewildered to find that what was really shifting their products was television or magazines from the next-door country.

The most serious change of all for Unilever was the one

which affected the whole of European corporation life – the American invasion. In England and America Unilever had become accustomed to American competition – particularly from Procter and Gamble and Colgate; in the field of detergents they are familiar rivals. About two-thirds of the total world consumption of detergents comes from four big companies:

Unilever	25%	(PERSIL, OMO, SURF, etc.)
Procter & Gamble	25%	(TIDE, DAZ, DASH, etc.)
Colgate	10%	(FAB, PALMOLIVE, AJAX, etc.)
Henkel	4%	(DIXAN, etc.)

In Britain the hectic advertising fight between Daz and Omo has become almost as familiar as the fight between the political parties. But on the continent, until recently, Unilever's main competition came from European rivals; and it was not till the coming of the common market that the Americans became aware of the potentialities. The result was spectacular; and the detergent war still rages through Europe. The two main contenders, Unilever and Procter and Gamble, approach the battlefield with opposite experience and 'philosophies'. Procter's men are accustomed to a single vast market, which they have learnt to dominate by exhaustive studies of marketing techniques and consumer needs, followed by massive campaigns aggressively directed from Cincinnati. Unilever has been accustomed to a whole array of very different markets, which they have captured and held by strong and sensitive local managements, tactfully guided from the centre. The contrast between these two giants is a pointer, not only to their own corporate characters, but to the future conflicts of Europe.

Procter's men moved into Europe with their usual thoroughness, boasting openly that, having held their lead over Lever's in America (where they had been established years before Lever started up there, about the turn of the century, and where their business is more than double Lever's), they could beat them in Europe, their home ground. They moved first into France, then Belgium, the Netherlands and Germany. They established a school in Geneva, to train continental managers in their business methods. And they launched the same products – Daz, Tide, Dash – everywhere, with the same basic methods. They made huge mistakes, but they also had huge successes; and they were always prepared to cut their losses.

Unilever was now in the midst of a new kind of international competition, with a new problem. On the one hand their greatest strength lay in their national managements, and their ability to adapt products to local markets. On the other hand, they needed to be able to plan campaigns internationally, more centrally and quickly, using the resources of the whole organization. The Unilever board decided to introduce a new kind of overlord into their high command – the 'Co-ordinator' – to supervise one group of products all over the world (except in America) to advise national managements on selling products; and to launch new brands internationally, with the same names, the same formulae, and the same kinds of advertising. The arrival of co-ordinators, on top of the already complicated international structure, at first bewildered managers, who feared that it was a step towards centralization. But it was a change in the shape of the continent itself, where the frontiers of trade were beginning to dissolve.

The battle between the Americans and Europeans continues, and the pace is still quickening. You can see the line-up in any supermarket in Europe, where the packages glare at each other with their panoply of advertising, slowly assuming the same shapes and names all over Europe. Dutch tourists come back from Italy and ask for spaghetti and gorgonzola, and the French are even beginning to take to soft drinks. Will TV advertising persuade Italians to eat würst, and the French to smoke cigars? Certainly marketing methods are becoming less national, more American. But as Lord Cole, chairman of Unilever Ltd., said: 'None of us is likely to see the day when Italian salesmen are selling our products to German shop-keepers or Dutch salesmen plying their trade in France.'

In this new spirited competition, while Unilever's delicate structure will have its advantages, there will be some agonizing reappraisals in the years to come, for Unilever as for other European companies. The American giants, by ignoring the frontiers, have made European giants behave in the same sweeping way.

MANAGERS INTERNATIONAL

The extent of the 'managerial revolution' at the top of big companies is often exaggerated. Even among the top twenty in Europe, there are still some boses, like Weinstock or Agnelli, who hold very personal sway, and among the next biggest companies large family interests are much more common: in France the Bercot family still effectively controls (with tight lips) the interlocked companies of Michelin tyres and Citroën cars, now augmented by Berliet trucks. In Britain Pilkingtons still control Pilkington's glass, Sachers and Sieffs control Marks and Spencer shops. In Italy, where taxation (or non-taxation) favours family fortunes, most of the great industrial empires are still controlled by families – Pesenti for cement, Pirelli for tyres, Olivetti for typewriters, Marzotto for textiles, Zanussi or Borghi for refrigerators. The industrial oligarchy is most striking of all in Sweden, after thirty-two years of social democrat governments; in 1968 a committee reported to the government that fifteen families, headed by the Wallenbergs, the Brostroems, the Kempes, and the Bonniers, controlled a fifth of Swedish private industry; the fifteen families' fortunes amounted to £132 million.

But it is much rarer to find a first-generation tycoon, who has fought his way up to the top; and the entrepreneur, from having been a hated bogy, has become regarded as a precious instrument of innovation and mergers. In France, where tycoons have always been rare, a tiny group of old autocrats – Boussac, Prévost, Martelet, Dassault – are trotted out as examples of enterprise; and even in Germany, the *wunderkinder* of the miracle are growing old, and giving way to the organization men. It is in Italy that tycoons still flourish most boldly – knocking down, among other things, the old notions that only Calvinists make good capitalists. Italian *neo-capitalisti* have cropped up all over the place, from the sleepy-looking province of the Veneto or Emilia, exporting all over Europe.

But in the biggest companies, the professional managers are entering their kingdom. Inside these new jungles, in spite of all differences of plumage and colouring, there is emerging a new breed of international technocrats, with their own nesting habits, patterns of migration and mating calls. Within the big corporations you will find often a flight of expatriates, who have risen up, much like diplomats, by circling from capital to capital. The international corporations, of course, tend to exaggerate the ease with which their men fit into each other's societies; there are always resentments between minorities and majorities – Dutch and British, Swiss and German, French and Belgian – and the expatriates readily gravitate towards a cut-off world of air-conditioned hotels, diplomatic parties and company houses. But the top managers are bound together by oil, steel or cars: they understand the same mumbo-jumbo, the same kind of industrial diplomacy or blackmail; and they quite often marry foreign wives. They are proud of their international outlook, and (within the continent at least) they can acquire great fluency in languages.

Many of the managers, too, have a definite European idealism; the generation now in their mid-forties saw an internationalized industry as a way of preventing new disasters; there is a quite thriving Federation of European Young Managers, with branches all over Europe, which arranges colloquia and exchanges, on such stirring common problems as 'technical development and its effect on management' and 'the remuneration of young executives'.

There has been one ambitious attempt at management education on a European scale: in 1959, at the high tide of the European movement, a European institute of business administration was set up at Fontainebleau, outside Paris, to bring to the continent the disciplines of the Harvard Business School, which has come to be regarded as the cure for all Europe's management problems. Fontainebleau was financed by big continental and American companies (but no British ones), much helped by Harvard and the Ford Foundation. It was run by Olivier Giscard D'Estaing, who comes from a family of technocrats and is a brother of the former Finance Minister; he himself went to the Harvard Business School after leaving the École Normale. He is something of a caricature of the busy new polymath – a bustling, white-rabbit figure, with the same athletic energy as his brother, talking in neat slogans and preaching the splendours of management; he has a flair for publicity. When I visited the institute, it seemed a gloomy harbinger of the new Europe. Its hundred and twenty students come from about twenty countries, with France, Germany and Britain in the lead, and they are supposed to be trilingual, though French and English predominate in lectures. But the common denominator of the nationalities is a bleakly materalistic one. The syllabus is purely practical, without cultural leavening – lectures on marketing, finance, quantitative techniques, with an hour a day for languages. And the school is in the exclusive mould of the French Grandes Écoles (most of the French students come from the commercial college, the HEC). Fontainebleu aims unashamedly to provide a new European élite. It is too early yet, since the school is only nine years old, to say how far it will rival the old-boy networks of Harvard or Standford, which are already making themselves felt in European big business. If it fails, it will not be for lack of self-promotion. But ironically, Fontainebleau has so far contributed more to America than to Europe: its best students mostly go into American corporations. 'We are creating a new kind of brain drain,' said one of their professors, Guy de Carmony.[1]

In the early talk of the managerial revolution it was often assumed that the managers would be recruited from all classes, rising from the factory floor or from technical colleges to take over the reins from the old bourgeois capitalists. Nothing of the kind has happened. The top layers of the middle-classes who had always produced the officers, the professional men and the top civil servants of Europe, have merely extended their field into the managerial class; even in Italy, where the scope for the self-made manager might seem greater, surveys have shown that most of the top managers come from the old bourgeoisie. The big companies insist on university degrees for their managers; and universities (as we will see) remain a very middle-class province.[2] 'So marked was the middle-class origin of the new managerial class,' concluded Professor Postan, after surveying the field, 'that hardly any recent sociological study of industry fails to bring it out. Indeed, the ability and willingness to demonstrate it are so manifest that they threaten to become the recognition call of the industrial sociologist.'[3] The narrowing class basis

1. *Conference on Industrial Integration in Europe*, Federal Trust, London, March 1968.
2. See chapter 21.
3. M. M. Postan: *An Economic History of Western Europe 1945–64*, Methuen, 1967.

of the managers appears to be a universal trend, whatever
the prevailing ideologies, governments or class structures –
whether in social-democrat Scandinavia, free-enterprise
Germany, or Labour Britain, or in America. But in Europe
the exclusiveness of the new managers is more striking, because they are grafted on to the old bourgeois traditions: the
old classes in which Europe took such pride, its armies,
priests, imperial administrators, have transferred themselves
into this new élite.

And even in eastern Europe and Russia, though statistics
are not available, it is clear that most of the top managers
are from a narrow middle-class sector, and probably increasingly so. German or English businessmen, going to Czechoslovakia or Poland to negotiate with their opposite
numbers, enjoy describing how they turn out to be more
obviously and flamboyantly élitist than they are themselves
– well-cut clothes, big office, large car. The encounter provides (as one worried French technocrat described it to me) a
kind of alibi, a *copinage technocratique*, a comfortable
knowledge that every country is moving in the same direction, and that not even Russia can find its top managers
on the workshop floor.

MULTINATIONAL COMPANIES

There is nothing a European dislikes so much as an expert from
overseas.

Thomas F. Watson (President of IBM), 1967

Faced with the Americans, a dominant question for
European industry is whether it will ever be able to construct
genuinely international companies, merging across frontiers
to produce single big units; and whether Europe can ever be
the logical context for such mergers. The need for European
companies has become part of the creed of the Eurocrats,
and in 1967 international lawyers were asked to work out a
legal formula for a 'European company' which would be
recognized freely through the western continent.

There have been hundreds of mergers and take-overs in
the common market, but they have been either within the
same country, or between a European and an American
company. The only major case of a European merger is the

link between the Belgian Gevaert and the German Agfa.[1] Lacking a common European company law, a complicated system of cross-holdings was devised; but the problems of that merger – legal, organizational and personal – have been so great that it has not been an encouraging precedent: the commercial secretary of Agfa-Gevaert, M. le Page, has explained how 'only at the very top are the minds merged'.[2]

The difficulties of forming a European company are huge. The whole field is a legal maze. Each country has a different system of company law, and different ways to protect shareholders; France has strong rules about pre-emptive rights; Germany provides a 'supervisory board'; Belgium limits the number of votes for a single shareholder. Rather than try to harmonize all company law, the common market now plans to set up a new legal entity of a 'European company' to run alongside national systems.

But the legal difficulties, it seems to me, conceal deeper psychological ones. In each country companies have a different and delicate relationship with their governments. The big engineering and electrical companies, like Siemens or English Electric, have grown fat with the help of massive contracts from their governments or nationalized industries. As national planning develops, the company gets more involved in notions of patriotism – Pechiney batting for France, Fiat for Italy, Krupp for Germany. This tendency is getting stronger, not weaker; a merger between BLM and Fiat seems as unlikely as one between Arsenal and Juventus. 'If Fiat were sold to another country,' one Italian banker assured me, 'there'd be a revolution.'

Moreover, to put it bluntly, companies in different countries do not trust one another. Given the choice between joining with an American company and with another European company, they nearly always choose the first. This is what worries the Eurocrats, for it causes a centrifugal force in the middle of Europe. Not only is the American company usually richer and technically more advanced; the whole history of European company relationships is filled with traumas. For instance, after each war, scores of German companies saw their patents and brand-names (as with Persil), taken over by their European rivals. Alfred

1. See p. 121.
2. *New York Times*, 13th March, 1968.

Conard, an American legal expert on mergers, concluded in a monograph on 'Corporate Fusion in the Common Market': 'The most important need is not technical but political. It is the need for a prospect of permanence in the European community and a prospect of genuine co-operation among its members in achieving its objectives.'

It is not an accident that some of the most successful multi-national companies are based in Switzerland (Nestlé, Ciba Brown Boveri, Hoffmann-La Roche) or Sweden (SKF, Ericsson, Alfa-Laval): their countries' neutrality, smallness and stable currencies have given the companies a basis of trust which makes collaboration much easier. Nor is it accidental that some of the most national or 'ethnocentric' companies are based in France or Germany. In this respect, the British aloofness from the continent, and the long British experience of international trade, have great advantages: they have given British companies an ability to come to terms with others, and a habit of looking at the world, which can make them effective cornerstones for multinational buildings. It is part of the weakness of the present structure of Europe that, while Britain is excluded from the common market, politicians who want to build up European companies must look towards Britain as a key component.

For the foreseeable future, by far the greatest number of multinational companies will be American-based. Their influence will grow and their relationships with nation states will become more delicate. The investment decisions of companies are increasingly affecting the European exchequers. A big deal in one year can transform a national balance of payments. The giant companies can plan for a decade ahead, ignoring the ups and downs of national economies. If they face difficulties in one country, they can move next door. When General Motors were not allowed by the French government to build a new plant in Strasbourg, they built it in Belgium instead, depriving the French of employment while still giving them competition.

Professor Vernon forecasts a 'long and stormy period of transistion' in relations between corporations and countries.[1] 'Today, it begins to be feasible to think of great international networks of mines and plants, straddling national boundaries, that are interlocked by supply lines which im-

1. *Harvard Business Review*, March/April 1967.

plement a common strategy in production, marketing and control'. He foresees growing resentments and obstacles against this common strategy. The corporations are likely to become less distinctively American, employing more Europeans and even losing some of their national identity. But the development will take time, since 'most modern men are raised in the system of nation-states'.

There are many Europeans (like Jean-Jacques Servan-Schreiber, the proclaimer of the 'American Challenge') who seem hopeful that the new American power will stimulate a European response, forcing companies and countries to come together. After this brief survey, I feel very doubtful. Many of the European companies (and the next chapter will show others) seem to be becoming more, not less, national in their character, and to reveal old rivalries in a new shape. The American giants, by luring European companies to collaborate with them, not with each other, can be more divisive than unifying. One is forced to wonder how much sense the context of Europe makes, when the continent has such a background of distrust, when so many of the keys lie outside it, and when industry has anyway become global. And it may be that the dominant question of the future will not be whether Europe should combine to resist the American challenge, but how European countries should control and humanize the new global technological industries, which can have a profound and unsettling effect on societies.

Chapter Six

Cars

The automobile makes them free. It is the last little bit of freedom left to man.

Professor Nordhoff

Of the industries that have transformed Europe, the car industry is still the prodigy. It provided the most spectacular manifestation of the post-war miracles, the glittering showpiece of the consumer society. It was at the centre of the first infatuation with prosperity, and the first disillusion with it. It employs some of the most prosperous workers, and some of the most militant. In most of Europe's current social problems – whether city planning, automation, over-production, the American challenge or the European response – the shiny monsters will be found somewhere in the middle. In the question of European integration and the breaking down of frontiers – a central theme of this book – the car industry provides key examples.

Compared to America, the automobile as a mass-product came late to Europe – thirty years late. But when it came, it came with a vengeance. Twenty years ago the factories of western Europe were producing half a million cars in a year; in 1967 they produced over nine million. In the first years after the war the 'civilization of the automobile' was still regarded as an American phenomenon, associated with wide open spaces and Hollywood suburbia; the idea of a car for every family seemed a fantasy in the context of Europe's crowded and needy cities. But as the continent recovered and then forged ahead, the European appetite turned out, after all, to be as unstoppable as that of the Americans. The four-wheeled boxes rolled out in their millions on to the winding lanes and narrow streets, clogging the cities and lining the seaside.

It is not surprising that the car has become an obsession

with European film-makers – not so much as a symbol of escape and adventure, in the American idiom, but as a lethal symbol of frustration and repressed violence. The obsession reached a new peak in Godard's *Week-End,* where a honking traffic-jam develops into mass-murder ending with a French woman eating (apparently) the flesh of an English tourist.

By 1967 there was one car to every six people in the common market compared with one to two and a half in the United States; Britain, having been in the lead in car-ownership after the war, has now fallen behind France and Germany. These were some figures for cars per thousand people, on January 1, 1967.[1]

Sweden	240	Holland	128
France	198	Italy	121
Germany	178		
Britain	172	United States	397
Belgium	161	Russia	4

There is still intense argument as to how many more cars Europe can produce before it reaches saturation; so much of the character and industry of the continent depends on it. But most car experts seem to think that the figure will come close to the American proportion.

Certainly the worship of the automobile in Europe is more intense even than in America. Marshall McLuhan believes that the age of the automobile is over, but it is hard to believe it in Europe; European intellectuals will talk about cars with an enthusiasm which amazes Americans; here, as in other fields, Europeans are becoming excited just as Americans are beginning to be bored. On Saturday afternoons, in the suburbs of Hamburg or the back-streets of Milan, you can see fathers washing and polishing their Volkswagens and Fiats as intently as soldiers polish their boots. In Paris you see gleaming Citroëns outside tumbledown shacks in a bidonville. In the economic boom, the car has taken precedence over the near-necessities of life, and the statistics prove it: more than half the French families have a car, but only a quarter have a bathroom.

There are differences between the European and American attitudes. The European cars are still much smaller,

1. *Basic Statistics of the Community,* EEC, 1967. See also chapter 13.

more varied, more eccentric than the Americans giants; the Europeans are more devoted to speed and acceleration: 'You still regard driving as a sport,' one American complained. And Europeans are still – for the time being – more loyal to old cars or old models. As they roll along the roads, the long and the short and the tall, they look like a mechanical zoo – the comic little Citroën 'deux-chevaux' with its hind-wheels sticking up like frog's legs: the Citroën DSs like sleek porcupines; the tiny Fiat 'topolini', the 'little mice'; and of course the Volkswagens, the timeless and unmistakable beetles. Compared to this exotic menagerie, the American cars look more alike and impersonal, like a school of sharks ('Not only do cars come to look like one another, and like other things,' David Riesman has remarked of American cars, 'but other things come to look like cars.'[1])

Gradually the European cars are fattening up, getting both longer and wider, and perhaps more alike in the process. But not even the most ambitious car-makers in Turin or Cologne imagine that their cars will swell to American proportions. For Europe is up against the one problem which no amount of prosperity can solve – the sheer shortage of space.[2] The intense urbanization of Europe makes cars a far greater problem. If every family insists on a car, how can the old cities remain habitable? How can Rome, an essentially pedestrian city, survive this overwhelming new passion? How can highways or fly-overs cater for the flood of machines, without criss-crossing the whole crowded continent with an ugliness which destroys the first purpose? Yet how can a modern democracy dare to restrict the most consuming of all consumers' demands? No prophet has yet dared to imagine the full social consequences of this steel procession on the old continent. My own hopeful guess is that after the first long infatuation, Europeans will at last begin to use the car less as a means of congregation, more as a retreat into a private hinterland; and that the European countryside, still being de-populated, will revive again when people realize the real benefits of cars. In the meantime, the infatuation will continue; for the motor-car is a symbol, above all the other things, of a new-found liberation.

1. David Riesman: *Abundance for What?* Doubleday, 1964.
2. See also chapter 11.

But the automobile is at the centre of economic as well as social problems; and the industry shows, more visibly than any other, the new scale of world competition. The car companies have grown since the war to be among the very biggest corporations in Europe. They are the hubs of their industrial states, reflecting not merely the state of the economy, but the national pride – a part-substitute for armies and battleships. The sales wars between Volkswagen and Fiat and their forays across frontiers have taken over some of the excitement of military invasions. In spite of the common market they still have national characteristics as obvious as sausages or cheeses, and their names are brandished like flags all over their home countries; a visitor from Mars could be forgiven for imagining that Fiat or Renault were the names of the nations.

For nearly twenty years the big car companies have steadily expanded, beating their own records year after year, bringing work to hundreds of thousands of employees; they have constituted the core of the European 'miracles', and their chairmen – Nordhoff, Valletta or Dreyfus – have been national heroes. But now, in the last two years, the miracles have come to an end, and the clouds have began to gather over the industry. The big companies dread the prospect of over-production and cut-throat competition which could close down whole towns. The prospect is brought closer by the mounting competitions and the massive investment from American companies, which force the Europeans to think in continental terms. Can the European companies, big though they are, hold their own without merging themselves to the same kind of dimensions as General Motors or Ford? Can they find enough new markets in eastern Europe, Russia or North Africa to keep up with the pace of expansion? Can western Europe cope with the same proportion of cars to people as in America without becoming virtually uninhabitable? These are questions that unite the car tycoons in a common angst.

Four continental companies can be taken as special national symbols, each leaders in its own country, and each now facing new problems: Volkswagen, Fiat, Renault and British Leyland.

These four have totally opposed legal entities: Fiat is privately owned, controlled by a single wealthy family; Volkswagen for years had no owner at all; Renault is wholly nationalized; British Leyland is owned by thousands of shareholders. Yet to the bafflement of economic theorists they have come to resemble each other, with corporate characters which belie their indifferent ownership structures. Fortified by their profits and exports, breaking outside their frontiers, they have become separate principalities.

They have nearly all been dominated by a single strong boss. In spite of all its hierarchies, automation, market research, the motor industry still rests in the end on huge hunches – gambling on two or three million cars; and the hunches rest, in the end, on one man.

FIAT

That brief word that in the genesis made the light.

Gabriele D'Annunzio

The most spectacular of these new powers is the city-state of Fiat. In the past seventy years, while governments, kings and constitutions have come and gone, Fiat has never ceased to expand, adapting itself to each new regime. Today Fiat encircles and dominates the big city of Turin more visibly than the kings of Piedmont ever did. Its Turin factories give work for a hundred thousand people, making cars, lorries, railway engines, aero engines, steel. Its private health service looks after nearly a third of the inhabitants of Turin. It owns a whole suburb of tall flats, two seaside resorts (one with a sixteen-storey skyscraper), a hospital and an alpine camp. It owns the Turin daily paper *La Stampa* – perhaps the best in Italy – the biggest Turin insurance company, and an apprentices' school of a thousand boys, 99 per cent of whom go into the Fiat works. At Turin university engineering professors are also employees of Fiat. It is difficult for any Fiat employee to go into a bar or restaurant in Turin without encountering another Fiat man: 'it makes it hard to misbehave,' one of them remarked wistfully. The enveloping paternalism is proclaimed in their shiny company magazine, *Illustrato Fiat*, with Fiat babies, Fiat weddings, Fiat football teams and above all Fiat cars, radiant with Italian showmanship, adorned with glitter and girls.

Turin, the former capital of Italy, still retains some of the grandeur of a royal city, with a palace, huge squares and long colonnades; and it still has the sense of military discipline of the kingdom of Piedmont. But Fiat have taken over the old military tradition and it seems to work better with cars than with armies. Young workers can enter the special Fiat apprenticeship school at the age of fifteen, and spend three years learning with regimental precision how to handle machines. The factories themselves are guarded like arsenals, and as orderly as barracks.

For seventy years Fiat has been a key part of the Italian economy. It was formed in 1899, at the beginning of the heroic age of motoring, by a group of Turin businessmen, and called the Fabbrica Italiana Automobili Torino or FIAT – soon shortened to its biblical-sounding initials. Its chairman was Giovanni Agnelli, a cavalry officer of thirty-three with extraordinary toughness and flair, who for forty-five years was to dominate Fiat, building up its diversified empire and making a colossal personal fortune.

When Agnelli died at the end of the last war, financial control passed to his eleven grandchildren. But for the next twenty years, the effective boss was a legendary technocrat, Professor Vittorio Valletta, who presided over the massive expansion after the war, relentlessly imposing his own stern paternalism, fighting the communist workers, expanding the factories with the help of American loans. Fiat became by far the largest company in Italy, a huge self-contained corporation with which governments interfere at their peril. In 1967 it even overtook its main rivals, Volkswagen, to become the biggest car-producers in Europe, and the fourth biggest in the world.

Valletta's last great coup is still reaching fruition. He had always had his eyes on eastern Europe, as a great new market where Fiat had an old reputation; when he met President Kennedy in Washington, Kennedy suddenly asked him why the Italians didn't make a car deal with Russia. For the next years Valletta worked away patiently, visiting Moscow, trying to sell tractors, inviting Kosygin to Turin, establishing trust. Then, quite suddenly in 1966, the Russians felt the need for a huge expansion in their car industry. Their minister for cars, Tarasov, came to Turin, and Valletta was asked back to Moscow. A sensational deal was announced.

Fiat would collaborate in constructing a huge plant on the

river Volga designed to turn out six hundred thousand cars a year – three times the current Russian production, and over half Fiat's. The car would be a modified version of Fiat's own new car, the 124. Work was to start immediately – and it did: the Italians, while a bit taken aback by Russian drinking habits, have been astonished by the speed of the Russians' switching of priorities.

It was a staggering agreement. The other car-makers insisted that the target of six hundred thousand cars couldn't be reached, and explained that this was really a barter deal between governments. But it put Fiat in the van of the movement to the east. It provided an ironic twist to traditional Italian politics. Fiat, the old bogy of the communist unions. Fiat the arch-capitalists, had become the trusted allies of the Russians. In a last-minute coup, to the fury of the Italian prime minister, the Russians had insisted that the factory-town would be renamed Togliattigrad, after the dead Italian communist leader.

Valletta had built up an ageing managerial hierarchy of narrowly-educated engineers; and he apparently expected one of them, probably Engineer Bono, to succeed him. But the Agnelli family controlled about twenty per cent of the shares, and the eldest grandson, Gianni Agnelli, who was deputy-chairman, was firmly in command of the main investments. Valletta, it seems, never took Agnelli very seriously and regarded him as a useful public-relations figurehead. But when Valletta retired in 1966, Agnelli took over as chairman. There was a good deal of astonishment: the managerial revolution, it seems, had gone sharply into reverse.

Gianni Agnelli has for a long time been a legend in Italy: he has a mythology not unlike President Kennedy's, with film-star good looks, a playboy past, and a heritage of easy wealth; and he likes to cultivate an atmosphere of power, as well as power itself. After the war he was one of the dashing international set, surrounded by girls and speculation; it was a time when Italy looked like going communist (he explains) so he might as well enjoy himself. Then he settled down, married a principessa, and became increasingly fascinated by politics and Fiat. Today he is a vulpine figure with a predatory charm; he casts some kind of spell on people near him. Italians sometimes refer to him as 'the King of Italy' and clearly his presence, like Kennedy's, fills some kind of psychological gap; there is endless gossip about him, his money, telephone calls and secret political influence. He fits easily into the part of a gay monarch and clearly enjoys every province of his empire – the Turin hierarchies, the weekly political visits to Rome, the private helicopter, the yacht, the tours of America. He combines his Italian passions with a great admiration for America and he enjoys importing American ideas into Italian business. The internationalism of modern technology gives Agnelli a special advantage; he is a director of the Chase Manhattan, and of the 3M company in Minnesota. His younger brother Umberto is head of Fiat International, and his family have recently made an exchange of shares with one of the French Rothschild companies.

The company that Agnelli took over, in spite of its success abroad, was still essentially a Piedmontese principality. At the top were engineers in their seventies, most of them speaking only Italian; the organogram (as one management consultant described it) was 'just a series of concentric circles, with Valletta in the middle'; and Agnelli was apt to find, when he gave instructions, that the old engineers would all go and see Valletta, to ask him what to do about them. With some difficulty, he set about rejuvenating and opening up the closed Fiat community. He retired scores of old men, made a retiring age of sixty-five, sent young managers over to America for training, brought in bankers and accountants from outside; he made it clear that he wanted to make Fiat an international company.

But the mainstay of Fiat's business was still in Italy itself, and it was here that Agnelli faced his first crisis. For decades, for Italians, the words 'Fiat' and 'car' had been almost synonymous; Fiat made four-fifths of the cars in Italy, and it was generally understood that their rivals, headed by Alfa-Romeo which was a nationalized company, would not compete with them in popular cars. Fiat had often been under fire from left-wing politicians for their concentration of industrial power in Turin in the rich heart of Italy and their neglect of the impoverished south. But Agnelli argued that intense concentration, as in Detroit, was essential for the car industry, and that what's best for Fiat is best for Italy.

One morning in May 1967, Agnelli without warning heard shattering news; that Alfa-Romeo planned to build a factory near Naples to employ fifteen thousand workers and to make three hundred thousand cars a year, with a model directly competing with Fiat. It seemed inconceivable that the government should break Fiat's monopoly. Agnelli rushed to Rome; experts and bankers warned of the dangers to planning and efficiency. But Alfa-Romeo could offer hopes of votes in the south; they believed that Italian car-production could be doubled by 1981, and that the new plant would be the cornerstone of new industries in the south. With elections looming, it was hard to argue against, and after two stormy months, the Italian government finally gave its approval to 'Alfa-Sud'.

Fiat people made it known that the project was bound to run into disasters, and that they would probably have to salvage it themselves. But the massive plans in the meantime went ahead: even in the face of such all-embracing industrial power, political pressures can win in the end.

VOLKSWAGEN

The present begins when one has cut off all connections with the past.

Professor Nordhoff

Volkswagen is the fading epic of the German economic miracle. The vast and symmetrical factory has, for the last fifteen years, been the showplace of German industry. It is not an easy pilgrimage: the factory stands in a bleak bit of country, at Wolfsburg, a few miles from the border of East Germany. As the train approaches you can see a solid mile of brick building, with four tall chimneys at one end, a sky-scraper at the other and a neatly laid-out town across the railway with hundreds of Volkswagens parked nose to tail alongside the station. It is a pure company town, made by, for and with Volkswagens. As you enter the station a fruity American accent comes over the loudspeaker saying 'The Volkswagen factory welcomes you to Wolfsburg'.

Inside, the building looks like a vast skeleton fairground, with familiar-looking bits of Volkswagen revolving from the huge roof, dangling like seats on the big dipper. Without much human interference, the bits of the beetle are fitted together; the climax comes when the front half meets the back half, and the two are automatically welded together with a clank, a hiss and a shower of sparks. A minute afterwards the roof, which has been waiting round the corner, is swung round into place and jammed on top, in another shower of sparks; and then the whole body trundles on, while the chassis arrives, to be screwed on with automatic screwdrivers. At the other end of the works the cars come out into the open air, painted and polished at the rate of five a minute. They are tested, checked, and driven on to special trains. This has been going on for two decades.

The Volkswagen story has become part of German folklore. It played a big part in transforming Germany's post-war fortunes. But it was not at all a typical German story: it rested on chance, and on a single personality.

The foundation-stone of the factory was laid by Hitler in 1938, who dedicated the promised car to the 'Strength-through-Joy' movement. The factory was built by Italian labour sent over by Mussolini: but the whole production was commandeered for the war. In 1945 a British officer, Major Hirst, allowed some factory engineers to work in the wreckage, repairing British army jeeps and lorries: he was one of the collection of British soldiers who, for a year or two, held Germany's future in their hands. He became interested in the bits of Volkswagen in the factory, and is credited with a legendary remark: 'Might even build a few cars.' It was at a time when much German industry was being dismantled, and proposals were actually made to transport the Volkswagen works to Britain or elsewhere as reparations. But the British car manufacturers thought that the car was too ugly and too noisy, with its air-cooled engine, to have much lasting success; and the factory stayed where it was. The Volkswagen, with its comic shape and its absurd history, was something of a joke – as it still is.

It was a time full of ironies. By 1947 the Allies, having stopped dismantling, were already preparing to hand back factories to the Germans, and Colonel Radclyffe of the British military government asked a forty-eight-year-old engineer, Heinz Nordhoff, to take over the Volkswagen works. Nordhoff had worked before and during the war for Opel's under General Motors, and he wanted to go back there. But the American authorities at that time took a stern line against anyone who had managed wartime industry, and so said no. So Nordhoff went to Wolfsburg, and soon afterwards took over the running of the Volkswagen factory. It was a unique situation; for although the factory was already turning out ten thousand cars a year, no one knew to whom it legally belonged.

It was a manager's paradise, a text-book case for the managerial revolution, and Nordhoff, as it happened, was a master-manager. A banker's son, he had been trained before the war by General Motors; he knew about servicing and sales as well as production: and he was prepared to gamble quite heavily on the future. He staked everything on the single 'beetle'; the parts were modified, details changed, until in the end (they said) only seven of the five thousand parts were the same; but the basic beetle remained. Nordhoff's confidence was totally justified. The Volkswagen soon dominated the German market, then spread through Europe and by the late fifties was invading America, where it quickly had a sensational success; in 1967 it was selling more cars in America than in Germany – an extraordinary but rather perilous achievement. It was by far the most exported car in the world – selling twelve times as many cars in America as the next rival import, the Opel (also German). In America Volkswagens were boosted by jokey advertisements which cunningly mixed snobbery with inverted snobbery. There was even a special Jokes-wagen book: in one advertisement a South American tycoon was asked if his Volkswagen had air-conditioning: 'No, but I've got others in the deep-freeze.' The advertisements (using the same American agency) then spread back into Germany with more elaborate messages such as 'Volkswagen, your second car, even if you haven't got a first', or 'for people who want to be different from people who want to be different'.

Nordhoff presided over his booming empire with magisterial calm, and with what he called 'the loneliness of unshared responsibility'. He fought off the claims of the pre-war 'Volkswagen savers' who had put money into Hitler's car. Isolated at Wolfsburg, unharried by shareholders or trade unions, his company became – even more than the other car companies – a state within a state. Until 1961 Nordhoff was technically a government servant; then Dr. Erhard, the economics minister of the 'miracle', decided to denationalize the company; the Federal government held on to twenty per cent of the shares and the Land government kept another twenty per cent; the rest were bought by one and a half million small shareholders.

Nordhoff was unassailable: by 1966 Volkswagen were producing 1,650,000 vehicles. He had brilliantly shown the advantages of sticking to one model. He once boasted: 'I shall never follow the fashion of bringing out a new car as though I were in the *haute couture* business.' But there was a snag in the Nordhoff success story; he had never had to plump for a new model. There were sidelines and variations – buses, vans, sports cars and bigger Volkswagens; but the Nordhoff empire was built on the beetle, and it remained the mainstay. As the beetle came up to its thirtieth birthday, and its ten millionth number, the question of what would succeed it became more and more anxious. By the autumn of 1966 Germany was facing its first recession since the beginning of the miracle, and Volkswagen were among the first to be hit. In January 1967 the unthinkable had happened; for a few days the great factory at Wolfsburg was silent, and the workers faced a spell of short time.

Recriminations soon followed. Nordhoff was ageing, and was accused of smugness and autocracy; the finance minister, Franz-Josef Strauss,[1] publicly attacked him for not developing a family car like Fiat's or Renault's, and pertinently asked: 'What happens when the Americans stop being amused by the beetle?' Nordhoff replied by inviting journalists round the experimental section, where four thousand designers and engineers were said to be working.

In the meantime the supervisory board, prompted by the government, persuaded Nordhoff to announce his retirement, and brought in a successor from outside his fief – Kurt Lotz, from the engineering company Brown Boveri. Lotz was a very different kind of *wunderkind* from a different world: he had been a policeman, then an airman, before he became a major under Goering. He is a rare case of a wartime officer, without a degree, rising to the top in post-war Germany; he likes to run a business with thorough delegation, controlling strategy while others look after tactics. He denied, after Strauss's attacks, that the slackening off of Volkswagen's sales had anything to do with the lack of a

1. See chapter 1.

new model; but clearly he was appointed to bring a new
policy and a new car to Wolfsburg. Soon after he took over
Nordhoff died, and the twenty-year legend was finally
over.

RENAULT

The year before Fiat was formed, a young amateur mechanic of twenty-one called Louis Renault constructed a
'voiturette' in a shed at the bottom of his family's garden at
Billancourt, just outside Paris – where it stands, in front of
the present Renault headquarters. Before Ford got going,
France became the world's leading producer of cars: even
London taxis were Renaults. In the pioneer age Louis Renault, a single-minded despot, was a national hero; six hundred Renault taxis took troops from Paris to the Battle of the
Marne in 1914. But in the second war the name lost its glory.
Renault worked closely with the German occupation, and in
1944 he was arrested by the French government and impris-
oned, charged with collaboration. His factories were
nationalized, and soon afterwards he died of heart-failure in
prison – brought on, it was said, by the humiliation.

The Renault company still bears his name; but now it is a
nationalized company, controlled – in theory at least – by
the French government. The present head of it, Pierre
Dreyfus, is a man of quite different background and temperament to Agnelli or Nordhoff. He is not an engineer or a
tycoon, but a professional administrator, a '*grand commis*'
in the old French tradition. He is altogether an odd man to
find at the head of an aggressive car empire; he sits in a vast
office, which looks over Louis Renault's original little hut; it
is the kind of room one imagines Pascal inhabiting. It has
bare white walls, no pictures or distractions, and a huge
empty desk with two empty ashtrays. It is quite difficult at
first to find M. Dreyfus: he is very small, neat, with a small
triangular face, sharp eyes and a long mouth which curls up
into a sly smile as he describes his adventures.

Most of Dreyfus's career has been in government administration: he comes from well-to-do Jewish parents, and is
distantly related to the Dreyfus of the Dreyfus Affair. He
started in his father's export business, and after spending the
war in the resistance he was involved in the post-war French
planning under Jean Monnet, then ran coal mines in Lor-

raine, and then became vice-chairman of Renault. He now presides with calm. He is absorbed in its problems, dislikes social life, reads Latin as a relaxation; he is, discreetly, a man of the left, a friend of Mendès-France and has been a member of the left-wing society, the Club Jean Moulin. But he has had no serious difficulties with De Gaulle.

Dreyfus is the undisputed boss of Renault: he likes to explain that the only sanction that the government has is to sack him and he is in a stronger position than many private chairmen: he has no obligations to consult his fellow-directors. At the same time, Renault feels very vulnerable to the public opinion: with its biggest factory in what used to be the 'red suburb' of Paris, with its visibility and its chequered past, it is constantly suspected; and it is, after all, nationalized. Pierre Bercot of Citroën, the private enterprise rival, is always accusing Renault of unfair advantages.

Dreyfus has made full use of his independence, in expansion and welfare. Before the war Renault had an evil reputation for labour relations, and the Billancourt factory was one of the main targets of the communists. Dreyfus has been determined to get the workers on his side, and provides long-term contracts to ensure their security, guaranteeing an annual wage increase of four per cent. In 1962 came the greatest show of independence, when he proposed an unprecedented four-week annual holiday for his workers. He enjoys describing how he achieved it. He pointed out to the government that an extra three days' holiday was quite workable; that the summer, when they were on short time anyway, was the best time, and that it would be simplest to extend the holiday period; the phrase 'four weeks' was not actually mentioned. The extra holiday was proclaimed, and soon became a rallying cry for the French unions, all demanding four-week holidays. There was vague talk of Dreyfus being fired by the government; but it would have been difficult for them to antagonize both management and labour. After that, conditions were further improved in the 1966 agreement, which gave senior workers up to *five* weeks' holiday.

Like Fiat, Renault has had difficult patches; they tried to expand too rashly, particularly into America, with too many faults; and their Renault 8, with its engine at the back, had an awkward start. For two years they made no profit.

But the Renault 16 established itself as a new family car, and the small Renault 4 has swept through Europe with a staying power that surprised its makers. They have merged with Peugeot, which has a tradition of brilliant engineering, and the marriage is gradually shaking down. They have also, like Fiat but less spectacularly, expanded eastwards; in 1966 they signed a big contract to re-equip the Russian Moskvitch car plant; to increase its production three-fold to 300,000 cars a year, and to exchange technical information; 'you see,' Dreyfus said to me wryly, 'we are good pupils in the school of De Gaulle.'

Renault has had such a stormy political history, and has been so much a symbol of France's post-war success, that it was appropriate that its factories should be at the centre of the revolt in May 1968. The holidays and high wages (which were anyway much lower than the German equivalents) did not deflect the old rebellious tradition; the young Renault workers were almost the first to catch the discontent from the students, and by occupying the factories forced the communist union to strike; when the union announced a settlement, the Renault workers rejected it, and they sat in their factories insisting on shorter hours and more pay. Dreyfus and his directors were staggered by this unexplained revolt, which set back all their prospects, and cut their production by 76,000 cars. With the factories at a standstill, and the petrol no longer flowing, the whole French car civilization stopped dead. But France could not survive long without cars; when De Gaulle spoke, the petrol came back, and the holiday-makers showed their relief; 'we should have realized', said Daniel Cohn-Bendit afterwards in London, 'that for the workers, the car is a fetish'.

BRITISH LEYLAND MOTORS

The British car scene is so obstinately different from the continent's that it is always tempting to see it as yet another sign of incompatibility: a fantastic array of different cars, different names and different traditions, some almost the same but not quite, still harking back to a horse-drawn age, and reflecting every nuance and subtlety of the English class system, so that people can argue happily about the differences between a Rolls man and a Bentley man, or the implications of a Jaguar. The factories are worlds of their own, grown up out of early beginnings, rooted like farms, resisting mergers as firmly as if they were regiments. British cars may provide many clues to British character; but what they indicate most clearly in comparison with the continent is the British continuity – picturesque but dangerously comforting. While most of the European car industry started more or less from scratch in 1945, the British came through with undisturbed smugness. Before the war British cars had grown up mostly in the Midlands, built up by rugged, self-contained men, without international sense: Lord Nuffield suffered from xenophobia, and after a disastrous attempt to invade the French market in the twenties he became specially Francophobe, and when meeting a Frenchman liked to remark 'oui oui, manure'.[1] In the post-war years, when they could have sold anything, the British car-makers missed huge chances to establish themselves in Europe or Australia.

All this historical clutter and diversity is visible in the components of the newly merged British company, British Leyland Motors, whose range makes it seem almost like a motoring museum. The first big merger happened in 1951, when the legacies of the two pioneers of the car business, Lord Austin and Lord Nuffield, were reluctantly put together to form the British Motor Corporation; but it was really a classic non-merger, with the same men producing their old cars, hardly speaking to each other between the two centres at Oxford and Birmingham. The managers took over from the tycoon, but lacked the powers, or the confidence to rationalize the business; they went on producing all kinds of cars, most of them unprofitable. An unlikely gamble was taken when BMC, breaking out of their Englishness, hired an eccentric Greek designer, Alec Issigonis, to design a reply to the bubble-cars: 'We just put him in a room to think out the answer.' The Mini, with its tiny wheels and feminine gaiety, broke the tradition of heavy, unsexy engineering, and incidentally launched the new mini-image of Britain. That car, and its big brother the BMC 1100, have been the staple of the corporation ever since. They marked a real break with the past, and an escape into the outside world, but they

1. For the story of Nuffield's French adventure, see *The Nuffield Story*, by Robert Jackson, pp. 116–18.

lacked the spectacular export success of Volkswagen; the Americans thought that the Mini's wheels were absurd.

BMC still carried on with its old factories and dear old names – Rileys, MGs, Wolseleys. They cherished 'badge engineering' – calling the same car by two different names. The Mini and the 1100 got older, with no sign of a new line to replace them; they had Volkswagen's problem, without Volkswagen's success. BMC men were a confident race on their own; their chairman, George Harriman, who took over in 1961, had worked his way up from the Hotchkiss carworks in Birmingham, where his father was works manager. He had the midlands mixture of homeliness and toughness – shy, tousled, innocent-looking, inarticulate.

By 1967, with a credit squeeze and mounting competition from the Americans, BMC were in trouble: most of their lines were making a loss, and their vaunted new family car, the 1500, was not very promising. The BMC merger which had looked so vast fifteen years before now looked too small; and in the meantime a rival giant was looming – the Leyland company, based on the solid business of buses and lorries, and now including Triumph and Rover cars. At the head of Leyland is an authentic tycoon, Sir Donald Stokes, who looks like a weather-beaten gargoyle. He is mad about engines; he has a schoolboy passion for buses, went into Leyland as an apprentice, from a minor public school; his office is full of Dinky toys of buses and trucks, and he still talks with the enthusiasm of a schoolboy. More important, he has a tycoon's detachment, and is able to break through the affectionate muddles which afflict the British motor industry and accepts the fact, quite gladly, that the car business needs some kind of dictator at the top. For months there had been much talk of a merger between Leyland and BMC, encouraged by the government, and awkward meetings between Stokes and Harriman. At last, in February 1968, it happened. The new company could compete, at least in size, with the continental giants. Stokes was determined that this should be a real merger, and that the jumble of cars and works should be put into shape; he moved in to redesign the BMC 1500, complaining it suffered from 'overengineering'; he was determined to establish British buses and cars in Russia and eastern Europe; he began to impose his personality on the old BMC hierarchy.

Most of Britain's hopes of breaking into the continental car market now rest with the new group, which has taken on the patriotic associations of Fiat or Volkswagen. The continental tariff is a big obstacle, and almost insurmountable for trucks; but for cars, some people think that the Channel tunnel will be a bigger benefit than joining the common market. (Harriman draws a map, full of figures, to show how Britain, with its higher density of cars, is bound to benefit much more than the continent from new links with Europe.)

Gradually the British business is coming closer to continental patterns; cutting out old names and quaint models, planning international lines for the world markets. It is hard not to mourn the passing of a more eccentric age, with its freedom of expression for everyone's ego; but international competition may be more interesting, and will certainly be more efficient, than the internal diversity.

THE EUROPEAN CAR

Whether car companies are public like Leyland, controlled by a family like Fiat, or nationalized like Renault, they play a key part in their nations' economies. Slowly they are penetrating into each other's territory, becoming more 'European' in design: Fiats roll into Germany and France, and Volkswagens go nearly everywhere (except France and Italy which still scorn them). But the companies are still very far from being international in attitude or structure; and in the meantime the competition from America has loomed steadily larger. When Pierre Dreyfus was once asked about the effect of the common market, he replied: 'It will be splendid for General Motors.' His fears were soon echoed.

These proud national companies, big as they were, became increasingly aware of their smallness compared to the Americans. There is nothing new about the American invasion; back in 1925 General Motors bought Vauxhall in Britain, and in 1929 they bought out Adam Opel in Germany. But it is only in the past few years that the American companies have become a major political factor. They still own almost nothing in Italy, but an eighth of the French industry, a third of the German and – now that Chrysler have bought out Rootes – half the British. At a time when companies all fear over-production, the American invasion is especially unwelcome. 'What I'm afraid of,' said one Fiat director, 'is that the Americans insist on seeing Europe as if it were the United States. They think there's tremendous potential here because there are only seven people to each car, compared to two in America. But we don't think Europe is like America – it's denser, and cars aren't so essential. I'm afraid that if the Americans go on increasing their capacity, the smaller firms will go under.'

Faced with the American attack, in this industry as in others, the Europeans have gone in for mergers. The car companies have been gobbling each other up: Renault took Peugeot, Citroën took Berliet, Volkswagen took Auto-Union, Leyland merged with BMC. But only inside their own country. The bigger the mergers inside countries, the less likely seem mergers across frontiers. For years, whenever business has looked bad, the continental tycoons have talked to each other; Dreyfus proposed mergers with Valletta of Fiat and with Nordhoff of Volkswagen; but Nordhoff did not want to be tarred with an anti-American brush, and he and Dreyfus, it was said, never really talked the same language.[1] Then in 1966 there were secret talks between Nordhoff and Pierre Bercot, the master-mind of Citroën, and plans were made for a Citroën-Volkswagen agreement; but then Nordhoff became ill, and his successor, Kurt Lotz, did not show the same interest. In October 1968 there was a sudden prospect of a real European merger, when Fiat announced that they were buying a large share in Citroën from the Michelin family, who controlled it. The news set off speculation about a succession of continental links, cutting across nations; but De Gaulle's government vetoed the arrangement, and Fiat had to be content with buying a fifteen per cent share – though this may prove to have a potent effect on the ailing Citroën company.

The prospect of a 'European General Motors' seems still a long way off; but the idea was never very convincing, or perhaps very desirable, for such a huge instrument of power and uniformity would bring as many dangers as benefits. The European giants, after the first shock, should now be big and lively enough to hold their own with the American

. See *L'Express*, 9–15th October, 1967.

invaders, and may even – with their special skill in small cars – make more inroads across the Atlantic. It is a more straightforward and emotional industry than the new ones, like aircraft and computers, in which Europeans cannot hold their own. Europe seems to be settling down quite happily to a car nationalism, which cannot be regarded as very menacing, and ensures a diversity of a kind; alongside the mass producers there will still be room for small companies, like the Swedish Volvo or the Czech Skoda, to join the traffic jam.

Chapter Seven

Bankers

> We want peace at any price. What do we care about
> Germany, or Austria or Belgium? That sort of thing is
> out of date.
>
> *Anthony Rothschild, 1866*

While the international corporations have come to be seen as
the greatest hope for bringing Europe together, the prophets
of this promised new unity are not so much the businessmen,
as the bankers. Most of the industrial managers are too
caught up in their own commodities and organograms to
look far beyond them. But the bankers can see, through their
balance sheets, profits and rates of exchange, into every
corner of the Western continent; and with their perpetual
flying and telephoning, they can keep in touch and make
links more effectively than anyone else. In my travels, I have
found bankers the most international profession (except
perhaps the new students), and in discussing Europe, the
most interesting; they can compare countries, perceive
trends, observe companies, detect flaws, understand motives.
That is not surprising. For the Europe that is so far taking
shape is a bankers' Europe; its heroes are Rothschilds and
Rockefellers, and a whole new hagiography has grown up to
celebrate them. Their creed is not much questioned, and
there is no comparable group of international trades unionists or even international socialists to criticize it. The
bankers' press is much the most internationally-minded, the
bankers' conferences are the most sophisticated. Yet their
limitations are still evident in most of their conversations;
and their view of the continent, preoccupied with financial
solvency, is necessarily very incomplete. A British journalist
visiting continental bankers faces the special hazard of being
lectured in the style of a Barclays manager, as if one was
oneself in debt to the tune of several hundred million

pounds: 'it's gone far enough' ... 'really must pull yourself
together ... have you no discipline? .. but why *can't* you
work harder?' Listening to the neat equations of Swiss or
German bankers – more discipline, fewer strikes; more unemployment, less inflation; less public expenditure, more private investment – it is hard to suppress a polite question: is
this really all that Europe is about?

No profession looks back to the gay old days before the
First World War with more evident nostalgia than the
bankers: and their style and cosmopolitanism still seem to
belong to that age. I talked to one of their elder statesmen,
certainly the most picturesque of them, Raffaele Mattioli, a
bird-like old man of seventy-three with bright eyes and a
head like a hairy nut, who still runs the Banca Commerciale
Italiana in Milan. Many bankers like to see themselves as
custodians of culture as well as money, but Mattioli really
is: he translates Shakespeare into Italian, owns a publishing
house and a Chianti vineyard, and he insists that he sees no
essential difference between a poem and a balance sheet. He
works in a big room overlooking La Scala which is massively
untidy, piled high with books of poetry and bank statements
– which can evidently only be sorted out by an old retainer,
with whom Mattioli exchanges comic repartee. Mattioli was
born in the Abruzzi in 1895 (he even took part in
D'Annunzio's attempt to capture Fiume); the bank he now
runs, the BCI, was set up at the same time by a consortium
of German banks, helping to finance Italy's industrial revolution. He talks with longing of the easy internationalism
before 1914: 'To understand how we feel,' he said to me,
'you should read Keynes's introduction to his *Economic
Consequences of the Peace*.' So I did. It displays both the
freedom of that old world, and its solid limitations.

'What an extraordinary episode in the economic progress of
man that age was which came to an end in August 1914! The
greater part of the population, it is true, worked hard and lived
at a low standard of comfort, yet were, to all appearances,
reasonably contented with this lot. But escape was possible, for
any man of capacity or character at all exceeding average, into
the middle and upper classes, for whom life offered, at a low cost
and with the least trouble, conveniences, comforts and amenities
beyond the compass of the richest and most powerful monarchs
of other ages. The inhabitants of London could order by telephone, sipping his morning tea in bed, the various products of

the whole earth, in such quantity as he might see fit, and reasonably expect their early delivery upon his doorstep; he could at
the same moment and by the same means adventure his wealth
in the natural resources and new enterprises of any quarter in
the world, and share, without exertion or even trouble, in their
prospective fruits and advantages; or he could decide to couple
the security of his fortunes with the good faith of the townspeople of any substantial municipality in any continent that
fancy or information might recommend. He could secure forth-
with, if he wished it, cheap and comfortable means of transit to
any country or climate without passport or other formality,
could despatch his servant to the neighbouring office of a bank
for such supply of the precious metals as might seem convenient,
and could then proceed abroad to foreign quarters, without
knowledge of their religion, language or customs, bearing coined
wealth upon his person, and would consider himself greatly ag-
grieved and much surprised at the least interference. But most
important of all, he regarded this state of affairs as normal, certain and permanent, except in the direction of further improvements, and deviations from it as aberrant, scandalous and
avoidable.'[1]

In that golden age of international banking, London was
the hub, at the climax of its hundred years of financial supremacy. Even after the First World War there was a partial
revival of international markets. But the crash of 1929 shook
everyone's confidence, and the failure of the Austrian bank,
the Creditanstalt, in 1931, began the creeping restrictions on
international banking – exchange control, tariff barriers and
attempts at economic self-sufficiency. The City of London
found its role as Europe's banker more and more cut down,
and turned towards the Commonwealth and home industry.
After the Second World War, the European countries were
at first preoccupied with the need to rebuild their own economies, and were distrustful of all foreign currencies except
the dollar and the Swiss franc. On the continent only Zürich
emerged with a stable currency, large savings, and the
prestige to attract international funds.

Switzerland has for three centuries been a special paradise
for bankers. The Protestantism of Calvin and Zwingli
favoured these austere self-reliant capitalists; when the Hug-
uenots fled France in 1685, much of their money went to the
Protestant cities of Zürich and Geneva. The Swiss came to
regard the acceptance of foreign money as part of their liberty, and took pride in the fact that 'anything circular cir-

1. J. M. Keynes: *Economic Consequences of the Peace*.

culated'. The two world wars increased the flight of money
to Swiss banks, and their legendary secretiveness allowed
them to take in money from all sides: there is now one bank
to every 1,500 Swiss, and the national aptitude for dealing
with strange currencies can be seen in any frontier *bureau de
change*. Since 1945 Zürich has been the favourite banking
place for rich men all over the world, whether Arab sheiks,
South American politicans or American expatriates; and
because some of the money is shifted anxiously from one
currency to another – from pounds to dollars to gold –
Zürich has become the by-word for currency speculation.
The 'Gnomes of Zürich' – a phrase which first emerged in
the mid-fifties – have become the favourite bogies for countries with shaky currencies. To the British, Switzerland has
become more famous for gnomes than for cuckoo-clocks,
and to the Italians, '*i gnomi*' are almost equally unpopular
when they take in lire smuggled out by rich Italians: the
Swiss-Italian frontier has a special tension. Certainly the
gnomes deserve their reputation for right-wing political
views, and for cynicism and speed in speculation. They are
not speculating for themselves, but for rich men or
companies all over the world, including Englishmen and
Italians; they are the convenient scapegoat for the loss of
confidence in a currency – which begins in the country itself,
and is merely reflected and amplified by the telephones of
Zürich. The power of the gnomes to wreck a currency is no
greater than the power of a stockbroker to wreck a share, or
a bookie to ruin a horse; and even the damage done by
speculation has now been limited by the new willingness
of central banks to help each other out. But for the City
of London, built up round a proud international currency which is now so vulnerable, Zürich is a convenient
object of hate. The 'gnomes' remain a useful caricature
of the irresponsibility and insecurity of international
money.

It was not until 1958, the year of De Gaulle and the
common market, that, encouraged by the new prosperity of
France, the western European currencies again became convertible. Money could flow freely across the frontiers, as had
happened up to the thirties. At last there were the beginnings
of a return to internationalism, and foreign money helped to

finance the succession of miracles, particularly the Italian miracle, which changed the face of Europe. But Europe was still very far from the free flow which Keynes described, for the whole machinery of international banking had been limited by the decades of restrictions. No continental capital had the resources and machinery to act as a proper clearing-house for large international loans; wars and inflations had led to a deep distrust of banks and savings. The only capital that could manage it was London, unequalled in Europe, with its huge conglomeration of banks, exchanges, insurance companies, discount brokers and foreign banks, accustomed to shift huge sums of money at short notice. But London, while it had the market, lacked the convertible capital to finance the new European trade; whereas the continental centres increasingly had the capital, but lacked the markets. The obvious conclusion, that London and the continent should get together, was drawn by many bankers and econ-omists, including a few Frenchmen like Mendès-France: but the French government regarded Britain's perilous balance of payments as a main disqualification for joining the common market.

In the first post-war years inevitably the main centre for raising capital had been New York, which had a machinery far greater and faster than that of the Europeans, and which had a currency that was trusted. Then, from 1958 onwards, the American balance of payments was in deficit, as a result of its heavy investment abroad and later the Vietnam war, while the continental countries had a large surplus. New York bankers were restricted in foreign dealings by the Interest Equalization Tax of 1963, designed to prevent the flow of dollars outside America, and New York ceased to be the centre for raising capital for Europe. But this did not diminish the importance of the dollar. By a strange irony the isolation of the American capital market led (as we shall see) to the most spectacular expansion of American banks into Europe.

GERMAN BIG THREE

The big continental banks evoke a much deeper dread than the British, partly because they have embraced industry with a closer hug. Their power goes back to the nineteenth

century, when their role in controlling the sudden industrialization was much more decisive than the British; the
French Rothschilds helped to finance the railways in France
and beyond, and their rivals the Pereires set a pattern for the
'universal bank', collecting savings from small savers and
deploying the capital for the development and control of
industry, which was followed elsewhere in the continent. The
French banks (partly because of the proverbial suspicions of
the peasants) soon fell behind the German banks, who
played a key part in the new industries, and used their deposits, and their customers' proxies, to establish controlling
shares in the big companies. 'A German bank, as the saying
went, accompanied an industrial enterprise from the cradle
to the grave, from establishment to liquidation throughout
all the vicissitudes of its existence.'[1] The German pattern of
'mixed banking' is forbidden by law in Britain, France or
Italy, where the big banks cannot hold shares in industrial
companies.

Through two world wars the big German banks maintained
a continuous influence over industry. The core of German
banking is made up of the 'Big Three' commercial banks, the
Deutsche Bank, the Dresdner Bank and the Kommerz Bank,
which have acquired permanent stakes in a huge range of
companies. They do not hesitate to use their power, to sack
chairmen, change managements and if necessary withdraw
their support. They are not only clearing banks, but issuing
houses and members of the stock exchange as well. The biggest, the Deutsche Bank is, as one London banker put it, 'as
if the Midland, Barclays, Hambros, Barings, Rothschilds
and Cazenove's were all rolled into one': in their huge headquarters in Frankfurt, their men talk about the whole range
of industry, finance and government with a terrifying omni-
science. The banks' pre-war histories were very disagreeable.
All three were involved, as early as 1930, in support for
Hitler, and after the war the Allies resolved to split them into
thirty-three regional components. But like other businesses,
the banks still held together, and before long had merged
back to nine, and then back to three. The visible proof of the
banks' continuity is their doyen, the ubiquitous Dr. Her-

1. Alexander Gerschenkron: 'Economic Backwardness in Historical
Perspective', chapter in *The Progress of Underdeveloped Areas*, University
of Chicago Press, 1952.

mann Abs, whose trim moustache, vast conceit and conservative views still pop up everywhere. He joined the board
of the Deutsche Bank in 1937, and by the outbreak of the
war was its chairman. After the war the British detained him
for three months but soon found him indispensable, and
made him their financial adviser. He was soon once again
running the reunited Deutsche Bank.

The German miracle gave new scope to the bankers, and
as the first boom subsided, so some industrialists crashed,
and bankers moved in to take over their companies. In 1968
came the greater fall. The Krupp firm for years had been
wobbling, and had been shored up by loans from a row of
banks, led by the Deutsche Bank. Finally the loan had
become so colossal and the owner Alfried Krupp had
become so intransigent, that the banks in league with the
government had to fore-close. They insisted that, in return
for a further huge loan, Krupps cease to be a privately-run
empire and become a public company, with a supervisory
board. At the head of the board was Dr. Hermann Abs, who
was just stepping down from the chairmanship of his bank.
In their long war with industry, the banks had won a Pyrrhic
victory.

The German banks are so powerful and so much disliked
that they are often depicted as an 'Establishment' secretly
guiding the future; it is sometimes said that government
planning is not necessary in Germany because the banks
already do it. But the Krupp case, at least, seemed to suggest
the opposite. As one private banker remarked at the time: 'If
they were seriously planning ahead, would they have poured
so much money into a company with so little future?'

BELGIAN VEGETABLES

Perhaps the most depressing instance of the domination of
bankers is to be found in Belgium, whose banks control
whole sectors of industry and often overshadow the government. Their influence might be guessed from their premises
in Brussels, leading off from the king's palace behind a long
classical façade, facing across the park. (Opposite one of the
offices is a large statue of two sad, nude figures. 'Who are
they?' a tourist asked a taxi-driver. 'Ah, those are victims of
the Bank!') The old interlocking families at the top which

control them are appropriately known as '*les grosses légumes*'. Their wealth dates back to Belgium's hectic industrialization, when they helped to finance coal, steel and textiles, and they have retained their supremacy. The biggest groups – Banque de Bruxelles, Lambert, Solvay, Coppée, Empain – divide Belgium between them. The power of the banks became so overwhelming that in the economic crisis of 1955 an Act was passed to separate the banking businesses from their industrial holdings: but '*Les Holdings*' were quite big enough to retain their power, and they continued to be run by the same kind of people as the banks, sometimes related, and working in the same premises.

The biggest and oldest is the Société Générale de Belgique, whose tentacles stretch from the Congo to Newfoundland: 'It isn't that we're too big,' their chairman, Max Nokin, has explained, 'it's that Belgium is too small.'[1] Its holdings control about twenty per cent of Belgium's industrial output, thirty per cent of its coal production, twenty-five per cent of its steel, seventy-five per cent of its non-ferrous metals. It is older than Belgium, and was set up in 1822 by King William I of the Netherlands to exploit church lands and finance new industries. It survived Belgian independence, and moved in on the heavy industries: for Belgian investors La Générale, like Royal Dutch/Shell to the Dutch, has been the pre-eminent national share.

The biggest and most notorious of La Générale's holdings was its share in the Congo copper company Union Minière, until it was eventually nationalized by the Congo government. The company took over the Congo interests from the infamous King Leopold II, and ran them with apparent enlightenment: the copper mines of Katanga were a model of African paternalism, with hospitals, schools and housing far better than in neighbouring Northern Rhodesia. But while taking vast dividends from the Congo, they took no responsibility for its political future; when riots began in 1959, the Belgians quickly granted independence, having made no preparation; and when Tshombe led the secession of Katanga, the Union Minière supported him, maintaining that they could not interfere in politics. As the Congo crisis deepened, first the UN and then the Belgian government tried to press the Société Générale, and through them the Union

1. *Business Week*, 26th May, 1962.

Minière, to pay their taxes to the central government; but the die-hards of La Générale stuck to their support of Tshombe and their government could not over-ride them: it was not till the bitter end that the Union Minière came to terms with the central government. It was an ugly example of what Trotsky called 'Belgianization' – the abandonment of national responsibility in favour of totally commercial values.

The power of Les Holdings, as of other old financial groups, has begun to diminish with the waning of their basic industries, mining, steel, or cement, and with the growth of the big manufacturing corporations.[1] The banks have been slow to initiate the necessary management reforms. The newer industries, dependent on technology and know-how, come from outside the bankers' groups, and predominantly from outside Belgium. As industry begins to become part of a European context, so the scope of Les Holdings is less, and their character more out-of-date.

CHASEMEN AND CITIBANKERS

The heavy conservative traditions of the old European banks have been much shaken by the arrival of American bankers, in the wake of the corporations: their gay and glassy premises have sprung up in every capital in the last few years, next door to the old stone morgues. Up till 1961 the American banks had not been much concerned with expanding in Europe; the United States was booming, and since foreign bankers were banned in New York, and bankers depend on reciprocal business, there was no great incentive to move into Europe. But the common market flourished, America suffered a short recession; and the ban on foreign banks was lifted. The big American banks quickly made up for lost time. They spread out through the world and particularly to Europe: in 1959 there were a hundred and thirty-two overseas branches of American banks; by 1965 there were two hundred and twelve. They moved into Europe, like the other American businessmen, as if it

1. For a discussion of the disabilities of Les Holdings in the new situation, see *Morphologie des Groupes Financiers*, Centre de Recherche et d'Information Socio-Politiques (CRISP), Brussels, 2nd edition, 1966, pp. 421–37: this fascinating study is quoted as a guide by the bankers themselves.

were another America, with the additional freedom of starting from scratch, and with an insulation from local surroundings and tribal customs which is aptly summed up in
their magazine advertisements; the Bank of America's 'Man
on the Spot' walking with his dark suit and thin brief case,
always with a dotted red circle round his feet; the Chase
Manhattan 'the bank with the worldwide reach' with its
smooth, sharp-eyed 'Chasemen' reassuring residents of
exotic cities; the armies of pale-faced 'Citibankers' from the
First National City Bank, posed against European ruins –
'Historians concentrate on Rome's past. Citibankers concentrate on its busy present and bright future.' As the *Herald
Tribune* said (23rd November, 1967): 'Europe almost seems
like home these days for the American banker talking in
English to American clients and doling out dollars.'

They are a formidable army. I listened to some Frankfurt
bankers (themselves no mean battalion) complaining about
their new American rivals; how they keep themselves quite
separate from German life; how they mix only with other
American businessmen, advertising men, military men; how
they regard a posting to Frankfurt as an exile to a distant
province, which the best men would turn down; and how
they have no regard for gentlemanly German traditions:
'They try to take over a firm without even talking to the
directors!'

What most distinguishes the Americans is that they really
believe in the profit motive, both for themselves and for
others – a belief that shows itself most vividly in the empire
of Bernard Cornfeld which we see in Chapter 9. The Americans are openly aggressive, eager to advertise themselves
and really want to *lend*: the idea of actually encouraging
people to borrow money has been firmly against European
banking traditions, particularly the French. Gradually the
American brashness has stirred up the European parlours –
to compete with loans, investment trusts or credit cards. And
European banks have begun to pull themselves closer
together on a continental scale. The big clearing banks – for
instance the Deutsche Bank and the Banca Commerciale
Italiana – have co-operated much more closely in raising
international loans. The biggest French merchant bank, the
Banque de Paris et des Pays-Bas, has combined with the
Bank of America to form an international subsidiary called

Ameribas in Luxembourg, providing medium-term capital for European industry. Lazards have formed a new company, run by Claudio Segré, the Italian financial expert, to co-ordinate their branches in London, Paris and New York. Rothschilds' have renewed their old family connections, between London, Paris. New York, Zürich and Brussels. As with the giant corporations, the American invaders are pressing the Europeans into the same shapes; but the Europeans still have their own shackles – not least their proliferation of currencies.

EURODOLLARS

The most extraordinary of all the American arrivals in Europe has been a major new currency, which is one of the most baffling phenomena of post-war Europe: the 'Eurodollar'. It is full of mysteries, and no banker I spoke to claimed fully to understand it. It could be defined as a dollar which, having been banked outside America, can then be lent to another bank or company, still outside America, thus acquiring an expatriate status independent of European restrictions, with a mobility that makes it the nearest thing to a world currency. In spite of its name, there is nothing specifically European about the Eurodollar.

Its story is very odd. The word is said to have originated from Russian banks in Europe; the Russians, having built up large dollar balances, did not wish to keep them under their own names in America; so they were kept in Europe, and were borrowed by other European banks; the Russian bank in Paris had the cable address 'Eurobank', and from this (it is said) came the expression Eurodollar. Meanwhile, as the Americans moved into deficit, companies in Europe were earning more and more dollars, which they did not convert immediately into their own currencies, but kept in Eurodollars, which were more mobile and international. In the early years when London banks, led by Kleinwort Benson, began lending Eurodollars to customers, it was regarded (like anything new in the City) as a rather dangerous activity. But soon the lending and borrowing of Eurodollars became an important new part of the City's business. 'They've got everything but the money,' one American banker said, 'and every banker knows that money comes to people who know how to handle it.'[1] While the pound was hedged round with restrictions, the Eurodollar could go anywhere, and the new business gave scope to the bankers' old skills. Eurodollars could not be made from nothing; they had to originate with real dollars owned by expatriates. But as their usefulness became more apparent, so they were lent and re-lent from bank to bank: only when a Eurodollar is finally converted into a mark, franc or pound, does it disappear from the Eurodollar market. In 1968 there were reckoned to be about fifteen billion Eurodollars in existence.

This strange new currency grew up spontaneously, with no encouragement from governments, and with much disapproval. Central banks, including the Bank of England, were and still are alarmed at the independence and uncontrollability of the Eurodollars. Because they originated with American banks abroad they were not subject to restrictions; the banks could 'borrow short and lend long' – which central bankers most dislike: and there was no 'lender in the last resort' who was bound to rescue them. They were 'money without a home'. They could float between countries, and defy credit squeezes: for the moralizing German bankers, most notably the inescapable Dr. Hermann Abs, they represented the depths of wickedness; while German banks were insisting on high rates of interest, the big German companies found they could borrow Eurodollars at a better rate. But they became more and more useful as an easy vehicle for international capital, even for the governments. The spread of this maverick currency is astonishing, but no odder than earlier cases when foreign money has been more trusted than local money (it might be rudely compared to the Maria Theresa dollar, which still holds sway in the Red Sea area – this was first minted in Vienna in 1780, then outlived Austria-Hungary, and came to be minted in Rome, London and Vienna to finance Oriental trade).

While the Eurodollar was spreading, there was also a growing market for 'Eurobonds', or bonds issued in dollars by companies in Europe, which romped ahead after the American Interest Equalization Act of 1963. Since Europe could not provide its own capital market, the Americans in Europe built up their own system. Eurobonds are issued all over Europe, often by syndicates of banks and particularly in

1. *The Times*, 8th November, 1967.

London and Brussels, where many American corporations have their headquarters. 'The growing internationalization of the market,' wrote Jacob Rothschild in 1968, 'has inevitably and rightly changed the emphasis away from London, or any other centre as such.'[1] Since President Johnson's 1968 restrictions, the American companies have had to raise their new capital in Europe; and European investors are apt to prefer American-run companies to their own. The success of these bond issues rammed home the fact that it was not capital the Europeans lacked so much as good management. When in 1967 the American Gillette company bought out the German Braun company for fifty million dollars, they promptly issued bonds for fifty million Eurodollars to pay for it. By May 1968 the big companies' demand for Eurodollar loans was becoming a stampede, and was beginning to seriously worry the other potential borrowers.

EUROPEAN MONEY

Anyone who is familiar with the part that the New York capital market played in the economic unification of the United States cannot but conclude that a European capital market is an absolute necessity as the driving force for industrial integration.

Robert Marjolin, December 1966

The more people and goods flow freely through Europe, the more absurd seems the jumble of currencies. This is obvious to any tourist when, in a few hours' train journey, he can accumulate three or four different currencies in his pocket, with bank-notes and coinage of all shapes and sizes. Stewards, airline hostesses or shopkeepers on frontiers have to be able to talk in two or three currencies at once. Every country in Europe has its own currency, including Luxembourg (though its franc has the same value as the Belgian one), and every currency has its own social history, and its own associations with disaster. The French franc, which was invented after the Revolution, was devalued five times between 1945 and 1958, and since 1914 has sunk to about a 250th of its value. The German mark has the most traumatic past, with two periods of runaway inflation in the last fifty years; in the first, in 1923, the new mark was established worth 1,000,000,000,000 old ones; in the second, in 1948, the

1. *The Banker*, April 1968.

new Deutschmark had a value ten times the old one. The pound has been devalued twice since the war, but can look back to a much more continuous past; the new decimal system will be the first major reform since before the Norman Conquest.

There have been many proposals for a European currency. One suggestion, made by Fred Hirsch of the International Monetary Fund, is that each European country would convert into a new currency, the European thaler (the thaler was the original German silver coinage, before the mark took over in 1873, from which the dollar was named); it could be based on the French franc, and would still be separately managed by each country, but it would be a great psychological and practical help in doing business across frontiers.[1] Any such plan seems a long way off; for the national currencies, after the troubles of the last fifty years, have acquired layers of national associations. Protecting the mark or saving the pound, like protecting farmers and fuel, is a recurring form of patriotism.

The success of the Eurodollar has only underlined the failure of Europe to form its own international currency, or a proper capital market. It was entrenched in the Treaty of Rome (Article 67) that member states should '... progressively abolish as between themselves restrictions on the movement of capital belonging to persons resident in Member States ...' In the subsequent twelve years there have been many attempts to study the obstacles and to overcome them. But the difficulties seem insuperable. Every country has a different system of taxation, and its own firm monetary policy, controlling the flow of money with different kinds of dams and sluice-gates. The French economic crisis of 1968, which swiftly imposed controls on the franc, showed how far away the common market still was from a common currency: German bankers were thankful not to be involved in the flood of inflation. All governments are worried that a free flow of capital would weaken their own control over inflation, and would undermine their planning, letting money rush into the existing rich centres, leaving the poorer areas still poorer. They dread, with some reason, the furtherance of a bankers' Europe without a political Europe to control it, and we are back in the familiar

1. Fred Hirsch: *Money International*, p. 338.

chicken-and-egg dilemma of Europe which is a recurring theme of this book: without economic integration, there is not the machinery for political integration, and without political integration, there is not the trust that is necessary for economic integration. The Eurocrats have achieved some closer financial co-operation: they have for instance a European Investment Bank, like a miniature World Bank, which gives loans to backward parts, mainly Italy. But the important moves towards financial integration are outside the framework of the common market.

There is another difficulty about the European capital market: the sheer shortage of capital. The bitter experience of inflation has left most of the continent – much more than Britain or America – with a deep distrust of investment. Many Europeans save more than the British or Americans, but are much more reluctant to make long-term investments, and many fewer are shareholders. In 1966 it was estimated that 17 per cent of the American adult population were shareholders, 7 per cent of the British, and 2–3 per cent of the continentals. More important, the insurance companies and pension funds, which own about a quarter of the shares in Britain, and make up the solid core of the market, are far less important in continental countries. In most countries pensions have been the responsibility either of the state or of the companies, and pension contributions are invested in the company. In Britain, the giant insurance companies and pension funds, headed by 'the Pru', have grown up quite separately from industry or government, and have helped to develop London as the most sophisticated capital market and stock exchange in Europe. The continental capitals do not have the same variety of institutions which can absorb private savings and turn them into long-term investments; the lack reflects a history of individual distrust on the one hand, and governmental direction on the other. A report prepared for the common market in June 1968 recommended that pension funds should be invested independently from the employees' companies, to increase the capital markets; but the big paternalist corporations are unlikely to stand for it.

In the end, the prospects for a European capital market depend not on the enterprise of private bankers, but on a different species – the central bankers who manage the currencies, and behind them the national governments.

CENTRAL BANKERS

The first quality of a central banker is to be cold-blooded.

Guido Carli

It has been a long-standing nightmare of the left that Europe might find itself being run by a committee of bankers; and in the last few years the bad dream seems to have been coming closer to reality. The dreaded figures of the central bankers, responsible to no parliament, elected by no constituency, and using a language incomprehensible to most laymen, have emerged more boldly from the shadows, outlasting governments and chancellors and pronouncing with growing confidence about their nations' needs. Once a month the European central bankers come together for a meeting of the 'Basle Club' in the bleak Swiss city; they spend the weekend talking and dining, and on Monday assemble for the conference of the Bank of International Settlements, the clearing-house where the central banks settle each others' debts. No announcement is made of their meetings, and no statement emerges from them. In most crises their movements are secret; when they flew to Frankfurt in November 1967, to try to check the gold rush, no one knew even where they held their meeting. Only in the most flagrant emergencies is the curtain lifted. The apogee was reached in March 1968, when the gold nearly ran out; the central bankers of the gold pool – Carli, Blessing, O'Brien, Holtrop, and Co. – flew off to Washington in a panic, to establish two prices for gold. Politicians and the public were confronted with an evident climax which hardly anybody could explain.

I visited some of these people in their financial fortresses, relaxed and assured in their sequestered power. Their whole background has cut them off from the populace, and they work in surroundings of nineteenth-century pomp. The vast pile of the Bank of Italy in Rome, staffed with uniformed flunkeys, makes the Bank of England seem modest and cosy by comparison; the great quadrangle of the Banque de France looms like a citadel alongside the Palais Royal, and inside has the atmosphere of some faded opera house. The bankers like to cultivate the image of being the friendly family bank manager, sympathetic to their country's troubles, smiling but stern; of being (as Fred Hirsch puts it) a kind of House of Lords, a safeguard against the more irresponsible decisions of democracies. Yet I cannot help wondering, as those troubles are analysed through a web of programmed data, how much they can understand the needs of their fellow-countrymen.

What has brought these men into the limelight in the past years has been, basically, the growing worries about 'international liquidity'. Much of the argument is inevitably obscure, and (I am warned) very dangerous to simplify; but the basic attitudes, at least, remain simple. The continental case against more liquidity (more ready cash) is that it will encourage inflation, financial indiscipline and the kind of lax attitude to balance of payments shown (for instance) by America and Britain; and that if currencies quickly cease to be backed by gold, financial anarchy will prevail. The case for increasing liquidity is that without it international trade will wither, and that the poor countries, much more than rich ones, will suffer from the lack of international reserves. Since most of the continental countries have had a continuing surplus in their balance of payments, they are angrily criticized for sitting on their hoards. On the other hand, Britain and America advocate greater international borrowing, and can both be accused of acting from obvious self-interest, since they have big international debts. But the real arguments for liquidity are not just to do with the relative positions of the countries of the 'Group of Ten' – who are all very rich anyway. They more crucially affect the poorer countries, to whom more expansion could make the difference between disaster and survival.

In this running argument, the influence of the central bankers can be exaggerated: the current personality cult (and sometimes their own vanity) builds them up as the final arbiters, whereas most of them are under quite firm political control.

Their powers in their own country vary widely, and are important to distinguish. A critical position belongs to the West German Bundesbank, whose decisions to deflate or reflate affect the whole economy of Europe, revolving round West Germany. Its president, Karl Blessing, can be very independent of his government; he can even put up the bank

rate without consulting them. Like many other central
bankers, he has moved between banks and big business: he
began as an aide to Germany's pre-war wizard, Hjalmar
Schacht, was fired by the Nazis in 1937; after the war he was
director of Unilevers in Germany before he took over the
Bundesbank in 1958. In the Bundesbank he has used his
power to oppose inflation, which infuriated many critics
inside and outside Germany. He is one of the most orthodox
of all orthodox bankers. In his obsessive dread of inflation
he represents a prevailing German attitude; for the generation who has seen these two inflations, the stern control of
budgets and public spending has become part of the basic
faith.

Perhaps the most influential single banker within his own
country is the governor of the Bank of Italy, Guido Carli.
His enormous prestige rests partly on the skill and de-
cisiveness with which he rescued Italy from its slump in
1964. In the small clique of Italian big businessmen who
carve up the country between them, he is the crucial figure.
One of them said: 'If we had to have a dictator again, it
would have to be Carli.' He is a fastidious long-faced man,
with a piercing personality. He sits in an exquisite damask
room in front of a painting of St. Sebastian. His influence is
greater than that of most cabinet ministers, and he is adept
in 'navigating' (to use the Italian phrase) between the political parties. He has become one of the strongest advocates of
co-operation between central bankers and of a European
currency: he has often tried to save sterling. He is a real
progressive among bankers: unlike most of them, he is able
to think much further than exchange-rates and growth-rates,
and is very conscious of problems of social stability.

While Germany has one of the most independent central
bankers, France has one of the most circumscribed. The
Bank of France has some very clever men; the governor,
Jacques Brunet, is an Inspecteur des Finances[1] who first
began work in the private office of Poincaré in 1924; his
deputy, Bernard Clappier, also an Inspecteur, is a very open-
minded 'European'. But they do not have great scope, for
monetary problems are closely controlled by the Ministry of
Finance, or by the Prime Minister, Couve de Murville, who
shows at least as much interest in monetary questions as in

1. See chapter 18.

diplomacy (he regards them as inseparably interconnected, which has been part of the strength of French diplomacy). And behind them is the ardent prophet of gold, Jacques Rueff (another Inspecteur), who has constantly insisted that only a doubling of the price of gold can restore international confidence. Behind him is De Gaulle himself, who has shown an almost religious belief in what he calls 'the immutability, the impartiality, the universality, which are the privileges of gold'.

In a position of special vulnerability is the governor of the Bank of England, Sir Leslie O'Brien, faced with a continuing balance of payments crisis which puts him in debt to his colleagues. O'Brien, who has worked his way up through the secret passages of the bank, is shy, non-political and much more professionally-minded than his predecessor, Lord Cromer. He has found himself suddenly, as governor, exposed to a limelight unprecedented since the days of Lord Norman, and immersed in the crises of devaluation and gold. He dropped a few bricks, and is now more circumspect in his remarks. The degree of independence of the Bank of England from the Treasury is still obscure, but O'Brien keeps up a critical posture towards government policy, advocating a measure of unemployment and criticizing the 1968 Budget measures for being too late.

On the sidelines in the consultations of the central bankers stands another Frenchman: Pierre-Paul Schweitzer, the chairman of the International Monetary Fund in Washington. But he has become less and less French in his behaviour since he moved from the Bank of France five years ago (he stopped wearing the Légion d'Honneur). Schweitzer comes from an Alsatian Protestant family of extraordinary abilities. Sartre is his cousin, the conductor Charles Münch is his uncle, and Albert Schweitzer was another uncle. He himself became (like three other bankers so far in this chapter) an Inspecteur des Finances. He joined the resistance, was captured, tortured and sent to Buchenwald. He was still there at the time of the Bretton Woods Conference in 1944, which set up the International Monetary Fund. He took a key part in French financial policy after the war, rigorously opposing inflation. When he joined the IMF there were great fears that he would be rigorous, too, in his defence of gold. But he has been insistent that he now owes allegiance to no government, and he has become steadily more insistent on allowing greater drawing rights from the Fund, to increase international liquidity. Towards Britain's debts he was been firm but friendly: after the devaluation crisis he was quoted as saying: 'I don't know how it strikes you, but I think that if you asked even your family bank manager back home for a loan of £1,000 million he might ask questions.'

The thought of these cold-blooded men gathering with increasing intimacy round polished tables in Basle, Frankfurt or Washington to settle their country's problems is not a reassuring one. With the appalling history of the unemployment in the twenties behind them, the bankers have a lot to answer for. Sometimes they make statements (like Lord Cromer's speech in Stockholm in May 1968, proposing an unsackable European Monetary Board) which arouse all the old fears. Yet it would be more alarming if bankers did not get together. The whole development of international trade depends on a trust in currencies which must be their main concern. The real nightmare for Europe is that confidence will collapse as it did in the thirties, that banks will fail and countries retreat into their own economic nationalism.

Certainly the central bankers have come closer together. They can claim, with good reason, to be more internationally minded than prime ministers, tycoons or trade-unionists; they have to be, in order to survive. They have done something to defend each other against speculation, and may yet do more to build up international liquidity. Yet their achievement is still very far from the post-war ideals of Keynes and others, who hoped that there could be a genuinely supranational approach to monetary problems, and they are as far away as ever from the prospect of a European currency. As one of them said to me: 'Central bankers can never get away from politics, because every country has a different idea of what money is for. You remember how when the Central African Federation broke up, they hoped they could have a single central bank for all three countries. Of course it was impossible. The differences between central bankers in Europe don't just arise from distrust; there are basic differences of national interest. The central bankers won't really be able to get together unless the politicians have got together first.'

Chapter Eight

Technology

La technologie, c'est la tarte à la crème!
Couve de Murville, 1967

It is neither socialism nor communism which reduces working hours, but automation.
Gaston Palewski, 1965

La locomotive, le téléphone, l'électricité, ça avait été bien! L'auto, l'avion, la radio, c'était mieux! La fusée, la télé, le moteur atomique, le laser, la greffe du coeur, c'est magnifique!
De Gaulle, June 1968

It became obvious long ago that technology had outgrown the size of nations. The existence of international corporations is justified by the fact that, spilling across the frontiers, they can dispense the precious fruits of their research – from frozen foods to computers – to nations too small to provide their technologies. Baulked at so many other stages, by De Gaulle and by other political obstructions, the Eurocrats have come to see the pursuit of technology as one of the most promising pressures towards integration, forging countries together with common enterprises. The very neutrality of the word technology makes it seem less subject to political divisions. But politics still raises its head, and the word still begs the question – technology for what?

CONCORDE

In big hangars outside Bristol and Toulouse, two long thin tubes have slowly taken shape, which make up the biggest and most controversial of all European ventures. In its building the Anglo-French Concorde has become a symbol for everything from European unity to the affluent society (even the final 'e' is controversial – the 'French letter' as the English plane-makers like to call it). It seems impossible to discuss it or to see it without some emotional involvement. I watched it being built at Bristol. It sat in a vast hangar, like a giant white fish, held up by a maze of scaffolding; the whole scene looked like a grown-up adventure playground, with a climbing frame built round this outsize toy; three hundred men clambered on and around it, lying on the wings, walking on the roof, squeezing in and out of the cabin, fitting, screwing, tapping, or just gazing at the aluminium creature. Next door was another shed made for showmanship; a full-scale model of the plane was lit up with changing coloured lights, glittering against the dark like a cinema organ; inside a complete cabin was fitted out in an American décor, and an excited salesman explained the fittings and comforts, the different arrangements of toilets and galleys, the variations of price around twenty million dollars, as if one was expected to buy one oneself.

It could hardly be more different from the even rhythm of a car factory making Volkswagens or Fiats. Here everyone's emotions centre round the thin white shape. This nervous industry was forged by wars and still has the tension, extravagance and romance of wartime: everyone in the hangar becomes mixed up in the great gamble, hovering between fiasco and triumph.

The Concorde has passed through so many storms and side-winds that its story is a kind of caricature of technological problems – a jet-age equivalent of the Channel tunnel.[1] It began in 1962 as an alliance between technology and diplomacy. The Tory Minister of Aviation, Julian Amery, one of the few English 'Gaullists', wanted to strengthen Anglo-French bonds at the time of the first attempt to get into the common market negotiations. The aircraft designers, both in France and in England, were coming to realize that they must collaborate or die. There were only four proper jet-plane industries in the world – in America, Russia, Britain and France; and the last two were too small to compete with the first two. The idea of a supersonic airliner was the natural next stage in civil aircraft, and the British had already done years of research into the 'slender delta' design of the Concorde. The agreement was signed, in November

1. See chapter 13.

1962, between the British Aircraft Corporation and the Sud Aviation, with an Anglo-French ministerial committee to 'chaperone' them. The governments were so keen that they made an agreement which neither side could break without the other, and they pressed ahead without bothering much who would buy the plane.

Political clouds soon loomed. The original estimate for developing the two prototypes was £150 million (about the same cost as three aircraft carriers). But as one Concorde engineer explained: 'There's always a kind of conspiracy to produce the lowest defensible estimate, between the politicians, the permanent secretaries and the manufacturers; you're lucky if it's within a factor of three.' The estimates steadily moved up – from £150 million to £200 to £300 and then to £500 million – as much as two Channel tunnels. When the Labour government came into power in October 1964, Roy Jenkins soon tried to cancel the Concorde altogether: it was anyway an un-socialist kind of plane, designed primarily for rich businessmen in a hurry, not for happy tourists. The French were outraged, threatened legal action, and the project went on.

Through all the political storms, the boffins went on as if nothing was happening; the top engineers commuted between Bristol and Toulouse, gradually making themselves understood to each other. There were plenty of difficulties. The British plane was designed in inches, and the French one in centimetres, but that was a familiar problem in NATO and elsewhere. More insuperable, the two sides had almost opposite approaches to technical problems: the French side, led by a *polytechnicien*, were determined to be wholly logical, assuming that all instructions would be rigorously obeyed. The English side, under the homely engineer Sir George Edwards, were obstinately pragmatic. They enjoy talking about their cross-purposes and encounters: how at first the French were baffled by the way the English called their bosses by Christian names and pulled each other's legs, yet still knew their place; how the English were amazed by the French calling each other monsieur and insisting on precise written instructions. But gradually they have been influenced by each other's habits, and they have even begun to have social relations, exchanging children for holidays, and inviting each other home.

The duplication, the travel and the higher cost of French labour, increased the cost (it was reckoned) by 30 per cent; though the wastage was said to be no more than when two rival British firms had to collaborate on the TSR2. Paradoxically, dealing with two governments can make it easier to get decisions. 'My experience of Concorde,' said Pierre Young, the chief engineer of Bristol Siddeley, 'is that you can get civil servants responsible for management to move more quickly because neither country wants to be holding the job up': or in the words of Sir Arnold Hall, the managing director of Hawker Siddeley, a multi-government project can be 'as fast as the fastest and not as slow as the slowest'.[1]

While the politicians dithered the project acquired its own momentum and prestige. The American rival was delayed by indecision, and the big American airlines were forced to take options on Concordes, to avoid being left out. Once PanAmerican, the biggest world airline, had decided to go supersonic, the others were almost forced to follow, however crippling the cost. The Concorde gradually became a symbol, not so much of Anglo-French friendship but of European competition with America. For the first time since the first Comet crash in 1952 Europe was ahead of America in the air-race. The Concorde became a political force in its own right. A few days after De Gaulle's second veto of Britain in 1967, it was wheeled out of its hangar in Toulouse, accompanied by a burst of celebration and only mild bickering about the 'e'. Soon afterwards a six-month delay was announced, and after the French strike in May there were more delays and still higher estimates. A Russian supersonic took off ahead of it. But the glamour remained.

For the British Labour cabinet it was a special embarrassment; many ministers openly hoped that the thing would never actually take to the air. Their dislike of it was understandable. It caused huge social problems, threatened to break windows, to terrify babies, and demanded still more space for airports, all for the sake of a few privileged transatlantic travellers. It seemed to represent European endeavour at its most absurd, competing with speed and noise, and

1. Conference on European Co-operation in Advanced Technology, UK Council of European Movement, July 1965.

quite unsuited to the crowded continent. Ministers turned with relief towards the 'airbus', for which Rolls-Royce had perfected a new engine, and whose very name sounds cosy and democratic.

Yet the awkward fact remains that Concorde has a unique sex-appeal; beside it, an airbus seems like a schoolma'am next to a model-girl. It appeals to the aggressive and adventurous instinct, in a way that can bring together thousands of engineers in two countries. It represents, like the American-Russian space race, some kind of substitute, a ritualization (to borrow from Anthony Storr) of war. It can be argued that these combative instincts are evil, yet to suppress them is as difficult as stopping small boys playing with toy guns. The Concorde is much less dangerous than battleships and bombs, and may yet be positively useful. The aircraft engineers and designers are a sophisticated and rarefied species, who cannot easily be switched to designing tunnels or health centres. If not working on Concorde, what else would they do? The accounting for Concorde finally enters the realms of sociology, politics and ultimately philosophy.

The Concorde, with all its ups and downs, represents a closer merging of national interests than the operations of multi-national corporations. The urgency and risks of the project, as in wartime, force rivals to forget their differences, and the Concorde is the most visible evidence of the fact that, whatever the other divisive influences, technology has now finally outgrown countries. In fact it has even outgrown continents. There are now only three major aero-engine companies in the western world – Pratt and Whitney, General Electric and Rolls-Royce – and each of them is anxiously watching the others. The Concorde is filled with American equipment, designed with an eye to the transatlantic market, and it may yet go into partnership with an American company; for the cost is so vast that only a world market can recoup it.

The Concorde, it seems to me, represents the real quandary of European technology. With all its extravagance and waste, it is perhaps the only European project to have caught the public imagination, and hence to be politically attractive. Yet the endeavour is just the kind of hectic pursuit of speed, at the cost of public comfort and peace, which Europeans most condemn in America: the price of taking up the 'American challenge' is that it must be taken up on American terms.

TECHNOLOGICAL GAP

The intensification of research in Europe is necessary for psychological, political and, in a certain sense, moral reasons in order to prevent the Europeans from losing confidence in themselves.

Robert Marjolin, 1966

It is odd how suddenly the hollow cliché 'technological gap' became a European rallying cry. In the first years of the European movement the word technology was hardly heard: in those days it was only science that people talked of. But by the mid-sixties the other old bogies that had stimulated European unity – communism, war or economic collapse – had begun to fade. In their place rose a new fear – that Europe would find herself hopelessly backward compared with America, and that in the next decades American advanced techniques of management and technology would reduce Europe to what Harold Wilson called 'industrial helotry'. You can hear the same laments in Paris, Rome or Bonn – that in another twenty years Europe will seem as backward as South America – or Canada, or the Arab world. And it is all blamed on the lack of the magic ingredient: technology. The new faith of technology began to be preached by people who had never understood the inside of a motor-car; diplomats turned from questions of détente and démarche, with rather embarrassing zeal, to talking about vertical take-off, or gas-cooled reactors. Technology has become part of the jargon – however garbled – of diplomacy.

The suddenness of this awareness seems the odder because the phenomenon is not at all new. The American zeal for technology and innovation, in the most obvious forms of gadgets and labour-saving devices, goes back to the mid-nineteenth century: as early as 1852 an English visitor to America was remarking that 'the American omnibus cannot afford the surplus labour of a conductor. The driver has entire charge of the machine'.[1] Americans (as Professor

1. H. Habbakuk: *American and British Technology in the Nineteenth Century*, p. 47.

Habbakuk has shown) were encouraged to new devices and to great productivity by many factors – the scarcity of labour, the rapid growth of capacity, the resulting standardization, the optimism aroused by opening up the new continent, and the 'emotional dynamism' coming from the new immigrants.

An early case of American technology coming back to Europe was the Singer sewing machine, an extraordinary epic of developing enterprise. It was invented by a poor German immigrant, Isaac Singer, who had been an actor, a farmer and a machinist before he turned to inventing. He launched his machine in Boston in 1851, in partnership with a shrewd lawyer, Edward Clark; in another year it was selling more abroad than in America. Singer himself got bored with it, and retired to build a big house called the Wigwam in Devon. But Clark revelled in the huge market, and virtually invented hire-purchase so that people could afford to buy it. The company soon over-ran Europe, revolutionizing people's habits both with the machine and with hire-purchase (the town with the first British factory, Clydebank, has a sewing machine in its coat-of-arms). Singer covered Europe with the advertising, and the sides of Greek cottages are still defaced with the words SINGER. For fifty years Singer had a virtual monopoly of sewing machines.

In 1901 an Englishman, Fred Mackenzie, wrote a book called *The American Invaders*, in which he complained: 'In the domestic life we have got to this. The average man rises in the morning from his New England sheets, he shaves with 'William' soap and a Yankee safety razor, pulls on his Boston boots over his socks from North Carolina, fastens his Connecticut braces, slips his Waltham or Waterbury watch in his pocket and sits down to breakfast.' Mr Mackenzie foresaw an imminent, total take-over: 'From shaving soap to electric motors, and from shirt-waists to telephones, the American is clearing the field . . . these in-comers have acquired control of almost every new industry created during the past fifteen years . . . the telephone, the portable camera, the photograph, the electric street car . . . the typewriter and the multiplication of machine tools.' His explanation for the success was not very different from that of critics today: 'Americans are succeeding today largely because of their climate, their better education, their longer working hours, their willingness to receive new ideas, their better plant, and perhaps most of all, because of their freedom from hampering tradition.'

Mackenzie's panic was premature; the Europeans gradually took over the new inventions, from shaving soap to watches, and built up their own electronics industry, helped by protection and war. American shoes or braces no longer threaten Europe. A new wave of inventions has taken their place, which might seem no more permanently menacing than the old ones – computers instead of telephones, nuclear energy instead of electricity, cornflakes instead of shaving soap, Boeings instead of trams. But the position is, of course, more serious; not only because the scale and expense of the new technologies make it harder for Europe to fight back, but because the American advantages that Mackenzie noted seventy years ago – better education, open-ness to new ideas and freedom from tradition – have now much broader scope.

The speed and success of the European miracles in the 1950s, catching up on existing technology and borrowing much from America, disguised the European inability to develop things: it was not till the end of the fifties that the big German industrialists (I was told by one of them) were aware that they were steadily slipping behind the Americans in technological innovation. In the first boom years the common market countries could boast that their growth was greater than America's; but by 1965 America was once again far outstripping both Western Europe and Russia: and it was now obvious that the key element in growth was innovation.

The problem of 'il gap tecnologico' was first publicized in Italy, by foreign minister Fanfani; he outlined a rather vague scheme in September 1966 for a 'new Marshall Plan', by which America would help Europe to cross the gap, which he put before NATO in December of that year. Not surprisingly, the Americans were unenthusiastic about sharing their industrial secrets with their competitors. One industrialist dryly remarked that the only way to achieve equality between America and Europe would be for America to put up barriers between the fifty states, and to introduce fifty different currencies.

Fanfani's cry was taken up by the British government,

who saw an opportunity to make new bargains with Europe through Britain's superiority in research; Harold Wilson put forward a scheme for a 'technological community' in which Britain could play the key role. But the community was never very clearly defined, and was not followed up. The British minister of technology, Wedgwood Benn, was not a convinced European, and during 1968 Britain backed out of two European projects, ELDO and CERN (see below), in a way which made Wilson's idea seem very hollow. The prospect of a technological community separate from a trading or political community is not a very hopeful one; for as we will see, technology and politics become increasingly intertwined.

BRAINS

Brains are like hearts. They go where they are appreciated.

Robert McNamara

> There were fifty scholars from Berne
> Whose rather peculiar concern
> Was learning to fly a balloon
> Via Florida right to the moon.
> Do you think they will ever return?

Dr Jakob Burckhardt

Europe has not doubted her ability to produce scientific brains, and the word 'science' has always had a splendour which 'technology' has not. For centuries Europeans have been responsible for most of the scientific discoveries of the world, and their originality shows little sign of drying up. Europeans often like to suggest that Americans are incapable of really original discoveries, and it remains true that a large proportion of American discoveries come from first-generation immigrants. For a long time Americans were worried about their dependence on Europe for original research, and a report to the President in 1945, 'Science the Endless Frontier', lamented this fact. Even among recent discoveries which have revolutionized the world, Europe (and specially Britain) was responsible for splitting the atom, penicillin, radar, television, computers and jet planes.

The convenient index for measuring original research is the Nobel prize, bequeathed as a guilt offering by the Swedish inventor of dynamite, Alfred Nobel, and awarded every year for the last seventy years. The table below shows the number of scientific prizes (for physics, chemistry, and physiology and medicine) gained by each country from their beginning until 1967. (It is not a reliable guide to achievements in eastern Europe and Russia.)

Western Europe has produced one hundred and sixty-one Nobel science prize-winners compared to seventy-four from America; and a large proportion of American prize-winners had emigrated from Europe – particularly pre-war Jewish refugees from Germany. Nobel prizes need deep roots, and much of Europe's achievements (and particularly the British ones) come from a few strong and exclusive scientific centres, where teachers have handed down their rigorous standards and methods to their pupils: no fewer than six British prize-winners have come from Lord Rutherford's Cavendish Laboratory at Cambridge. But since the war, the American proportion of Nobel science prizes has shot up – fifty-one between 1945 and 1966, compared to twenty-two from Britain, ten from Germany and only four from France. The German tradition was broken by the pre-war

Country	Total Nobel prizes
Sweden	9
Switzerland	7
Denmark	5
Austria	7
United Kingdom	47
Netherlands	9
Germany	46
United States	74
France	20
Ireland	1
Hungary	3
Belgium	2
Finland	1
Australia	2
Portugal	1
Canada	2
Italy	5
Czechoslovakia	1
Argentina	1
USSR	9
Spain	1
China	2
India	1

persecution and the war (in 1964 no fewer than thirty-six Fellows of the Royal Society in London were refugees from Germany).[1] Both America and Russia benefited from German scientists and engineers after the war, particularly in rocketry, where the competition boiled down, it was often said, to a question of 'our Germans are better than your Germans'. Only in the last few years has the flow begun again, with such prize-winners as Hans Jensen from Heidelberg, Karl Ziegler from Mülheim, Feodor Lynen from Munich and Manfred Eigen from Göttingen.

CERN

To smash the little atom
All mankind was intent:
Now every day
The atom may
Return the compliment.

Max Born

In pure science, Europe is not only inventive, but co-operative. The most striking proof of this is the European Centre for Nuclear Research, or CERN, which is run by thirteen different countries outside Geneva, and which represents the most expensive tribute to pure science. It is, to a layman, a delightful but wholly baffling place, like a factory without a product; it has all the dedication of the Concorde project, but nothing visible to show for it. Its centrepiece is a wide circular tunnel, two hundred yards across, with a row of huge magnets inside it, and two big sheds leading off it; this is the cyclotron, which cost ten million pounds, through which neutrons and protons are propelled at high speed. The surrounding equipment is thoroughly picturesque. There is a control room full of TV screens, flashing lights and numbers, coloured dots dancing across panels. There is a group of twenty-two computers said to be the biggest and most expensive in Europe. And in the sheds there are colossal bits of hardware and elaborate engineering, solid concrete blocks, more TV screens, endless coils of coloured wires. The cost of CERN about £20 million a year – seems less surprising in the face of these enormous workings, and the army of 2,500 people who watch them. But all this ex-

1. Laurence Reed: *Europe in a Shrinking World*, p. 135.

travagant engineering is directed to investigate particles of a million-millionth of a centimetre – which no one could possibly see, and whose behaviour is still maddeningly obscure. The spending of such huge sums on so abstruse an inquiry worries many scientists; the proposed next step, the giant ring generating three hundred billion electron-volts, would cost £150 million (and Britain has now refused to pay her share). No politician can understand its implication; when I asked one of the CERN scientists how many people in Europe really understood what went on there, he said 'perhaps twelve'. But to physicists, it represents the last great adventure in pure science, the ultimate attempt to understand the 'primeval history of matter', which *might* provide a new secret of the universe; as such it is irresistible.

Whatever its other achievements, CERN is a monument to European collaboration. It harbours few national rivalries, and it is not bound to national quotas for staff or contracts; it is run by Professor Gregory, a half-English Frenchman; the president, Professor Funke, is a Swede; the English scientists are most numerous, and the computers are English-manned; but no one seems very conscious of nationality. CERN has even managed to break down some of the suspicions between European universities, who share its equipment and settle its programmes, and some scientists hope that CERN itself might develop into a super-university, on a continental scale. Nor is the research imbued with European nationalism: it has American and Russian visitors, and exchanges scientists with its Russian counterparts. CERN seems to be a return to an earlier international age of science, removed from politics and threats of war. But it is the very uselessness of CERN which makes this co-operation possible. No countries will quarrel about their share, because it has no foreseeable practical results. It is too pure for politics. CERN scientists, in justifying their huge expenditure, are tempted to suggest that they will eventually make a practical discovery: their former director, Professor Weisskopf, quoted the story of Faraday, who, when asked the point of his discovery of electricity, replied: 'I don't know, but I'm sure that your successors will some day levy a tax on it.' But many scientists must hope that nothing practical ever comes out of Geneva – not only because of memories of Hiroshima, but because, if even their science became political, their academic paradise would be ruined.

BRAIN DRAIN

It is when scientific discoveries are leading to practical technology that Europe realizes her disadvantage. Over the past thirty years the pattern has become monotonous of inventions pioneered in Europe (most of them in England) then developed in America: and Europeans have realized their weakness in the most painful way possible – by having to pay for it. An early example was penicillin, invented in Britain during the war, given free to the Americans, who then invented the mass-producing process – which then had to be bought back at vast expense to Britain. While science is still a relatively international activity, with its sense of common purpose and adventure, as soon as it turns into technology it becomes much more national and local, circumscribed by balance-sheets and patents.

To measure the American advantage you can look at the numbers of patents and licences. Between 1957 and 1963, 17 per cent of all patents taken out in western Europe were of American origin, while only ten per cent of patents taken out in America came from Europe: and the discrepancy still widens. The cost of patents, licences and agreements weighs heavily on the balance of payments; in 1965 two-thirds of the French deficit and half of the German one came from their technological dependence on America.[1]

The most obvious reason for backwardness is the lack of researchers. America spends about *six times* as much on research as the common market countries; in terms of percentage of the gross national product, the figures for 1963–64 (according to OECD) were thus:

United States	3.4%	Japan	1.4%
France	1.6%	United Kingdom	2.3%
W. Germany	1.4%	USSR (?)	2.7%
Italy	0.6%		

Britain alone comes near the American proportion, and Britain's superiority in research is perhaps the most attractive dowry she could bring into the common market. But Britain

1. *OECD Observer*, February 1966.

has concentrated far too much of her research in two industries, nuclear energy and aircraft, which have produced very doubtful returns: research was apt to be regarded as an activity quite separate from manufacturing or marketing; as one minister put it: 'Research was thought of as a kind of substitute for the Empire.' And Britain by herself is technologically more and more at a disadvantage. Europe's ineffectiveness in research is more serious than the percentages show, because so much of the effort is duplicated or even quintuplicated by rivalries and frontiers. The scientific achievements of the future seem likely to depend on clusters of like-minded top boffins, as in the American 'centres of excellence' – MIT or the University of California. But the European disunity makes this impossible. America's research seems wasteful enough; but Europe's is split between nations, companies and universities, competing inadequately with each other. 'The situation is much the same as if, in the United States, each state of the union were to attempt individually to provide the whole apparatus of the contemporary science effort.'[1]

Few developments in post-war America have been more striking than the close linking of universities, industry and government; but in Europe the process has only just begun, and the interchange between universities is painful and slow. Experts on the technology gap now like to blame the 'management gap' for preventing European industry from exploiting new ideas. In January 1967 the OECD produced a seven-hundred-page report on technology which gloomily concluded that Europe would fall still further behind America: they recommended 'the rejuvenation of business management, the continued reduction of costs, the honouring or restoring to honour of mobility, initiative, risk and profit, the development of a climate of co-operation between government and administration, the universities, industry and the trade unions'.

The symptom of frustration is the 'brain drain' – a phrase which, first coined in Britain, has now become a lament all over the continent. Britain's position is not necessarily the worst, for she has at least another drain sloping in her direction, from the Commonwealth. Switzerland, which has

1. Alexander King: 'Science and Technology', *Daedalus*, Winter, 1964, p. 449.

taken great pride in taking scientists (including Einstein) from elsewhere, suffers even more seriously than Britain. Dr. Burckhardt, president of the Swiss Federal Institute of Technology, has reckoned that twenty per cent of the young élite of his country join the brain drain. He compares it with the 'blood drain' of the Middle Ages, when the sons of Swiss peasants and squires would go abroad to be hired as mercenaries by foreign kings.[1]

MIGRATION OF SCIENTISTS AND ENGINEERS TO
THE USA
(Annual average 1956–61)[2]

Country	Numbers	Percentage of total output
France	82	0.9
W. Germany	425	8.2
Netherlands	136	15.1
United Kingdom	662	7.4
Austria	66	7.0
Greece	64	10.2
Ireland	45	9.3
Italy	71	1.3
Norway	78	16.2
Sweden	105	8.8
Switzerland	134	17.0
Canada	1,239	32.3

All the governments lament this loss of their brains, and try to counter it: the new American immigration laws of 1968 will cut off the flow, but only temporarily. The lure is not simply financial; it is the lure of opportunity and respect. 'Mr. Brain Drain is among us,' warned Le Monde in December 1967, announcing the arrival in Paris of Mr. Douglass, head of Careers Inc. 'What does Mr. Douglass say? That the supremacy of grey matter and the mobility of talents are henceforth basic facts from which it will no longer be possible to escape; that the mastery of the world is linked to technology; that here is tremendous adventure for America, in which he, Mr. Douglass, is delighted to play a role. And why won't the Europeans work together? The young scientists and engineers of the old continent – (he finds proof of this every day) – are no longer faithful to their employers,

1. The Times, 17th October, 1967.
2. OECD Observer, February 1966.

but to their profession. Where else are the best conditions to exercise it, if not in America? The straightforward behaviour of the bosses over there, the relaxed relations which are established with them, lure over the young Europeans – that budding crop coveted by managers from New Jersey to California.'

This is the real humiliation for Europe; for it shows how much of the sense of opportunity and the shaping of the future has passed across the Atlantic. As the scale of technology grows, so a continent becomes the only viable unit for the researchers who are exploring it.

The great attraction of the drain to young scientists is that it leads to the future; and that is what makes it so worrying to others. However much Europeans may be able to catch up with existing industries, there is always the feeling of new industries, and whole new ways of life, evolving across the Atlantic. No conference or plan about the future can be assembled without reference to America. The suggestions that technology involves the 'mastery of the world' may not be borne out by recent history; but it is a preoccupation among those who do not have it. The desire to keep the brains in Europe, and to provide projects of a scale to combat the Americans, has become a prime argument for European integration. But the question is: which projects?

EUROPROJECTS

There are already a host of joint European projects: a list of them compiled by OECD in 1963 covered three hundred pages. As an Austrian senator, Mr. Czernetz, wittily remarked: 'To tell one from another is a science in itself.'

CONCORDE	(£800 million?)
	See p. 178.
AIRBUS	(£190 million?)
	A 300-seat 'jumbo jet', built by Britain, France and West Germany, scheduled to be ready in the summer of 1973 for BEA, Air France, Lufthansa, etc., but beset by quarrels and facing obvious competition from the American airbus.
JAGUAR	(£400 million)

T–G

A supersonic light strike fighter to be used by the British and French air forces in the early 1970s. The Breguet Company build the nose, cockpit and body; the British Aircraft Company build the wings, tail and the engines.

ELDO   (£180 million)
                The European Space Vehicle Launcher Development Organisation: see p. 199.

CERN   (£14 million a year)
                See p. 188.

ESRO   (£120 million)
                The European Space Research Organisation originating with a group of scientists from CERN; See p. 199.

EUROCONTROL   (£10 million)
                The civil air traffic control system, with the legal responsibility for upper space in the common market and Britain, and its own experimental centre outside Paris. (With supersonic planes streaking across a single country in five minutes, its problems will grow.)

NADGE   (£100 million)
                The Nato Air Defence Ground Environment – an automated early warning system which informs intercepting planes of the approach of attacking aircraft. Includes all NATO countries, and (significantly) France. See also p. 219.

DRAGON   (£30 million)
                A high-temperature gas-cooled reactor for nuclear research, jointly run by Britain, Euratom and five other European countries, at Winfrith in Dorset.

The difficulties and drawbacks of these polyglot bodies are familiar – language, duplication, cross-purposes, planlessness and above all different political objectives. As Jean-Jacques Salomon, secretary of the OECD's scientific ministerial meeting, described it: 'On the one hand, the international organizations end up obeying their own laws of expansion, which are to some extent independent of the joint decisions of member countries, and on the other hand, they draw up programmes which do not necessarily allow for the work being done in the same field by their member countries or by other organizations.'[1]

But as more and more projects become too expensive for any single government, so governments will be forced to co-operate with their neighbours. The remorseless logic of money is beginning to over-ride prejudices or political rivalries; a few days after the French second rejection of Britain's application to enter the common market in November 1967, a new Anglo-French agreement was signed for the Jaguar strike fighter. The tide seems slowly to be turning towards a pan-European technology; yet in the most important fields, the case-histories are not very encouraging. There are at present four crucial areas of the future: aircraft, computers, nuclear energy, space. Some problems of aircraft we have already seen, in the example of the Concorde; the other three areas need briefly to be surveyed.

COMPUTERS

It is not without reason that the computer has become an obsessive image in nightmares of the future; in France to judge from jokes and cartoons, it seems to play a specially haunting role, as the heartless agent of technocracy, watched by mad scientists, secretly dominating the innocent lives of so-called individuals. The more confident are the predictions about the computer's role in management – cutting out drudgery, by-passing bureaucracy, easing delegation, simplifying scholarship – the more worrying is the realization that this is a field where Europeans are trailing behind; and that, when the computer talks, it will talk American.

The idea of a computer was actually invented in 1820 by an eccentric Englishman, Charles Babbage, under the name of the 'Analytical Engine', but he got no support from the Treasury. The first working computer was made in Germany in 1941, when Britain was second in the race. The Americans, as in other discoveries, were quite slow to realize its importance; but once they got the point they raced ahead.

Ten years ago both France and Italy had promising com-

1. *OECD Observer*, February 1966.

puter companies. In Italy Olivetti had expanded from type-writers to computers:[1] but by 1964 it had over-extended, and sold out part of its computer side to the American General Electric. In France Machines Bull was, in spite of its name, an all-French company; it had begun in Paris in 1931, buying the patents of a Norwegian engineer Fredrik Bull, and had grown to be for a time the world's second biggest computer-maker. Then, like Olivetti, Bull got into difficulties and it, too, was rescued by General Electric. The subsequent marriage was an uneasy one. General Electric insisted on drastic sackings and rationalization, and then turned out to be having difficulty with their own computers: by early 1967 they had to retrench drastically. The French government had decided it must rescue the remains of the computer industry, and put together an odd group of five companies hopefully called the 'Plan Calcul', run by a 'Mr. Computer' directly responsible to the prime minister, but without, so far, much promise. In Germany the Siemens giant was backward, and had to make their computers under licence with the American RCA; only recently have they developed their own. The other electronic giant, Philips in Holland, 'the sleeping giant', was riding smugly on the television boom.

In the meantime the phenomenal IBM company, which makes 80 per cent of the computers in the world, moved into the European market in the sixties with subtlety and firmness. They could spend £60 million a year on research and development, compared with £5 million by the biggest European company, ICL; and their relentless marketing gave them footholds in nearly every big company. The European governments, while tut-tutting, had to buy IBM computers for their departments; and France had to order IBM machines for their nuclear force de frappe (first vetoed by the American government, but then pushed through by IBM). By 1966 IBM had three-quarters of the market in France, Germany and Italy and half the market in Britain. The growth rate of the industry will be colossal. M. Maison-rouge, the (French) president of IBM Europe, has forecast that between 1970 and 1980 computers will be the third world industry after oil and cars.[2]

1. See Chapter 5.
2. Quoted in Servan-Schreiber, *The American Challenge*, p. 99.

The dominance of IBM bothers most people – including themselves. 'If the Europeans do not find a way to slow us down politely' (said their president, Thomas Watson, in 1967) 'and if we ourselves in our enlightened self-interest do not find methods of making our operations abroad more acceptable to the nationals of the countries in which we operate, the Europeans in simple self-defence will throw up new barriers against further penetration of American industry on their continent, and will begin to restrict the positions we already have.'

Only the British have some hope. International Computers (ICT), after some unhappy beginnings, expanded quickly after 1965 and even made some progress in Europe; and in 1968 a shot-gun marriage was arranged with two rivals, English Electric and Plessey, to produce ICL, by far the biggest European computer group, and the fourth biggest in the world. But although computers do not need such vast government patronage as aircraft or nuclear research, they do need a huge market.

IBM, with its monopoly position, can afford brave gambles; their new 7360 computer, it was reckoned, cost five billion dollars to develop and introduce – as much as the total annual British defence budget. The future of smaller companies is not hopeless; for computers are becoming so common that specialists – as with cars – will still have a chance. But faced with the choice between linking with the British company – whose computers are not 'compatible' with IBM equipment – or following the Americans, the continental companies are not in much doubt. And IBM are subtle and confident enough to change like Proteus, and take on very European expressions. They use European researchers in Europe, exchanging findings between their laboratories. They set up local boards, and give them great dignity. They may even be on the way to becoming one of the first really 'geo-political' companies.

NUCLEAR ENERGY

A still sadder history is that of Europe's nuclear industry, which began with such high hopes. In Britain, ever since the war, nuclear research has been a special national pride, and £70 million a year has been spent on it. But as in other fields the scientists were not much interested in selling their wares, and the familiar lag developed between research and its commercial application. The research was impressive, and a succession of power stations grew up along the coast, the first in the world; but the consortia that built them were too small, or too slow, to compete on an international scale, and only two were sold abroad (to Italy and Japan). The continent, without the legacy of wartime research, was later to develop, and ran into greater difficulties. The formation of Euratom, at the same time as the common market, was planned as the centrepiece of nuclear research, and a nuclear industry; it was regarded by some (as we have seen)[1] as a more important potential unifier than the common market itself. But it was soon the centre of political rows, and its development was in contrast to the peace of CERN. By its tenth anniversay in 1967, Euratom had virtually disintegrated.

The real divisions are evident in the next stage of nuclear power, the fast-breeder reactor. Britain is first in the field, with the prototype plant at Dounreay, a huge white ball on the coast of Scotland, now almost complete and three years ahead of all others; but France and German both now plan to build their own rival prototypes, and the three countries will spend between them about £400 million pounds, each conducting the same experiments. Yet none of them by themselves have the resources to capture the European market.

The Americans, as with computers, were late in moving into nuclear energy; but once it became clear that it would be cheaper than coal or oil, they moved decisively and quickly. The two giant companies, Westinghouse and General Electric, heavily involved with government contracts, staked their futures on mass-producing nuclear power stations. They made huge mistakes, but they could afford to; they had already by March 1968 exported or licensed thirteen reactors abroad, and they had sold licences to Siemens and AEG in Germany, and to Ansaldo and Fiat in Italy. They are now pushing ahead with fast-breeder reactors – with some help from the British brain drain.

In producing nuclear fuel, the most rarefied of industries, Europe is still more contrary. The making of enriched

1. See Chapter 2.

uranium (U235), which all existing nuclear power needs, is
done by separating isotopes, which (like making aluminium)
consumes inordinate amounts of electricity; but the bigger
the plant, the cheaper the process. America has three plants,
each using as much electricity as (say) Bristol: Europe has
two, Capenhurst in Britain and Pierrelatte in France, both
much smaller, and so more extravagant. There could be no
more obvious case for collaboration. Both France and
Britain would like to share their costs, but neither wants to
share any secrets. Capenhurst, which has just been completely re-equipped, hopes that it can (with secret processes)
come close to the American price, and can build up a big
export market in nuclear fuel; and it is possible that the
Dutch may have produced a much cheaper process. But it
seems likely that Europe will not be able to produce enough
enriched uranium for itself, and may depend on buying
American.

SPACE

The most pathetic European story has been the half-
hearted attempt to join the space race. In 1964, the two
schemes were begun, first ELDO to make rockets, then
ESRO to make satellites. ELDO was based on the British
rocket Blue Streak, with France and Germany making the
other two bits: the common market and Britain shared the
cost, and since there was no room in Europe, Australia was
brought in for the launching site. ESRO, for space research,
was financed by ten countries, with Britain paying a quarter:
they build weirdly-named centres all over Europe, including
ESDAC in Germany, ESRIC in Italy, ESRANGE in
Sweden, ESTAC in Holland and ESTRACK, with stations in
Alaska, Spitzbergen and the Falkland Islands.

Both projects soon fell into troubles; ELDO was not
powerful enough to launch the most useful (geo-stationary)
satellites; by 1966 it was already out of date, and had to be
cut back. The French bit of the rocket was said to be useless,
and in 1968 Britain decided to pull out of it, to the approval
of most of the British experts (except *The Economist*) but
to the fury of many continentals. ESRO was left without a
launcher, dependent on using the Americans'; but they too
were having worries. They had four directors in three years,

culminating in a more hopeful one, Professor Bondi; the ten countries could not agree, and after mounting costs their two half-ton satellites TD1 and TD2, were cancelled in 1968.

Europe was back at square one, having either to drop out of space or start a much bigger programme. The European industrial lobby called 'Eurospace' insisted that space research was essential for other technologies, and even the Swiss watchmakers demanded a space programme. A plan for spending £1,200 million was put forward in Bonn in June 1968. But there is constant argument about how far space encourages other technologies with its 'spin-off' (according to one school, the non-stick frying pan is the only useful result of the American programme); and however much industries pressed for the space race, they themselves could not afford to pay for it. Of all the fields of competition with America and Russia, space is one that Europe can most obviously back out of: it may be that the lack of space in the continent itself makes it psychologically less attractive.

A CHALLENGE?

Last year the fashion was bigness. This year it's technology.
                                                          A Eurocrat, 1967

All these technological fiascos agitate top people in Europe, for to them they are a kind of personal humiliation. But how far do they distress the average voter? Christopher Layton has asked: Is the Briton, who shaves with a Gillette razor blade, eats Heinz beans for breakfast, drives to work in a Ford on Esso fuel and runs his office with Remington typewriters and IBM computers, while his wife Hoovers the house and shops in Woolworths, aware that all these are made by American owned firms?[1]

Layton thought probably not, and I have found the same unawareness on the continent. Even the average Frenchman is probably unaware that all his electric light bulbs and all razor-blades are made by American firms; few German drivers know that Opel cars are owned by General Motors, or Braun razors by Gillette. If they did, would they care? What would it matter to Europeans if the continent were to become a kind of Canada, dependent on American capital and American know-how? It can be, and often is, argued

1. *Encounter*, April 1967.

that this is a much more sensible future for Europe – not to spend vast sums on expensive research, on the space race, the jet race or the computer race, but to make use of American inventions and to concentrate capital and energy on improving the daily quality of life, and so building a more civilized society than that of the Americans. So much of the American effort, like the Russian effort, is linked not simply to population or wealth but to sheer size. The psychology of progress, experiment and wastage arises from the great open space of the hinterlands. Europe with a tenth of their area cannot possible compete without destroying its own character, its old traditions of privacy, roots and strong individualty. If Europe can only keep up with America by becoming like America, is it worth it?

Between competition with America on all fronts and the present inertia, there must be a half-way house. Europe can still concentrate on those technological frontiers which best suit the continent. Technology is not only a question of missiles, jet planes or H-bombs: hospitals, schools, housing and civilized leisure will all require the development of new methods. It is in these social fields, as much as in war-like ones, that Europe has been accustomed to lead. Yet here, too, Europe has slipped back so that 'Americanization' is synonymous with all modernization.

Europe will not be able to hold her self-respect, as Marjolin warns, if she does not contribute to the technological advance. But is technology in itself a strong enough incentive for unity? It is implicit in every discussion of the 'Challenge' that Europe can only fight back not through protection – which would cut her off from the stimulus and the know-how – but by building up a pan-European industry, with all the sacrifices of sovereignty that that implies. But Europeans will only make this effort if they have the political will – that is, if they feel resentful enough towards the Americans. In spite of the uproars of recent years, there is not much sign that Europeans have reached this boiling-point. In the midst of the clamour about integration, European companies still prefer to deal with Americans; Braun sells out to Gillette, Rolls-Royce signs up with Lockheed, the *force de frappe* buys from IBM: the Trojan Horse which lets America into Europe is (as André Fontaine has remarked) to be found not in England or Germany, but in the centres of European industry.

Perhaps it is not surprising that the pursuit of a technological Europe has so far lacked political sex-appeal. In the first place it cannot (as Monnet has said) be very closely identified with people's personal hopes; indeed it can add to their fears, evoking nightmares of a machine-made Europe with a computer in the middle, catching up populations not so much in a great new unity, as in a new kind of servitude. And in the second place, the greatest incentive to develop technologies in the past has been war; and in the sphere of defence (as we will see in the next-but-one chapter) Europe is specially divided.

Chapter Nine

Euro-Americans

The contest of the old with the new world in all departments of life will in all likelihood be the great overwhelming question of the coming century.
Werner von Siemens, 1889[1]

The third industrial power in the world, following the United States and the Soviet Union, could well be in fifteen years not Europe, but American industry in Europe.
Jean-Jacques Servan-Schreiber, Le Défi Américain, *1967*

No traveller, however jet-propelled, can miss the most obvious common signs of western European capitals: the letters IBM, looming up in identical blue letters from tall buildings on the road from the airport; *Time* magazine or *International Herald Tribune*, at every central kiosk; the same-looking Hertz girls at the airports, in their black-and-yellow uniforms, filling up the same forms; the long glittering façades of TWA and Pan-American, stretching along the most expensive shopping street; Hilton and Intercontinental hotels, always with the same insulation from the city, always (as Conrad Hilton put it) 'a little bit of America'. Posters for Pepsi-Cola and Coca-Cola, with their grinning teenagers, in small villages and even above the canals of Venice. These are the visible common denominators of western Europe. They are all not European but American, and they rub home the now familiar fact that it is only the Americans who see Europe clearly as a whole, and who can ignore its frontiers. 'Shouldn't you be able to rent a car in Italy and leave it in Holland?' says one advertisement: 'Hertz says Si!'

The American presence in Europe is familiar enough; it

1. Werner von Siemens: *Inventor and Entrepreneur*, Augustus M. Kelley, 1966.

was never more evident than in the first post-war years, when GIs and Marshall Aid were everywhere, scattering dollars or nylons. What is new is a different phenomenon, an apparently permanent American presence in Europe, in it, yet not of it. The European boom, the American deficit, the speed of jet travel and the vagaries of tax laws, have all encouraged American companies or individuals to settle in Europe, establishing factories and offices and often becoming virtually self-sufficient from America. They inhabit a separate world, an interlocking network of Americans-in-Europe, including American corporations, banks, management consultancies, advertising agents. They work in special air-conditioned office blocks where quite often every name in the entrance-hall is American. They seem almost as separate as an army of occupation. Yet they impinge increasingly on Europeans, acting as a catalyst which can quickly release unsuspected energies and ambitions. In the old days the source of the American strength in Europe seemed obvious – it was their money. But today Americans make money out of Europe: they thrive not on dollars but on Eurodollars. As Servan-Schreiber puts it: 'we pay them to buy us'. Their strength rests on something more than wealth.

A Belgian economist said: 'If you are trying to study Europe, you must go to America'; an American publisher said: 'The trouble with you Europeans is that you decide that you have got to get together, and then what do you do? You fly off to New York to talk about it.' Both remarks ring painfully true. Even the academic studies about the future of Europe are likely to come not from Paris or Cambridge but from Wisconsin or Chicago. The language of European integration and federalism – including those last two words – is an American language.

It is impossible, as I have found, to discuss new Europeans without also discussing Americans. The common threads of European unity that we have so far followed all seem to lead off the map, westwards. The search for power, whether coal, oil, gas or nuclear: the structure of international corporations; the quest for a common currency; the integration of trade unions; the co-operation in technology – in none of these does the context of Europe, or western Europe, appear at all self-contained. In each the trend is towards more, not less, involvement with America. In pursuing these clues, I find myself, as in some maze of mirrors, each time turned back towards the Atlantic.

Americans, clearly, find it easier to believe in Europe; their picture of the continent is far simpler than the Europeans'. Their Europe is just another land-mass, with the same kind of population; frontiers, languages and nationalisms can be ignored. It is not just a commercial view but an attitude of mind which is evident in any plane journey cross Europe, when Americans persist in thinking that countries are no more different than states: they like to imagine the all-European man, as they imagine the all-American. The American obliviousness makes Europeans aware, perhaps more than the common market itself, of their own psychological constrictions: 'They talk about Europe as if it really existed,' said one top Italian industrialist: 'They come out with conceptions like "the southern European market", which I never thought about before.' (This simplification of geography is of course familiar enough; it is not very different from the British habit of talking and thinking about 'West Africa' or 'South-East Asia', which seems similarly extraordinary to the inhabitants.)

There are, of course, all kinds of layers of Euro-America (as I shall call this separate land). At one extreme there are the academic havens, which reconstruct a Jamesian world of studied elegance, like the Villa Serbelloni on a promontory of Lake Como, or I Tatti, Berenson's old villa outside Florence. At the other extreme is the vast brown slum in Frankfurt, which was once the centre of the German chemical combine, the IG Farben, but which now contains the headquarters of the American army in Europe. Walking inside, behind the colossal façade with 2,500 windows, you are transported immediately away from Germany, into a shabby outpost of the Pentagon: American GIs, true to their caricature, wander through a vast drug-store, gazing at American comics; and the Germans working in the building look almost indistinguishable. Frankfurt is the capital of Euro-America, and more than one in ten of the population is American, as the vast consulate suggests; their self-sufficiency is conjured up by their paper, *Frankfurt American*, recording their socials, outings, theatricals, without much reference to the native population.

In all these places Americans are very separate; yet their influence extends far beyond their walls. Their real power, like that of the British in Victorian India, stems from their capacity to animate the natives. If you go into a German-American advertising agency, a French-American airline office, a British-American bank, it is not always easy to know which of the staff are Americans. It is the extraordinary ability for American companies or even individuals to unleash the hidden drive and competitiveness of young Europeans which has, perhaps more than anything else, shown up the limitations of European management. In the last five years, since the American success has become so visible, there have been endless discussions among industrialists to trace and analyse their special ingredient; the search has shifted from American capital, to know-how, to size, to mobility, to technology, to management, to education. The discussion reached a new frenzy on the continent (though less in Britain) after the publication of the book, *Le Défi Américain*, by Jean-Jacques Servan-Schreiber, editor of *L'Express*. Servan-Schreiber, observing the ability of the Americans to exploit the common market far more successfully than the Europeans, inspects the European weaknesses and concludes (much as de Tocqueville did 130 years before) that the real ingredient is the American trust in the individual. He contrasts the willingness of American companies to gamble on giving young people their head and to decentralize their divisions, with the 'presumption of incompetence' and the centralized directions of the French technocrats; he decides that 'this wager on man is the origin of America's new dynamism'.

Certainly this release of individual energies is a large ingredient in the American success; whether in a young Frenchman working for IBM, a young Oxford graduate in Procter and Gamble, or a young German in J. Walter Thompson, the signs of bursting confidence are the same; it comes not just from the brainwashing of the companies, but from the sense that they can do anything, express themselves, take risks, argue and above all make more and more money. It cannot be regarded simply as an American influence; it is also a de-Europeanizing influence – an escape from the tribe. The released energy is not so unlike the energy of the Chinese in South-East Asia, of Indians in Nairobi, of Greeks in America. The migration, whether from one continent to another, or across the unseen divide, from Europe to Euro-America, brings a surge of energy and self-reliance, and all the straightforwardness that comes from grappling with problems *from outside*. Yet this release is clearly not all gain; in all these expatriate business communities, away from the rules of the tribes, there is the danger of going too far. The Americans' confidence in the individual may be the secret of their success, but it may also be (as in their insistence on carrying guns in their own country) the source of growing troubles.

A VISIT TO CORNFELD

> No army can withstand the strength of an idea whose time has come.
>
> *Victor Hugo, quoted by Bernard Cornfeld*

Of many vivid manifestations of Euro-America, I will take one as a kind of caricature: Bernard Cornfeld, who at forty-one has probably made more money out of Europe than anyone in the last few years. He is not at all a typical American; in fact his methods have been repudiated by the New York stock exchange. But he has shown, perhaps more sensationally than anyone, how transatlantic energy can transform Europeans and their habits. He has built up a corps of ten thousand salesmen, selling investments from door to door, held together by their commitment to money-making; and he has brought this high-pressure salesmanship into the passive world of European finance, whether in Spain, Holland, Germany or England, adding his own personal element of showmanship. His case, though singular, is worth a close-up.

Cornfeld is only American by adoption; he was born in Istanbul, where his Rumanian father was in a film-distributing business (providing the showbiz background): he came to America as a boy, went to Columbia University, became a left-wing social worker, and then switched to selling mutual funds, the American equivalent of British unit trusts; he came to Paris when he was twenty-nine, started selling on commission for an American mutual fund, to GIs and others. Then the French government stopped him, and he moved to Geneva, where he could spread his net much

wider and started up on his own; quickly he built up his own
'Investors' Overseas Service' (IOS), by-passing existing
banks and institutions to go straight to his potential customers – the middle-classes who wanted to invest money in
American stock, where it would be safe, and grow faster. He
formed a 'Fund of Funds' (a brilliantly portentous name)
which invested in other American fast-moving funds; and he
geared his operation to high rewards, both for salesmen and
investment experts. His selling methods and the secrecy of
this operation soon cut across the SEC, the watchdogs of the
New York stock exchange. Eventually he had to agree to
cease selling to any Americans, in or outside the States; but
by now his European customers were so many that he could
do without Americans, and Europeans were outside the jur-
isdiction of the SEC. By 1968 his various funds had assets of
over a billion dollars; and nearly a third of his customers
were in the stronghold of financial orthodoxy, Germany.

Flying out to Geneva to visit Mr. Cornfeld, I got a preview
of the fund business from overhearing a fast-talking American in the seat behind me, explaining that he was trying to
break into Cornfeld's market: 'They just told me to go and
take over Europe ... the whole thing's wide open – they're
just so backward here, like the States ten years ago. ...
You've just got to educate them, and then there's nothing to
stop you. ... Of course we have no address in the States,
we're not recognized by the SEC. ... We've just got a very
unfavourable write up in *Time* – that doubled our business ...'

In Geneva I went to Cornfeld's headquarters, in a big
apartment block overlooking the lake, entirely filled with his
staff. Inside, it is like a sexy advertising agency, with a suggestion that something tremendous is happening next door.
There are a lot of handsome girls in dark-blue military uniforms with brass buttons; there are rice-paper walls, bustle
and sense of purpose. I talk with Cornfeld's young public
relations man called Hal, from the American diplomatic service, who then takes me to an ornate lakeside chalet which
used to belong to the Colgate toothpaste family. We wander
round the gloomy rooms, pick up drinks from the kitchen,
and then a bald little man comes in, all eyes and mouth, like
a toad. He looks gloomy and untidy in spite of a fashionable
buttoned-up jacket with flowery tie and handkerchief, which

turn out to be done by Cardin. He has a thick neck, but
sensitive hands. His face is fat, but still shows the muscles
working nervously beneath. He is forty, but looks fifty.
I'm introduced to Bernie Cornfeld, and he says, 'Ah, the
gentleman from the press,' in a tiny tired voice: he talks
desultorily with a slow stutter: he explains about 'people's
capitalism' and the absurdities of European banks: 'All
they've got to sell is their façades. They think that people
have got to come to them. What we sell is *performance*.'

Then one of the dark blue girls comes in, looking menacing, and says: '*Monsieur, le hélicoptère vous attend*.' Hal
expresses surprise. But Cornfeld says quietly: 'Just going
over to have a look at my castle – they're doing paintings on
the ceiling.' He turns to me: 'Why don't you come along –
we can talk on the way. We'll be back in half an hour.' I say
yes, of course, and soon afterwards the girl comes back to
say again, *le hélicoptère*. So we step into Bernie's Corvette
Sting Ray convertible, and whizz off to Geneva airport,
which happens to be almost next door. In the entrance hall, a
young Austrian pilot comes up and then an elegant Swiss-
French architect called Serge. Bernie does not quite carry off
this fantasy-life, his big eyes wandering round the airport,
his hands always fidgeting. As we pass the Customs, I realize I haven't got a passport (the castle is in France), but
this little local difficulty is brushed aside with the explanation that I am coming back in half an hour. The helicopter awaits us on the tarmac; on the way we inspect a little
Mystère jet which Cornfeld shares with a friend who sells
Volkswagens on the Pacific coast. We climb into the helicopter: Bernie shows signs of life for the first time. We rise
above Geneva, circle briefly above the frontier-post; on the
way Serge points out rival châteaux, and asks the pilot to
hover over them, while he exclaims about the formal
gardens. After twenty minutes the Cornfeld Château appears
– a twelfth-century pile with a drawbridge and steep turrets
shining with new black and gold tiles. We hover over a
double swimming pool surrounded by statuary, and slowly
descend on to the grass alongside, which shivers with the
wind as if with apprehension. We get out, all stooping below
the rotating blades although they're well above us. Even
Bernie is not used to helicopters.

He bought the castle three years ago, but there are still

about twenty workmen there. Bernie and Serge walk round
looking at the roof-paintings: Bernie rejects them: 'They
don't *do* anything to me.' The château is full of *bric-à-brac*.
painted washbasins, white wicker furniture, old mirrors,
tapestries – with a few mundane objects like a ping-pong
table and a miniature billiards: Bernie clambers up and down
the ladders, his huge eyes seeing everything, but still lug-
ubrious, talking more and more softly and sadly. I try to ask
him what the place is *for*: he says faintly 'just weekends': he
admits reluctantly that it will have fifteen bedrooms. It
seems it will be used for entertaining senior managers and
master-salesmen; the décor is strictly for business. Serge gets
more and more eloquent, gesturing into each new room, but
still fails to arouse gaiety from Cornfeld. He seems most
interested in a scheme to fill up the moat, so that ducks can
float on it: he is also very fond of two vast dogs, which
bound up every stair with him.

After an hour, we pile into the helicopter and whirr up
again, back to Geneva: Bernie is still enthralled by the view,
as though it emphasizes his own detachment. We drive back
in the Sting Ray to his office: 'Won't you come up?' He has
the top floor, with mustard velvet walls, still full at eight
o'clock of odd people – a man from the Philippines, a girl
showing friends around. In Bernie's office, his elder brother
is playing cards. Bernie talks a bit about America and LBJ –
'everything the States does nowadays seems to be bad PR' –
but there is still a portrait of LBJ in the room.

It is the blend of showbiz and finance that European
bankers find so maddening and unnerving: bankers' phrases
like stewardship or trusteeship certainly sound strange in
these playboy surroundings. Most of Cornfeld's directors are
under forty, and like to run the business in a casual, theatrical style. The salesmen are the key to it, and everything is
done to heighten the intensity of their faith. High-pressure
courses instruct them how to attract customers with every
gambit – promising, above all, security against inflation.
Nothing could be more alien to the mahogany traditions of
European bankers, who cultivate an atmosphere of rock-like
conservatism. Their reaction to Cornfeld's intrusion can be
imagined; they have made sure that the past history of the
dispute with the SEC is thoroughly known.

As his business has romped ahead, he has acquired a much

more reassuring superstructure. He has hired the former
leader of the German liberal party and Vice-Chancellor of
the Republic, Erich Mende, to run his German business. He
has taken on a respected English mandarin, Sir Eric Wynd-
ham-White, the former secretary of GATT, to join his English board; and he has taken on *two* Roosevelts. One of them
is the late president's eldest son, James, an ex-diplomat
whom Bernie likes to refer to repeatedly as Ambassador
Roosevelt; he is sixty, very tall, and seems to be a kind of
father-figure to Bernie; he runs the diplomatic side, the setting up of 'national funds' to be invested in Europe, which
helps to offset resentments about the drain of money to America. The other Roosevelt, Ted, runs the bureaucracy of the
business. The office workers, in a different way, are as extraordinary as the high command. They were expelled from
Geneva after a row about labour permits, and are now
housed across the frontier in France, in the village of
Ferney-Voltaire (where Voltaire took refuge when *he*
crossed over from Geneva: a lot of play is made with that
parallel). The village has been transformed by the arrival of
this young international army; a blue prefabricated block
was built in three months to house 400 workers, and apartment blocks sprang up all round it. Most of the office
workers are European, from twenty different countries, and
many of them English; yet the place seems more like some
American business-school. The average age is twenty-three;
at noon, the girls and boys troop across to the company
restaurant, the Chuck Wagon, for a strictly non-alcoholic
lunch. The offices are informal, but hard-working; along the
corridors hang photographs of Bernie making speeches to
assembled salesmen. It is hard to remember that this is a
small French village; in the square the grinning statue of
Voltaire surveys the extraordinary scene.

Most financial people seem to think that Cornfeld's outfit,
in spite of its chequered past, has come to stay;[1] and already
it has prodded some European banks into similar selling
methods. It might be compared to the revolution of the
Brothers Pereire one hundred and thirty years ago, who
founded the new popular bank, the Crédit Mobilier, which
challenged and eventually transformed the old banking es-

1. For Cornfeld's eventual fall, and its consequences, see Introduction.

tablishments led by the Rothschilds. Rothschilds, in the end, broke the Pereires; but this time the big banks have already followed Cornfeld's ideas. The consequences of Cornfeld, if he does not come to grief, may be equally far-reaching; if he devotes more of his investments to Europe – as he says he will – and others follow, they can materially affect the European stock exchanges, turning savings into investments. 'This is only the beginning,' Bernie assured me: 'The first billion dollars is the hardest.' His current ambition is to get into France, to extract the gold from under the mattresses, and turn *that* into investments.

Clearly Cornfeld is anxious to 'Europeanize' himself, to adapt his operation to suit each government, and he may well have the political skill, or advice, to do it. But his whole success depends on his capacity to look at Europe from outside it – as if from his helicopter – ignoring its old institutions and frontiers, and regarding Europe as if it were much like America in the wild old days of capitalism, before the Great Crash.

TWO CONTINENTS

It's at precisely the moment when public opinion stiffens with regard to American policy that habits in general tend to become Americanized.

Raymond Aron, September 1967

In spite of all the interactions with America, there is still not much difficulty in distinguishing Europeans from Americans. Americans have paradoxically helped to unite Europe in two opposite senses: first, by regarding the western continent as a whole; secondly, by showing Europeans that they have at least one thing in common – that they are not American. As an Englishman travelling through the continent, often wondering what I had in common with other Europeans, I became aware of at least one common bond when the subject of Americans came up. Nothing makes Europeans feel more European than talking about Americans. But behind this lies another paradox; that it is the Europeans who are most 'Americanized', most fascinated by transatlantic ideas, who feel most strongly the need to counter them. No example could be more fitting than Jean-Jacques Servan-Schreiber, the whizz-kid editor of a French

imitation of *Time* magazine, itself financed by American
capital. He is the epitome of a French-American, crew-cut,
brisk, relentless in his pursuit of the Kennedy image and the
methods of the Harvard Business School. But it is he who
emerged as the propagandist of the 'American Challenge'.
The paradox points to the basic European weakness in talking about America; that however resentful the attitude,
there is no clear conception of an alternative civilization;
when they discuss Europe, they discuss it in American terms.
Conversely, the more thorough anti-Americans are also anti-
Europeans (whether Charles de Gaulle or Douglas Jay):
their alternative is embedded in the nation-state.

The differences between the continents seem so strong that
it is difficult to remember that Americans are, after all, only
transplanted Europeans – some of them, like Cornfeld, very
recently and temporarily transplanted. The contrasts seem
the more extraordinary in the countries which provided
millions of emigrants to America – German, Italy, England,
Ireland – where all the cousin-hoods, the common grand-
fathers or great-grandfathers, do not bridge the gulf. In
France, which provided far fewer emigrants to the United
States (about half a million), the strangeness is less surprising; but even in French-speaking Canada, the relationship was not much heard of until 1967. Each European
country, I noticed, assumes that others have a special relationship or understanding with Americans: and each relationship seems to dissolve inside that country.

Yet the recurring contrasts between Europeans and
Americans can lead to a dangerous oversimplification. The
exaggeration is encouraged by the fact that Euro-Americans
are, of their nature, more extreme than Americans at home;
they are liberated from the rules of their tribes, as Cornfeld
is liberated from the SEC, and their expatriate life encourages a special ruthlessness and detachment. The Europeans only see the wilder edge of the American world, and they
are faced with a series of extreme choices; would you choose
the maverick enterprise of Cornfeld, or the deadly monopoly
of the old German bankers? A reasonable answer might be
something in between, but that synthesis is still far off. The
danger (it seems to me) is that Europeans, rightly impatient
with their own gerontocracies and patriarchal traditions, and
demoralized by the phenomenal American success, will

accept every aspect of the American system, without looking
far enough into its social roots and consequences. The
European's viewpoint, observing the invasions of industry,
technology and banking without seeing the society from
which they stem, is inherently misleading. European managers have become so used to seeing America as the land of
the future, the forerunner of all 'post-industrial' societies,
that it becomes difficult to imagine a future which is not like
America. The effort of imagination is made harder by the
fact that in many respects America already *is* the future; so
many of the American innovations, like cars or Cornfeld,
arrive twenty or thirty years late. To visualize a specifically
European future, appropriate to the size and the complexity
of the continent – to select some joint projects (like computers or CERN) and drop others (like Concorde or Space) is
the most obvious need if Europe is to re-establish her self-
confidence and pride; yet in all the fields we have seen –
through industry, finance and technology – Europeans betray
a deep sense of inferiority towards America.

I have often been struck by the parallels between the
remarks that are now made by Europeans about Americans,
and the comments of nineteenth-century continental writers
about Victorian Englishmen. The obsession with hygiene:
'The English think Soap is Civilization,' said Treitschke. The
obsession with money: 'Money is the hallmark not of wealth
alone,' said de Tocqueville in England in 1835, 'but of
power, reputation and glory.' The speed and size: 'Everything here is on a larger scale,' wrote Taine of London in
1862, 'the clubs are palaces; the hotels are monumental; the
river is an arm of the sea; the cabs move twice as fast.'
Above all, the continentals' sense of their commercial backwardness. To many visitors, the technological dominance of
Victorian England seemed, like the Americans' to us now, to
be something which they could never see the end of; that
technological gap seemed unbridgeable. They need not have
worried: the English were soon to lose their supremacy. But
the change came from where the continentals did not expect
it – from inside Britain. The Victorians lost interest in trade,
they could not take industrial research seriously, they were
distracted from money-making by imperialism and they had
the fatal illusion of permanence. The industrialists' sons re-
treated to country estates and eccentric hobbies, and grew

roots. According to one recent account 'by 1914, there was hardly a basic industry in which we held technical superiority except perhaps pottery'.[1]

Are there comparable signs of demoralization inside America? European tycoons, giving up hope of catching up, hopefully ask the question: 'I know that every civilization is supposed to carry the seeds of its own decay,' said one Unilever director; 'but I just can't find those seeds in America.' I, too, cannot see them: there are not many real parallels between contemporary America and Victorian Britain (though the Vietnam war has resemblances to the Boer War, particularly in its capacity to frustrate and demoralize a vast technological machine). There are few signs of the American economy running out of steam, of businessmen neglecting research, or even of Rockefellers retiring to the land. To hope that the technological gap will be closed by America slipping back seems forlorn, and it is anyway hardly something to be hoped for. Yet it may be that the Europeans (like their nineteenth-century forebears) too readily equate technological dominance with political dominance.

To emphasize the competition between the two continents can easily obscure the changes and revolts inside America itself, and the extent to which technology is causing the same huge problems on both sides of the Atlantic. It is this which makes 'anti-American' so difficult to define; for (as we will note in Chapter 21) the anti-Americanism of young European students is itself inspired and influenced by America. The Vietnam war, with all its consequences – particularly the rebels and draft-dodgers that have escaped to Europe – has brought a new ironic kind of Atlantic community, of students united against American policies; and in the targets of the students' revolt – against the consumer society, the repressive tolerance of the Establishment, the manipulation of mass media – the Europeans take many of their ideas, their slogans and their techniques of protest from America. For the radical students there is no question of Europe having to answer an American challenge; the question is whether individuals can maintain their freedom and integrity in either continent. For this problem young Am-

1. D. H. Aldcroft: 'The Entrepreneur and the British Economy, 1870–1914', *Economic History Review*, August 1964.

ericans look towards Europe at least as much as Europeans
look to America.

From whatever viewpoint, I suspect the preoccupation
with the 'American challenge' may soon diminish. In the first
place, the battle for the future – at least the immediate
future – has anyway clearly been lost; computers, nuclear
energy, space rockets will all continue to come from America for the next decade. In the second place, the biggest
American companies in Europe – perhaps led by IBM – may
well succeed in Europeanizing themselves sufficiently to
maintain at least the semblance of a 'geo-political' character. But most important, the American political dream
shows signs of losing its splendour, both for Americans and
Europeans; and while Europeans look westwards for their
technology, Americans may begin to look more to Europe
for political ideas. It is central to the argument of Servan-
Schreiber, in pressing Europeans to respond to the challenge,
that American technology brings with it political domination,
and that Europe will cease to control her own destiny. But
the events of the last year do not confirm this; and America's
huge internal problems raise further doubts. The preoccupation with the technological challenge – with all the
bleak mathematical calculations that it entails – is always in
danger of obscuring the real questions of political structures
and responses; and in this Europe may have a more interesting role to play.

Chapter Ten

Defence

> NATO will have fulfilled its military task only when we have fulfilled our political one.
>
> *Willy Brandt, 1967*

> If one looks back, one is impressed by how much security Europe has achieved; if one looks ahead, one is impressed by how little the *status quo* is likely to last.
>
> *Pierre Hassner, 1968*

Driving into Brussels from the airport in the summer of 1967, I could see only an empty muddy space in the flat land on the way to the city. A few months later I came back to find a hive of long low buildings, three stories high, sitting as separate and immaculate as if it had been dropped from the sky. In front flew fifteen flags which suggested that this was NATO, the North Atlantic Treaty Organization: it was confirmed by slogans on walls round about, saying *'En Dehors OTAN'* – 'Get out NATO'.

NATO's precipitate move gives some indication of its massive resources, and its detachment from the rest of Europe. In October 1966, after the French government had given NATO notice to remove its military installations, it was decided to move the headquarters to Belgium. In December the Belgians offered a temporary site. In May 1967 work began, by a consortium of Belgian, Dutch and German companies. By October the building was finished, and a convoy of trucks brought one hundred and forty tons of documents from Paris. The building has 1,320 offices and fifteen conference rooms, housing two thousand people, and it cost eight million dollars to build. And in theory, at least, it is only meant to last five years, before another building in Brussels is ready.

Inside, if you can get through the security barrage, you pass through a glass wall to find a bleak no-man's-land, with the same sense of emptiness and uniformity as other regions of internationalia – as FAO, the common market, or UNESCO. A wide plastic corridor half a mile long leads into other wide corridors, past unending doors of strange-sounding people and even odder departments – ALLA, OTO, LOG, PERS. There are banks, bars, post office, TV studios, a travel office, showing that the building could quite easily cut itself off from the mainland; and there are jokes about NATO being mistaken by foreigners for a small country, and about 'How's the weather in NATO?'

Few people nowadays know much about NATO, even in Brussels. In theory its arrival should give it close contact with the common market, but in practice the two might inhabit different continents. Major countries now have three ambassadors in Brussels – one for Belgium, one for the common market, one for NATO – and they overlap very little. If you ask a NATO man about the common market, he looks blank; and the common market people have always steered clear of defence. One commissioner told me how Hallstein would sometimes warn them: 'Don't waste time talking about defence. In the first place we don't understand it. In the second place we'll all disagree.'

NATO is separate, not only because of defence and secrecy, but because it is American: the biggest of all the provinces of Euro-America. Behind the panoply of European co-operation, the alliance is built round American money, influence, equipment, ideas and management. The NATO language, though officially English-and-French, is really a mid-Atlantic accent, often closer to American than English – 'center' and 'labor'. And the whole structure of NATO emphasizes that Europe is incapable of defending herself.

The defence system is not apparent to the public. It is part of modern military policy, particularly American policy, to keep soldiers tactfully apart from locals; they live in their own encampments, with their own cinemas, girls, and PXs, importing food, drink, toys, books, even milk from home. The American air bases, from Norway to Turkey, are islands cut off from national surroundings; their airmen move in and out, accompanied by vast impedimenta of household equipment, large cars and families, but are cut off like ghosts from the local communities. (We have lived next door to an American air-base family in Suffolk: their children were taken by bus to a special school, and the family had no visible contact with the village.) The four hundred thousand American troops in Europe (a population greater than Luxembourg's) only come to the surface in such towns as Frankfurt or Heidelberg – where the town is Americanized, with cafés called Klein Amerika or Smugglers' Inn, and signposts to 'Shopping Center', 'Patton Barracks', or 'Mark Twain Village'. The British Army of the Rhine, which contributes 50,000 men to the NATO numbers, is almost equally detached from the German cities near which it quarters; in spite of urgings (notably by General Hackett), the officers speak little German, their family and social life revolves round the camp, and their girls are brought over from England. There are sometimes suggestions that closer contact would improve Anglo-German relations, but worried memories survive of the time when the Cameronians made their name as the 'poison dwarves'.

Nor are the actual defences easy to see. There is a colossal NATO 'infrastructure' (a word borrowed from French railways, which has come to denote any kind of network of communications and engineering) which up to 1967 had cost £1,300 million: but not many people know of it. There are two hundred airfields, each costing between two and four million pounds; hangars built into the mountainside in northern Norway; 5,600 miles of underground pipelines, carrying jet fuel and petrol; a row of radio transmitters like giant up-ended saucers, curving from Turkey, through Greece, Italy, France to Denmark and Norway, bouncing messages via the troposphere from one to another; a few thousand Nike or Hawk missiles, mostly in West Germany, sticking up like giant fireworks; and an elaborate radar system, linked by computers with missiles, with the hideous name of NADGE (NATO Air Defence Ground Environment), being built along the same semi-circle from Turkey to Norway.

All these expensive devices are cut off (both geographically and organizationally) from other European institutions. They belong to a different world from that of the corporations, universities or the common market. But defence is unlikely to remain so separate. Firstly, the American influence seems likely to diminish. Secondly, Europe is finding that so many other problems – industrial mergers, technological backwardness – have at the back of them the problem of defence. Of all the motives for uniting, the strongest is a common fear; and of all the incentives for advancing technology, the most powerful has been war.

The complex arguments concerning the defence of Europe are beyond the scope of this book; what is relevant here is its bearing on Europe's integration. Defence is something which many people prefer not to mention, in the context of larger idealisms of reconciliation, peacemaking and international understanding. But it must be faced that many of Europe's most valuable institutions – whether French railways, Greek roads, British nuclear power stations, the Marshall Plan or the École Polytechnique – owe their origins to war or the threat of war. However rarefied and subtle the new nuclear defence, its involvement with industry and politics remains as real as ever. But it is one of Europe's present paradoxes that whereas in previous times more spending on technology has been urged as a means of improving defence, today it is common defence that is urged as a means of improving technology.

FUNK AND FEAR

The real father of the Atlantic Alliance was Stalin. It is he who has a right to a statue in each of our countries.

Paul-Henri Spaak (and others), 1967

NATO people nowadays are conscious that their role and *raison d'etre* have changed since the early cold war, and they look back to the beginnings with a kind of embarrassed nostalgia. Twenty years ago the North Atlantic treaty was signed in Washington by twelve countries in April 1949; it was soon after the Czechoslovak *putsch* and the Berlin blockade, with civil war still raging in Greece. Faced with all that, Western Europe came together with unprecedented speed. The Western Alliance with Russia faded into history, and the communist parties in France and Italy bitterly turned against the new North Atlantic Alliance. Its first years, under Generals Eisenhower and Ridgway, were hectic and heroic; Paris was its political battleground, filled with the slogans like 'Ridgway go home', and facing a strong neutralist faction, including *Le Monde*.

The common threat gave an impetus not just to NATO but to the whole movement for European recovery and integration; the Marshall Plan, the Coal and Steel Community, the European Defence Community, and the common market itself. The immediacy left little time for squabbling or resentments. General Lord Ismay, the first secretary-general of NATO, was heard to say privately that it was held together by 'funk and fear': or, as one British diplomat developed it at the time—

> The NATO's one foundation
> is based on funk and fear
> And all co-operation
> is strictly ad hoc here.

The fear achieved amazing results, which would not have been dreamt of a few years before; by 1955 there were fifteen countries acceding to the treaty and West Germany, only ten years after the war, had become a key part of the alliance: the reversal of alliances had come full circle. The NATO headquarters moved from London to Paris – first in huts in the Palais de Chaillot, then in a brand-new permanent block at the Porte Dauphine. The fifteen foreign ministers met twice a year. Of course, their solidarity was never as great as the pious statements made out. France in Algeria, France and Britain in Suez, showed how divergent military interests could be. But the fifteen countries have nevertheless maintained a joint defence system for nearly twenty years, almost unprecedented in the history of western Europe. I asked one top NATO official if he could think of any equally long-lasting alliance. He could only think of the Hellenic League, centred on Athens in the fourth century BC.

Its strategy underwent several transformations. After the Korean war both American and European armies wanted to cut down on manpower, and NATO leant more heavily on the American nuclear deterrent, which seemed more effective than the Russian. Then came the Sputnik in 1957, and the sudden American panic and reaction, leading to inter-continental missiles which could attack Russia, without needing Europe. Then came the Berlin crisis in 1961, with its

new military threat to Europe, and the American doctrine
soon afterwards followed by NATO of 'flexible response' –
which required large troops as well as the massive nuclear
deterrent. The idea of a multilateral force to integrate
Europe with the American deterrent was first vigorously put
forward, then quietly dropped. Then came the creeping
détente between western Europe and Russia, and the new
American involvement in Vietnam, bringing a new lessening
of American interest in Europe. As the 'funk and fear'
became weaker, so NATO became less solid. De Gaulle determined to break out of the integrated system of the alliance. In 1966 the General told NATO to move its bases off
French soil and the next year both NATO and its military
organization SHAPE moved to Belgium.

De Gaulle had realized that the immobility of the two
superpowers gave France the opportunity, with firm leadership, to play a much more flexible role, recruiting the support of smaller nations; he was reverting to an earlier idea of
France's role which had, in fact, been brilliantly expounded
by one of his first mentors, Charles Maurras, in 1910.[1] De
Gaulle became increasingly hostile to America and friendly
to Russia, while adopting an ambiguous defence policy, culminating in the cry of *'tous azimuts'* – her weapons in future
would face all directions. The doctrine was forcefully described by General Ailleret, the French defence chief in
1967, just before he died, in an article in *Revue de Défense
Nationale*.

The *détente* left NATO politically weaker. It had the
difficult problem of maintaining a unified system of defence
without appearing to perpetuate the division of Europe. A
good deal of anxious thought has been devoted since 1966 to
explaining the new role of NATO, particularly to a younger
generation who had grown up with little idea why it's there.
The second object of NATO – to contain Germany – was
much harder to explain when the first object – to resist
Russia – seemed less pressing. By 1969 members will be able
to leave the alliance, which adds to the sense of imper-
manence. In 1968 a dull but worthy report called the
'Harmel Exercise' was published – prepared at the suggestion of the Belgian Foreign Minister, Pierre Harmel – to

1. See the account of De Gaulle's foreign policy by Pierre Hassner in
Preuves, Paris, February 1968.

propose how the alliance should be adapted to the new situation; and a succession of rather negative speeches proclaimed a new role for NATO. 'There exists an artificial image of the alliance,' said the secretary-general, Manlio Brosio, 'as a belligerent military agency unwilling and unfit to create conditions of peace. This is a caricature of all that we stand for.'

The military commanders of NATO stressed more obscure dangers. Sir John Hackett, the most articulate British general, wrote to *The Times*: 'It is perhaps a little unfortunate that the stability in east-west relations which is so important upon both sides and everywhere so much hoped for should be commonly described by the term "*détente*". What we are engaged upon here in Europe is peace-keeping by military stabilization.' What Hackett meant, it seems, was that NATO is now more worried about its allies than its enemies: but that was an awkward basis for an alliance. Certainly the choice of fifteen hastily brought together since 1949 now looked very odd. The real core of NATO is made up of the United States, Britain and the common market countries. Greece and Turkey, both dictatorships, are not central to Western Europe's defence, and hate each other more than a conceivable NATO enemy: in Greece the colonels rule with the help of NATO arms, which is presumably not what General Hackett meant by 'peace-keeping by military stabilization'. Portugal was first brought in because she owned the Azores, which are no longer much wanted; her disgraceful African policies caused her allies to attack her at the UN, and she has threatened to leave NATO in protest. In Scandinavia, the neutralist movement appeared to be growing; the Danish Labour Party was doubtful about NATO, and in early 1968 an energetic 'Get Norway out of NATO' campaign was launched.

Perhaps more alarming to NATO was the radical student movement, which decided in mid-1968 to launch an international campaign against the alliance, in most countries in the West: for the new generation, NATO was a sitting target – American-dominated, outdated, bureaucratic, hypocritical; and NATO has not got a straightforward message with which to confute them. With all these dissident forces inside the alliance, NATO seemed unlikely to survive in its old form; and by the time of the Russian invasion of Czechoslovakia in August 1968 it was in evident disarray.

FIFTEEN ALLIES

In its political structure NATO is an assembly of fifteen scrupulously co-equal countries. It is an 'inter-governmental' organization, not (like the common market) a 'supranational' one; that is, it can only act through the official representatives of each country, reaching unanimous decisions, and is therefore not built for wider independent decision-making. The top body is the North Atlantic Council, who meet about seventy times a year round the big circular table in the NATO building; this is usually made up of the fifteen national ambassadors to NATO (each country has big delegations in the same Brussels building). But twice a year the foreign ministers meet and once (in 1957) heads of government. Each year one of the foreign ministers acts as president of the council, by a quaint procedure in alphabetical order. But the major figure of the council (as at the United Nations) is not the president, but the secretary-general, who is there all the time; and it is he who is the boss of the international bureaucracy and the scores of committees which inhabit the NATO building. There have been four secretaries-general; the first was Lord Ismay, the British general who was Churchill's chief-of-staff in the war; the second (1957) was Paul-Henri Spaak, the exuberant Belgian; the third (1961) was Dirk Stikker, a Dutch diplomat; the fourth (1964) the current one is Manlio Brosio, an Italian ex-minister and diplomat. The progression indicates the decreasingly martial role, and Brosio is an elegant embodiment of NATO tact, a tall smiling figure, every inch a diplomat; he is now seventy-one, and has been ambassador in turn to Russia, Britain, America and France. He can steer his fifteen colleagues decorously towards a pre-arranged agreement.

Brosio rules the political structure of NATO, with polite balance between the fifteen nations. In theory the tiny members are as important as the giants. Iceland has a population of 200,000 (less than Croydon's) and no army at all, and for a time it had a communist in its cabinet; Luxembourg has a stage army of 600 and no aeroplanes. Both of them have their own delegation and ambassador to NATO, and the same vote as the United States. Behind the NATO council, as a kind of inner ring, is the curious political body called Western European Union, which was set up in 1955, at Eden's instigation, as a kind of salvage operation from the ruins of the European Defence Community (see p. 55). WEU consists of the six common market members and Britain; they have headquarters in London, and an odd parliament which meets twice a year, supposedly to discuss defence questions; but they tend to get diverted, to the fury of the French,

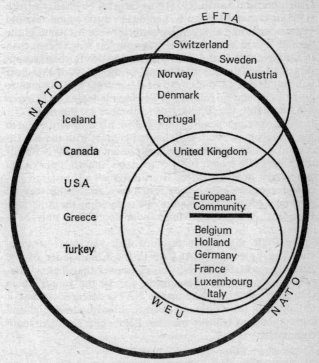

into discussing Britain's attempts to join the common market. The chart above shows the complicated overlaps between NATO and some other European groups.

Alongside this intricate political apparatus is the military apparatus, which reflects the stark truth of NATO – that the fighting power and expertise comes from America. The

T–H

European military headquarters of the Alliance, called SHAPE (Supreme Headquarters Allied Powers Europe) is in a separate building thirty miles away – likewise hurriedly built on Belgian soil. At the head of the European operations is a man called 'SACEUR' (Supreme Allied Commander Europe) who since the beginning of NATO has been American. The first (1950) was General Eisenhower; the second (1952) was General Ridgway; the third (1953) was General Gruenther; the fourth (1956) was General Norstad; the fifth (1963) is General Lyman L. Lemnitzer, a sixty-nine-year-old veteran who, like all his predecessors, made his name in the Second World War. SACEUR is now less magnificent than in the days of Norstad, who was, as Alastair Buchan has put it, a kind of 'Viceroy of Europe' in the midst of the great political decisions; the spread of the *détente* and the greater hold of civilians on military policy has made SACEUR seem less important, the secretary-general more so. But SACEUR is still a very independent power, with his own direct line to the Pentagon and with very limited contact with the NATO council. It has sometimes been suggested (even by Norstad) that SACEUR might, for a change, be English, but NATO people are not very keen. Constitutionally, American nuclear forces can only be controlled by a American; they all have dual control, and can only be released by the American President. A European commander could thus only be a figurehead.

SACEUR shares responsibility with two other strange-sounding potentates, SACLANT, the Commander of the Atlantic, and CINCHAN, who rules over the Channel. Between them they are responsible for all the forces which would, in wartime, make up the NATO defences – about a million men, four thousand aircraft, three hundred ships and a few thousand ballistic missiles. Below him are three main commands:

> Northern Europe (Kolsaas, Norway).
> Central Europe (Brunssum, Holland).
> Southern Europe (Naples, Italy).

Below them is the whole network of commanders and commands which make up the European defence system – with exotic names which baffle outsiders, including BALTAP (Baltic approaches) and COMNAUNORCENT (Commander Naval Forces Northern Area Central Europe).

DEFENCE AND INTEGRATION

Questioner: Why is there not more standardization in weaponry, or unity in strategic thinking?

General Norstad: There are three reasons. The first is the United States, the second is the United Kingdom, and the third is France.

It is remarkable that, after a twenty years' alliance, the European armies are as separate as ever. The table below shows the total European defence strength (not just NATO forces) compared to the American; but the sums do not indicate the real weakness of the Europeans – that their spending on defence is not co-ordinated or standardized. Among the thirteen European NATO countries there are twelve armies, eleven navies, eleven air forces, and twelve ministries of defence. Each of them orders its own equipment and makes its

DEFENCE STRENGTH OF NATO COUNTRIES[1]

Country	Armed Forces	Defence Budget*	Military Service (Months)
Belgium	99,000	501	12–15
Britain	427,000	5,450	Voluntary
Canada	102,000	1,589	Voluntary
Denmark	45,500	292	12–14
France	505,000	6,104	12–15 Selective
Germany	456,000	5,108	18
Greece	161,000	318	24
Italy	365,000	1,940	15
Luxembourg	560	7	Voluntary
Netherlands	129,000	898	16–18
Norway	35,000	320	12–15
Portugal	182,500	305	18–48
Turkey	514,000	472	24
United States	3,500,000	79,576	24 Selective

* $ million

own dispositions. Each of them reserves the right to plan its own defence system; the bigger countries, France and Britain, have never confined their defence planning to a European context. The two most easterly members, Greece and Turkey, have been close to war with each other. Allowing for the wastage and inefficiency that this produces, the European defence strength is not a quarter of the American, but nearer to a tenth.

1. Source: Institute for Strategic Studies: *The Military Balance*, September 1968.

It is not only the armies and navies which remain separate, each with their own commander-in-chief, but the whole system of buying or making arms, aircraft, or ships. At a time when the costs are rising on an exponential curve, the military attempts of European countries to go it alone look increasingly ridiculous. It has often been hoped that arms contracts could force European industry into more rational ways: but the arms now seem even less rational than industry.

NATO has constantly tried to standardize its members' equipment: but in no field is national obstinacy more apparent. Robert Rhodes James has said: 'The problem of standardizing equipment, even in national forces, is as old as the history of war. In 1915 two British units which had made a joint landing on the Gallipoli peninsula discovered that they were using different rifles and ammunition, with disastrous consequences. In 1951 the army of one NATO member-country had nine different types of rifle in service, requiring nine different types of ammunition. In November 1957, in the course of a bombing, navigational and reconnaissance competition organized by the US Strategic Air Command in Florida, it was found necessary to fly a hundred and seventy-six tons of special equipment from Britain in order to enable British aircraft to take part. It was said at the time by a British Air Ministry spokesman that "the wheel chocks constituted the only equipment common to the British and American aircraft taking part in the competition." '[1]

'Each one wants to keep his rifle, his machine-gun and his tanks and his shells,' lamented Spaak in 1960: 'each one, above all, wants his air force, his own national aircraft, which can only be used under restricted conditions.' 'Our armies employ fourteen different types of small arms ammunition,' said General Lecomte in 1961, 'While Russia and all the satellite countries have only one type of round for all small arms.'[2] One of the few successful European ventures was the patrol aircraft, the Atlantique, designed by the French Breguet company with propellers made by De Hav-

1. Robert Rhodes James: *Defence, Technology and the Western Alliance*, No. 3. Institute for Strategic Studies, 1967, p. 1 – a critical survey to which I am much indebted in this section.
2. *Ibid.*, p. 4.

illand in England the middle section made by Fokker in Holland, the rear fuselage and fins by Dornier in Germany. It went through ahead of time; but when it actually came to be produced, all but two of the six countries which had ordered it – France and Germany – decided that they didn't want it after all.

With the Europeans at odds, 'standardization' is apt to mean standardization to American equipment – as in other fields. The only really working European collaborations have been in producing equipment designed by American companies: the most expensive and celebrated case was the Starfighter plane, designed by the American Lockheed company, and then produced under licence in West Germany, Belgium, Italy and Holland: it became a 'NATO project', supervised by a special body called NASMO. About a thousand Starfighters were built in five years; but the deliveries were late, there was no proper system for repairs or spares, and each of the four countries insisted on its own assembly line. Finally, when the planes came to take the air, a succession of them crashed in West Germany, and nearly brought the Erhard government down with them: by August 1968, eighty-six had crashed. The Starfighters left bitter memories, not least because Lockheed's profit from licences was reckoned at over a billion dollars.

Still, other Euro-American joint adventures have gone ahead; in 1958 American Hawk missiles began to be built in Europe by a consortium including Thomson-Houston (France), Philips (Holland), Telefunken (Germany) and Finmeccanica (Italy) – with Britain staying out, building her own Thunderbird. There were great difficulties with the scattered factories, and with lack of trained people, but four thousand missiles were built. In 1962 the Sidewinder and Bullpup missiles were both built by European consortia: the Bullpup was shared by a curious foursome of Norway, Britain, Denmark, and Turkey, with Norway oddly enough (for political reasons) having the main share of production; in the end only five NATO countries bought Bullpups; the others preferred to buy a French missile, the AS–30.

The current orders for strike aircraft reveal the NATO divergencies at their most absurd; the Dutch are buying the American Northrop F5, the Italians are buying the Lockheed CL 985B, the Belgians and French are ordering the

Mirage V, and the Danes are buying the Swedish Saab Draken – which is from outside NATO altogether.

The weight of American technology and the relentless salesmanship present growing problems. The American government, not surprisingly, welcomes the flow of foreign currency which helps to offset their own colossal military expenditure in Europe. Since 1963 they have tried to set off at least half the cost of their overseas troops by arms sales, bringing in about one and a half billion dollars a year; in Europe American sales make up about twenty per cent of the arms business – the most sophisticated and promising part of it.

The American arms salesmen have become new bogies in Europe, particularly to the left. (European arms salesmen, on the other hand, are not able to sell much of their out-of-date wares in their own continent, and therefore concentrate on the much more disreputable traffic of selling them to the Congo, Nigeria or the Arab states.) The word 'arms' is misleadingly emotive, conjuring up high explosives and machine-guns; whereas the vast majority of American sales revenue comes from aircraft. It is obvious that, with or without salesmen, European governments would turn to American companies for their military aircraft, because they are more highly developed.

But the American pressure does make it still more difficult for European governments to collaborate. Just when a deal is about to be fixed, the man from Northrop or Lockheed or Boeing calls in, suggesting a still more advantageous joint venture; and we have seen how many European governments, faced with a choice of collaborating with an American or another European, feel safer with the former.

It is here that NATO comes obviously into conflict with the common market's hopes for industrial integration. A common alliance should in theory have helped to build up a western European defence industry, with other industries ranged behind it; but in fact NATO, by providing such a convenient market for American companies, is a disruptive force for Europe's own technology. It has only increased the centrifugal forces that we have seen elsewhere.

EUROPE WITHOUT AMERICA?

All discussion of European arms, with all that lies behind them – common aircraft, research, space projects – revolves round the more fundamental question of whether Europe will ever form its own defence system, independent or interdependent of America. The question has moved back and forth like a hot potato over the past fifteen years. Now, with the Americans preoccupied with the Pacific, with Russia reasserting her military domination, and with Britain again coming closer to Europe, it again looms: will Europe want to, or be able to, defend itself?

The Russian invasion of Czechoslovakia might be expected to generate a new sense of cohesion among the NATO countries, and certainly the fact that Russia could muster 650,000 troops at such speed to overrun a neighbouring state gave Western Europe an abrupt shock, and a sense of inadequacy: the Russians had replied to the Western policy of 'flexible response' in their own ruthless fashion, insisting that Russian troops must be up at the frontiers of Germany, and not trusting the Czechs to defend them. The invasion led to anxious rethinking at NATO, and some Europeans even saw it as providing a new spur to Western political unity. But at the time of writing this (September 1968) it seems unlikely that the Russian threat will be worrying enough to press the Western Europeans closer together, or to revive the old spirit of NATO in the fifties; for the real barrier between Czechoslovakia and the West remains the nuclear one, and Western countries still feel safe enough under the nuclear umbrella. Only West Germany is likely to be more seriously alarmed; but her only real guarantee would be her own nuclear deterrent, and that is something that her allies still dread, almost as much as the Russians'. Germany remains the confusing factor, the piece that does not fit into the jigsaw. The Russians still retain an obsessive fear of both parts of Germany which has scarcely diminished in the past twenty years. The Americans still dread that, without their presence, a flare-up in Germany could set off a frightened counteraction from Russia. The distrust on both sides perpetuates the cruel division of Europe and of Germany.

With more uncertainty about the continued American presence, there has been more talk of an independent European defence system. Many of the 'Europeans', even the least militant of them like Jean Rey or Monnet himself, are influenced by the realization that power now resides not in Europe but in Washington and Moscow. The only real remedy for that must be some form of supranational defence alliance, which cannot make sense if it does not have effective nuclear force.

Some prominent Europeans, including Franz-Josef Strauss and Edward Heath, advocate a European nuclear force, based on a pooling of Anglo-French resources. But that immediately comes up against the problem of German participation. An Anglo-French nuclear force would assume an American withdrawal; the German involvement with a nuclear force would immediately terrify both Russia and eastern Europe; NATO would probably split, with smaller powers seeking alliances with America; and the division of Europe would be still more firmly kept. Europe would find itself committed to vast new expenditure and new dangers, only to find its real power in the world still blocked. Not surprisingly few politicians develop the idea to its conclusion.

It may be that western Europe, still under the NATO alliance, could build up a European defence community parallel to the United States system – eventually developing its own general staff, its own weapons, and its own integrated technology: not attempting to integrate the nuclear efforts of Britain and France (which are probably not much use anyway), but in all other fields achieving genuine equality with the United States. As the defence policies of the European members diverge, so the plan becomes harder. But the withdrawal of American interest and troops might pull them together; and a European Defence Community of some kind is the only solid basis for all other communities – whether economic, technological, political or simply social.

The alternative is bleak; and is now happening. The European countries, lacking any common defence policy, sink back into their national defence systems and forces, building up not only their own armies and aircraft, but round them their own national technologies and research.

The results are increasingly absurd compared to the super-powers, turning European armies more rapidly into a kind of comic Balkan *imbroglio* – full of clever but ineffectual people, determined to preserve their national independence, but in the process becoming more dependent on America. The example of France, though it may fascinate the rest of Europe, will become increasingly misleading; since the French show of national independence is only plausible under the secure awareness of the American umbrella, and the escalating costs of aircraft, missiles and anti-missiles will make it impossible for a nation of fifty million to keep up with the race.

Europe's basic dilemma, of being caught between two super-powers, remains not very different from twenty years ago – less dangerous, but no more soluble. Its defence problem, however intricate in detail, is very simple in substance; that neither of the super-powers trusts Europe on its own; and Europeans do not trust each other – all with good reason. In this predicament, the only possibility of a reunited Europe will come by permission of the two super-powers, and is likely to depend on some kind of neutralization in central Europe (as proposed in the two Polish plans of Rapacki and Gomulka) guaranteed by the other powers. Europe has involved the other continents in its two catastrophic civil wars, and will still have to accept their conditions for the final peace.

In this straitjacket Europe cannot seriously hope to be a 'third force', or even a fourth force, in military terms. Even if it could, it is doubtful whether it would; for it seems to me that Europeans, after their appalling experiences, have lost much of their will to fight. Will Europe, then, be able to unite its energies without the ultimate motive of becoming a nuclear super-power? Will the ambition to have its own super-technology, super-industry, or perhaps super-government, be sufficient to overcome national rivalries, and to provide the new spur to unity? Will European laboratories, universities, hospitals or highways provide a substitute for aggressive ambitions, for a European army or a European bomb? It would be pleasant, for the pattern of this book, to be able to say Yes. But after surveying the divisive fields of energy, industry, technology, or finance, the frank answer can only be No.

A further question remains: can Europe, without its own defence and technology, still have a major influence in the world, in the field of ideas, civilization and societies? Can Europe acquire a unity – or at least a common character – of a more interesting and creative kind, in keeping with the other side of its history; not the history of self-destructiveness and aggression, but of an overflowing inventiveness in devising new kinds of society, new political ideas, new philosophies? It may be that the military domination of the two super-powers has given Europe too great a sense of inferiority, and that with both the super-powers facing vast new internal problems the attractions of a thoroughly unified continent will become less prominent. The emphasis in the future may be more on the problems of holding societies together, maintaining the consent of the governed in the face of the great technological structures; and in this situation Europe may find her very diversity gives her advantages. Europe may be able to reply to the American challenge in a different form, by questioning some of its assumptions; for technology is not the only commodity in demand. To quote one recent American critic: 'There was a time early in the past era when Europe looked to America for help: the time has come early in the next era for America to look to Europe for help.'[1]

1. Theodore Draper: 'World Politics, a New Era?' *Encounter*, August 1968.

Part Three

Chapter Eleven

Consumers

Cache-toi, objet!
Paris students' slogan, 1968

In the first chapters of this book I tried to show how the industrial and economic structures of Europe are gradually being pressed into new relationships and patterns – giant companies, joint technology, international finance. It is these material forces, in the absence of political and ideological ones, that have preoccupied the 'Europeans' in recent years in their search for ways of unifying the continent; and it is these that, for the time being, seem the most successful in breaking down frontiers. But these forces have two great limitations. First, as we have seen, they do not press Europe to stand alone, but rather to be more linked with America, more dependent on her and hence (probably) more like her. In none of these economic fields does a purely European movement at present make much sense. Secondly, these forces are not likely to excite the mass of the population, or to inspire anyone with high ideals. The Europe that will be forged by international corporations, banks, car companies or even trade unions may make the continent more prosperous, more efficient, more rational. But it will be a Europe of unprecedented materialism and boredom – particularly for the young. It will be Europe held together not by isms or ideals, but by cars, oil, detergents and computers. Without more passionate objectives, the pursuit of industrial growth imposes its own bleak system of government. The direction of the economy depends increasingly on a small group of technocratic men, whose decisions – given the need for sustaining growth rates, preserving stable currencies and com-

peting with rival industrial countries – are governed by
narrow technical choices. The greater the industrial competition between countries, the more each country is pressed
by its neighbours towards policies not of its own making; the
discussion of what kind of society people want, how it
should be shared, has seemed increasingly irrelevant to what
actually happens.

The 'consumer society' which revolves round the motor-
car has overwhelmed Europe – more suddenly than it en-
gulfed America – and transformed its politics. The socialist
parties, whether in Britain, Germany or France, have seen
their old ideologies undermined by the attractions of this
new bourgeois life, and the acceptance of the necessity for
growth has reinforced the tendency towards a 'consensus'
government. The left-wing parties have lost much of their
ideological content. Many prophets have forecast that the
preoccupation with property, spreading down the social
scale, would become a fixed feature of European politics,
dissolving the old class quarrels and perhaps virtually an-
nihilating the left: and the last decade has been an apparent
'depolitization' in western Europe.

But it would be doubly surprising if this change were to be
so permanent. In the first place, it is against all precedents of
continental history. There have been periods before of astonishing prosperity, followed by a sudden surge of indig-
nation and boredom, and ideological revolt: Europe,
through all its industrial revolutions and booms, has always
kept a fascination with political ideas. Secondly, for a
younger generation who have grown up in this consensus of
comfort, drained of high purposes and cut off from involvement outside Europe, the 'consumer society' is bound
to appear as a kind of padded cell of intolerable narrowness.

The economic and industrial machinery will continue to
extend its cogs and levers through Europe; but it is hard to
believe that the expansion of corporations or the march of
technology will, by their own momentum, dictate the real
shape and character of the New Europe. As the first consumers' rapture subsides, the questions of 'what kind of
Europe' is bound to come up to the front: technology, however sophisticated, cannot provide the answer by itself.

Of course there is nothing new about a preoccupation

with objects and comforts; what contemporary figures are more materialist or avaricious than the characters of Balzac or Galsworthy? To condemn the new household machines, in themselves, as corrupting and undesirable, is an untenable position in the context of a genuine democracy: they are only condemned by people who already have enough of them. But what has been specially gloomy about the European consumer society has been that, coinciding with the retreat from ideologies and the new indifference of Europe towards the rest of the world, the machines have seemed to become ends in themselves, a convenient solace for lost empires and causes. The European car has, as we have noted, become an object of much greater adoration than the American one, partly, I suspect, because it has nowhere particularly to go *to*: the preoccupation with gadgets and furniture that emerges from the European magazines is a sign that, having acquired comforts, people cannot stop talking about them. The consumer boom through Europe has suited the politicians well enough; they have nothing much else to be proud of. The catch-phrase of Harold Macmillan, 'you've never had it so good' was echoed in Germany: Sie haben es nie so gut gehabt. The Refrigerator, the Washing-machine and the Car almost seemed to have become political leaders themselves. It is the supremacy of the machines, rather than their existence, which marks the special nightmare of the contemporary consumer society, and which makes it (I believe) so stifling yet apparently inescapable for the new generation.

In the rest of this book I will look at some of the social and political forces that are changing, or reflecting, the shape of Western Europe. I begin with some of the new patterns of consumption, and communications, before passing to the new structures of politics and government.

SUBURBS AND DURABLES

The American exerts his egotism through the proprietorship of home and land and by family isolationism. The European accepts the anonymity of the big city, assured of the individuality of his intellect, less dependent upon material possession.

Humphrey Carver.[1]

1. Humphrey Carver: *Cities in the Suburbs*, 1962.

Whichever way you travel along the surface of Europe
you can easily be fooled. Along main roads, the continent
seems to consist of advertisements, garages and towns.
Along autostrade or auto-routes, there is nothing but fields,
forests and signboards. By railway, it turns out to be entirely
factories, sidings and the backs of cities. It is only by air, as
the plane circles down to land, that you can see plainly the
most spectacular change – the relentless spread of the
suburbs. The neat new houses huddle round the main roads
like fungus, or perched in neat criss-cross patterns; on the
edges are raw holes and clearings for yet more estates.
Flying above many of the cities, between Rotterdam and
The Hague, between Bradford and Leeds, between Frankfurt and Mainz, it is hard to see where one city becomes
another.

The landscape seems to cry out for space. The six
common market countries have a total population (188
million) just below that of America (200 million), and a
land-area one-eighth of America's; the density is 156 people
to the square kilometre, compared to 21 people in the United
States. The densities of European populations progress from
the emptiness of Scandinavia to the congestion of Holland
and Belgium, as this table shows:[1]

Country	Population (millions)	People per square kilometre
Sweden	8	17
Spain	32	63
Austria	7	87
France	49	90
Denmark	5	111
Switzerland	6	145
Italy	53	172
United Kingdom	55	225
West Germany	60	240
Belgium	10	312
Netherlands	12	372

Western Holland, the most crowded of all, in in danger of
becoming a single continuous suburb: in the whole country
there is only half an acre per person. The ring of three cities
(Rotterdam, The Hague and Amsterdam) called the 'Rand-
stad' is the magnet for the rest of the country, and desperate attempts are being made to lure people to the north. In
south-eastern Britain the problem is almost as acute, and the

1. *Basic Statistics of the Community*, 1967.

Channel Tunnel will encourage the extended urbanized strip from the Thames to the Channel and eastwards to the Rhine and the Ruhr. These agglomerate urban areas of north-western Europe, as they spawn their suburbs still further out into the country, will present future planners and politicians with insoluble problems – problems still worse than those of 'Boswash' (the urban strip from Boston to Washington). The inhabitants, as their wealth increases, will each want their own one-family house, garden, car, second car; the roads will cross and recross the cities; and this uniquely crowded corner will be right up against the one immutable fact of the continent – the shortage of land.

The centres of cities conspire to provide a false façade, and the tourist industry magnifies the illusion. The excitements of the Reeperbahn in Hamburg, of Montmartre or Soho, tell more about the fantasies of visitors than about the character and habits of the residents. The architecture of capital cities, treasuring their history and eccentricities, caricatures the national differences; and the city hall, the Hôtel de Ville or the Rathaus express a self-conscious patriotism.

The real rhythm of local life, away from bright lights and shop-windows, shows itself in suburbs. And what first appears is the likeness of one to another. Staying in suburbs of Hamburg, Brussels or Bonn, I found it often hard to remember that this was not England or America. There were the curious local habits, it is true, like the German ones of putting mattresses out of the window every morning or scrubbing the pavement in front of the house. But the rhythm of life seemed the same; the same small family units, with their car in the garage, to be washed on Saturday; the television set (sometimes showing the same English programmes); the neighbourhood cinema often, too, showing the same films; the same little status-symbols, garden objects, gnomes, old lamps, fancy letters on the gate; the same kind of supermarket at the end of the street, selling Daz, Ajax or Persil. Even the smells in the suburbs are the same: the unmistakable city smells of local food, sanitation or sweat give way to the supranational soaps, antiseptics and petrol fumes.

The sameness of suburbia, of course, has limitations.

Metropolitan intellectuals, particularly in America, have always enjoyed generalizing about its horrors – the conformity, joylessness, *embourgeoisement* or sheer boredom; but when they have actually gone into the suburbs, the generalizations have fallen apart. As David Riesman has written of America: 'The city is not necessarily the seat of urbanism, and the suburban way differs from the city way only at the polarities of each and is based on variables not entirely dependent on ecology or visible from a helicopter.'[1] Yet the suburbs do impose a new pattern of living and leisure, which is common to western Europe; and they remain a convenient symbol for the common retreat to a more home-based community. Above all they are the show-places for the sudden invasion of 'consumer durables', which have so abruptly changed living habits. This table shows the percentage of wage-earners' households in the common market that owned various services in 1963–64.[2]

	France %	Nether-lands %	Belgium %	Italy %	Luxem-bourg %	Germany %
Motor-Car	48	24	37	20	41	31
Motor-Cycle/Scooter	41	41	24	22	17	9
TV Set	37	57	48	55	27	51
Washing Machine	43	78	73	20	82	65
Refrigerator	55	36	36	57	70	68
Telephone	6	27	19	29	40	9
Domestic Servant	5	9	8	1	4	4
Garden	47	21	58	17	81	45

Some people have seen in this consumer boom the makings of a new common European consciousness; thus Uwe Kitzinger, summing up the evidence of the 1963 *Reader's Digest* Survey, wrote:

If this survey leads to any one important conclusion it is this: that the countries of Western Europe, Britain and the Six (if we except central and south Italy) now really look substantially alike. The homes of the Dutch have much the same durable goods as the homes of the north-west Italians, the homes of the Germans have much the same amenities as those of the British ... We may not have reached Salvador de Madariaga's ideal where Frenchmen think of 'our Goethe', Germans of 'our Chartres' and Englishmen of 'our Michelangelo' – though on the continent there is an increasing reluctance to think of these as

1. David Riesman: *Abundance for What?* Doubleday, 1964.
2. *Family Budgets, 1963–4*, EEC 1968.

'theirs'. We do on the other hand seem to have arrived at a more humdrum international affluence when Philips shavers, Grundig tape recorders, Beaujolais wines and Vespa scooters are accepted as natural items in each country's aspirations of ownership and consumption rather than as exotic imports from the outside world.[1]

The affluent Europe of shavers and tape-recorders may be a common pattern for the future. But for the bulk of the population it is still quite unattainable. The horrors of the 'consumer society' are so much talked about, conjuring up nightmares of luxury and leisure, that it is often difficult to remember that most of the population are still struggling to buy a car and to pay rent on a small flat. Even the sameness of cars and refrigerators conceals vast discrepancies in real standards of living. In both France and Italy housing has lagged far behind, and millions of households have cars but no bathrooms. In 1966 France had one car to every five people – a higher proportion than any country in Europe except Sweden (see page 282); yet less than thirty per cent of French homes had bathrooms, and more than twenty per cent had no inside running water. In Italy there was one car to nine people, one television set to eight people, but less than a single room for each head of population.

HORIZONTAL V. VERTICAL

In spite of the sameness of their refrigerators, cars or factories many Europeans can still maintain contrasted ways of life: it is hard to be confident of standardizations about 'post-industrial society'. In their pattern of living, London and Paris have always been at the two extremes. As you drive out of Paris along the tall grey boulevards, you pass seemingly endless rows of high apartment blocks, six or seven storeys high, with steep slate roofs and courtyards behind. The city does not straggle or dwindle into greenery, as London does, but keeps up its high skyline almost to the end: the so-called suburban Paris does not look suburban in the English sense, of being low and green. On the dingy fringe of Paris there are still high blocks of flats, rising abruptly from the jumble of surrounding houses, factories or junk-yards. Then quite suddenly Paris stops, and gives way

1. *Reader's Digest*: 'The New Europeans: A Commentary on Products and People', 1963.

to fields and farms and cows; only ten miles outside the city, even now, you can look across wheat fields with not a house in sight. The statistics (for once) support the traveller's impression; the density of the City of Paris, even including its two big woods, is 114 people per acre, almost three times the density of Inner London (43 per acre). Even the Paris suburbs contain 31 people to the acre – not far off from the crush of Inner London.[1]

The contrast has always been remarked by travellers. Hippolyte Taine, travelling to London, was astonished to see the low self-contained houses stretching all the way to Hampton Court. Paris and London both began as Roman cities, and in the Middle Ages were huddled inside their city walls. From Elizabethan times London spilt over into the villages, and railways, buses and underground took people farther and farther out. But Paris right up to 1860 kept inside wider fortifications, commemorated in the names of the 'Portes' at the end of the Metro lines. The Paris skyline rose higher and higher; the apartment, ever since the Middle Ages, has been the normal unit of housing in Paris, even for the very rich – as in other European cities, including Edinburgh. But in Victorian London even the poorest families in back-to-back houses had their own front-door, and the 'flat' only came in the late nineteenth century, with the extremes of Peabody dwellings for the poor and Queen Anne's Mansions for the rich. Even then the idea of flats never really became popular, and Londoners preferred a suburban semi-detached to an urban flat.

The extreme urbanism of Paris stems from interlocking causes – the lack of transport, the lack of urban investment, the military past, the extreme centralization of French authority. The general pattern of Paris is repeated, less spectacularly, in other cities in France, Italy and Spain; the self-enclosed city remains a Latin phenomenon, which is even perpetuated in South America, in contrast to North America. Ancient Rome, with its high walls and multi-storeyed houses, was the prototype for modern Rome which still, in spite of its huge overspill of suburbs, has the same break between town and country. it is the fear of the countryside, as much as the love of cities, that marks the Latins. 'Le weekend', spreading through the continent since the war, has

1. For further comparisons, see Peter Hall: *The World Cities*, pp. 61, 65.

helped to tame the countryside; but Latin weekenders prefer to live in clusters, in small towns or seaside resorts. The English, and to a lesser degree the Dutch and Germans, have never really accepted their exile from the country – in spite of, or because of, their being the most urbanized people in Europe (eighty per cent of the British live in urban areas). The English rural fantasies show themselves in the eccentricities of suburban architecture, the love of golf, and the refusal to plan city centres seriously, but above all in the quantity of gardens. Seventy-two per cent of the British have gardens, compared to only sixteen per cent of the Italians: forty-six per cent of the British have lawnmowers, compared to one per cent of the Italians.[1]

The post-war expansion of Paris has broken out into new suburbs, which have become a favourite subject for satirists and writers. Many of them are proudly vertical: modern French architecture is still much influenced by Le Corbusier, the prophet of tall building, dedicated to the 'intensity of life': clusters of small skyscrapers have risen up round Paris, close up to each other as if to shelter from the rough country weather. This contrast between French and English habits has been fundamental and full of consequences, affecting the patterns and pursuits of leisure, and the rhythm of daily life. The difference between the sense of tension in Paris, and the relaxation and expansiveness of London is psychological as well as architectural. It is difficult to resist correlating the crowded Paris flats with the continuing passion for street demonstrations; and the rows of small London houses and gardens with the phlegmatic conservatism of the English workers.

Yet even this traditional cross-Channel contrast is beginning to diminish, and Parisians are beginning to accept and even to welcome the horizontal suburb. You can see signs of it in the spate of advertising in *Figaro* or *Le Monde*, showing low bungalow houses and gardens: 'What could be more intimate, what nicer, more friendly, than a log fire, *at home?*' The most surprising sign is the success of the American Levitt Company, the arch-suburbanites, who in 1963 moved into two countries with 'underdeveloped' housing – Puerto Rico and France. I called on the President of Levitt France, Andrew L. Lorant, inside one of those all-American

1. *Reader's Digest* Survey, 1962.

Paris buildings, in an office with thick curly carpets, soft-spoken secretaries and pictures of Levitt palaces on the walls. He insisted that he did not come to France as missionary for the American way of life, but he talked with fervour; he explained how Levitt's bought land south-east of Paris in the unfashionable direction, and planned their first estate on American lines – putting houses four to the acre, without hedges and even with restrictive covenants to stop hedges being built. The houses are copied from the American ones; the 'Arcy' is the American Ardsley, a steep-roofed bungalow with a big sitting-room and a built-in garage. For the French the kitchen, of course, was cut off from the dining-room, the bathroom had to be bigger for the bidet, the refrigerator was smaller and there was no ready-made kitchen unit. But there was no question of the traditional cellar. The houses were bought, nevertheless; and other builders soon started copying Levitt's.

Mr. Lorant enjoys the sociological changes that the new houses induce. 'There's much *less* privacy in these garden communities than in a tall apartment block – my French friends can't understand that. In the apartments the people never need meet each other at all; but as soon as they're in the country people can see everything their neighbours do – their cars, their friends, their mail, their children. They *have* to join committees' (at this, to underline his point, a man from the gas company rang up, to complain about a recalcitrant Levitt resident who wouldn't join in the home-owners' association). 'Though I don't tell them so, we're teaching the French a lesson in government. You know they thrive on anarchy, but on our estates they really feel part of the community: they can't paint their house pink without asking their neighbours.' He even sees the French Levittowns as a democratizing force; in one street, he says, there is a duke living next to a self-made Corsican, and their children actually *play* together. It is all going so well that Levitt's want to expand elsewhere in Europe: they do not see much scope in England or Germany, where mass suburb-building is already highly developed, but they have their eye on Scandinavia. In any case, they reckon that from now till A.D. 2000 both in America and Europe the total number of houses will have to be doubled. 'We're not just in the housing business,' Mr. Lorant likes to explain; 'we're in the shelter industry.'

The low houses of Levitt and others are still only for a prosperous minority; the mass of Paris workers can only afford to live in an apartment block, and the fastidious bourgeoisie of Passy or Neuilly would feel lost and isolated. The plans for Paris in A.D. 2000 visualize a row of sky-scraper satellite cities. But the demand for a house of one's own is steadily growing, in France as elsewhere, and will not be easy to resist, as the consumer society gathers its own momentum, with luxuries turning into necessities. It would be rash to suggest that bricks and mortar will in themselves diminish the French passion for anarchy; but suburban estates will make Paris a duller, and perhaps less explosive city.

FOOD

The destiny of nations depends on what and how they eat.
Brillat-Savarin, The Physiology of Taste

The oldest of all consumer industries is food, and the kitchen still reflects most European problems. The proportion of the family budget spent on food, drink and tobacco is still colossal. These were the proportions in manual workers' households in 1963/4:[1]

Italy	49.1 per cent
France	45.4 per cent
Germany	42.6 per cent
Belgium	39.2 per cent
Holland	37.2 per cent

But as the flight from land continues and family incomes rise, so eating becomes less important and other things more; even the powerful tradition of French farmhouse cuisine is being broken up by the movement of labour. Anyone can observe the new generation of Europeans are noticeably thinner, taller and more alike than their predecessors: the images of the jolly fat Italian or the strapping mädchen are very out of date. As one European sociologist, Leo Moulin, has put it:[2] 'Fashions, sport, fear of coronary thrombosis, the desire (and possibility) to appear and remain young for a long time, the continual lengthening of the average life-span

1. EEC: Basic Statistics, 1967.
2. *European Community,* January 1967.

together with the determination to grow old gracefully, the heavy demands of present-day work, and the strains of car-driving all cause modern man to bridle his appetite constantly, at least in the North Atlantic countries. For the first time in history the gnawing fear of hunger, that old bugbear of the human race, has given way to the equally acute opposite fear of cholesterol.'

Tinned food, dried food, pickled food and frozen food are all beginning to standardize eating, both within countries and within the continent. The international companies – Findus (Nestlé) and Birdseye or Iglo (Unilever) – wage war with tins and packets across the western continent. Talking to these food industrialists, one glimpses the battles of the kitchens. Countries extend very different welcomes to new foods. Sweden is the most open-minded (they have even taken to an 'instant breakfast' from America); Britain, Germany and Switzerland are not far behind. Northern Italy is very receptive (spaghetti after all was one of the first processed foods), but southern Italy very suspicious. France is still the most resistant. The Germans (like the Americans) are much the most faddish, very keen on supposedly health-giving foods such as decaffeinated coffee or non-fatty margarine. Frozen peas, the top vegetables in Britain or Sweden, give way to frozen spinach in Germany and Holland. There are still plenty of foods which do not travel outside their own country, like German lentil soup, Dutch *loempia,* or Scots faggots; and the division between Teutonic and Latin tastes remains very deep. But movements are quickening: spaghetti and other pastas are spreading northward quite fast; cheese is becoming very mobile, and the same kind of processed Emmenthaler sells in Germany and Italy. New sub-food from America has swept quickly across Europe; broiler chickens invaded Britain, Holland and Germany. One food expert explained: 'Marketing and processing goes from west to east, and tastes go from east to west'; frozen pizza, for instance, is now second only to frozen orange juice in America.

If there were to be a 'new European meal', equally acceptable to all countries, I was told it would probably begin with minestrone, go on to steak and chips with mixed vegetables, then to vanilla ice-cream with strawberry sauce, then cheddar or Edam cheese. But if there is one single new European food, it is – frozen fish-fingers. First invented in 1955, the fingers swept first through Britain, then to the continent, with special success in land-bound countries like Austria, where fresh fish takes three days from the coast. The fingers are the same everywhere, fish sticks in Belgium, bastoncini in Italy, fischstäbchen in Germany.

If Europe is to be united on the basis of fish-fingers, one might think, it had better not be united at all. Of all the nightmares dreamt up by the anti-supranationalists, the most alarming is the vision of Europe, like North America, suffering the same tasteless foods from coast to coast, munching cole-slaw, T-bone steaks or thousand-island sauce all the way from Oslo to Torremolinos. Sometimes in aeroplanes the nightmare comes true. But away from the mass-produced foods, the European tastes remain stubbornly separate. Wurst hardly moves out of Germany, pâté does not get down to Italy. Food everywhere is the evidence of roots. The people who have in the past been most drastically uprooted by industry, like the British and the Germans, have the dreariest diet; the most embedded in the land, like France and Italy, have the most individual. The sheer contrasts in climate enforce a variety, and the choice of diet remains astonishingly national, as the table below, taken from the common market survey, shows.

Habits still conform closely with traditional clichés, with the French as champion wine-drinkers, Belgians the top potato-eaters, and Dutch the champion milk-drinkers. As *Le Monde* commented (27th December, 1967): 'The common

Amounts of food consumed annually by household[1]

Products	Germany	France	Italy	Holland	Belgium	Luxem-bourg
Bread (kilos)	84	108	122	86	122	94
Meat (kilos)	53	56	43	37	58	72
Milk (litres)	100	103	87	153	111	122
Eggs	248	170	222	215	198	254
Butter (kilos)	10	10	3	2	13	13
Fresh fruit (kilos)	51	52	59	54	50	41
Fresh vegetables (kilos)	26	46	40	42	29	32
Potatoes (kilos)	120	102	34	130	190	165
Wine (litres)	7	116	95	2	6	18
Beer (litres)	46	28	2	11	54	37

1. *Study of Family Budgets in 1963–4*, published by the statistical office of the common market, 1967.

market in agricultural products has hardly affected the specific national culinary traditions.' Historically, it is not surprising; food has always travelled more slowly than other things. The potato, which was brought to England by Sir Walter Raleigh in 1586, was used only as an ornamental plant in France until the end of the eighteenth century, when a chemist called Parmentier in 1773 wrote an essay on the potato as food. Wars (as with the other technologies we have seen) are the main incentive to innovation: sugar beet spread through France during the English blockade of Napoleon, but was not developed in Britain until the German blockade during the First World War. Today, in spite of deep-freezers, working wives, supermarkets and a common agricultural policy, kitchens in the common market remain bastions of national character. Not only food, but the apparatus of kitchens defies standardization; the kettle, which was known in Tudor England has never really caught on in Germany or Italy. Matches are frail and waxen in Italy, thick and well-timbered in Germany. Even corkscrews and tin-openers have their national twists.

The kitchen is slowly losing its dominant position in the house, even in Latin countries – as lunch hours diminish, wives go to work, and quick-lunch snack-bars take the place of long lunches at home. No doubt many housewives will breathe a sigh of relief. But the total industrialization of food is one of the most doubtful of all material blessings. The kitchen, having been thankfully forsaken as the prison of drudgery, may thankfully be restored as the sanctum of creative leisure. Britain offers a special warning; having so thoroughly abandond its country cooking in the last century, housewives now have to painfully relearn the secrets of home cooking from continental recipes. It may be that a synthesis will be found between the benefits of mass-production and the special splendours of home cooking; but watching the uniform rows of frozen packets and tins lining up in the continental supermarkets, and succulent colour advertisements spreading through the magazines, it is clear that the battle for individuality will be a tough one.

CONSUMER NIGHTMARE

Each country, of course, has its own version of the consumer nightmare. It was in Germany, out of the post-war chaos of the cities, that the new world grew up most suddenly and immaculately, enveloping its inhabitants with all the trappings: staying in flats in German suburbs we became very aware of it. The traditional pride of the hausfrau – a justified cliché – was more intense after the years of desperate shortages, when a house could be found; for refugees from the east it was still more intense. The special relationship of a German family to their house or flat is unmistakable. A visitor is shown around the house as soon as he comes in; the objects, furniture and gadgets are laid out as if in a contemporary shop-window, or a Victorian front parlour. Young married couples when they move must always 'sich einrichten' – set themselves up – by buying all their suites, carpets and consumer durables, so that the scene will be ready for visitors. The completed stage leaves little room for development or disruption, and it helps to give that frozen look to German homes. There are no old sofas, junk or messy corners: and in this formal stage, people move uneasily, and the objects seem to acquire a power of their own.

The precision and tidiness of German homes seems to extend through all classes. Even among intellectuals or artists, we found little signs of disarray or defiance of the domestic discipline; the objects and décor were different, but the museum-look was the same. White walls, sharp rectangles and Scandinavian purity of style all help to make intellectuals' flats look more like offices, or vice versa. The proverbial passion for cleaning and polishing remains entrenched: one German friend, when she came to visit our untidy flat in Bonn, would automatically but apologetically begin cleaning up the kitchen: 'I just can't stop myself.'

The trouble is, there is less scope for cleaning. German housewives, more than any others, have been afflicted by the problems of the sheer comfort of the modern suburb. The hard-working traditions of scrubbing and polishing have been undermined by the new machines and new cleaners, and advertising men enjoy describing their difficulties of selling labour-saving devices: the most successful car-polish (Johnson's), I was told by an ad-man in Frankfurt, is the one that needs most muscle. An advertisement for a German wax that made polishing look much quicker had no success until the rider was added: 'So that you can do more cooking.' But even cooking, with frozen spinach and tinned spaghetti, takes far less time. German women after the age of forty, with their children away, suffer from alarming neuroses of boredom and unwantedness: 'An older woman can feel particularly alien in an environment in which everything works so perfectly, as today . . .' explains Professor Schulte[1] of the Tübinger Nervenklinik, 'even more so when the washing and patching, rinsing and potato-peeling are withdrawn from her.' In a single generation the hausfrau has seen her mother's values overturned; a job in an office, from being a harsh necessity, may now be prescribed as a therapy, to rescue her from the boredom of the home.

The sterile world of German suburbs, for those who were brought up in the earlier chaos, must remain something of a miracle, which must at all costs be preserved. But it would be surprising if the boredom had not produced a fierce reaction from the younger generation. The German students have not actually forsworn the benefits of washing machines and cars: but behind their fury with the 'fat-belly thinking' of their elders lies a deep-rooted sense of frustration and immolation in the luxurious prison of the consumer society, without knowing how to escape from it.

France appears to show a complete contrast. The way of life of the French bourgeoisie in the cities, living in small flats in dark old buildings, without gardens and with antique plumbing, has always struck foreigners as peculiarly uncomfortable, even defiantly austere; the hard straight chairs, the dim lighting and the lack of fresh paint all conspire to spread gloom and to keep the twentieth century in its place: it would seem the complete opposite of the German acceptance of every new comfort. But the French bourgeoisie have willingly, if more discreetly, succumbed to the new gods. Even the advertisements in *L'Humanité*, the communist daily, now present luxurious visions of the consumer society. The change in ten years is well expressed by the difference between the old weekly magazine *L'Express*, with its passionate polemics and arguments through the Algerian war, and its reincarnation since 1964, as an imitation of

1. Quoted in *Spiegel*, 18th December, 1966.

Time, preoccupied with money, cars, fashions and holidays.

The French intellectuals, freed from their passionate ideologies, have joined the material pursuit. A novel called *Les Choses*, by Georges Perec, 'a history of the sixties', described the lives of a young couple, both market-researchers, who lived in a world preoccupied by special objects and status: 'their flats, studios, attics, bedsitters in ancient houses, in chosen parts of Paris (Palais Royal, Place de la Contrescarpe, St. Germain, Luxembourg, Montparnasse), all looked alike: one found the same filthy sofas, the same so called "rustic" tables, the same tangle of books and records, the same old pots, old bottles, old glasses, old jugs – filled haphazardly with flowers, or pencils, or small change, or sweets.' The couple, frustrated in money-making, try to escape to Tunis to get away from it all, but finally settle down to public relations in Bordeaux, trapped in their material cage.

LEISURE

Work is more fun than fun.

Noël Coward

Leisure may become what workers recover from at work.

David Riesman

Of all the alarms sounded from America about the consumer society, the most worrying are the warnings about leisure. The whole point of the mass-production of consumer durables is that they remove drudgery, and give new scope for individual leisure; yet the industrial and marketing machine that provides the durables threatens to move over into mass-producing the patterns of leisure itself. The appeals of the mass media and advertising have become so enveloping and so seductive, and mass-production has invaded so many leisure activities – holidays, food, television, films – that to retain or recover a creative and private style of leisure requires a constant opposition and questioning.

The fear has been growing in America that the industrial propaganda will leave no room for independent expression; 'the danger to liberty,' writes Professor Galbraith, 'lies in the subordination of belief to the needs of the industrial system

... If we continue to believe that the goals of the industrial system – the expansion of output, the companion increase in consumption, technological advance, the public images that sustain it – are co-ordinate with life, then all our lives will be in the service of these goals ... If, on the other hand, the industrial system is only part, and relatively a diminishing part, of life, there is much less occasion for concern.'[1]

The ability to keep the industrial system in its place, and not to allow it to move over into private life, should be a less worrying problem for Europe, with its strong traditions of privacy, its firm roots, its old patterns of leisure. The American authors of *The Year 2000*, surveying the problems of growing leisure and alienation, are envious of the European traditions: they contrast the American businessman, who justifies his rest or play mostly in terms of returning to do a better job, with the European who seems to 'enjoy his vacation as a pleasure in its own right'. 'In the post-industrial society that we are describing, in continental Europe the middle and upper classes could in effect, return to or adopt the manner of the "gentleman".'[2] But looking round the continent I do not find signs of an incipient Europe of Gentlemen. The pressures towards uniformity increase, without very much effective resistance: the flight from the land makes individuality harder to maintain; the leisure industries, led by the tourist industry – as we will note in the following chapters – become increasingly competitive, highly-organized, mass-produced. And anyway Europe is up against the same old problem – that there is not *room* for everyone to be a gentleman.

In the meantime among all classes the 'leisure problem', as it is gloomily described, is gradually growing in Europe. In the last ten years the hours in the European working week have gradually fallen. In Germany, where the unions are most insistent on a forty-hour week, the average hours per week went down from 45.6 in 1959 to 43.7 in 1964. The legend that the Germans work longer than others dies hard; in fact the British put in longer hours. These were the average hours per week worked in manufacturing:[3]

1. J. K. Galbraith: *The New Industrial State*, Houghton Mifflin, 1968.
2. Herman Kahn and Anthony J. Wiener: *The Year 2000*, Macmillan, 1968, p. 213.
3. *UN Year Book*, 1966 (ILO).

	1965	*1966*
Holland	46.1	46.1
France	46.1	45.9
Great Britain	46.9	45.0
Switzerland	45.4	44.8
Germany	45.6	43.7
Belgium	40.9	40.4

A more fundamental contrast shows itself in the matter of holidays; and here there is a spectacular difference between America and Europe, with Britain (as so often) somewhere between. The *minimum* annual holiday with pay in America is only a week: only Portugal, Switzerland and Canada have such a low minimum. All other European countries have at least a two-week minimum, France and Scandinavia have a minimum of three weeks, and Sweden has four weeks.[1] But in most cases the minimum has been left well behind; this table shows how metalworkers' holidays with pay compare. after five years' service, in different European countries:[2]

Country	*Vacation Days on Pay*	*Paid Statutory Holidays*	*Total*
Austria	24–30	13	37–43
Finland	25–27	11	36–38
Sweden	24	10	34
Germany	22	10–13	32–35
Norway	24	8–10	32–34
Italy	14–18	16–17	30–35
Luxembourg	19–26	10	29–36
Belgium	18	10–13	28–31
Denmark	18	9	27
Netherlands	15	5–7	20–22
Switzerland	12–24	8	20–32
Great Britain	10	6–8	16–18

In France the left has steadily pressed for longer holidays; the two-week holiday was one of the reforms of Léon Blum's Popular Front government in 1936, and the three-week holiday was achieved twenty years later by Guy Mollet. The four weeks was achieved by Renault workers in 1963,[3] and quickly spread to the other big industries. In 1968 four weeks was about to become compulsory; now the senior Renault workers get five weeks.

1. Source: *Working Holidays with Pay*, ILO, Geneva, 1964.
2. Source: International Metalworkers' Federation.
3. See chapter 6.

The month of August hardly exists for continental industry; the furnaces go out, the production lines stop, the shops close down, the theatres go on tour, and the population moves out in a furious cavalcade to the south. And the public holidays, both religious and secular, pop up on the continent far more frequently than in Britain: in Germany there are ten to thirteen (according to Land), in Italy sixteen or seventeen a year. In Rome in May there is a holiday each week. With a holiday on a Thursday or Tuesday, many office workers can often 'make a bridge' to the weekend, to give a four-day exodus – so that the week can have more holidays than work days. The British cult of the long weekend has been overtaken, to leave British workers lagging behind with often only six public holidays a year. British trade unions have always been much more interested in pressing for wages than for longer holidays, and here again, the popular image of the British worker is misleading: he works longer hours than many continental counterparts, has shorter holidays, earns less – yet still has difficulty in competing.

Long holidays clearly have important political consequences, though it is not easy to define them. One viewpoint was stated in 1967 by Gilbert Trigano, president of the Club Méditerranée, the chain of French holiday camps,[1] writing in *Communauté Européenne*. 'Compared to their neighbours, the Frenchman has the most holiday and the least leisure: the Englishman has the most leisure and the least holiday,' explained M. Trigano. 'In France we have learnt to go on holiday, perhaps because our leisure organization was not ready – it is not altogether ready at the moment, and if we left all our work at 5 p.m. we would find it very difficult to occupy our evenings.' M. Trigano predicts that in ten years' time Europeans will all be having six weeks' holiday, rather than a shorter working week, because 'it is impossible to concentrate on an important job for only thirty-two hours a week', and thinks that long holidays (provided they are staggered) are much more economical and healthy and could be very democratic: 'in a bathing costume, there is no longer the boss, the executive, the worker; in ten years' time, we will see bosses, workers, farmers, employees, mixing in the same holiday places – whatever the desire of millionaires

1 See p. 265.

to be among themselves on the Aga Khan's beaches in Sardinia, and in spite of the efforts of some big corporations like Fiat and Volkswagen who try to organize the workers' holidays in a vacuum.'[1]

The prospect of workers enjoying long holidays on the Tahiti-like beaches of the Club Méditerranée does not please the old school of French trade unionists – particularly since they run their own austere camps – and Trigano's article set off a lively controversy. Many of them believe[2] (as one communist unionist, M. Barjonet, put it) that 'man makes himself through work', and another unionist described the clubs as 'the excuse which capitalist societies provide to support insupportable conditions'. The communist unions are, of course, the most insistent on 'workers' holidays'; but all the big unions are agreed on giving priority to a shorter working week of forty hours, as opposed to a fifth week of holiday. They want shorter working days à la Russe and longer weekends, to restore the workers after the rhythm of the factories, and to enrich their daily lives. For the student rebels, the escapist holidays of the Club Méditerranée are a symptomatic of the industrialization of leisure, the substitutions of mass-fantasies for individual spirit. One slogan at Nanterre proclaimed: 'See Nanterre and live: See Naples with the Club Méditerranée, and die'.

It is not perhaps surprising that it is in France, more than anywhere, that the complaints against the consumer society and its encroachments on leisure have been most vociferous; for it is there that leisure has been most valued, and the new industrialization has been most sudden. A protected country, with slow and eccentric local patterns, has been thrown into the currents of international competition, at the deep end; the peasants have suddenly become townspeople, the soldiers' sons have become industrial managers, restaurants have been superseded by quick-lunch bars. *Les Choses* have taken the place of ideas. The increase in holidays, though spectacular, has been accompanied by a much greater pressure in the rest of the year; 'if France is the country which owns most cars (wrote *Le Monde*, 1st July, 1968), it is also the one which can least make use of them. If she has overtaken most countries in the extension of holidays . . . she also

1. *Communauté Européenne*, June 1967.
2. *Le Monde*, 17th and 18th July, 1967: 'Les Syndicats et les Vacances'.

has the poorest daily leisure, and it is perhaps in France, at least in the cities, that escapist holidays, even future escapist parks, are the most denounced as alibis for a degradation of daily life . . .'

The revolt against the 'manipulation' of the consumer society, and particularly of leisure, has been a common theme of Western students' movements; but in France the students' questioning has overflowed into a national debate, fed by speeches, clubs and newspaper articles. It may be that France will be the first Western country seriously to try to check or counteract the pressures of advertising.[1] The French students have pressed home the point – for the time being at least – that 'the industrial system is only part of life'; and that the individual must assert himself constantly against the pressures of conformity. The character of the revolt itself, with its happenings, slogans and romantic rhetoric, was a defiant gesture against these pressures; summed up in the slogan: *'dessous les pavés, c'est la plage'* – the beach is under the paving stones.

Few people seriously believe that the consumer society could or should be destroyed; what its critics hope for is to keep it in its place. In the commercial enthusiasm for the unification of Europe, there is a real danger that the machine will ignore and submerge the individuality and diversity which is still Europe's pride; and a united continent, however desirable, cannot have real health or stability, if there are not strong balancing forces on the local levels.

1. See Pierre Drouin in *Le Monde*, 11th June, 1968.

Chapter Twelve

Travellers and Tourists

What I gained by being in France was learning to be better satisfied with my own country.

Dr. Johnson

No convention on tourism is complete without a fulsome reference to 'increasing international understanding'. Nineteen sixty-seven was designated 'International Tourist Year' by the United Nations, and U Thant opened it with a special reference to the role that tourism can play in 'promoting peace by fostering understanding'. The statistics are splendid, particularly for Europe. In 1965 a hundred and fourteen million tourists in the world arrived in foreign countries; three-quarters of them arrived in Europe. The number of international tourists grows by about twelve per cent a year. Tourism according to OECD, is 'one of the most spectacular features of the "leisure civilization" which is gradually developing in the western world'.

Tourism has become very big business. In the post-war years it has become a heavy industry, on the scale of steel or cars, and a much bigger earner of foreign currency. For Spain, Italy or Greece it is the largest source of foreign exchange, and even for Britain it is the fourth. Faced with this huge new source of income, no government can afford to look down on the business; questions of hotel bathrooms, beach umbrellas and icecream sales are now discussed by ministers of tourism with solemn expertise. Before the war the tourist industry was widely regarded as being unmanly and frivolous; d'Annunzio complained that Italy was becoming a 'honeymoon country'. 'Nowadays no one thinks that tourism is servile: that was a form of nationalism,' the Italian Minister of Tourism, Signor Corona, said to me: 'Ever since the recession in 1963 we've had to take tourism very seriously; after all, it earns twice as much foreign currency as Fiats.'

Tourism has blazed new trails, as armies used to; in Spain, Italy, Greece and much of eastern Europe, new road systems have opened up the country, first to tourists, and then to industry and locals. Much of tourism is a nationalized industry, a key part of national planning; only a few individuals, like the Aga Khan in Sardinia or Edmond de Rothschild at Mégève, are rich enough to build whole resorts and set the style. In Greece or Italy the governments are the style-setters. In Languedoc, west of Marseilles, the French government is killing the mosquitoes and building six big resorts, to hold nearly a million tourists. In eastern Europe, a whole new seaside culture has sprung up in the last few years: the governments are patrons of leisure. Tourists from the west multiplied from half a million in 1962 to nearly two million in 1965 – the most visible breach in the iron curtain.

The scale of the industry and the huge stake of governments and big companies are in themselves alarming to those who hope that leisure can bring individuality. 'There is a tendency already perceptible in France,' wrote Le Monde in June 1968,[1] in the wake of the revolt against the consumer society, 'towards making holidays like automobiles, towards considering the holiday-maker not as a worker who has stopped working, but as a consumer who has begun to consume. ... We are thus moving to "passive holidays" where, whatever he thinks, the individual is not the master of the date of his holiday (imposed by the industrialists) nor of the cost (largely imposed by the state transport industries) nor of the content, which is dictated by the imperatives of mass production, and conveyed by the suggestions of advertising.'

The mass-production of tourism clearly limits the extent to which it can really improve understanding between countries. The obsession of the new mass tourist is not to see a new country, but to find two commodities – the sun and the sea – with least possible inconvenience: the huge migration of Germans to Spain and Italy is not primarily caused by an interest in Latin culture, but by the shortness and coldness of Germany's coastline. The trainloads, planeloads and coachloads of tourists who rush through Europe are sealed off

1. J. F. Simon: 'Les vacances vont devenir des marchandises': Le Monde, 2–3rd June, 1968.

from the countryside, and their destinations are well prepared to receive them with their own language, their own food, and their own mealtimes.

The insulation is getting thicker. The new 'tourist centres' which account for much of the current expansion are growing up along empty coastlines, built from scratch on previously uninhabited land. Here there is not a chance of getting to know the inhabitants; there are no inhabitants. Everything and everyone, including tourists, waiters and cooks are brought from outside. I stayed in one of the newest of them, a hotel on the Gargano peninsula, on the Adriatic coastline of Italy, built as the first part of a tourist complex by the Italian government agency, ENI. We approached it by half an hour's journey on a switchback road carved through thick woods. The hotel, like a bright white honeycomb, stood out from the bare hillside of pines and rocks. It was very like an ocean liner; three sun-bathing decks looked over the sea, with swimming pools, and a band. Inside were wide promenades, humming with air-conditioning, where guests could walk and watch each other; a shop, a bar and a barber removed any need to go ashore. In the evening a pop group called 'Noi I Gentlemen' in purple uniforms were wailing English tunes; a large outing of Italians from Agip, the oil company in Rome, danced frenziedly, while a party of German 'Scharnow' tourists watched and discussed. It had all the determined do-nothing routine of shipboard life, worshipping the sun and sea. The two groups, turning in their own circles, never touched. To find an Italian village was a major expedition.

TOURISMUS

For years the dominant European tourists have been the Germans, far outnumbering English or Americans. The English (the experts say) are still the most pioneering; the Scandinavians are the first to arrive, the most passionate sun-seekers; the Americans are still the most hectic. But the Germans are the most. In 1966 $5\frac{1}{2}$ million of them arrived in Italy, $1\frac{3}{4}$ million in France, $1\frac{1}{4}$ million in Spain, 700,000 in Yugoslavia. A fifth of the German population go abroad each year, and each year they spend a bigger slice of their income on travel; in 1951 they spent 0.2 per cent of their total private income; in 1966 2 per cent.

In his own country the German tourist is thoroughly circumspect. We visited a favourite resort, the island of Sylt at the top of Germany's short coast, alongside Denmark; a railway embankment carries trainloads of bright white Mercedeses on to the island, where they distribute themselves according to income. In the richest village, Kampen, there are rows of almost identical new cottages, each with neat red brick, steep thatched roof, half-round windows, and a romantic name. In the front gardens are nautical objects – anchors, ship's lights or old bollards – and inside are ship-pictures, facetious notices, miniature bars. Social life, as in a ski-resort, is governed by a daily timetable of bars, tea-places and night-clubs. Couples in two-tone sweaters, with little white wellington boots and perfectly pressed trousers, sit up on bar stools sipping whiskies or walk systematically along the dunes. There is a mild air of naughtiness; husbands flirt elaborately with each other's wives, and on hot summer days the island is famous for nudist beaches, called 'Abyssinia', which have become a kind of national daydream. The dream is self-conscious and regulated; and everyone can see what everyone else is up to.

But once abroad, the German tourist becomes driven by a wild search for self-expression; and Germans now worry a good deal about their image abroad. They have taken over from the Americans the reputation as the loudest, the rudest, the most cliquish nation. One German writer, Gerhard Nebel, described how 'southern beaches are an inferno of brown-baked, probably drunken, entangled flesh, fat buttocks and floppy breasts'. Italians enjoy describing how the 'Latin lover' industry has developed among fishermen along the sea-coast near Rimini, to satisfy the fantasies of young German girlhood. The discipline at home produces a wild reaction.

Each year the net spreads wider. The names of the two biggest tourist companies, Scharnow and Touropa, can be seen all over Europe, on special trains, planes, coaches; they vie to provide distant but perfectly organized excursions: 'just pack your bags, Scharnow will do the rest'. They pride themselves on their world connections: safaris in Kenya, gold-digging holidays in Alaska, sledge-journeys across

Greenland, camel-caravans across the desert with stops in Bedouin tents. But however far away, the tourist is always assured that he will be supported by German guides and German comforts.

German tourists are only the extreme examples of how the modern traveller is cut off from his destination, not just by the machinery of the industry, but by the mental carapace that surrounds him, which leads him to find only what he brings with him. Two recent writers have inspected this self-defeating mission. Professor Daniel Boorstin, in America, has analysed the 'Lost Art of Travel'[1] He insists that travel has never been the same since it became comfortable; he warns us that the word itself is derived from travail, and that until the last century travelling across Europe was really perilous. Since the railway, the aeroplane and the hotel, travel has become a spectator sport, and the old interest in people has been lost: 'The traveller used to go about the world to encounter the natives. A function of travel agencies now is to prevent this encounter.' Travel has become a bland and riskless commodity, and 'whether we seek models of greatness, or experience elsewhere on the earth, we look into a mirror instead of through a window, and we see only ourselves'.

The theme is developed more acrimoniously by the German critic Hans Magnus Enzensberger, in an essay 'a theory of tourism'.[2] After debunking earlier critics of tourism for themselves sharing the tourists' illusions, he explains that the whole idea of tourism, which began a hundred and fifty years ago, is based on a hopeless quest for 'freedom' from the trammels of bourgeois and industrial society; 'the very tours which were designed to free people from society ended up by including this society. . . . As a result tourism has become a mirror image of society which it shuns.' The aristocrat and the farmer never had a great desire to travel, but the upstart bourgeoisie goes in search of what he is denied at home: 'The freedom which he hopes to attain as a tourist is not represented only by historical or geographical distance, but also by a way of life he considers socially superior. His search includes not only history as a museum, not

---

1. Daniel Boorstin: *The Image*, Harper Colophon, 1964.
2. Hans Magnus Enzensberger: *Eine Theorie des Tourismus*, Einzelheiten I. Suhrkamp, 1963.

just nature as a botanical garden, but also a social climb towards his picture of "high life".' Enzensberger concludes gloomily that: 'While we finger our return tickets in our pockets, we admit that freedom is not our goal, that we have forgotten what it is.'

GRAND TOUR

These severe onslaughts on the tourist are worth examining because, if true, the role of tourism in helping to integrate Europe is clearly useless. These critics offer no formula to liberate the modern tourist because they believe his whole premise is false. But if the new tourist is really so doomed, was the eighteenth-century grand tourist really much different? The Grand Tour looms so large in European nostalgia that it needs to be looked at.

The heyday of the grand tourist was the last half of the eighteenth century, before the Revolution and the railways destroyed their leisureliness. The English were the models, and a succession of writers helped to build up the mystique – Boswell, Smollet, Sterne, Dr. Burney, Walpole, Gray, Goldsmith. But no reader can be struck by their contact with the natives. Horace Walpole was one of the best-connected – prime minister's son, Old Etonian with diplomatic relations – but even he was very cut off: 'We have seen very little of the people themselves,' he wrote from Paris, 'who are not inclined to be propitious to strangers, especially if they do not play, and speak the language.' Back in London he said, 'I talk no French, but to my footman; nor Italian, but to myself.' Thomas Gray, Walpole's companion until they quarrelled, was no better, and admitted, 'Eleven months, at different times, have I passed at Florence; and yet (God help me) know not either people or language.'

Hazlitt travelled through France and Italy in 1828, full of good intentions ('the rule for travelling abroad is to take our common sense with us, and leave our prejudices behind'); but he met very few foreigners, and only seemed at home in Switzerland, where he was relieved to find *The Observer* and *The Edinburgh Review*. 'It is well to see foreign countries,' he decided, 'to enlarge one's speculative knowledge, and dispel false prejudices and libellous views of human nature; but,' he added piously, 'our affections must settle at home.'

These literary travellers had an adventurous time. They were carried across the Alps in snow-storms, stayed in foul inns and sometimes faced highwaymen. But they moved from one English enclave to the next, like Boorstin's Americans. They stayed at the Hôtel de Londres, or in the Piazza di Spagna, and called on Sir William Hamilton in Naples. Nor was it only an English failing; even Goethe, a great internationalist and Italophile, is worried by his inability to join in the life of the country: 'Were I not impelled by the German spirit,' he wrote from Italy 'and desire to learn and to do rather than to enjoy, I should tarry a little longer in this school of a lighthearted and happy life and try to profit by it still more.' In Naples he was enchanted by Lady Hamilton and chatted up by a pert young princess, but most of his time in Rome was spent with German savants. Hippolyte Taine, who found the Italians very distrustful, wrote from Rome that 'A foreigner here, who has entertained for the last twenty years, remarked that if he should leave Rome, he would not be obliged to write two letters in six months, so few friends had he in this country.'

There were more enterprising men. Boswell, who did the Grand Tour in 1764, boasted that 'I am not so rude as Diogenes but I am, like him, in search of men'. He lived with princes in Brunswick, mixed with professors in Leipzig, forced his way in to see both Rousseau and Voltaire. He avoided English society, and was struck by the tedium of diplomats. His internationalism was stimulated partly by his ruthless quest for famous men, partly by his lechery, which ensured an interest in local habits. Many other travellers, from Sterne to Casanova, were likewise internationalized by lust.

The romantic picture of the grand tourist, moving casually through the salons of Europe, is not really borne out by memoirs: they only broke through into continental society with great effort. The most international travellers – and this is the key point – were usually journeying not for general education, but for a specific purpose, whether pursuit of famous men, or girls, or more normally some kind of business. Writers in search of copy or culture were insulated by their own self-consciousness, and the really informative books were often the by-product of some other mission. De Tocqueville went to America not primarily to study democracy, but to investigate penitentiaries. One of the most detailed accounts of pre-revolutionary France was by Arthur Young, who was studying French farming methods just before the Revolution: he stayed with French aristocrats, talked business with them, invited them back to Suffolk, and noticed much in common. He found 'a great approximation in the modes of living at present in the different countries of Europe'.

Boorstin and Enzensberger, like other writers on travel, blame the railways as we now blame the airlines. Boorstin quotes Ruskin's complaint that 'going by railway I do not consider as travelling at all; it is merely being "sent" to a place, and very little different from becoming a parcel'. But Ruskin's complaint about the new travellers was not that they were insulated against foreign countries, but the opposite. In *Praeterita*, he rhapsodizes about the old days in open carriages, cut off both by comfort and ignorance. 'There is something peculiarly delightful – nay, delightful inconceivably by the modern German-plated and French-polished tourist – in passing through the streets of a foreign city, without understanding a word that anybody says!'

HOTELS

It was not, I think, the railways that insulated the new travellers, so much as the hotels. Their full melancholy history has yet to be written. The English word hotel is first recorded only in 1765, used by Smollett, appropriately enough, in the sentence 'the expense of living at an hotel is enormous' (the same year marks the first use of the word restaurant – a phenomenon which began in Paris just before the Revolution, and multiplied after it, with the help of chefs from abandoned châteaux). Many of the hotels were merely renamed inns, but some were more luxurious. By 1824 Hazlitt was complaining about the Paris hotels 'where you are locked up as in an old-fashioned citadel'. With the arrival of railways the citadels grew up all over Europe.

There is, I have noticed, a vast psychological difference between staying in hotels and apartments. In a hotel, the whole atmosphere inspires restlessness – like school on the first day of term. The cramped bookless bedroom, the hall-full of people waiting for something to happen, the black-coated crows at Reception, the jangling of keys, the clanking of lifts, the to-ing and fro-ing of chambermaids – they all add to the unreal melodrama. But a flat is immediately part of the city, sharing its smells, problems, dust-bins and cost of living. Plumbing, telephones or concierges may be exasperating, but they are authentic; getting food may be complicated, but it provides daily contact with the city. In hotels there are no everyday objects to remind you of who you are and where you are: while in flats those homely tin-openers, corkscrews, kettles or window-latches all have local oddities. Flats attract their occupants back, while hotels drive them out into the streets.

Hotels are still booming. In 1966, 194 were built in France, 230 in Spain, 99 in Britain; 770 were built or modernized in Italy. The coming of Jumbo jet planes will bring a new wave of Jumbo hotels, designed for the transitory habits of air passengers as the first big hotels were designed for the railways. They will become still more like annexes to airports, and be still more cut off from the native city.

But even more tourists are looking for places outside hotels – camps, youth hostels, apartments, villas or mountain huts. In 1966 'supplementary accommodation' went up 14 per cent in Spain, 30 per cent in Yugoslavia, 9 per cent in Italy. And tourists are spending proportionately less on their hotels, and more on other services – excursions, shopping or entertainment. Watching German campers putting up their folding latrines and nylon cathedral-tents, complete with porches, aisles and transepts, one realizes that modern camping has its own kind of insulation. But it is at least exposed to local weather, food, and people, and to the liberating influences of the open air.

New fantasies take the place of old; as hotels cultivate aristocratic grandeur, so camping nourishes the Noble Savage. The high priests of the new mystique are the Club Méditerranée, the chain of holiday camps which now stretches from Bulgaria to Tahiti, and which has (as we have seen) become an object of ideological controversy about the function of leisure. The club was started in 1950 by a Belgian diamond-cutter, Gerard Blitz, and a camping manufacturer, Gilbert Trigano, operating a camp in the Balearic Islands to provide holidays that were both exotic and cheap, 'beyond the bounds of everyday life'. Today it is a public company, backed by Edmond de Rothschild, with forty-five 'villages' and a membership of half a million, still increasing by thirty per cent a year. The villages foster a special escapism – a mixture of relaxation, eroticism and unworldliness like the Garden of Eden, which has little to do with the country they are in. Their special image is Tahiti – straw huts, wild sunburnt girls, beads instead of money – and they now even have a camp in Tahiti itself, much frequented by Americans. Partly as a result, they are now invading the American mainland, linked up with American Express – an interesting case of tastes moving westwards.

Trigano is an eloquent European, and believes that 'it's through holidays that Europe will be made'; thirty per cent of the club members are non-French. He insists that only holidays can provide the human motivation to eliminate barriers, though he sees limitations: 'In spite of everything there's a real barrier of language. On holiday you want to find yourself among your own kind; it's a bit irritating to sit at the table with people who don't speak the same language.'[1] His clubs cannot be said to offer a very educative picture of Europe; but at least they catch up all kinds of people in their fantasies, in a more hospitable and gregarious way than the old grand hotels.

FRANCO–GERMAN EXCHANGE

In terms of making social contacts, the most effective travellers are still, as in the eighteenth century, the people who have some definite purpose; the artificiality disappears in the common pursuit. This has been the lesson of the most ambitious scheme of subsidized travel, the Franco-German exchange – the one lasting achievement of the treaty signed between de Gaulle and Adenauer in 1963. It is on a lavish scale – an expansive gesture of the friendship by two ex-enemies, the hopeful tribute of two old men to a new generation. The two countries spend £4 million a year sending 350,000 people across the frontiers: for Germany, the sum represents the lion's share of spending on youth and cultural activities abroad.

I spoke to the Secretary-General of the German side, Dr.

1. *Communauté Européenne:* June 1967.

Krause, an enthusiastic European who was the last German Rhodes scholar at Oxford before the war, and has been Anglophile ever since. He was involved in the July Plot against Hitler, and rescued from prison by the Allies. He now runs the youth exchange from an old hotel on the Rhine near Bonn, decorated with huge French and German flags.

In the last three years a million young people have been through exchanges, ranging from Franco-German scout camps to full scholarships for men of thirty. With the younger groups, it is not easy to find common interests: the French talk about culture; the Germans talk about reunification. Language is by far the biggest difficulty, and the organization spend eight per cent of their budget on language-teaching.

Dr. Krause carefully analyses the after-effects. As soon as there is some real joint activity, whether ski-ing, mountain-climbing, or amateur journalism, the people are much more likely to keep in touch afterwards. But the most enduring contacts are the full scholarships (there have been seven hundred in three years), which can have a real influence on politics in twenty years' time. Dr. Krause, with his own Oxford past, is convinced of the diplomatic value of the exchanges: 'If Britain doesn't wake up to it, she'll find herself an underdeveloped country.'

AU PAIR

In Britain, the biggest influx of working foreigners comes from the odd system known as '*au pair*'. Every week hundreds of girls arrive in strange capitals, labelled and speechless, as if to a new slave market. It began as a genuine exchange but now has become a commercial bargain between families who need help and girls who need to learn a language. As languages have become more important, so numbers have gone up. About forty thousand *au pair* girls now cross over every year – sixty per cent of them to Britain, whose language is most in demand. Thirty per cent of the girls in Britain come from Germany, fifteen per cent from France, twelve per cent from Switzerland, and ten per cent from Denmark.

In its main aim, to teach girls languages, the system succeeds fairly well, by the ruthless device of throwing them in

at the deep end; but from the accounts of agents who deal
with the girls, it is debatable how far it increases international friendship. There is a basic conflict of objectives –
the hosts want cheap labour, the girls want leisure and the
language. The girls (particularly French ones) usually come
from a richer home than their hosts; and they can easily be
exploited. They often find it hard to meet English people of
their own ages: the language schools and clubs are made up
of other foreigners, and the English boys only go 'for the
wrong reasons'. The cross-purposes are so frequent that the
Council of Europe is setting up a charter, under which *au
pair* girls will be called firmly 'student help', and will have
written agreements about hours of work. English girls who
go abroad – mostly to France and Italy – usually have an
easier time; servants are more common, and since the girls
have a useful language, they are apt to be treated (as one
agent put it) 'more like cheap governesses than cheap
maids'.

In spite of its perils, and occasional scandals, the *au pair*
system has played some role in breaking down frontiers; the
British Vigilance Society has reckoned that fifteen per cent
of the girls are very unhappy, fifteen per cent very happy,
and seventy per cent more or less content; but only a small
minority keep in touch after they go back home. The *au pair*
system leaves some links. But it is a reminder of how many
barriers there are – of age, class, language – between easy
interchanges.

UNDERGROUND EUROPE

Below the formal structures of exchanges, work permits
and the tourist industries, there is a growing young under-
world who slip easily across frontiers and regard the continent as their playground; the students' papers, like the
fortnightly *International Times,* convey the flavour of this
neo-tourism:

Foreigners coming to Copenhagen this summer can contact
SUPERLOVE at Larsbjornstraede 13 in the centre of town.
Underground papers including *IT* can be had here and a booklet
is being prepared in English for the hip-sub-tourist. A word of
warning ... it is getting increasingly difficult to get through the
borders without a show of bread. Finding a place to sleep is also

a big problem in Copenhagen but can be overcome by the resourceful. There are plenty of girls with pads.[1]

The underground network allows much more mobility than the superstructure. Beatniks, flower people or drug-takers are hardly distinguishable across the frontiers; since they talk very little, language hardly matters. The Gammler in Germany, the Capelloni in Italy or the Beatniks in London all look the same. More intellectual flotsam is to be found in the Café Select in Montparnasse, the Queen's Elm in Chelsea, the Jamaica Inn in Milan. English pop groups wander from town to town, as English jig-dancers did in the sixteenth century. The Beatles were first discovered on the Reeperbahn in Hamburg. The student rebels show a breath-taking mobility, popping up in one capital after another, if necessary defying the police and frontier-posts.

Hitchhikers, though loathed by consuls, have a much wider range of experience than car-drivers. Picking them up on the autobahns, I became aware of the underground of hospitality and exchange which leads off from the road. As usual, the most international travellers are often in pursuit of girls. A young Scots apprentice on his way back from Munich had spent a hectic international month moving from pad to pad. A young German law student on the Frankfurt autobahn had acquired an impressive knowledge of international affairs, largely from talk in cars. Some months later he called on me in London, after six weeks in England where he had been washing-up in St. Ives, staying with one girl in Sevenoaks, and three in Fulham. For such people as him, it is nonsense to say that modern communications cut them off from 'real' travel: it has opened up a huge, cheap new field, with far easier contacts than Horace Walpole's.

The young Europeans may not take the idea of 'making Europe' as seriously as their elders; with no memories of war, the talk of reconciliation is just boring. But they are able to live Europe much more casually, to pick up movements far more quickly, and to have a common aim, at least, in wanting to get rid of the Old Europe. It may not be quite the kind of aim that their parents had in mind; but then nothing in Europe has worked out quite as planned.

1. *International Times*, 3–16th May, 1968.

Chapter Thirteen

Transport

> If you cut the communications of Europe we should fall back plumb in twelve months from the twentieth century to the tenth.
>
> *Leonard Woolf*

Beneath all the fantasy and escapism of the tourist business, there remains the solid fact that the means of transport in Europe are providing unprecedented mobility. With each new development of communications, over a hundred and fifty years, there have been new hopes and convictions that the continent would gain a new unity; yet at each stage, Europe has stubbornly reasserted its differences. In the early nineteenth century, the traveller to Italy still had to cross the Alps on foot, or be carried on a chair by porters, or take a ship from Marseilles to Livorno, risking pirates. Then, in a few decades, railways and tunnels pierced the Alps and brought the two sides within hours of each other. But it is hard to be sure that the extra speed made for extra internationalism. The new jet-propelled Eurocrats are not obviously more cosmopolitan than the medieval scholars who rode on horseback through the continent. The spread of rapid communications through Europe is full of paradoxes, and the ease of movement may also have the effect of making people more conscious of their roots and their regions.

RAILWAYS

No invention held out more hope of unity than the railways. The first line on the continent, from Brussels to Malines, was opened in 1835; in each country trains brought a frenzy of activity and hope. In Germany the railways helped to create the nation, and the Germans 'discovered the pleasure of getting to know one another' (Treitschke). The first international line crossed between Prussia and Belgium in 1843, when officials shook hands on the frontier. In Italy the railways (partly financed by Hambros in London) likewise came just before unification, and soon provided a spectacular link with France. The Mont Cenis tunnel was begun in 1857, enthusiastically backed by Cavour, and was opened in 1871; the St. Gotthard was begun a year later.

Italy was obviously brought far closer to the rest of Europe by railways and tunnels. Cavour, in 1845, wrote a prophetic article about railways. He foresaw that the new line to Turin would make it a European city, and he hopefully saw Italy regaining its medieval commercial supremacy, through railways which could take people from the north through Italy to Brindisi and by ship to the East. More remarkably, he warned that the flood of tourists arriving by train, while bringing big profits, would be a great danger: 'This will hardly favour the development of industrious moral habits; it may engender a spirit of guile and servility which will damage the national character. As a sense of its own dignity is of prime importance to a nation, we do not care for profits at the price of insolence and arrogance.'[1] Cavour's hopes of Italy becoming again the gateway to the East were not to become true: but his fears about the corruption were to be echoed.

By the late nineteenth century the railways were able to cross frontiers without fuss. The first Orient Express left Paris in 1883, and took sixty hours to reach Istanbul. By 1907 there were twenty-eight Grands Express Européens, with their dark blue coaches, including the Bombay-Marseilles express and the St. Petersburg-Vienna-Nice-Cannes Express. The great anarchist Prince Kropotkin, who had great faith in the new inventions as a means of international co-operation, had a special enthusiasm for the sleeping-car expresses as an example of voluntary association.[2] The railways vied with each other across the continent. In 1914 the train journey from London to Paris took 25 minutes less ($6\frac{1}{2}$ hours) than the Golden Arrow does today.

1. Cavour's review of Count Petitti's article on Italian railways in *Revue Nouvelle*, 1846, quoted in Denis Mack Smith: *The Making of Italy, 1796–1866*, pp. 101–110.
2. See James Joll: *The Anarchists*, 1964, p. 159.

Railways demanded practical co-operation, and a succession of organizations were set up to regulate and standardize railways, posts and telegraphs. International exhibitions flourished, with Paris as their centre: in 1889 there were no fewer than eighty-seven international congresses there. The Grand Palais and the Petit Palais, built for the great exhibition of 1900 are monuments to that technological optimism. Many prophets believed that the railways would bring a new age of peace; the German economist Friedrich List believed they could bring a release from nationalism and ultimately abolish war.

But railways were much more effective in preparing for war. The German network was organized from the start on a semi-military basis, with 'three-quarters of a million men who stood stiff at attention when their superior spoke to them'. As it happened, it was completed in time for the Franco-Prussian war in 1870, and greatly contributed to the speed of the German victory. By 1914 railways had reached their peak of internationalism; but they were also the indispensable structures for the mass-destruction that followed.

Since the last war the railways, like other troubled industries, have fallen into the laps of their individual states to be protected and revived. All now are nationalized, and all make a loss. The British are *not* the biggest losers: they lose £150 million a year, the French £250 million, and the Germans £300 million. Even the Swiss are now losing money.[1] The German trains, for all their spotless efficiency, are now facing the same old intractable problems – too much track, too much staff, too much protection. Their basic problem, like that of all railways, is one that passengers are not aware of – the problem of goods. The socialist Minister of Transport, Herr Leber, has had to cut down the lines and to tax lorries on the road – infuriating Dutch lorry owners and setting back the prospects of a common market transport policy. In transport, as in energy and agriculture, the state remains the patron and nursemaid of ailing industries.

Airways and motorways have taken over from railways as the international fantasies. The Orient Express has come down to a single through coach, shunted from one stopping-

1. *The Times*, 7th February, 1968.

train to the next without even a restaurant car. The international 'Sleepings' have become rarer, and only a few national night trains keep their old glory – from Milan to Rome, London to Edinburgh, or the Blue Train, now eighty years old, from Paris to Nice. (The most sumptuous I have been on is the Russian 'Red Arrow' which glides slowly overnight on the wide gauge from Moscow to Leningrad, with a whole coach for a dining-car, open most of the night. It is a train of Victorian splendour, which belongs firmly to the world of Anna Karenina.)

New technocrats' trains have appeared, brisker and covering much shorter runs – leaving longer journeys to the air. The Trans-Europ Expresses glide, always by day, between capitals, stopping only a minute at each station. They were thought up in 1954 by Dr. Den Hollander of the Dutch railways, who realized that efficient fast trains could compete with airlines over distances up to four hundred miles. A special agreement between six countries allowed engines to cross frontiers without stopping. The TEE now move between a hundred different cities in Western Europe, at up to a hundred miles an hour – always within a day. The longest journey is from the Hook of Holland to Geneva, in twelve hours.

Trans-Europ Expresses have their own mythology, evoked by Alain Robbe-Grillet's sexy fantasy-film with that name. But the excitement cannot compare with the associations of the old sleeping-car expresses, and the nostalgia of *The Lady Vanishes*. It has become a favourite cliché to picture Eurocrats speeding through the continent in the Trans-Europ Expresses: but in fact most of the trains are based on Germany, full of silent businessmen, with a few formidable fraus in pudding-basin hats, glaring at fellow-passengers; the compartments are littered with discarded *Spiegels*, the dining-cars serve German food and expensive wine. Most passengers are middle-aged and male; the stenographers tend to plumpness and the absence of sleeping-cars inhibits sexual fantasy. But the Trans-Europ Expresses have achieved their aim – to compete commercially with airlines on shorter journeys; and they are a visible symbol of the breaking down of frontiers.

The interaction of railways with Europe is not over. Many European railway executives have their eye on Japan, where

the new Tokaido line runs three hundred and twenty miles
on concrete pylons in just over three hours. French railways,
the boldest, are pressing ahead with the 'Aerotrain', the most
science-fiction project on the continent, which will shoot
silently over a cushion of air on a single rail between Paris
and Orleans in half an hour, at up to two hundred miles an
hour: French planners hope it may produce a new solution to
the over-crowding of Paris. In spite of their crises and vast
losses, European railways may still achieve a new revolution.
Between the dissociating experience of plane-travel, and the
frustrations of driving on the roads of Europe, the railway
may provide not only a *via media* but a more adaptable and
meaningful interpretation of a united European land-
mass.

AIRLINES

For too long we've been kidding ourselves that anything
to do with flying is fun, glamour, excitement. Well, it
isn't.   *Lufthansa advertisement, 1968*

No European country was prepared for the air boom. Between 1960 and 1966 the air passengers in western Europe
went up by twelve per cent a year, reaching nineteen million
in 1966. Airports, springing up in small resorts, have transformed them. The tenth busiest airport in western Europe
(busier than Milan, Düsseldorf or Hamburg) is at Palma in
Majorca. The air boom has given insoluble new problems to
every major city in Europe, of noise, congestion of entry and
re-entry, and above all of space: but the real problems are
still to come, with the supersonic and jumbo jets. Airports
have moved further out into the precious countryside,
spreading their ancillary activities and noise and using up
more farming land; among the big cities only Berlin can still
use its pre-war airport, Tempelhof, ten minutes from its
centre. London has the biggest problems of all: by far the
busiest airports in Europe are the two London ones. Heathrow and Gatwick, which took over thirteen million passengers in 1966 – nearly twice as many as Paris and more than
three times the number for Rome.

   Compared to the emptier continents, particularly America
and Australia, Europe is still not air-minded, and the airports still deploy an atmosphere of anxious and unnecessary

fuss. The shuttle-service has not yet reached Europe, and the departure of a plane is still regarded as an event heralding possible danger and disaster. Hostesses bossily usher passengers from one pen to another, calling them long before departure time. The atmosphere is curiously like early continental railway travel, as described by a writer in the *Athenaeum* in 1846: 'You must arrive just half an hour before the departure of the train. ... Until the half-hour sounds no tickets are granted; until the tickets are taken no one is admitted to the waiting salon. ... The ceremony of weighing the luggage ... is performed with a decorous gravity'[1]

The fuss is augmented by the co-existence of no fewer than fifty-six airlines in western Europe, ranging from British European Airways, which carried six million passengers in 1964, to THY, the Turkish airline, which carried three hundred thousand. Nearly all of them are nationalized; but Lufthansa was partly de-nationalized in 1966, and France and Britain allow private companies (Air Inter, UAC, BUA, British Eagle) to compete on some routes. Olympic Airways is the private property of Aristotle Onassis. Attempts have been made to bring airlines together, and to establish a common European system called 'Air Union', partly to compete with the Americans on transatlantic routes; but it was smashed, like other plans, on the rocks between French *dirigisme* and German *laissez-faire*. In the meantime the airlines collaborate for time-tables and price-fixing through one of the most hated cartels in the world, the International Air Travel Association. Not surprisingly in this uncompetitive climate the air fares in Europe are far higher than in America; in 1968 the fare from London to Paris, a distance of two hundred and fourteen miles, was £11: from New York to Washington, an equivalent distance, outside IATA's control, it cost 16 dollars or £6-14-0.

International airports have already driven their sharp wedges into the cities, bringing in sudden new problems. But the strains ahead will be far greater. By 1970 the jumbo jets will bring a change much greater than was brought by ocean liners. The new Boeing 747 can carry five hundred people and will, as one British airport official described it, be 'as wide as the front of Victoria station in wingspan, as long as

1. Quoted by Geoffrey Trease: *The Grand Tour*, p. 233.

the Palace of Westminster, their tails as high as Cleopatra's
Needle. The cars and taxis needed to bring the passengers
to the airport would stretch for over a mile'. In October
1967 a meeting of air experts was held at Lucerne to try to
decide what to do: the director-general of IATA, Knut
Hammerskjöld, warned them that two hundred million
people travelled by air in 1967, five hundred and eighty
million were expected in 1975, and seven hundred and
seventy million by 1980 – a four-fold increase in thirteen
years. He viewed the future with 'considerable alarm'.

They are quickening the pace of travel all right, but what
do they leave behind? I often wonder, watching the whey-
faced passengers glaring at each other, traipsing across the
tarmac, along the clattering airport corridors, into those
eerie supranational halls, gazing at advertisements imploring
them to go somewhere else. What is this gay cosmopolitan
Europe, this new international set? In Germany, with all its
rival cities and without a proper capital, the question is
specially relevant. German businessmen are perpetually
flying, and there is even a notion that there is a kind of
'capital in the air', where top people meet each other, settle
matters, and form a longed-for kind of establishment. But
the very speed of air journeys can easily diminish the real
contact with other cities. 'In the old days,' one veteran Eurocrat said, 'when I went to Milan by train, I stayed a few
days, went to the opera, and saw my friends. Now I can fly
there and back in a day, and I don't do anything except
business.'

So far, air travel has created as many new problems for
Europe as it has solved. It manages to be both the most
expensive and the least comfortable form of travel: planes
dry people up, as trains make them relax. In the next few
years air travel may become cheaper and more casual, but
concomitant disadvantages will grow. A small urbanized
and mainly industrial continent may not be best served by
air travel; the social implications of this drastic type of communication are much more important and far-reaching than
the airway planners are prepared to recognize. Airlines make
no real attempt to treat passengers as individuals: one BEA
hostess told me that her colleagues referred to their passengers as sheep: 'how many sheep do you have on board?'

The most unattractive feature of the airlines is that they

have become 'flag-carriers' of the most chauvinistic kind,
basing their advertising on appeals to patriotism and
national caricatures – finicky Lufthansa, spotless Swissair,
glamorous Air France, steady old BEA. They depend on their
countrymen for the bulk of their business – sixty per cent of
BEA passengers are British, fifty per cent of Air France's are
French. They are extreme cases of what Professor Perlmutter calls the 'ethnocentric' company;[1] for their whole
character is bound up with flag-waving. Worse, their scope is
being steadily extended by the buying-up and building of
hotels, which allows them to establish little bits of Britain,
France or Germany in the middle of other capitals, and to
protect their passengers still further from foreign influences.
The pattern was set by the American TWA, who own the
Hiltons, and Pan-American, who own the Intercontinentals.
In 1968 Airport Catering Services (a subsidiary of BEA and
Charles Forte, the snack-bar king) bought up three of the
best hotels in Paris, the Plaza Athénée, George V and La
Trémoille; the employees, joined by some guests, marched in
protest against the take-over, with a banner saying *'Nous
defendons le patrimoine hotelier'*. The airlines, with their
vast capital and dependence on advertising, represent one of
the most potent and dislikeable forces in the consumer
society. Their determination to package their passengers into
narrow national boxes is far from encouraging to the social
integration of Europe.

MOTORWAYS

Cars don't help you to know people.
Norman Douglas, Old Calabria

A century after the coming of the railways, the motorways are transforming Europe's patterns of travel and her
countryside, even more drastically. The tenfold increase in
cars in ten years (see Chapter 6) has strained the old roads to
their limits. Every country in western Europe is now building motorways, autobahnen, autoroutes or autostrade,
bringing a new international scope to the motor-car.

There is nothing new about the idea of motorways: the
Italians, always brilliant road-builders, built the first one in
1922, from Milan to the Alpine lakes. Hitler, mainly for

1. See chapter 5.

military reasons, had built thirteen hundred miles of autobahnen by 1942. But the real boom in motorways has come
since 1950. Germany and Italy kept their lead; in 1967 the
total mileage of motorways stood at:

Germany	2,200
Italy	1,300
Britain	620
France	490
Holland	450
Switzerland	260
Austria	250
Belgium	203
United States	23,000

For the demon driver, the change is already spectacular.
In Europe, except in Britain, there is no speed limit. At
ninety miles an hour on an empty road, he can drive from
Antwerp to Munich, a distance of four hundred and sixty
miles, in six hours – stopping only for frontiers and petrol.
From Hamburg to Naples the motorways are only broken
by Switzerland, where the roads shrink into country lanes,
and wind slowly up the valleys to the passes: but eventually
– when the Swiss cantons have agreed – the whole stretch
will be motorway. In two years' time motorways in Europe
should make up the network shown on page 282.

Drivers' relationships with their roads are still very varied.
In Germany the motorways are part of the strongly-pat-
terned everyday life – with processions of heavy lorries, and
powerful Mercedes cars driving doggedly and slowly. In
Italy roads have a fantasy quality, like an advertising film,
with fast sports cars swinging from one lane to the next, and
garage attendants jumping and running round the petrol
pumps, as if performing a ritual dance. But everywhere the
motorways have the same sense of being suspended between
land and air. They skirt the cities at their industrial edge,
providing a landscape of refineries, breweries, sewage farms
or chimneys; only the huge names of the towns loom up, like
modern poems, to evoke associations without reality. The
motorways provide their own weird images – the Agip six-
legged dog, the Esso tiger, the white-booted Shell supergirl –
and their own bleak furniture. The Germans have bare little
parking-places, with concrete tables, green dustbins and

keep-clean notices. The Italians have the bright red palaces
of Pavese, on the Italian autostrade, which hang over the
autostrade as if to emphasize their dependence on it. Here
one might expect to find a special international motorway
life, romantic, seedy, or passionate, like the world of *Lolita*
or *The Wild Ones*. But no, they have a suburban primness:
the tourists sit at their tables, watching cars go by, shopping
at tourist markets, and eating bought sandwiches from poly-
thene bags, in little groups as if still in their cars.

AUTOSTRADA DEL SOLE

The longest and most beautiful of all is the Autostrada del
Sole, which runs the 469 miles from Milan to Naples, across
113 viaducts and bridges, through thirty-eight tunnels, past
five special chapels and 572 flyovers, and provides – as its
makers proclaim – a new 'spinal cord' down the middle of
Italy. No road in Europe has so many social implications.

Its progress is majestic. It begins with a row of filling
stations south of Milan, cuts in a dead straight line through
the flat plain of Lombardy, past crumbling old farm houses
and shining new factories, until, just south of Bologna, it
faces the timeless obstacle of the Apennines. It swoops
through the mountains in double tunnels or on vast arched
viaducts, looking down on the squiggling bends of the old
road. It curves down into the plain of Florence and through
the valleys of Tuscany and Umbria, passing hill towns and
olive slopes on either side. It joins the valley of the Tiber,
and drives straight through the wild, hot countryside of the
Campagna to the outskirts of Rome.

After Rome, interrupted by a ring-road, it carries on
through Frascati vineyards, by the edge of the Alban hills,
and passes below the monastery of Monte Cassino into the
plain north of Naples. Beyond Naples a new motorway takes
over, along the bottom of Vesuvius, past Salerno and Eboli
into the mountains, until you have to turn off it; you can see
the half-finished bridges and viaducts winding their way
towards Calabria, where the road will finally end at Reggio
at the tip of the toe.

As soon as you drive off the autostrada into the sleepy
villages of the hills, you feel a few centuries behind; looking
back, the flow of lorries and cars appears like a futuristic

intrusion. Little has changed alongside it; only a few brand-new factories, flourishing tourist centres and spas. Though the motorway seems to belong to a different era, it is already hard to imagine it not being there: it sweeps so boldly through the mountains that it seems as permanent as an old Roman road.

Its building was one of the great epics of post-war Italy, and typified its problems. The Ministry of Works was too hamstrung by its bureaucratic restrictions to face it; so in 1956 a special Autostrada company was formed by the nationalized IRI organization, to build it with a mixture of public and private capital. It cost in the end a hundred and sixty million pounds (a year's loss on British railways, or a quarter of the cost of developing the Concorde). Part of the cost is being paid back over thirty years by the tolls, which are worked out to cost half the saving that the motorway would give to the motorist. The choice of the route was fraught with politics. Modena was furious because it was left out, and the building south of Florence was delayed for two years by arguments with Umbria. The citizens of Siena were so cross at being missed that they had to be placated with their own special spur. As the road was completed, each stretch was opened with religious dedication and Italian aplomb. The Archbishop of Milan blessed the fleet of motorway ambulances; the Archbishop of Florence laid the foundation stone of the autostrada church; the Pope himself descended on the Orvieto motorway to bless it and drive to Rome on it. Finally, in October 1964, the Prime Minister, half the cabinet and the Archbishop of Florence sang a *Te Deum* at the autostrada church (dedicated to the men killed working on the road) and cut the last tape.

EUROPEAN ROADS

The motorways will soon be achieving a continental pattern. They began in a strictly national framework, ignoring next-door countries and stopping well short of the frontier. So far only one motorway, from Liège to Aachen, completed in November 1965, crosses countries as if nothing had happened. But the common market, through the European investment bank, is encouraging special roads to break through the frontiers – including the motorway up the Val

D'Aosta, which winds up through the Alps to meet the Mont
Blanc tunnel into France; and a road to connect the Italian
network, across the Brenner Pass, to Austria and Germany.
The map on the next page shows how European motorways
should look by 1970.

Countries are racing each other to provide links through
Europe: the French want to push through their motorways
to Le Havre, to bring new traffic from the Atlantic, to compete with the Antwerp and Rotterdam motorways. Three
routes will eventually compete for traffic from north to
south – through Paris and Lyon, through Basle and Milan,
and through Munich and Innsbruck. It is still hard to assess
what differences these roads will make to the patterns of industry: a first survey of the effects of the Autostrada del Sole
suggested that, although many factories have sprung up near
the road, they belong mainly to industries already in the
same region, which therefore would have been put up
anyway. But the trade takes time to evolve, and the extension
of the autostrada to Calabria will be the real test.

For the tourist the motorways represent a fundamental
contrast with the railways and *their* first impact. The trains
encouraged travellers, laden with impedimenta, to stay for a
week or a fortnight at their destination; the grand hotels
round the termini are their memorials. The railways were
powerful centralizers, not only for hotels, but for museums,
galleries, offices. But cars encourage travellers always to
move on: not just because of the obvious mobility and the
boots full of luggage, but through the obsession of car-
drivers, in their glass-and-steel boxes, always to be somewhere else. The Italian Ministry of Tourism confirms this
trend. Tourists are staying at more places for shorter
times.

A large sector of the future character of Europe, as we
have already seen, depends on the future of motor-cars; they
are still transforming the pattern of the countryside, the
suburbs and cities. Western Europe is still infatuated with
them, and the obsession is still spreading eastwards and
southwards. But in the next generation, the car may yet be
the means, not of the rush to the centres, but of a retreat
back to the countryside. As a means of decentralizing (an
issue which looms in later chapters) the car can be as
effective as the railways were in centralizing.

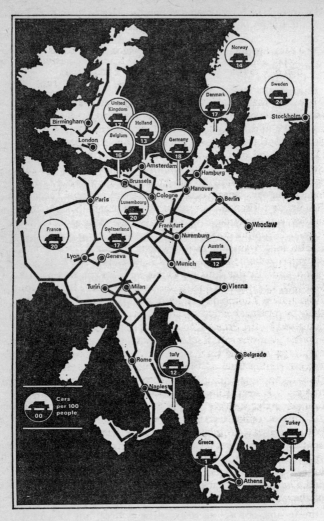

European motorways planned for 1970, with present car population

CHANNEL TUNNEL

> There are few projects against which there exists a deeper and more enduring prejudice than the construction of a railway tunnel between Dover and Calais.
>
> *Winston Churchill, 1936*

There are many bold schemes to forge new links through Europe. One of the most ambitious is a road bridge between Denmark and Sweden, and another bridge, costing a hundred and thirty million pounds, from Germany to the Danish island of Lolland; between them they will connect Sweden to the heart of Europe, and will carry still *more* sun-seeking Scandinavians to the south. But no scheme is more expensive, or older, than the Channel Tunnel between Britain and France. For anyone who imagines that technology can easily cope with politics, the extraordinary history of the tunnel is a melancholy lesson.

The idea was first seriously put forward by a French engineer, Albert Mathieu, in 1802, who enthused both Napoleon and Charles James Fox; but Napoleon was soon at war with England.[1] It was taken up again in 1833 by another Frenchman, Thomé de Gamond, who planned first a bridge, then an artificial isthmus, and then a tunnel; he was encouraged by the Prince Consort, but opposed by Palmerston, and the plan was squashed by fears that Napoleon the Third might try to invade England. There was a new technological fervour at the time of the construction of the Suez Canal (1867) and a new plan was drawn up by an English coal-mining engineer, William Low, with double self-ventilating tunnels. After a delay caused by the Franco-Prussian war and money difficulties, the project was taken up by a flamboyant railway promoter, Sir Edward Watkin. In 1880 he actually began tunnelling inside the cliffs of Dover, and invited politicians and royalty to champagne parties inside the tunnel: he met heavy opposition led by Sir Garnet Wolseley and *The Times*, but actually tunnelled a mile and a quarter of the way to France until he was stopped by the Board of Trade.

A new scheme was proposed in 1907, with electric trains

1. See Thomas Whiteside: *The Tunnel under the Channel*, 1961, to which I am much indebted.

and a special viaduct on the French side which could easily
be destroyed in time of war: but the scheme was turned
down again on the eve of the First World War. In 1924 the
project came up again; Ramsay MacDonald after consulting
four ex-prime ministers and the Defence Committee, rejected it as a dangerous experiment. In 1930 the Defence
Committee rejected it again. During the Second World War
there were worries that the *Germans* might secretly build a
tunnel.

At last, after the war, the military anxieties seemed al-
layed. In 1956 Baron Leo D'Erlanger, who had inherited the
tunnel company from his uncle, revived the project with
support from the Suez Canal company, who had just lost
their canal. A twin tunnel was proposed which did not differ
much from Low's plan of a century before. *The Economist*
attacked it as 'Pie Under the Sea', and *The Times* continued
their century-old opposition, but the success of the common
market, and Britain's application, brought new enthusiasm.
The problems were now not so much technical or military,
as financial. The plan was passed from Tories to Labour in
1964, without being axed, and now (September 1968) it
seems very likely to go ahead, at the cost of two hundred
million pounds, to be completed by 1976. The tunnel will be
able to take an ordinary car and driver by train, through the
channel in half-an-hour, at the cost of £5-16-0. The train will
take four and a half hours from London to Paris.

The history of Europe would have been very different if
the tunnel had gone ahead a hundred years earlier. Marshal
Foch even believed that the first war would have been won
two years earlier. For the future, it will certainly transform
industries and tourism. So far Britain has been largely cut off
from car-tourist traffic: only nine thousand foreign cars
came into England in 1967, while fifteen million came into
France. The tunnel will be able to carry a million cars a year
into Britain and, served by new motorways, will bring Dover
within three hours of Paris; the London-Paris route will
become one of the main axes of Europe. Industrially, the
tunnel must increase the concentration in the south-east of
England, and the French are planning two autoroutes from
the coast which (they hope) will revive the desolate old textile towns in the north of France. Some British industrialists
believe that the tunnel will be more important than joining

the common market as a stimulus and quickener for British industry. The effect of the new invasion of Britain by car tourists may be comparable to the invasion of Italy a hundred years before, which Cavour worried about. But the real political effects (as with Italy) can never be analysed; for, as Thomas Whiteside ends his history of the project, 'Among Englishmen, the Channel has been not only a body of water, but a state of mind.'

All these new technological wonders – motorways, tunnels, airlines – look like straightforward additions to the integration of Europe. The planners have conceived them with such hopes, and they are the outward signs of the internationalism of capital. But the boldest schemes still come up against intransigent local reactions; the Channel Tunnel story shows how a simple link can be thwarted; the Suez Canal shows how an international lifeline can become a bitter cause of war, and be destroyed by it: we can no longer have the confidence of the engineers of the 1860s. In all schemes, what matters in the end is the assent and involvement of local communities. Motorways might be taken as test-cases for the conflicts between central and local authorities; in Britain or Switzerland (where local government is strongest) the technocrats lay out their munificent plans, only to see them frustrated by local lobbies and landowners, and ending up years later with twists and curves; the compromise is exasperating but magnificent: the old winding roads are the tribute to a rooted democracy. The more Europe is criss-crossed with new international lifelines, the more essential is the defence of local interests and the participation of the communities. Without that, the new networks will be no more a force for real integration than were Hitler's autobahns.

Chapter Fourteen

Languages

> Dante, Goethe and Chateaubriand belonged to Europe
> in the measure that they were eminently Italian, German
> and French. They would have little served Europe had
> they thought and written in a sort of . . . Volapük.
>
> *De Gaulle, May 1962*

> I speak Spanish to God, Italian to women, French to
> men and German to my horse.
>
> *Emperor Charles V*

In discussions about European travel and integration, the
problem of languages, like the Emperor's lack of clothes, is
so obvious that it tends to be ignored. Yet the problem is
inescapable. In the whole continent there are no fewer than
forty languages, not including dialects – ranging from Ro-
mansh, spoken by 50,000 people in Switzerland, to Icelandic,
spoken by 192,000, or to Lapp, spoken by 1,500. Languages
divide not only the continent but the countries; Switzerland
has four official languages, Belgium and Finland have two.
Even in the United Kingdom there are three spoken
languages.

Behind the obvious barriers of language – the sheer in-
comprehensibility – there are all kinds of secondary pitfalls.
Anyone in a foreign language is likely to be a bore, and the
thoroughly bilingual can be the most boring of all; the best
linguists in Europe, such as the Dutch or the Swiss, can
easily drain all languages of overtones and fun. Even with
quite a competent linguist, great bogs of muddle can appear
to confuse a simple subject; and interpreters have a knack of
multiplying muddle. People who *enjoy* speaking foreign
languages can be a special menace, for what they enjoy is all
too often the patter and snobberies of language, not the real
content: some people, I have noticed, can understand almost
everything in a foreign conversation except the real crux.
Anyone is something of a fool outside his own language, for

language represents his dignity, his style, his self-confidence. Particularly the French. I remember interviewing one very smooth French cabinet minister, listening to him answering my questions in long, immaculate French sentences, linked with faultless logic; his talk, his gestures, his expressions all seemed to fit perfectly together. Then suddenly, for a few sentences, he broke into stumbling, slightly comic English – probably rather like my French. The whole performance seemed to collapse, to go out of sync, like a badly-dubbed film. He never seemed the same again.

And languages harbour not only misunderstandings, but all kinds of subconscious associations and prejudices, which lurk in words long after they have been exorcised elsewhere. Whole armies of German words came back from the war crippled and deformed, for foreigners' ears, with new association, either sinister or comic. I have found, at the end of a tiring day in Germany, harmless words looming up like ghosts, fraught with grim meanings and encouraging travellers' paranoia. Innocent everyday German words like *Rundfunk* or *Herr Professor* still contain echoes of old battles or old jokes (there are people who still cannot hear the word *fünf* without laughing) and road signs acquire a specially alarming quality – *ACHTUNG! ABFAHRT! ANSCHLUSS! EINGANG! VERBOTEN!* (But road signs in any language are specially fierce; what could be more menacing than *'CHAUSSÉE DÉFORMÉE'* or *'GET IN LANE'*, or more baffling, even to a Londoner, than *'DO NOT ENTER BOX UNLESS YOUR EXIT IS CLEAR'*?)

CONFERENCES

Traduttore, traditore (translator, traitor).

One soon notices the practical obstacles of languages, listening to the international conferences, seminars, colloquies, round tables or parliaments that are part of the machinery of European unity. The greatest difficulty (it soon becomes clear) is that it is much harder to interrupt people. Politicians, of course, are the worst. Speaking their own language, protected by a microphone or an interpreter, they feel complete freedom to bore everyone else, to avoid the question or the theme, and to make a speech which sounds,

very often, as if it was meant for their own constituency.
The other delegates – those that are present – spend their
time reading papers, scribbling, or perhaps removing their
microphones in silent protest. Since they will often have the
speech roneoed already in front of them, there are no sur-
prises in store.

Politicians have built their career round the mastery of
their own language, with all its tricks, double-meanings and
evasions, and they feel uneasy in other languages. Among
major countries, the Germans are noticeable exceptions: in
the German cabinet, a majority speak both English and
French, including Kiesinger, Strauss, Brandt, Wehner and
Schroeder. But the French and English are much less impressive; in the British cabinet only Richard Crossman
speaks French and German well, and he is not very keen on
Europe; in the French cabinet, only Couve de Murville
speaks good English, and he prefers not to use it. Any comparison of top people's languages shows up the English particularly badly. The inadequacy of languages deprives
conferences of a good deal of their piquancy; there have, I
was told, been trade union conferences at which no delegate
on either side has known the other language. But politicians
who like showing off their foreign languages can be a greater
danger than those who know none. Macmillan's insistence
on speaking French with De Gaulle at Rambouillet without
using an interpreter has been blamed for the consequent
misunderstandings; and when Kiesinger came to London in
1967 he was much criticized by the Germans for insisting on
speaking English. Even for a statesman who knows the other
language perfectly, an interpreter gives a valuable breathing-
space to think out a reply.

It is the interpreters who are the key figures at any
European conference, and to understand the strains and
cross-purposes between languages one has only to talk to
them. They are the unsung martyrs of European unity. They
sit behind their glass boxes, with their earphones making
them look like pixies or moonmen. If you listen first to the
speaker, then to the translator, you are soon reminded of the
width of the bridge; an Italian orator will fill whole sentences with stirring rhetoric, closer to the language of music
than words; the interpreter sits staring vacantly into space,
waits for the last cadence, and then translates politely with a

brief platitude. Translating German involves special suspense; the interpreter must wait for the last avalanche of verbs at the end of the sentence, and then translate back-to-front. The best interpreters can enliven dreary speeches with new energy, and the really great interpreters to statesmen can invest their masters with a supererogatory wit. But the run-of-the-mill interpreter deals in a language which often borders between sense and nonsense – a kind of Muzak of words, flowing on and on in a succession of dignified nouns, in a nasal supranational accent.

I visited a school for interpreters at Heidelberg, where young men and girls (the girls in general are better) are trained. Conference interpreters are a tiny profession – only a thousand in the world – and competition is intense: only twenty per cent from the schools make the grade. At the school they sit in mock-conferences, interpreting and re-interpreting each others' speeches from German to Italian to Dutch to Russian. The tension is agonizing; pretty girls sit frowning intently, breathing heavily, staring with that mesmerized look that interpreters all seem to develop, their fingers strumming nervously on the desk, struggling with the jargon of diplomacy or technology. They interpret for only twenty minutes at a stretch, but even this leaves them exhausted at the end of a day. They have to learn to interpret both simultaneously (sentence by sentence) and consecutively (repeating a whole speech at the end); the second is the greater strain, particularly for the girls, because there is time to think and worry; but it gives most scope to the best ones, because they can really improve the original. 'They need to have nerves of steel,' said one of the teachers, 'and it can make them tense for life; some of them crack up after twenty years. They can earn sixty-eight dollars a day at conferences, but it takes it out of them: at conferences they're treated like dirt.' In the top jobs the responsibility is alarming; diplomats are full of stories about misinterpretations causing disaster – like translating *éventuellement* as eventually, or *demander* as demand, or *prétendre* as pretend.

AN INTERNATIONAL LANGUAGE?

Up till the sixteenth century there was no real problem about a common language for Europe; for scholars at least, it was Latin. 'This was surely the polite and enviable age of letters,' wrote Hazlitt, travelling in France in 1824, reflecting with envy on the journeys of Milton two centuries before; 'when the learned spoke a common and well-known tongue, instead of petty, huckstering, Gothic dialects of different nations!' But the new nationalisms of the eighteenth and nineteenth centuries thrived on the differentiation of languages, and even French, which had taken over part of the role of a *lingua franca*, began to lose its dominance after 1870. (The phrase '*lingua franca*' originally referred not to French or Latin, but to the mixture of languages, based on bad Italian, which was used by traders in the Levant in the seventeenth century.)

Two brave attempts were made in the late nineteenth century to achieve an international language. The first was Volapük, or 'world-speak', invented by a South German priest, J. M. Schleyer in 1880, and based on an odd kind of English (*vol* means world, and *pük* means speak). It had a sensational but short-lived success; at the third Volapük conference, in Paris in 1889, everyone including the waiters talked Volapük, and there were over a million Volapük students. But there was soon a rift in the Volapük Academy, and its director, M. Rosenberger, went on to found a new international language 'Idiom Neutral'.

The most famous successor to Volapük was Esperanto, which, as one Esperantist has kindly put it for me, was

> *publikigita sep jaroj poste kaj elpensite de iu ideala pola doktoro, Lazarus Zamenhof. Esperanto estas basita sur la latina lingvo kun germanaj aldonoj kaj estas pli facila lernebla ol Volapük; en 1905 okazis internazia konferenco ce Boulogne, citiukaze oni montris la* 'Forced Marriage' *de Molière en Esperanto kaj la aktoroj venis el nau diversaj landoj.*

The optimism for Esperanto has waned since the last war – partly because of the new importance of Asian and African languages, which give less hope for world languages based on European roots, and partly no doubt because of the growing importance of the Americans, who have very little enthusiasm for learning another language. But Esperantists still make up a loyal international club; there are Esperanto centres where people talk it at high speed, under the portrait of Zamenhof. They claim to have eight million people in the world who speak it, and to have Esperanto broadcasts from twenty-one radio stations in thirteen countries: Fiat and Philips actually provide special advertising brochures in Esperanto. One correspondent in Yorkshire tells me that 'my wife and I have during the past four years visited twenty countries in four continents, and in almost all of them have been entertained by Esperantists in their homes, clubs, etc. ... There is a camaraderie and brotherhood among Esperantists of all nations which is what is needed throughout the world among all peoples, and until Esperanto, or some other NEUTRAL international language is adopted, tourists will not have the best opportunity of mixing with the natives of different countries and understanding them.'

FRANGLAIS V FRENGLISH

> I am afraid that Frenglish is the vernacular of Europe or
> perhaps its Desperanto.
>
> *Professor Hallstein*

In Europe since the war, with all its hopes for unification, the need for a single international language has become much more obvious; but the prospect is still as distant as ever. Instead, the battle has intensified between the two languages which can claim a world following, English and French. Behind much of the French antagonism to Britain there lies the simple fact that with Britain outside the common market, the French language is the natural language of communication between the six members; and language opens the way to French ideas, French oratory, French logic and French culture: while with Britain inside the market, the English and American languages would almost certainly become dominant. The word-war is waged through every international organization, and even the 'e' on the end of Concorde can become a hot political issue ('a humiliating defeat at the hands of De Gaulle,' as one ex-cabinet Minister, William Deedes, called it).

After the war English, or American, seemed well set to become the international language of western Europe. (English and American are becoming increasingly different, and some language schools now offer two separate courses. In international organizations a good deal of time can be happily wasted by changing labor to labour, zee to zed, or faucet to tap.) The Americans moved into Europe with bland unawareness of languages, assuming that anyone of importance would speak English. In the British and American zones of post-war Germany, English seemed the key to all employment and promotion, and the new language of defence and high technology was predominantly English. The American commercial invasion promoted English still further; to rub home the point American companies often advertise in English for staff, in French or German papers. Computers on the continent are an Anglo-American preserve. When they learn to speak, it will be in English. When a European company is taken over by an American one (I was told by a taken-over director), a new hierarchy is likely to arise of proficient English-speakers who can get on with the new American management. Englishmen are apt, to the fury of Continentals, to equate knowledge of their language not only with efficiency, but with moral excellence. 'When they say that someone's a great guy,' a Dutch employee complained to me, 'they really mean he speaks very good English.'

French, in the meantime, has been on the defensive. Eastern Europe has been a bastion of the French language (even up to 1917 it was the official language of the Russian foreign office), and after 1945 the spread of Russian from the east and American from the west left French with much less influence. It seemed that the French language, in spite of its magnificent past, would retreat to its original frontiers. But from 1950 onwards, it began miraculously to recover. Its come-back, as Marc Blancpain, secretary-general of the Alliance Française, explains it,[1] was partly due to French becoming regarded as 'the Latin of the modern world', taking the place of Latin in schools in North and South America; but also to the continuing hold of French in diplomacy. The French African states, even after independence, continued to use French as their diplomatic language, and now at the United Nations (as the French often boast), a third of the delegations speak in French. And, more important,

1. Marc Blancpain: 'L'Honorable Seconde Place du Francais dans le monde': La Revue des Deux Mondes, 1–15th December, 1965.

the common market, conceived by Frenchmen, planned in French, and permeated with French notions, became a powerful new field for the French language. Officially the common market has two dominant languages, French and German; but at Brussels some of the top Eurocrats have never learnt German, while all the Germans speak French. Translation remains a massive industry at the common market headquarters (in 1968 there were 400 translators, a sixth of the staff): but French effectively dominates. Not surprisingly, the prospect of English-speaking members is not welcome. 'The irruption of newcomers, all Anglophones, would be a very hard blow for the French, all our partners, including the new generation of Italians, knowing the idiom of Albion as well and sometimes better than our language'.[1]

Yet the international position of French remains tenuous, for outside France it is essentially a language for a small élite: only sixty-three million people speak French as the mother-tongue,[2] and even adding others who speak French with ease, there are less than eighty million, compared to 140 million who speak Spanish as their mother-tongue, 120 million who speak German, 309 million who speak English-American, 697 million Chinese-speakers. The prestige of the French language, particularly in English schools, is out of all proportion to its importance in the world. As a commercial language, in spite of its revival in Eastern Europe, French is constantly threatened, and M. Blancpain records his horror at discovering French equipment in Asia and Latin America with directions printed in *English*. Not surprisingly, the French regard their language, as De Gaulle showed at Quebec, as an instrument of prestige and power, and of French *rayonnement*. 'The decline which French knew at one time was due to a diminution of France's influence,' explained M. Peyrefitte at the opening of the new headquarters of Alliance Française in June 1967, and continued cryptically: 'To name is to create, and to create is to name; it is not by chance that many railway terms are English and that the first satellites were all called Sputniks. We must see to it that French is no longer the language of a certain aristocracy, but that it is also a living language of creative people.'

1. *Le Monde*, 19th January, 1968.   2. See Blancpain: *op. cit.*

Passionately the French defend the purity of their language in the face of the English invasion. The French language, unlike the English, has never suffered the indignities of transatlantic vulgarization; and the French, while themselves bad linguists, still maintain a pained and scornful attitude to any foreigner who speaks their language badly – as if to imply that the only solution to the language problem is for everyone to speak French perfectly.

The defence of the French language against intrusions has become a militant crusade. In 1964 the best-seller *Parlez-vous Franglais* by Etiemble first thoroughly exposed the menace, and traced the infiltration of English words from the first trickle in the early eighteenth century (club, haddock, baby, lord, etc.) to the present flood. The book began with a sexy short story about *une stewardess,* written entirely in Franglais:

> *Tout la tentait dans ce grand magasin, les robes baby-doll, les twin-sets du dernier new look, les homespuns, les pulls-chasubles. 'Moi, je n'achète plus que des pulls fully fashioned!' Egoistement, Pierre s'intéressait aux trench-coats et aux blue-jeans. Mais la jeune femme lui montrait de ravissants smokings bleutés, des spencers très Eaton, des raglans de loden ou de camel-hair, des pardessus fourrés de teddy-bear . . .*

The battle for pure French is a matter of concern both to academics and journalists. Once a week members of the French Academy meet in Paris to discuss which new words should be allowed in the Dictionary. In the weekly magazine *L'Express*, 'Logophilus' regularly laments new atrocities, such as the disappearance of the semi-colon or the plague of inverted commas. *Le Monde* provides solemn articles on the Defence of the French Language, in which the author, Robert Le Bidois, tries to stem the rising tide; he combs the dictionaries for authorization of new words, and sadly inveighs against the latest monstrosities. He breathes a heavy sigh over the prefix 'Mini', spreading from Britain to France by way of the *mini-jupe*; and the introduction of brand-name advertising on French television gave him new nightmares about advertisers, shouting their ungrammatical slogans, like '*telex-consommateurs*' or '*demain-vous-serez-butane*', across the sound waves.

The pedants protest in vain; the combined bombardments of advertising, television, Americanism and technology are battering down even the strong ramparts of the French language. The most humiliating insurgents are not the sensible words which have no equivalent in French, like *le timing, le weekend*, or *le parking*; but the words which sound English, but are not, like '*le standing*' (prestige), '*le coming-man*', '*le pull*' (pullover) or '*le dry*' (martini) – which betray a treacherous fondness for using English for its own sake.

To observe the invasion, one need look no further than *Le Monde* itself; its Christmas supplement of 1967 included such items as

> *la robe de nuit hippie en liberty, fleurie de tons vifs, style baby-doll des robes 'home wear relaxe'*
> *le sac shopping*
> *attaché-case*
> *mixer*
> *gadget*

On the other side of the battleground, English has long resigned itself to being corrupted by French – from the earliest intrusions of the Normans, through the huge eighteenth-century infiltration, up to the twentieth-century assaults of the *boudoir*, the *cuisine* or *haute couture*, or the earlier technological invaders like aileron, fuselage or chassis. English, too, has its quota of nonsense words – like bon viveur, petite suite, or double entendre, which sound French but aren't. But the English use of French is more snobbish, more *nuancé* and more nostalgic than the French use of English. A rival short story could easily be written in Frenglish. It might perhaps be based on an aide-de-camp hors de combat and his nouveau riche fiancée, with a louche ambiance, and a galère of roués who are passés, and femmes fatales who are manquées. But the mélange would seem rather fin de siècle, not to say déjà vu. And since the last war, the flow of new French words to English has almost dried up. A few frivolous words have crossed the channel – discothèque, son-et-lumière, cassette, cinéaste, après-ski, culotte, sportif, musique concrète, chi-chi – but most of them are redolent of some pretentious Alpine resort, and they are hardly more numerous than the Italians, who have provided such pleasanter post-war exports as *espresso, pronto, gran turismo,* Vespa, *dolce vita* or simply *ciao*. As for German, the movement into English has almost stopped. After the earlier philosophical and psychological invasions, with such heavy artillery as *weltanschauung, zeitgeist, angst, schadenfreude* or *gestalt*, there was a spurt of Hitler-words like *blitz, lebensraum, ersatz* or *diktat*, and joke post-war words like kaput, nix, prima or hausfrau; but since then, the German language has hardly penetrated its neighbours. And the German language has, much more than French, retained its own character. International words like telephone, airport, television are all firmly translated to *Fernsprecher, Flughafen, Fernsehen*: the resistance to imports was encouraged of course by the Nazis; and since the war many more Americanizations have crept in. But German, helped no doubt by the complexity of its constructions, remains more impregnable than French or Italian.

The journeys of words are becoming increasingly rapid, and also more devious; for they can cross and re-cross frontiers, acquiring new shades of meaning. Pre-war refugees from Germany brought over words like *spiel* or *delicatessen*, which then came back to Europe with new meanings. Americanizations anyway often have their roots in Europe: campus, which is now spreading from America to France is a going-back to an old Latin usage. The word budget began in France as *bougette*, and has now come back to France in its anglicized form.

What kind of hybrid language will eventually emerge from the New Europe? Certainly once internationalism has descended from the arid heights of diplomacy into the rough-and-tumble of the market-place there is not much prospect of maintaining purity of languages. Travelling through the continent, one can see how pidgin-English and pidgin-French are taking over; when two people converse in a language which is the mother-tongue of neither, the possibilities of debasing it are infinite; English and Italians can converse in bad French with no sense of guilt, and even with relish. In international companies a desiccated Germanized kind of English takes over, consisting largely of nouns strung together; and American itself is full of German-sounding constructions, including the extraordinary new nouns teach-in, love-in, sit-in.

If and when Europe moves towards political unity, then languages will be knocked about, Frenchified, Germanized, or Anglicized in a way that will make American seem pure by comparison. It is a prospect which can alarm intellectuals. J. G. Weightman, the English critic of French literature, wrote in 1963, 'What keeps me awake at nights is the problem of the future of the various languages and literatures of Europe when we return to medieval universalism, intensified by great mobility of population, multilingualism from childhood, and international television. ... Suppose there is no unilingual mass, as may very well be in two or three generations. Europe will go through a terrible period of linguistic uncertainty for which there is no precedent.'[1]

TEACHING

> You taught me language; and my profit on't is,
> I know how to curse: the red plague rid you,
> For learning me your language!
>
> *Caliban*

Whatever the eventual prospects of international languages, Europe's most obvious immediate need is to teach them properly. For small trading nations, like the Dutch or the Swiss, the necessity has been obvious for centuries. In the case of Germany, the need after the war was much more sudden; yet it is astonishing how many Germans in middle age, faced with the arduous prospect of having to do their business in an unknown language, have mastered idiomatic English. I find it hard to believe that the Dutch or Germans are inherently better linguists than the English. But the English have not only lacked incentive, doing business with the English-speaking Commonwealth and with America; they have also lacked any frontier people (except for a few desultory Channel islanders) who, in most countries of Europe, whether in Alsace-Lorraine, Alto Adige or in all Switzerland, help to make bilingual bridges. The role of such people, caught between two cultures, has been central not only in languages but in the wider unification of Europe; Alsatians, for instance, have played a role in the common market quite out of proportion to their numbers.

1. 'Going into Europe,' *Encounter*, February 1963.

Who are the best and worst linguists? My own random observations would put Americans well at the bottom, closely followed by the Spanish and French, with the British and Italians not far ahead: the Germans in the middle, but always advancing; and the Swiss, Swedes, Dutch and nearly all Jews at the head. But one could also classify people by their professions – with hall-porters, waiters, playboys, and barmen at the top, and politicians, trade unionists and customs men at the bottom. A more scientific study is provided by the *Reader's Digest* survey in 1962 of the common market countries and Britain (though the high figures for France can be partly explained by Alsace-Lorraine, and the low figures for Belgium by the fact that there are two official languages):

45% of Dutch speak a foreign language: 39% German, 16% French, 1% Italian, 31% English, 1% Spanish.
22% of West Germans speak a foreign language: 7% speak French, 1% Italian, 1% Dutch, 14% English, 1% Spanish.
21% of French speak a foreign language: 9% speak German, 3% Italian, 1% Flemish, 7% English, 4% Spanish.
16% of Belgians speak a foreign language: 9% German, 1% Italian, 1% Dutch, 8% English.
15% of British speak a foreign language: 4% German, 9% French, 2% Italian.
14% of Italians speak a foreign language: 3% German, 9% French, 4% English, 1% Spanish.

At last Europeans are grappling seriously with language teaching. Up till the end of the nineteenth century modern languages were taught at schools as if they were dead languages, with a pronunciation that had little to do with the actual spoken language: generations of English schoolboys and even undergraduates – were taught a French which still left them speechless in Calais. In the 1880s the 'Direct Method' began to come in, with the revolutionary technique of teaching children languages as if they were their mother tongue. But in England, at least, the real teaching revolution has begun only in the last few years, and it has come not from Europe but from America. The 'language laboratory', based on the use of the tape-recorder, reached England in 1961. It was received with some apathy (the first one was used by Shell to teach Indonesian), and the French were quicker at accepting it; but by 1965 there were 452 language laboratories in England, including 190 in secondary schools.

The new system is now much used by businessmen in crash-courses, and British industrialists have belatedly realized that speaking a language, however imperfectly, is vital.

Slowly the European governments are trying to move towards bilingualism at schools. In 1965 the European ministers of education, meeting in Vienna, proposed a programme for improvement in modern language teaching, and in Strasbourg the Council for Cultural Co-operation (CCC) set up a 'modern language major project' to pool research and information about language teaching; in 1967 the Council of Europe launched a 'long-term action plan' which reckoned that by 1988 every European will have to know at least one foreign language. How far this ambition will succeed depends largely on the teachers, who all over Europe are the main obstacle to linguistic innovations – particularly to the language laboratories. And effective language teaching has to be started at a very early age – in the first years of primary school, which required a drastic revision of the time-tables. Most experts agree that, given a drastic reform, general bilingualism in Europe is quite attainable. But the problem remains; *which* other language?

LANGUAGE AND NATIONALISM
La langue ... le signe principal d'une nationalité.
Michelet

Since the disappearance of Latin, the assertion of languages has become inextricably involved with nationalism and regionalism. Gaelic, Flemish, Erse, Breton have become rallying cries, and the linguistic battles are still hotting up. Belgium is the angriest linguistic battlefield, as any motorist can see from the disfigured road signs, substituting LIÈGE for LUIK or LUIK for LIÈGE. The battle between Flemish and French in Belgium is splitting the country with growing ferocity: in 1968 the row spread to the ancient Catholic university of Louvain (Leuven) where the Flemish students deeply resented the domination of the French-speaking section, and insisted that they should be thrown out of Flanders – thus precipitating the fall of the Belgian government, and threatening the whole existence of Belgium. The row at Louvain, with its medieval heritage as a centre of international scholarship, is the extreme case of the bitterness and destruction that language can provoke.

Many other language battles are brewing up, and this linguistic fury, together with the regionalism that goes with it, might well seem destructive of European unity. Even in Switzerland, sometimes quoted as having an ideal settlement, the troubles between German, French and Italian seem to be growing. In languages as in some other fields, we find Europe apparently moving back towards a medieval variety, rather than to a new uniformity.

But the variety can be culturally enriching, satisfying to local pride, and can provide the sense of local identification which Europeans may need more, in face of the technological conformity. The multiplication of languages is not necessarily disunifying – provided that, as in the Middle Ages, there is also a common language which is regarded as neutral. The more emotional the language battles, the more essential is a universal language, which can ride above them. Already in Belgium there are signs that English has become more popular as a compromise between Flemish and French; and in Switzerland, too, English is welcome partly for its neutrality. The combination of its neutrality and its links with American business and technology seems to be pressing English inevitably – in spite of Britain's exclusion from the common-market and the victories of M. Blancpain – to become the new Latin of Europe.

Chapter Fifteen

Press

> The crisis of newspapers and magazines is nothing but the emergence and consciousness of the crisis of the democratic system itself.
>
> *Rudolf Augstein, 1968*

To be reminded of the different assumptions of European countries, you have only to look at the newspapers. The news that on one side of the frontier has hit the headlines every day, in the next country may not be mentioned at all; vast scandals loom up in one country, and are ignored in the next. Even in reporting events outside Europe, two papers as close geographically as *The Times* and *Le Monde* seem to be looking at quite different maps, with different projections. Crossing into Eastern Europe, the change of newspapers proclaims more clearly than anything the continuing difference of perspective. Only in 1968 were Western newspapers allowed into Moscow, and crossing between West and East Berlin it is still forbidden to take in a copy of a Western newspaper.

In spite of faster communications, by air, rail or road, many of the newspapers are more localized than before the war. In Germany and Italy the press still reflects the rival prides of the big cities, as they were before Bismarck and the Risorgimento. In France the Paris mass-papers have never recovered the provincial readers they lost in the last war, when the south was cut off by the occupation and bad communications. Only one newspaper in western Europe, the worst, *Bild Zeitung*, has a circulation (above four million) which compares with the big British dailies. The British newspaper industry is more highly developed than in any continental country, and the British remain the most addicted newspaper-readers – only excepting the Swedes, with their long winter nights – as the table following shows.[1]

1. *UN Year Book, 1966.*

The fewer newspapers on the continent may be partly explained by their discontinuity. The last war cut like a knife through the traditions of the press, and in the common market countries most of the big newspapers are no more than twenty-three years old.

Number of newspapers sold per 1,000 inhabitants, 1965

Italy	113
France	245
Belgium	285
Netherlands	293
Germany	326
Luxembourg	425
UK	479
Sweden	505
US	310

Yet Europe was the birth-place of newspapers. The first recorded newspaper was the weekly *Avisa Relation oder Zeitung*, published in Strasbourg in 1609; its thirty-seventh issue had a scoop about Galileo's invention of the telescope in Venice. Weeklies appeared in Frankfurt (1615) and Berlin (1617), but the Thirty Years' War set back the new industry. The oldest surviving newspaper in Europe is thought to be the *Gazzetta di Parma*, founded in 1735, fifty years before the London *Times*. (I met its editor in Parma, Baldassare Molossi, the son of the previous editor; it is, not surprisingly, a conservative paper, opposed to change of most kinds, and owned by local industrialists.) A few other surviving newspapers date back to the eighteenth century; the *Neue Zürcher Zeitung*, started in 1780; *The Times* in 1785; *The Observer* in 1791. Several major European papers are more than a century old, including the Vatican paper, *Osservatore Romano* (1860), and *Figaro* (1866).

But the Second World War left much of the press so corrupted and discredited that it had to begin all over again. The French newspapers had a particularly shaming history, and hopeful revival. During the war the old Paris newspapers, led by *Le Matin*, collaborated with the German occupation with unnecessary zeal, so that after the liberation only one of them, *Figaro*, was allowed to continue. In their place, the resistance papers came out into the open in a mood of magnificent idealism; their names – *L'Aurore, Libération, L'Aube, Combat* – breathed the hopes of the new age, and the Communist *L'Humanité* sold more copies than any other. The newspapers were determined to avoid the pressures of big business, and set out to achieve 'the separation of money and ideas'. But the dream soon faded, and money gradually regained control of ideas. Two textile millionaires, Marcel Boussac and Jean Prouvost, moved in to control two profitable papers, *Figaro* and *L'Aurore*. The advertising tycoon, Marcel Bleustein-Blanchet, controller of the Publicis advertising agency, acquired a share of *Figaro* and *France-Soir*; an Italian, Cino Del Duca, after introducing the comic-strip to France, started a chain of women's magazines, bought the resistance paper *France-Tireur*, and turned it into a noisy popular, *Paris-Jour*. And, most infuriating of all to the left, the old octopus of Hachette gained control of the two mass-circulation afternoon papers, *France-Soir* and *Paris-Presse,* thus still further enlarging their interlocking empire of newspapers, advertising agencies, books, banks and distributing agencies. In 1945 there were twenty-three morning newspapers in Paris; by 1950 only eleven; today there are ten (two very small) – see the following table.

	Printing 1968	Politics
France-Soir	1,300,000	Centre
Le Parisien Libéré	900,000	Centre Gaullist
Le Figaro	506,000	Right, Gaullist
L'Aurore	460,000	Right
Le Monde	381,000	Independent
Paris-Jour	340,000	Gaullist
L'Humanité	235,000	Communist
La Croix	125,000	Centre (Catholic)
Paris-Presse	60,000	Gaullist
Combat	40,000	Radical

SPRINGER

In West Germany, the worries about the press have a special seriousness; partly because, with a weak parliamentary tradition, and without other strong institutions for voicing public opinion, the press has taken over some of the functions of parliament, and indeed often seems stronger than parliament. And partly because Germany has the most alarming press concentration in Europe of newspapers under the ownership of a single man. The German press monopolies are not only an apparently insoluble problem for German democracy; they are also a warning of the future that may face other countries, and the endemic diseases of the capitalist press.

It began, like other German 'miracle' stories, in an almost surrealist way. After the war the Allied occupying powers found no newspapers working, and with democratic fervour they resolved to start papers themselves and later to give licences to carefully selected Germans, guaranteed anti-Nazis. Paper of any kind was in desperate demand (I remember in the winter of 1946 seeing rough grey sheets for sale at exorbitant prices), and newsprint was wanted as much for lavatory paper as for reading. The British occupying Hamburg and the Ruhr had a special role, and a small group of young captains and majors suddenly for a few months enjoyed an unprecedented power of patronage: for a newspaper licence (even more than a British licence to run a television station in the fifties) was a licence to print money. A licence provided both newsprint, which was a kind of currency, and also for a few years a virtual publishing monopoly.

Not many candidates for newspapers knew about journalism and yet had clean records. One of the few was a handsome young journalist called Axel Caesar Springer, who was living on his wits in Hamburg. His father had owned a publishing business in Altona, outside Hamburg, which went back to 1789: he had lost most of his money in the war, leaving Axel with enormous frustrated ambition. Axel, astonishingly, had managed to spend the war as a playboy, pretending to be ill and working for a time as a cinema-operator. He tells the story of three candidates for newspaper licences being cross-examined by a British officer. Two of them told implausible tales about their anti-Nazi careers and their persecution by the Gestapo. Springer came in and was asked, 'Well, who was persecuting you in the war?' He replied 'only women'. He got the licence.

One of his British friends described to me his personality at that time. 'Very witty, clever at organizing parties, full of funny stories and gossip about Hamburg life. Expert at judging people's moods. He had a trick of telling stories which had some particular object, then turning his head away and watching out of the corner of his eye to see your reaction. He was really a philistine, but he dearly loved to play the Maecenas. He was very easily bored. I always knew if I wanted to get rid of him, the best way was to talk about one subject: he very soon got restless. He was a tremendous egoist: he had two charming wives in three years. He had an extraordinary capacity to look ahead: before the currency reform in 1948 he would talk at length about its likely effects. He was always more a tycoon than a journalist. He always suspected that people were intriguing against him. But at that time he still could laugh at himself. He seemed too superficial to be dangerous.'

Springer's first big job was printing a magazine for the Hamburg radio, then run by the British under Hugh Carleton Greene. Springer was given the licence, and the radio magazine called *Hor Zu* (Listen) became the keystone of his fortune: it now sells over four million copies a week. At first he was not involved in newspapers, but when independent newspapers were allowed in 1948, Springer applied for a Hamburg newspaper and got it: the *Hamburger Abendblatt* is still the main Hamburg evening paper. In the meantime the British had started a prestige paper, published twice a week, called *Die Welt*. It was first planned by a *Daily Express* journalist, Sefton Delmer, to resemble the *Express*; but German journalists preferred it to look like *The Times*. It came out in 1946, supervised by another British journalist Peter de Mendelssohn, with short paragraphs and brisk sentences in the British style: but long German sentences later reasserted themselves. When the British gave it up in 1950, Springer, now well-established, put in the highest bid. There was a tussle between the British Treasury (who wanted the money) and the Foreign Office (who were alarmed by Springer). The Treasury won.

Die Welt remains the most prestigious part of Springer's empire – beautiful to look at, dull to read, variable in its policies. One of its editors said: 'We have not yet found ourselves.' It is one of the most national of Germany's quality newspapers, selling a quarter of a million copies. But before Springer took over *Die Welt*, he had started up a much more profitable venture at the bottom of the market – a raucous popular daily, *Bild Zeitung* (picture paper), partly modelled on the *Daily Mirror*. The *Mirror* people resent the comparison and *Bild* soon made the *Mirror* look old-maidish and gentle by comparison. It is a wild red-and-black explosion, with joke pictures and impertinent comment: the contrast with the staidness of *Die Welt* is made more extravagant by the lack of any German paper like the *Daily Express* or *France-Soir*: *Bild* looks like an eruption from a chaotic subconscious.

Springer was now as strong as Northcliffe at his prime, and he had got there quicker. He has become the fantasy-tycoon of Germany – a kind of Northcliffe-Beaverbrook-Thomson rolled into one. He flies between houses in Berlin, Sylt, Hamburg, Mayfair and Switzerland. He patronizes artists – particularly Kokoschka. He cultivates expensive English décor and English clothes. He has now had three wives. He exasperates his editors with his egotism and interference, and charms his junior employees with generous actions. He has made reconciliation and reparations towards Israel his personal mission: he has given half a million pounds to the National Museum in Jerusalem, and insists that all his papers take the Israeli side.

He came to see himself as a passionate patriot, even the saviour of reunified Germany. In 1966 he took a full page in the *New York Times*, which announced: 'My name is Axel Springer. I am a German. My city – Berlin – is divided by a wall. My country is divided by ignorance, prejudice and fear.' Like Northcliffe his politics were largely an extension of his egotism: he travelled around the world interviewing presidents and prime ministers and attacked them if they wouldn't see him. As an aggressive symbol of reunification, he has built a skyscraper in West Berlin, now right up against the wall, blazing the neon letters *Axel Springer Verlag* across the dark streets of East Berlin. For its opening in 1966 he gave a huge champagne party attended by everybody from President Lübke to Günter Grass, and presented each of the four thousand taximen in West Berlin with a twenty-pound watch.

Springer dominated the press, and in the popular field *Bild* had no rival. These are the four German national papers – two of them Springer's:

	Circulation 1968	Headquarters
Die Welt	270,000	Hamburg
Frankfurter Allgemeine Zeitung	268,000	Frankfurt
Süddeutsche Zeitung	221,000	Munich
Bild Zeitung	Over 4,000,000	Hamburg

In newspapers he could not go much further. But his ambition moved on to politics, and also to television. He argued that only by giving newspapers a share in television (as in England) could they become financially secure. But the strongest argument against commercial television in Germany was Springer himself: for in any grant of TV stations to newspapers, his group would be likely to end up in a dominating position.

By 1967, when the German students were first making themselves felt, Springer's papers, particularly *Bild*, had become a main symbol for the 'manipulated society'; they hated Springer's own crude political views, his monotonous anti-communism and his support of '*das Establishment*' of the Grand Coalition. Springer's papers, in return, depicted the students as irresponsible thugs. By the autumn of 1967 Günter Grass was accusing Springer on television of fascist methods; the intellectuals of 'Group '47' were refusing to write for any of his papers; and at the Frankfurt Book Fair I watched students and even publishers parading with buttons saying 'Dispossess Springer'. In the spring of 1968 the anti-Springer campaign became more violent after the attempted assassination of Rudi Dutschke. The Berlin skyscraper was besieged, and students marched on Springer buildings all over Germany; a single newspaper tycoon had become a scapegoat for the whole consensus system.[1]

I went to see Springer early in 1968, at the top of his skyscraper: the gaunt brown building is heavy with symbols – a big Calder sculpture outside, a gaudy Kokoschka painting of Berlin in the cavernous hall. At the top of the tower is a huge empty journalists' club-room, like a caricature of English clubland, all brown leather, brass and old cartoons. On a private floor above is a library with pale pine walls, decorated with antique lamps, and with a big brass telescope by the window trained over East Berlin. Here, in this self-conscious eyrie, sits Springer. He is an exuberant tycoon; athletic, almost boyish, bouncing up and down in his big leather chair, swinging his legs around, immaculately dressed, with the letters AS on his shirt. He vibrates with calculating charm; one is aware immediately of his celebrated feminine intuition, watching people ironically, smiling subtly, almost flirting.

1. See chapter 21.

Springer's office looks over both parts of Berlin, and he likes to gesture to the east and west as he talks. 'I've got little hope that those people in red – ' he said, pointing east ' – are any better than the Nazis in brown were. It will be a tragedy if we recognize East Germany – we must not recognize criminals. We must never forget the six million Jews that were murdered – that will take fifty years; but we must not forget that other concentration camp over *there*.'

He talked about his papers. He was, he said, much influenced by the Scandinavians, particularly the Bonnier papers in Sweden, and by the British. His own favourite paper is the *Neu Zürcher Zeitung*. He spends half an hour reading *Welt* every day, and seven minutes reading *Bild*. He believes that if *Bild* had been going before 1933, it could have stopped Hitler: the press at that time was against Hitler, but was too highbrow to penetrate the masses. He wants to start a new intellectual paper, with an easier style, and much more about Europe. He said that he could give his highbrow papers independence, because the popular ones subsidize them; and he quoted a pre-war Berlin song: 'I love money because it gives me freedom.'

'I don't think the movement against me will die out. You see, young people hate this "Establishment", as I did when I was young, and they are pushed on by politicians who want to change our whole system. My reply to them is that I am fifty-five, and in my lifetime I have lived under four systems – first the black, white and red flag, then the black, red and gold, then the Swastika, now the black, red and gold. I must admit that our present system, with much freedom and wealth, is not perfect; but we can do a lot with it, and we must not change it again.' I asked him if he admired any German politician: '*Admire?*' he asked with a frowning smile: 'No, there is no one of the size of Adenauer.'

Springer's views were not, it seemed to me, of any great interest or originality: they represented the generation who had turned with relief to rebuilding and money-making; and with his own record clean of Nazism, he could equate any new rebellion with threatening to subvert the democratic system. What is worrying is that, in West Germany, Springer *is* the system, and parliament has so far not been strong enough to break his monopoly. In early 1968 an official commission reported that a concentration of more than twenty per cent would endanger press freedom, while forty per cent would directly prejudice it; Springer, with thirty-nine per cent, came close to the second. Springer walked out of the commission during its sitting, and after selling some of his magazines, rejected the commission's findings in August 1968, as 'anti-constitutional'. It is doubtful whether any government will dare break up Springer. and that fact alone is demoralizing enough; as Dr. Bucerius, the owner of *Die Zeit* and *Stern* and one of Springer's fiercest critics has complained: 'the worst phenomenon is not Springer's influence, but the undermining of democratic self-confidence in large groups of society – for instance among students.'

SPIEGEL

In the press, as in politics, Germany remains a country of extremes. At the same time that Springer was printing his radio magazine, a young British officer, Major John Chaloner, was setting up small news-sheets around Hanover. Chaloner had the idea of producing a German version of *Time* magazine, to break through the readers' apathy. He got together young German journalists, including a shy, rather spotty man called Rudolf Augstein, who was the same age (twenty-three) as himself, and who had a real flair and a passionate conscience. Chaloner, Augstein and others put together an improvised news magazine called *Diese Woche*; the first covers showed pictures of Ernest Bevin and the ship *Queen Elizabeth*. The first numbers appeared in November 1946 with a long article about hunger in the Ruhr; the early copies vividly evoke the misery of 'point zero'. It worried the British military government, but after a few weeks a licence was granted to Augstein and two others: to enable them to buy it, Chaloner with two friends sold 10,000 cigarettes on the black market. It appeared under a new name, *Der Spiegel* (*The Mirror*) and soon romped ahead. (Soon afterwards Chaloner started a distributing agency in London: Augstein sent him 250 copies of *Spiegel* each week and so paid the debt.)

So began the most spectacular venture in post-war European journalism. Augstein was not merely a brilliant editor: he was a man of unusual political seriousness, and even more unusually, an intellectual. To meet, he is refreshing and stimulating. He is still, at the age of forty-five, a boyish, rebellious figure: he has wide eyes, a sceptical mouth, and big spectacles which enhance his owlishness: at a party he seems almost like a student who has wandered in amongst socialites – detached, self-contained and revelling in argument.

Armed with his licence and political courage, Augstein could soon give *Spiegel* a national following. He at first admired Adenauer, but was then appalled by his cynical manipulation of power, and saw himself as his special scourge. He also at first admired Franz-Josef Strauss and then turned to hound him. *Spiegel* had the guts which the parliamentary opposition lacked, and often seemed to be the only real opposition. It provoked armies of enemies – not only Adenauer's men but also the critics of its vulgarity, ruthlessness and distortion of language, the '*Spiegelsprache*' which outdoes *Time*.

Augstein's crusading reached its climax in the Spiegel Affair in 1962, when Strauss finally hit back by having the magazine raided and its editors arrested.[1] His time in jail profoundly influenced Augstein. After three weeks he wrote in an open letter to *Spiegel* readers that, 'I abhor myself and repent in dust and ashes': the letter revealed a very different personality from that of the swashbuckling *Spiegel*. As one observer wrote: 'The powerful boss of the *Spiegel*, who had identified himself with his great apparatus, showed himself, as soon as he was separated from this apparatus, to be small and powerless. He had not kept pace with the growth of his work. And since he was still clever, he despised himself in front of himself and his own powerlessness.'[2] The Spiegel Affair, which brought down Strauss, was in a sense Augstein's triumph. But when he came out of jail he was now detached from the fray. He still writes an outspoken column every week, but he cares less about the working of the magazine. Between Augstein the sensitive intellectual and *Spiegel* the brash money-maker, there has always been a discrepancy, and Augstein, though now very rich, has always preserved a bohemian detachment from the big business of Hamburg. Politically, he remained passionately involved.

1. See above p. 47.
2. Bernt Engelmann: Meine Freunde die Millionäre: *Deutscher Taschenbuch Verlag*, p. 152.

He has campaigned consistently against the Grand Coalition, against Strauss's excesses, and in favour of Britain
joining the common market. He never tires of attacking
Springer and demanding a 'Lex Springer' to split up his
empire. (The German press, even more than the British,
loves writing about itself. The cut-and-thrust between newspapers has taken some of the place of argument in parliament.)

Spiegel does not now have quite the same following
among students; it lost some support when it criticised Rudi
Dutschke, and a wilder, much sexier magazine *Konkret* has
stolen some of its political thunder. *Spiegel* itself, with its
cocky confidence and virtual monopoly in its field, represents a kind of 'Establishment', bound up with advertisers
and the consumer society, and the fact that it is now printed
on Springer's presses increases students' suspicion. Augstein
himself is clearly worried by the problems of all German
papers, including his own: 'I feel that confidence in the institution "press" is decreasing,' he said at Königswinter in
March 1968: 'the press itself feels this lack of confidence and
is reacting with business efficiency on the one hand, and with
resignation or the attitude of a Chinese mandarin on the
other. If my fears are justified, then this crisis is worse than a
crisis of parliament; because it is simpler to reform parliament – a clearly outlined institution – than to reform a
system of information that is as diffuse as society itself.'

ITALIAN RHETORIC

In different countries newspapers seem to inhabit different
centuries. To escape from the concentrated commercialism
one has only to cross the Alps to see newspapers still basking
in the leisurely style of the nineteenth century – before the
mass-readership revolutions of Northcliffe and Hearst,
catering for the bourgeoisie with a diet of politics and rhetoric. Most Italians read no newspaper at all: the total daily
sales of all their newspapers are less than the *Daily Mirror*'s.
The big Italian papers have no illusions that they are anything but an extension of politics; nearly all are subsidized
by parties or industrialists, and only two big ones – the *Corriere della Sera* and *La Stampa* – make a trading profit.
These are the 'Big Five' of Italy:

	Circulation	Politics	Headquarters
Corriere della Sera	444,716	Right CD	Milan (Crespi)
La Stampa	345,257	Centre	Turin (Fiat)
Il Messaggero	224,577	Centre CD	Rome
Il Giorno	201,690	Left	Milan (ENI)
Il Tempo	167,860	Far right	Rome

As in other young nations, journalists in Italy have played a key role as propagandists and prophets, and they still enjoy special prestige and special salaries. Sacked editors in Italy can collect huge sums for *liquidazione*, and intellectual communicators are in a sellers' market. Mazzini and Cavour were both journalists, and among the editors of the socialist paper *Avanti* have been Nenni, Saragat and Mussolini.

Italian papers have become used to weathering revolutions and dictatorships, and they were not cut down by the war like the German or French. They change their editors, but not their names or owners. Under Mussolini, the owners of *La Stampa* handed over the editorship to fascists, and the *Messaggero* in Rome quietly conformed to the Duce, as it now conforms to the Christian-Democrat right wing. The most historic and influential, the *Corriere della Sera*, has had an action-packed past – a kind of miniature history of Italian liberalism. It was founded in 1876, just after unification, to cater for the bourgeoisie on the model of the London *Times*. By 1914, under its liberal editor Albertini, it had become 'more of a political force than the Chamber of Deputies'.[1] But after the war Albertini was too worried about socialist strikes to realize the greater danger of Mussolini, whom he actively supported. He soon regretted his support; when eventually he became critical, Mussolini confiscated whole issues. Eventually the Duce persuaded its owners, the Crespi family, to replace Albertini with a fascist. After the last war the Crespis still owned it, and turned it back into a businessman's, vaguely liberal paper, supporting the right wing of the Christian-Democrats, as it still does. The *Corriere* has the biggest circulation in Italy, but to an English journalist this fact seems amazing; for *Corriere* makes few concessions to popular readership, and still caters for the same kind of educated bourgeoisie for which it was founded.

Some attempts have been made to produce flashier news-

1. Denis Mack Smith: *Italy*, University of Michigan Press, p. 293.

papers. *Il Giorno* was set up in 1956, at the instigation of Enrico Mattei, financed by his state-owned company ENI, and modelled partly on the *Daily Express*. Its first number pledged itself to 'suppress that tendentiousness which inevitably comes from mixing opinions with facts'. It is printed in a shiny glass building in Milan, with a jazzy front page and snappy paragraphs: its strip cartoons include Carol Day and Jeff Hawke. But they have not lured the established readers. Rizzoli, the magazine tycoon, also tried to start a popular daily, and even acquired a press and a staff; but he found it impossible to distribute it cheaply enough through the long peninsula.

Italy may never have a national mass-circulation press. Television, radio and picture magazines have already got in first, with fewer problems of distribution, and seduced their new millions into audio-visual habits. In a country where there is still mass illiteracy, picture magazines have boomed; their readership is reckoned at twenty-three million, about twice as many as the newspapers, out of the population of fifty-one million. You can see quite prosperous men solemnly turning over comics in a train. Since the last war a bumper crop of gaudy photographic magazines has burgeoned, including *Oggi*, *Epoca*, and *ABC* (which profitably combines anti-clericalism with sex). Unlike British ones, they can happily combine sex and politics. The most spectacular hotch-potch is to be found in *L'Espresso*, the left-wing weekly founded in 1955, with huge theatrical photographs, six-inch headlines and exposures of political intrigue, which nearly brought down the government in 1967 with its revelations about a planned *coup d'état* three years before.

L'Espresso exemplifies the special trait of Italian journalism – that it is closer to speech-making than to the news: the photographs, displaying huge heads of politicians looking noble or absurd, underline the polemic. Marshall McLuhan claims that television and picture-images are ushering in a new audio-visual age; if so the Italian viewers, having never really succumbed to print, will be in the forefront.

LE MONDE

In the midst of this hectic money-making, a few newspapers have managed to withstand the pressures, calmly presenting news to an assured élite. The *Neu Zürcher Zeitung* from Zürich, with tiny headlines surrounded by large white spaces, is regarded by many conservatives as the best paper in Europe: it is regarded with special dread in Britain as the mouthpiece of the Zürich bankers, 'the gnomes' own daily'. In Munich, the *Süddeutsche Zeitung*, edited by a small, out-spoken Bavarian, Dr. Proebst, maintains a large network of foreign correspondents, and keeps a watchful eye on Bavarian politics and Franz-Josef Strauss. In Stockholm, the *Svenska Dagbladet* is one of the last papers in the world to have only advertisements on the front page.

The most influential of these highbrow papers is *Le Monde*, which casts such a spell on the continent that it deserves inspection. It defies most of the rules. It is printed on grey paper in small type with a lot of italic. Its headlines are proper sentences, with none of the 'cable-ese' of *The Times* or *Die Welt*. It appears in the afternoon. It is wary of scoops, and tells correspondents not to waste time on them. Its front page is dominated by an editorial which is always about foreign affairs, and long reflective articles, often about obscure places: it likes to have long grey articles stretching over three days. It makes few concessions to women. It has never in all its twenty-five years published a photograph. Yet its circulation has nearly doubled in ten years, and is more than that of *The Times* or *Die Welt*.

Its workings are equally remarkable. There are only ninety members of the editorial staff (compared to four hundred on *The Times*) including eight foreign correspondents, and only five reporters. Contributors are paid very little, and *Le Monde* men have an almost monkish dedication. They start work at eight o'clock, and put the paper together in the morning. Their fewness helps to give the paper its most important quality – of giving a unity to the news, linking and 'orchestrating' it. While other papers present a huge *hors d'oeuvre*, *Le Monde* cooks up an *entrée*, for serious eating. On days of crisis, it will give five or six pages to the same subject, with long headlines across the top; when the pound was devalued in 1967, *Le Monde* gave seven pages to its consequences – as much as *The Times*.

The special character of *Le Monde* is largely the work of a legendary figure, Hubert Beuve-Méry, its editor since the beginning, who has forged its character with his high standards, his pessimism, and deep distrust of America. After the liberation, the then prime minister, General de Gaulle, wanted a paper to take the place of the discredited *Le Temps*, and he turned to Beuve-Méry, an ex-professor of law who had been *Le Temps*'s correspondent in Prague until he resigned over Munich. Beuve insisted on complete independence and moved into the old printing-presses of *Le Temps* with a staff of twenty-six hand-picked journalists. The first great test was in 1951, when Beuve-Méry was insisting that France should be part of a third force outside the Atlantic Pact. The board objected, Beuve-Méry resigned. But most of the staff stood by him, and a new structure was worked out to allow the journalists more than a quarter of the shares, thus giving them (for instance) a veto over a new editor. Other troubles followed. In 1956 a group of big businesses brought out a rival, *Le Temps de Paris*, which threatened *Le Monde*'s frail finances; but it soon foundered. In 1962, after *Le Monde* had attacked the atrocities of the OAS, a bomb was thrown into Beuve-Méry's flat. But *Le Monde* thrives on trouble and with each new crisis its circulation (dutifully recorded each day) takes a new jump.

Le Monde is often accused by the British of being Gaullist. But from the beginning Beuve-Méry kept his distance from the paper's originator, and in the last years he has become a fierce critic. After De Gaulle's press conference of November 1967, Beuve-Méry ('Sirius') denounced his 'Machiavellian genius and insatiable urge for power'. *Le Monde* has repeatedly publicized British arguments for entering Europe and gives extensive and sympathetic coverage to British institutions, showing special admiration for its television, parliament and universities.

Le Monde showed its independence to the full in the students' revolt of 1968. From the beginning it publicized and discussed the students' ideas, and Beuve-Méry returned from a trip to Madagascar to find that his paper was the main organ of revolutionary thought; he was not himself so enthusiastic, but bowed to the majority. The paper continued printing and distributing itself through the strike – Madame Beuve-Méry herself was observed selling papers – and at one point its circulation topped 700,000. Since then, being relatively unworried by advertisers (who have nowhere else to go) it has published a series of discussions about the problems of consumer society: in total contrast to *Die Welt*, it has welcomed the stimulus of new ideas.

What gives *Le Monde* its special importance to Europe is its internationalism: true to its name, it takes the world as its stage, and assumes readers to be its citizens. The perspective is crucial; for the influence of a newspaper stems as much from its assumptions as from its opinions. Most quality newspapers, when pressed for readers, have cut down their foreign news: in the British press as competition gets fiercer, foreign news gets scarcer. But *Le Monde* always regards France as part of Europe – not only by giving space for foreign correspondents, but by quoting other newspapers, making international comparisons and connecting events. Their special perspective is apparent in the sample opposite, of a week's headlines in May 1968, from four major newspapers: the sample confirms what any reader can observe, that *Le Monde* is the most international, and *The Times* the most national.

Is there a flaw in this paragon? There is a hint of it in the lack of letters from readers. Sometimes (as when *Le Monde* criticized Israel in 1967) there is a sudden burst of letters; but in general the great flood of reports and opinions is met with resounding silence. As one of the editors put it: 'In France, they are always saying "I must write to *Le Monde*", but they don't. In England, they say "I must write to *The Times*", and they do.' The difference, I think, is a significant one. It corroborates the view that is often expressed by foreigners, that 'public opinion' in Britain is still a more tangible and credible force than in most parts of the continent. No feature of *The Times* is more reassuring than its letters, giving reactions to any crisis from all over the country: it can become a kind of ante-room to the House of Commons, and often more effective. No other paper that I have seen can achieve this *rapport*: with *Le Monde*, which assumes such intelligent readers, the lack is most glaring.

'Why cannot we have an English paper of similar calibre and why, if we had, could it not make a profit?' asked Mr. Cecil King in 1967: 'The answer is that *Le Monde* has no real competition for the subscriptions of the French intellectual and administrative élite, and, small though its circulation is, it commands a sufficient share of the market.'[1]

1. 'The Newspaper in Europe', Royal Society of Arts, 14th February, 1967.

	Le Monde	The Times	Die Welt	Corriere della Sera
May 6th	Hanoi and Washington agree on Paris	Race-problem towns to get funds	New wave of Vietcong counterattacks	Vietcong offensive in S. Vietnam
May 7th	Attack launched against 122 objectives in Vietnam	Study is likely on ethics of transplants	Parliament wants to press the Länder on high schools	Vietcong offensive falls off round Saigon
May 8th	Three days before the Paris Vietnam peace talks	Nationalists gain in Scots elections	Parliament speeds up high school reforms	Moro: no to impatience
May 9th	Before the opening of the Paris peace talks	$3\frac{1}{2}\%$ limit left out of new pay Bill	Paris hopeful on Vietnam peace talks	Kennedy victory in Indiana
May 10th	The day before the Paris peace talks	Conseratives sweep the country	Growing concern over Prague	Dramatic appeal from Prague
May 11th	The Paris peace talks	Mr Wilson rebuts Cecil King's statement	Americans meet North Vietnamese	Massing of Soviet troops at frontiers

Le Monde is protected from fierce competition by having a virtual monopoly of intellectual readers. It does not have to strain for a mass readership outside that class, and its excellence is one of the strongest arguments for protecting the press elsewhere. As a solitary exception to the national-minded newspapers, it points towards a future united Europe in which readers would not think of their country's problems in isolation; the price of that intellectual unity is the exclusion of less informed readers, and a stratification of the press.

A EUROPEAN PRESS

The newspapers of the wealthy countries of the free world are suffering from dangerous diseases.

Axel Springer, Kiel, 1967

In the meantime, the highly commercialized press, which appears in its most developed form in Britain and Germany, is likely to be less and less able to act as forum for free and intelligent debate. The new technical processes, particularly colour, will require heavier investment, and the advertisers will become still more dominant. To quote Augstein again:

What really matters are circulation figures, profits and con-centration. The contents shrink until they are invisible. Only the presentation counts. Not the reader but the advertiser wants colour. So give us new machines which force greater concentration. The perfumed paper with multi-coloured letters is our future. It may even play a melody while it is being read. Seriously, newspapers and journalists in Germany and I fear in Britain too, are becoming more and more perfect and more and more trivial. I have no doubt that if this development is not stopped it can, indeed will, bring about a collapse of our political system one day.[1]

Augstein's prediction is extreme (perhaps editors are always inclined to exaggerate the importance of the press). But it seems inevitable that newspapers competing heavily for advertising and circulation will find it increasingly difficult to give an all-round critical view to their readers. The advertisers press newspapers, consciously or unconsciously, to omit some news and to over-emphasize others. As the critique of the present industrial systems becomes more angry, so the stately newspapers of Europe will reveal their weaknesses and omissions, and become more vulnerable to the charge of being organs of 'the manipulated society'; for they cannot afford to discuss the real faults of the industrial system for fear of offending their advertisers. There may be a difficult choice between an outspoken semi-monopoly press, exemplified by *Le Monde*, or a competitive but compromised one, like *Die Welt*.

In the meantime new printing techniques will also favour smaller, cheaper papers; and students are already reacting against the 'Establishment' papers with more and more news-sheets, pamphlets or 'extra-blatt' papers which can pay their own way with the help of exotic advertising. An 'underground press' is emerging, on the American model, with the informality and scurrilousness of eighteenth-century pamphlets, but often with a more international perspective than the big papers.

One solution to the crisis facing the commercial press, as in other industries, might be to forge links between European newspaper companies, to share the massive new costs – which could also provide a broader context. There are some slender connections across frontiers. The news magazines *Spiegel, L'Express* and *Newsweek* use each other's material. The Paris magazine *Réalités* appears in two languages. The Italian *Epoca* publishes in German. A maga-

1. Königswinter Anglo-German conference, March 1968.

zine called *Capital* was planned between *Paris Match,* the
Financial Times and Springer. Some trade magazines, about
plastics or mechanical handling, appear in several languages.
But in daily newspapers not much can be transferred into
another country and language without seeming flat; for
journalism, like conversation, depends on its audience; on
context, timing, shared knowledge and prejudices.

I asked Springer why, since he could not expand further in
Germany, he had not set up a European paper or magazine.
'I've thought about it since 1945, but it's still too early. Only
the top layer are interested in Europe, and you can't give
everyone the same news. Take the Olympics; the British will
always want to have headlines about *their* athletes, even if
they came in fourth; and so will the Germans. And anyway,
it's difficult for me as a German to buy a paper in Britain or
France; they would always complain about foreign
influence.' Other press tycoons have found similar objec-
tions: for newspapers, more than any other medium, are
sensitive to every nuance of national emotion.

In picture magazines, being liberated from language, a
new universal idiom appears. All over Europe the same
small cast crops up – including the Queen of England,
Sammy Davis, Jackie Kennedy, the Beatles, Queen Soraya,
Barbarella, Charlie Brown, Mary Quant, James Bond or Brigitte Bardot. The same fashions and thrills sweep through
magazines – the Pill, LSD, Carnaby Street, Provos or
Hippies. Comic-strip characters cross the frontiers more naturally than statesmen, and any historian of European unity
must surely pay tribute to these intrepid new Europeans.

Real people and news are much more confined within
national frontiers. As in other industries, the nearest thing to
a European press is the American press in Europe; in the
kiosks the common element is the *Herald Tribune, Time* or
Newsweek; and most of the joint publishing ventures in
Europe are not between neighbouring countries, but with
America. *Life* and Mondadori share the Italian magazine
Panorama; McGraw-Hill and *L'Express* produce the French
business magazine *L'Expansion*. American news is more
interesting to readers than news of neighbouring countries.

We are back with the fact that the newspapers of Europe
are, in the end, the mirrors of their own societies; and they

reflect, perhaps magnify, the stubborn separateness of the countries. To anyone who feels tempted to generalize about 'The Europeans', it is a useful corrective to glance at a stallful of European newspapers, with their parochial headlines and loyalties, their introverted presuppositions, and their language-puzzles. Their growing commercial difficulties do not seem likely to encourage greater internationalism, and as their troubles get greater, they will be still less prepared to take risks. But newspapers no longer have a monopoly of news. For the hopes of a new Europe, we must also look to new media.

Chapter Sixteen

Television and Songs

> Europe is now getting a unity under the electronic auspices of compression and interrelation.
>
> *Marshall McLuhan*

Of all the consumer durables that have swept into Europe, the most obviously potent is television. The motor-car, however masterful it may seem, is still the servant of its owners. To ascribe to washing-machines or refrigerators an insidious influence is absurd. But the television imposes its will on whoever watches it; there can be no answering back. Most people, watching the spread of the antennae through Europe, feel that it must be doing something to the old continent.

In five years the number of TV sets in western Europe has almost doubled; in 1967 there were forty-seven million – about one to every five people. For some time after the war the British were well ahead, which helped to give the BBC a strong influence on the rest. The British still have the most sets per head of population (one in four); but the Germans are very close and others are catching up. Interestingly, as the figures on page 240 show, it is the countries which have more cars which tend to have fewer TV sets, and vice versa.

In the early years television was a much more communal activity; Italians would sit in rows in the village bars, watching television like a cinema audience. But with the increase in sets, TV has become everywhere a more domestic pastime, taking people out of the pubs, the cinemas or the open air, into the sitting-room: in Holland, which has tall blocks of flats without curtains, you can see the rows of TV sets flickering at night.

No European country has resisted the lures of television: the new luxury has taken precedence over old ones, and Italy

has more television sets than baths. But in many parts of
Europe the intelligentsia are still fighting a stubborn rear-
guard action. French or Italian intellectuals are still proud of
not having a television set. While in Britain a mass programme like Panorama or the News at Ten provides a
common talking point, the French élite will often be quite
unaware of the programmes that the rest of the population
are watching.

European governments were determined that their television should not follow the American horrors of free enterprise; they set up television stations primarily financed by
licences, sometimes augmented by advertising, with varying
degrees of autonomy as the following table shows. The most
decentralized of all is Germany, originally at the insistence
of the French and the Americans after the war. Each of the

Some European TV Networks

	France	Britain	W. Germany	Italy	Switzerland
	State monopoly (ORTF)	State-owned corporation (BBC) Commercial companies (ITA)	2 channels controlled by Länder 1 channel by Federal government	Mixed corporations controlled by state (RAI)	State concession to single company (SSR)
Number of channels	2	3	3	2	3 (one for each language,
Annual licence fee	£9	£5	£6 10s.	£8 10s.	£8
Number of sets	8·9 million	15 million	14·3 million	6·9 million	1 million
Per 1,000 people	178	270	237	130	150
Advertising	Coming	ITA only	2 channels	2 channels	3 channels
Maximum daily length (advertising)	(?)	7 mins an hour	20 mins	26 mins	15 mins

eleven States of Germany, even Bremen, has its own station
and its own big staff; they all exchange programmes on the
first channel (ARD) so that an evening's viewing can seem
like a round-up of German cities – Munich talking to Frankfurt, Hamburg to Cologne: there are as many as nineteen
'magazine' programmes. There is also a second national programme (ZDF), from Mainz, established with high ideals
about programmes being 'conducive to the reunification of
Germany in peace, and freedom and understanding between

nations'. The two channels muster a huge army of television reporters and producers, predominantly liberal and inter-national-minded: they revel in exhaustive and learned docu-mentaries from all over the world. In some respects Germany is a television man's paradise: reporters can mix comment with fact, and, as in America, can get in almost anywhere. At national events the cameras and microphones move forward relentlessly, like an army of mechanical cranes. Their staff is enormous; in Frankfurt they occupy a huge circular palace, designed for the parliament, and in Baden-Baden TV men have taken over from invalids as the dominant population. But in spite of their freedom the German reporters are very respectful. They do not cut short or contradict the long-winded speeches of politicians: the discussions have the formal pontifical sound of the old BBC, before it was knocked sideways by the arrival of commercial television. German television seems limited by its own high-mindedness, projecting a polite world which is too good to be true, and which seems to bear no relation to *Bild Zeitung*.

In the polyglot countries of Europe, television has to reflect all the sections with scrupulous fairness; Belgium has Flemish and French, and Switzerland has German, French and Italian – creating extravagant problems for advertisers. The most complex of all is Holland which has five separate programmes, with religious *and* political divisions – AVRO (general), KRO (Catholic), NCRV (Protestant), VARA (Socialist) and VPRO (Liberal-Protestant): each (except the last) is allowed exactly 5/21 of the broadcasting time.

Watching the continental programmes, I found most of them less adventurous than the British; and Britain can well claim to have the best system. To have a state service com-peting with commercial enterprises is – as with schools or doctors – a classic British compromise; it has manifest faults, but it arouses envy in both Europe and America. The com-mercial competition, with its elements of showbusiness, ruthlessness and sheer exploitation of the medium, breaks up the aura of reverence that so easily settles round state-owned broadcasting; while the nationalized service provides a safeguard against the excesses of the American system. Com-pared to the continental programmes, the British are fiercely independent – and for this commercial competition must take some credit. It is ironic that Britain, a supposedly socialist country, should be the only one in Europe with commercial TV companies; while Germany, the most militant champion of free enterprise, should have all broadcasting publicly owned.

TELEVISION POLITICS

Most countries have felt the influence of television on their own national politics. It has provided prime ministers and presidents with a medium, far more persuasive than radio, for talking direct to their electorate; and it may yet be that television will turn all European countries into *de facto* presidential systems, whatever constitutions may say otherwise. It has taken some time for leaders to learn the techniques of this new style of demagogy -- the mixture of sympathetic concern with firm authority - 'like a family doctor', as Harold Wilson confided to the Irish Prime Minister, Sean Lemass. Whoever can develop this role has a new means to by-pass both parliament and cabinet. A successful performer can, at least for a time, establish a relationship with the viewer which makes other politicians seem small and unreal. He can go much farther than the heart-to-hearts of the radio speakers. For on TV he can *be* the news, and *make* the news when he needs to.

The classic example of television enhancing the power of a single leader has been in the case of De Gaulle. The French government's hold on television did not begin with him; in fact, under the fourth republic De Gaulle himself was banned from the screen, and throughout the Algerian war French TV gave a very partial account. Thus, when he came to power in 1958, De Gaulle easily realized how invaluable it would be. '*La télévision, c'est le gouvernement dans la salle à manger*', one of his ministers remarked; and De Gaulle insisted that, since nearly all the press were against him, he must have the screen on his side. The new medium provided the perfect extension of his theatrical personality; it by-passed parliament, penetrating straight to the voters, and it fitted neatly with the use of the referendum. We have seen how his style of press conferences gave full scope to the monarchic splendour which television so enjoys (in case anything goes wrong, the conferences are not transmitted till an hour later); and outside his formal appearances, De Gaulle's spectacular world tours increased his domination of the screen. The tall figure with outstretched arms, moving through the cheering crowd – in South America, Canada, Poland – became a recurring sequence, not just on French screens, but all over Europe. Television enabled De Gaulle, unlike any previous head of state, to *act out* his foreign policy – to provide a travelogue of world affairs with himself in the middle of it, to bring a province of Canada, which few French knew or cared much about, into the middle of the world's stages. All politicians have realized how television favours an extrovert style of diplomacy – helicopter journeys, sudden departures, windswept encounters – but De Gaulle, using all the freedom of his presidency, went a stage further in making history in public.

The French public, and the television staff, accepted the control of the medium with a passivity which surprised foreigners. An interministerial committee sat every morning to discuss controversial programmes, and suppress a few; but the most effective control was through *autocensure*: most producers did not try to put on doubtful programmes, because they could not face the trouble of arguing and risking suppression. Many others thought that television should not be too controversial anyway, for fear of stirring up anarchy.

Then, in the 'May days' of 1968, the censorship really burst into the open. For the first week of the student revolt the events were covered with blatant partiality. Demonstrations and fights were shown without voices; the security police were well hidden, and no student leaders appeared on the screen. A commentary was provided by a careful civil servant on the staff of the Minister of Education. At the end of the week, a student programme by the French Panorama was suppressed at the last minute. The journalists and technicians, enraged, staged a partial strike and demanded to be allowed greater objectivity. They were ignored, and they then formed a committee of ten, to try to enforce objectivity; they successfully insisted on televising the censure debate in parliament, and when De Gaulle gave his first television speech they demanded that opposition leaders should be allowed to make comments. They went as far as recording them, but their screening was stopped. All the journalists except twenty-three then voted to go on strike; for the next five weeks television was reduced to the bare minimum laid down by statute – of one bulletin a day.

The television strike went on long after other industries had gone back to work – and with some reason, for the freedom of television went to the heart of the complaints about authoritarian rule. De Gaulle was furious that the television should have (as he is reported to have said) 'stabbed me in the back when I was on my knees'. Eventually the journalists went back to work without having won their case, and without much support from the public, who were fed up with the skeleton programmes. De Gaulle retaliated by dismissing or demoting a hundred of the strikers, including some of the most distinguished commentators, like Léon Zitrone and Michel Honorin. Some concessions were made, including the ending of the interministerial committee, and more staff representation on the board; but the new director of television, André François, made it clear that the government would not tolerate an independent television service. For the time being the opposition had been broken; but the ruthless control of French television, alongside the comparative freedom of her neighbours, stood out as the most obvious and provocative sign of De Gaulle's domination.

It is often debated whether TV can strengthen a potential dictator, whether for instance it would have helped Hitler. Marshall McLuhan insists that television is a 'cool' medium, unsuitable for dictatorial frenzy. 'Radio is the medium for frenzy, and it has been the major means of hotting up the tribal blood of Africa, India and China, alike. TV has cooled Cuba down, as it is cooling down America.' On the other hand, it is argued that a convincing personality can always extend his powers of conviction through the screen (certainly Goebbels was very keen to develop television for the Führer). One French socialist leader assured me: 'If TV had been invented twenty years earlier, we wouldn't be here today.' Between the two views, Sir Hugh Greene (who ran the BBC German service in the war) argues that, 'I do not believe that television would have changed the course of history in the slightest degree. Those – the great majority – who surrendered to Hitler's influence would have found him at least as persuasive on the television screen: those who did not would have found him perhaps even more abominable. There is a theory – perhaps a true one – that television shows up insincerity. But the most dangerous people, like Hitler, are not insincere.'[1]

Perhaps Sir Hugh is correct; but the most important influence of television, I believe, is not in projecting a single leader, but in purveying one view of the world, and leaving out others. It is this that can make it such a dislikeable instrument, not just of dictatorships, but of any complacent regime. By using spectacular film, by asking searching questions and showing angry interviewers, television can conceal or forget the other questions. The dependence on film, in itself, leads to blatant omissions, and favours the acceptance of existing bosses and governments; foreign dictatorships, like Spain or Greece, have learnt that if they do not want to be attacked on television, they have only to keep out the cameras; for without film, television usually prefers not to report at all. It is the bland propagation of the *status quo*, offering no chance to answer back, which has made television on the continent specially suspect to the younger generation.

The doctrine of Marshall McLuhan, revolving round the misty notion that 'the medium is the message', is naturally attractive to the practitioners: for it makes it appear that television is an independent power. But TV is never as independent as it looks; behind all its arguments and exposures, political and commercial decisions can still discreetly control it. Controversial programmes, if not squashed, can be relegated to the afternoon.

The most dramatic example in history of the apparent power of television was in Prague in 1968, when, after Dubcek became first secretary, the screen was suddenly filled with argument, criticism and free speech, bringing a sense of liberation and revival to the whole country. It looked like a heroic victory of the medium over the rulers. But in fact the liberation depended on the courage of Dubcek himself, who told the television controllers to put out whatever they liked, and used public opinion to strengthen his position against Novotny. As John Morgan described it: 'The medium was not the message, but the means of transmitting a revolution-

1. H. Carleton Greene: *Two Threats to Broadcasting*, Bad Schwalbach, May 1959.

ary message.'[1] In the next months television and radio became the bastions of free speech and truthful reporting: when the Russians moved in, they went straight for those bastions.

The role of television as a forum for democracy, even as a part-substitute for parliament, is growing rather than diminishing; the fact that so much discussion is now outside parliament – culminating in the student revolts – presents television with new scope and new conflicts. All over western Europe, there has been argument as to how far television should give publicity to the students, and the rebels' provocative tactics – themselves designed with half an eye on the camera – have brought the question of selection and control of programmes into the forefront. The extra-parliamentary medium is faced with extra-parliamentary movements, and this provides a new kind of test of democracies: if the movements are ignored both by television and parliament, then the anger (as in France) will be bottled up for a future explosion. Britain has so far, I believe, managed to keep television open to most new controversies, more successfully than most. As one BBC producer, Anthony Smith, has put it to me:

The beauty of the position in Britain as opposed to France and Germany is that everyone in this country knows that every major controversy will find its way on to the screens; British television is organized in such a way that it can't be prevented from making the semi-conscious guilts and languishes of the British conscious and official. It is one of the things that enables us to achieve quite rapid change in a context of social stability; the French thought that by a process of selection you could control the actual information that circulates in a country, ignoring the fact that television distributes very little information anyway. Its function is more ritual than educational. Dubcek on the other hand realized that the more you open up television to express the truths (or the facts) that everyone accepts anyway, the greater stability you can achieve. Television is therefore purgative and anti-revolutionary where it is established as a truly mass medium; dictators or would-be dictators naturally think that the medium is revolutionary, and in suppressing it create certain of the conditions within a country that actually do form the basis of revolution, namely disbelief of the public media.

1. *The Listener*, 11th April, 1968.

ELECTRONIC VILLAGE

Idealists of broadcasting have seen television as an international force, helping to shrink the world. But, in purely
technical terms, television is much less international than
wireless; an efficient radio set can pick up programmes from
all over Europe, and can give a linguist listener a real sense
of travelling along sound-waves; while television is much
more hemmed in by its short range.

There are significant overlaps. German television, for instance, spreads across the frontiers into eastern Holland and
Belgium, and bits of Switzerland, France and Austria.
Many Dutch and Austrians prefer to watch German programmes, the Dutch marketing men have discovered sudden
unexpected boosts in sales of products when they have been
advertised on German TV: the influence of German TV is
said to have humanized the image of Germany among neighbours. In parts of Holland there are central aerial systems,
on top of high flats, which can pick up programmes from
Germany, France and Belgium. In Belgium, French television can penetrate across the flat fields of Flanders, with
unexpected results; for instance, after De Gaulle's veto of
British entry to the common market in 1963, the Flemish
were found to be surprisingly unsympathetic to the British –
partly because, it turned out, they were influenced by French
television versions of the news. In Brittany, and round Boulogne and Calais, there is a small vogue for watching BBC2.
In France, Belgium and Holland – which do not have any
television advertising – the glimpses of TV commercials
from neighbouring countries increases the anger of advertising men at their exclusion from the new gold-mine.

But most viewers are shut in to their own national networks, and the frontiers in the air have been strengthened by
the coming of colour television. It is a pathetic example of
Europe's inability to co-operate – not simply perpetuating
old divisions, but creating new ones. The old black-and-
white barrier between the screens – 405 (Britain), 819
(France) and 625 (the rest) – was bad enough. But colour has
provided much more expensive rivalries. In 1967 the major
European countries, including Russia, all started programmes in colour – fourteen years later than America, and

seven years after Japan. The delay has allowed Europe to
produce better colour – but also to produce two irreconcilable systems (both of them different from the American
system, NTSC), the German PAL and the French SECAM,
which in spite of all efforts to unite them now split Europe
down the middle: the PAL empire stretches from Scan-

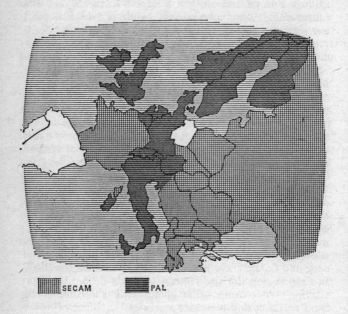

dinavia to Italy, including Britain and Iceland, while
SECAM embraces Russia and most of eastern Europe. Sets
made for SECAM cannot pick up programmes from PAL,
and vice versa, so that the division creates a new curtain
through Europe. People in small countries like Belgium and
Holland, who have been able to pick up foreign TV programmes in black-and-white, will be cut off by the colour
curtain; and only expensive two-way sets will provide both
systems.

Both in colour and black-and-white, the great majority of

viewers see (and want to see) only their own country's television: and watching it through Europe one is struck by how
far it reflects, or even magnifies, the national distinctions; the
unrelenting long-windedness and rhetoric of Italian political
discussion; the overwhelming solemnity of the German, the
smugness of the French, or the self-criticism of the British.
The advertisements dwell lovingly on national clichés, particularly with relation to sex; on German commercials the
women seem still to be perpetually polishing, on Italian ones
they seem always to be floating in long dresses through eth-
ereal backgrounds. It is not easy to remember that all this is
one continent.

Some massive events, it is true, do bring viewers together,
through the engineering system of 'Eurovision' in Geneva,
so that for a few minutes the whole continent is under the
same spell: the funeral of Churchill, the selection of Miss
World; the deaths of the Kennedys; the 1966 World Cup
final between Britain and Germany. On these rare occasions
television really does project an 'electronic village', emptying
the streets from John o' Groats to Calabria and producing
the same universal topic of conversation the next morning.
But otherwise Eurovision has been something of a let-down.
After the first excitement the viewers find the supranational
context impersonal and remote, and national stations now
like to add their own local commentaries and 'anchor men'
to interpret the programmes.

Several companies make 'European' gestures with special
programmes about other countries. In Germany on Sunday
morning there is the '*Frühschoppen*', a discussion with international guests; in several countries there is the '*Jeux Sans
Frontières*', an international quiz-game. In Britain there is
the programme 'Europa', which now has imitators in Germany, Belgium and French Canada; it gives film reports on
one country by another – a Swiss view of English gambling,
or a German view of Albania. 'Europa' provides an odd
glimpse of national cross-relations, but it also reveals how
much of the excitement and guts of television come from its
national basis. What makes the programme is not the
European consciousness, but European rivalries and cross-
purposes: like football matches, symbolizing or even car-
icaturing the national differences.

But the biggest traffic across the frontiers, as with printed

magazines, is not in facts but in fantasy. The main common
element in European television is now the common addic-
tion to British serials. They pop up in increasing numbers in
every country except Russia: Mrs. Thursday in Sweden,
Coronation Street in Holland, Dr. Finlay in Poland, Sher-
lock Holmes in Hungary, Tom Sawyer in Belgium, the Saint
in Rumania. The television magazines of small countries
look uncannily familiar to an Englishman, with pictures of
the Forsytes, Dr. Who or the Troubleshooters. The most
successful of all, like Danger Man, the Saint, or Z-Cars, span
almost the whole continent: the English Maigret appears
nearly everywhere except France (which has its own Maigret). The top seller is The Avengers, which crops up in
various disguises. In France it is called 'bowler hat and
leather boots'; in Germany (where it is almost a national
obsession) it is called 'with umbrella, charm and bowler hat'.
(For an Englishman to watch it dubbed in German is an odd
sensation; for although the character of Steed is extrava-
gantly English, the voices seem to shift the whole setting to
Germany, adding a new dimension of mystery and kink-
iness.) In the last few years the British traffic in serials has
pushed still further behind the iron curtain; the audiences
sometimes (but not too often) complain that the villains are
Russian.

The basic reason for this trade is the high cost of serials.
Only America and Britain have big enough markets to
afford large numbers of fast-moving series – say £50,000 for
an hour's performance – and other countries have to look to
them to fill the hungry maws of the television screens. In the
last two years British exports have gained on Americans;
Europeans have reacted against the American style and American political assumptions, and have turned more towards
British alternatives (although British serials often themselves
have 'mid-Atlantic' character, having an eye on the American market). British television is thus beginning to play
the same kind of role as purveyors of international fantasy
as Hollywood played before the war. It is slightly alarming
to reflect what kind of image of Britain must emerge from a
mixture of Coronation Street, the Saint and Z-Cars.

ELECTRONIC LIMBO

Outside the fantasies of songs and serials, it is hard to find proof that television has helped to break down frontiers or to build up an integrated Europe. It may well be in ten years' time, with the development of satellites, that sets could be made, each with their own miniature 'dish' to pick up distant programmes; but would governments encourage them, or viewers enjoy them? Here we reach a matter of more general speculation. The ultimate barriers are as much cultural as technical: the appeal of television, like that of newspapers and politics, depends on national assumptions, national hopes, national involvements; and attempts to produce non-national programmes, like the United Nations' ones, are apt to be lifeless and flat. Television producers find that, except on astonishing occasions like Russian space flights, or world cups, attempts to present the world as the 'electronic village' end up as an electronic limbo. Some old BBC hands believe that radio has a more decisive influence abroad, by carrying straight information and unvarnished facts. But even the old motto borrowed by Reith, 'Nation shall speak peace unto nation,' proved inept: for radio turned out to be much more effective speaking war.

Yet television still has a unique capacity to bring the world into a room. It has been able to convey a sense of familiarity with foreign people, and foreign leaders, which radio and newspapers never could. It has very easily confuted old clichés about lazy Italians and fat Frenchmen, and it has certainly quickened the sense of competition between countries: among farm workers it has been found to have a special impact, by showing how much better off people are in the towns. In all countries television has been associated with the materialism of the new affluence, and everywhere it has been attacked as the voice of 'the Establishment'. But the love of spectacle, which has helped to bind television to the national establishments, can in the end be exploited by the opposite side. There can be little doubt that the fires of student revolts, spreading from university to university, have been fanned by the television cameras; for if there is one thing that suits television even better than pageantry, it is violence. Television cannot stir up movements and debates out of nothing. But once there are great events and high emotions to be reached (as in the Paris revolts), television can reflect them and pass them from country to country with a sense of urgency and intimacy that is shared by no other medium.

SONGS

It is quite fitting that the most successful Eurovision link-up should be the preposterous song contest, the annual climax of fantasy and romance. Here at last is an event which the whole continent witnesses collectively. In the 1968 contest, held at the Albert Hall, two hundred million people (twenty-two million in England) watched singers from seventeen countries. They appeared on a star-spangled stage in long glistening dresses, and looked at the audience with the dreamy look of girls in romantic postcards. The audience in the hall, predominantly middle-aged, gazed back with longing. Most of the songs conformed to their national caricature: all the French-speaking songs were about *l'amour*, the Italian was about *il sole*, the Norwegian was about stress. The winner was a Spanish song with no language barrier, called 'La-la-la', sung by a jolly little girl with huge smiling teeth, who looked like a simple peasant but who turned out to be the daughter of a millionaire impresario. (The voting for each country was an interesting index of national allegiances: Scandinavians and Iberians voted loyally for each other, Ireland and Yugoslavia exchanged votes, Britain voted heavily for Germany, and Germany voted decisively for Spain.)

Songs travel much better than politicians or jokes. The winning Eurovision song is immediately released in several languages, and blared out by juke-boxes from Helsinki to Brindisi. Songs have a really common market, if nothing else has. They are among the few art-forms where foreign names and place names are positively *welcome*. They exude a sense of geographical restlessness, with inarticulate longings to be always somewhere else. 'Wonderful, Wonderful Copenhagen!' 'Arriverderci, Roma!' 'Come Back to Sorrento!' 'California Here I Come!' 'I Love Paris!' 'Goodbye to the Isle of Capri!' A few places, like Bootle or Woking, may not yet have been serenaded in this way, but there was even a nostalgic French song called 'Manchester and Liverpool', which was tactfully translated into English as 'Where have you been, Pussycat?' Foreign names, particularly English names, are always appreciated. The top four German singers in 1968 were called respectively Roy Black, Ronny, Peter Alexander and Freddy Quinn. Among the favourite Dutch groups are the Down Town Jazz Band, the Mops and OK Wobblers. The British singer Gerry Dorsey attributes some of his success to changing his name to Engelbert Humperdinck (in Germany, at the request of the composer's son, he drops the Humperdinck).

The internationalism of songs is familiar. The troubadours strummed through France, Italy and Spain in the twelfth century. Chevalier and Dietrich were international names in the thirties. What is new is not the traffic, but the scale of it.

Songs still show, as emphatically as food, the classic division of tastes between Latin and Teutonic peoples. The Italians still take their songs more seriously than anyone. Italy has three hundred record companies, which produce an average of thirty-eight new songs *a day*; there are a dozen pop song festivals a year, culminating in the one at San Remo in January, where villages from all over Italy send in their votes, and see the results on television: the competition is intense, and when Luigi Tenco failed to win the contest with his 'Ciao, amore, ciao' he committed suicide: soon afterwards it became a world hit. Ten years ago the Italian position seemed secure, with singers like Marino Marini and Domenico Modugno, and world-famous songs like 'Ciao Ciao Bambino' and 'Arriverderci Roma'. Inside the country, Italian songs still hold their own; of their top singers in 1967, the first ten were Italian. But in the last few years the Anglo-Saxons have moved into Italy with relentless wails, defying all the rules of *'bel canto'*: I Beatles, I Rolling Stones and I Procul Harum have become part of the language. Perhaps the invasion of machines has demoralized the old romantics: in any case, as the Fiats have boomed, the Italian songs have slumped.

France is a more formidable stronghold; and in spite of foreign bombardments, the French song has kept its fastidious character. On *France Inter*, the pop radio station, the Gallic sounds keep up the fight, with their rolling rrr's, their lilting cadences, and their tinkling pianos or echoing flutes – rudely interrupted by the harsh batterings of Anglo-Saxon drums, and guitars and echo chambers. One should not underestimate the resistance of the French song. The prevailing style is unmistakably Gallic, with some songs that could have happened twenty years ago, with the same old backgrounds – gipsy violins, accordions or Mantovani-type strings – and the same old rhymes: *amour, jour, toujours*; *pluie, nuit, Paris*. They are still fortified by a special intellectual snobbery. One singer, Georges Brassens, has already had a thesis written about him, and was rumoured to be going to be elected to the Academy. Another, Antoine, went to the exclusive Sciences-Po. Another, Gilbert Becaud, has composed an opera and written a song in praise of De Gaulle, Jacques Brel – now a film star – is the object of a special eggheads' cult. Singers are not only literary, but political: Sheila is known as a Gaullist, Jean Ferrat as very left.

The French tradition still casts its spell, attracting singers from all over Europe. Two of their stars, Adamo and Jacques Brel, come from Belgium: so does the 'Singing Nun', Luc Dominique, with her guitar called Adèle. Aznavour, the tiny actor-singer, is Armenian, Dalida is half-Italian; Petula Clark began as a rather square English singer and has been transformed into a sophisticated French star.

But even in France, the Anglo-American invasion has transformed the scene, and the Beatles and their followers have broken the barriers. As with television serials, the French can ascribe their defeat partly to the sheer size and professionalism of the Anglo-American market. The record companies can build their expertise on the huge teenage market, to develop more elaborately noisy recordings. The giant EMI company has twenty per cent of the world market, and of the top eight record companies in France only two are wholly French. As patrons of pop, the English and American teenagers are a more formidable army than any continentals: they are louder and freer, they work less and play more.

But the roaring victories of the Beatles cannot be explained away just by the strength of the Anglo-Saxon market. What has swept the British pop singers through Europe has been their vitality, their freshness, and above all their ability to express the liberation of youth; and it is this which makes their sounds so exciting and significant in eastern Europe (a BBC man transmitting programmes behind the iron curtain complained that for every letter he received about political and cultural talks, there were a hundred asking for more pop songs). It is an odd experience to twiddle the knob of a radio in London, and hear, in the midst of the jabber of incomprehensible talk, the same tunes and singers bursting out from stations all over the continent. No one will ever be able to assess the real influence of this mixing of noises. Songs are part of that mysterious international sub-culture – including fashion, comic-strips, advertising gimmicks and pop art – which, not dependent on words, can move easily through frontiers, on television or films, or in picture magazines. Their influence is very visible; when the French star Sheila sang a song called 'Le Kilt', sales of tartan shot up in Paris; when Julie Driscoll appeared in Europe, fuzzy hair appeared too. The influence of songs may be superficial, but we cannot afford to ignore them; for the throbs and wails of pop music are about the nearest we have to a common European language.

Chapter Seventeen

Films

One day in Rome we went out to lunch with a friend who works at the film studios of Dino De Laurentiis, the Italian film tycoon. Along the Via Latina, just before the twenty-third kilometre stone, two great grey cubes rose out from the flat plain; in front of them stood a shiny white office block with round penthouses on top (where the boss lives); an automatic gate let us into the car-park filled with big Fiats. Inside, the offices could just as well be in Hollywood. There were international unpronounceable names on the doors: everyone had to be able to speak English. In a big foyer there was an elaborate model of the battle of Waterloo, made with toy soldiers, guns and farms, laid out to impress prospective American backers for the film. In one of the big cubes, bits of Padua from *The Taming of the Shrew* were being dismantled to make way for *Barbarella*.

After lunch at the Restaurant of the Stars, we drove along a rough track behind the studios, to explore this fantasy territory. Cologne cathedral loomed up on the left, looking tattered. We came to a rondavel village, left over from some African epic; then an Indian wigwam camp; and rounding a corner we suddenly found ourselves driving into the middle of a wild west town, with a Wells Fargo coach in the middle of it. We parked quickly, to avoid getting into the film, and got out to watch. It seemed curious, on this hot May afternoon, a few miles outside Rome.

There was all the familiar western scenery – the marshal's office, the saloon, the Colonial-style church, the provision store – with their batwing doors, their gingerbread balconies and faded lettering, all propped up with scaffolding. The stage-coach with two horses was drawn up outside the saloon, while two girls in bonnets and long velvet dresses clambered into it. A casual young director and a fat continuity girl stood by a camera on the other side of the street;

small boys, barmaids, a grocer with an apron, lurked behind
the façades: cowboys were lying on the grass chewing straw
lazily or walking around practising their slouch, as if they
had been living all their lives on the range. A megaphone
blared, the extras emerged from behind the marshal's office,
the arc-lights were rolled up. The stage-coach was galloped
off, followed by the camera. Then the girl's bonnet flew off
by mistake, the director shouted 'Cut', the horses were
stopped, and the cowboys went on chewing straw.

It was, of course, yet another of the famous Italian westerns, the most far-fetched of all the cinema success-stories.
They began when Sergio Leone, who had been an assistant
director of *Ben Hur*, decided that American television had
consumed so many westerns that Hollywood could no longer
make good ones. He decided he could just as well make them
in Europe. He got together an Italian cast, gave them English names, and found a deadpan young American television
actor, Clint Eastwood, to play the lead. He changed his own
name as director to Bob Robertson. He took over a Japanese
plot, adapted it to a western, added extra blood and violence,
and made *A Fistful of Dollars*, which ended up making over
four million dollars. It set off a boom – two hundred Italian
westerns in the next two years, half of them with the word
'dollar' in the title; in 1967 a third of all films made in Italy
were westerns, led by *The Good, the Ugly and the Bad,* and
there were more westerns made in Italy than in America.
The whole mythology of the wild west – the goodies and
baddies, tin stars, lone hero – was transported to Roman
studios and Spanish hills. It was a rare case of a piece of
folk-lore moving from west to east.

It might seem odd that Italy, with its twenty centuries of
culture and history to draw on, with Dante, Boccaccio, Cat-
ullus or Vergil to furnish national romances, should turn to
mass-producing the corniest American myth; and the 'Spaghetti Westerns' or 'Dollar Bang-Bangs' have been much
mocked by critics for their bloodthirsty clichés and ham
acting. For myself, after seeing *For a Few Dollars More*, I
felt that Leone had in fact resuscitated the dying western. His
crude villains speaking broken English and his cheap Spanish shacks are much more evocative of a frontier society
than the glossy new Hollywood westerns, which long ago lost
confidence in their plots. Leone reminds us that the west was

peopled by uprooted and confused Europeans, perhaps not unlike his own actors. He himself has no doubts of the relevance of westerns to Europe. 'The universal attraction of the western,' he told the *New York Times* in 1968, 'is that it is a great fable, a myth like Achilles. For me personally the attraction is the joy of making justice oneself without asking permission – bang, bang. It is especially appreciated today with these long lawsuits. Look at me – I am now in my fourth year of lawsuits!'[1]

The dollar bang-bangs are an odd reflection on Italian filmgoers, who are the most dedicated in Europe: these were the box-office receipts (according to *Variety*) in the biggest European markets of 1966:

Millions of Dollars	
Italy	265
Great Britain	175
Germany	156
France	156
Spain	100

Of the two hundred and sixty-five million dollars from Italian audiences, a hundred million went to American films; but the traffic has recently become more two-way. As with food, Italian films, led by the westerns, have been booming abroad, and in 1966 forty-five million dollars' worth were exported – three times as much as in 1958.

In its golden age just before the First World War, the Italian industry led the world in spectacular productions. Before the days of talkies, films could travel across the world with extraordinary ease, not needing translating or subtitling: the film was itself a new international language. The Italian *Quo Vadis* in 1913 had huge reconstructions of Ancient Rome with real lions for the circus; it lasted two hours, cost £7,000, and made a profit of £70,000. It set a new pattern for silent spectaculars. But after the First World War Hollywood emerged all-powerful and the Italian industry lost much of its talent. Mussolini tried to revive it; he built Cinecittá outside Rome, and started the first film festivals; but he made the Italian cinema into a propaganda weapon, and directors like Rossellini and de Sica stopped making films and became critics. At the end of the Second World

1. Interview with Mary Blume, 6th March, 1968.

War Cinecittá was a refugee camp and the industry was in chaos: but the very lack of equipment contributed to the neo-realism of the post-war films, like *Bicycle Thieves* or *Rome Open City*, which set a new and seminal style for Europe. This burst of creativity spent itself, but the Italian industry regained its commercial strength: a shrewd lawyer, Eitel Monaco, who still runs the Italian Motion Picture Association, built it up into the best-organized industry in Europe. But it has become increasingly geared to the American market, and even films primarily intended for Italian audiences are sometimes shot in English and then dubbed into Italian. (For Italian westerns, each actor speaks his own language, and is dubbed later.) While the Americans have moved into Italy, the Italians have moved into America, to conquer more effectively the American market. In 1967 there were as many Italian pictures made in America as the other way round, and one film *An Italian in America* was near the top of the box-office successes. The links between Italians and Italo-Americans, so little evident in diplomacy or industry, are very apparent in films. Italian directors and actors often use anglicized names, with exotic results: the checklist of Italian pseudonyms in the *Monthly Film Bulletin* in January 1967 included Jeff Frank (Jesus Franco), Anthony Daisies (Antonio Margherita), Red Ross (Renato Rossini), Montgomery Wood (Giuliano Gemma) and Olga Sunbeauty (Olga Solbelli).

A GLOBAL INDUSTRY?

The cinema is visibly capable of sweeping across frontiers. You can see the same film, in different linguistic disguises, turning up in every capital: a weird-sounding name turns out to be all too familiar – 'Loin de la Foule Déchainée' is only 'Far From the Madding Crowd', 'La Bisbetica Domata' is just 'The Taming of the Shrew': these old familiars tend to increase the sense of unreality of jet travel. The fashionable cinema districts, the Champs Elysées, Leicester Square or the Piazza Barberini, have a shiny family likeness, and often enough the cinemas turn out to be American-owned. Big hits like the James Bond films can leave their wake of toys, pullovers or slang all over the continent. Films are a prime influence in propagating the sub-culture of fashions and styles, with extraordinary speed, all through the western world. *Bonnie and Clyde* swept through every capital, leaving a boom in berets and maxi-skirts.

There is nothing new about this global uniformity. For twenty years between the wars the great Hollywood studios provided a universal mythology: the Europeans fought back with quotas and subsidies, but Hollywood could scoop up most of the talent and outbid them in sheer size. After the Second World War the great Hollywood studios broke up in the face of taxation and television (for people of my generation, the collapse of Hollywood seemed as momentous as the Fall of Constantinople). It looked for a time as if America was losing its grip over the world's film industry; in fact the grip was becoming stronger, though more concealed. The big studios bought up world distribution networks; and more and more Hollywood money and Hollywood directors moved over to Europe, escaping from taxation or from Joseph McCarthy, or in search of cheaper extras or better actors. New Californias were discovered first in Italy, then in Spain and then in Yugoslavia.

Television forced the cinema to become even more of a world industry. The film companies put their money on the big blockbusters which could provide the spectacle which the small screen couldn't. As with other technologies, the sheer cost of these films forced them to look beyond their own frontiers. Breathtaking scenes involve breathtaking expense (the climax of *You Only Live Twice*, where the roof of a volcano opens up, cost £350,000). The really big moneymakers are all spectacles. These were the all-time box-office hits in North America up to 1967, according to *Variety*:

1 *Sound of Music* (1965)
2 *Gone with the Wind* (1939)
3 *Ten Commandments* (1957)
4 *Ben Hur* (1959)
5 *Dr Zhivago* (1965)
6 *Mary Poppins* (1964)
7 *My Fair Lady* (1964)
8 *Cleopatra* (1964)
9 *Thunderball* (1965)
10 *How the West Was Won* (1962)

(No global figures exist, but the top ten in Europe would not be very different, except that musicals have not had much success on the continent.)

The European film industries, to fight back, have had to

collaborate across frontiers: it is curious to note that European films with all their problems of language and cultures, have managed to internationalize themselves more effectively than chemicals, cars or computers. They have devised elaborate 'co-production' agreements, in which two or more countries share the finance of a film, and undertake that production costs and employment of nationals will roughly balance. Scenes are shot twice, once in each language; or the stars speak their own language and are dubbed later. The result is an odd kind of stateless film. *Barbarella*, for instance, was shot at De Laurentiis's studios in Rome, co-produced between France and Italy; the director was French, Roger Vadim, the star was his American wife, Jane Fonda, and other stars were Ugo Tognazzi and Milo O'Shea. In the common market countries co-produced films now outnumber national ones: of eighty-eight films made in France in 1967, seventy-three were co-productions. The British did not come to co-production until 1967 – in time for the political move towards Europe; in September, just before De Gaulle's second veto, there was a Franco-British agreement, and two months later an Anglo-Italian. Among the first Anglo-French pictures were *Mayerling*, a remake of the old romantic film, with Omar Sharif and Catherine Deneuve; and *La Motocyclette*, with Alain Delon and Marianne Faithfull.

But co-productions have not been able to counter the invasions of American capital, and in the last few years the Americans, as well as making their own films in Europe, have increasingly financed the Europeans. In France they are having a large impact, offering both finance and distribution. In Italy Americans are moving into 'co-participation', and they arranged to invest fifty million dollars in 1968. Many Italian westerns are American-financed, and even Franco-Italian co-productions are often made with American money.

The American influence is most evident in Britain, where between eighty and ninety per cent of films are American-financed. The American invasion is encouraged by a subsidy of 'Eady Money' (named after its inventor, Sir Wilfred Eady), which helps films made in Britain with a levy collected from the box-office. But the main attraction is the 'reservoir' of actors, directors and technicians, cheaper and sometimes better than Americans, who speak more or less the same language.

Without the flow of American capital, the British or Italian industries would be in very serious straits. But the involvement in the transatlantic market must change their perspective; as one British director put it: 'When you're dealing with Americans, you have to put on Hollywood spectacles; and then it's difficult to take them off.' In Italy the association of film authors (ANAC), with a majority of left-wing documentary-writers, accused the big directors of being '*tutti Americani*' – after which the hundred members, including Fellini and Visconti, walked out. The association then deplored the 'depersonalization of the works, conditioned by the requirements of the international market; the cheapening of any original research; the automatic deafness towards anything worrying for the system.'

It is perhaps in France that the conflict is most extreme, between a sensitive national tradition and the pressures of the international industry; for the French directors have always – and still more in the last decade – imposed their own personal, poetical style on their films, and have succeeded in integrating films into their whole culture, blending poetry, painting and acting. The French industry has always had a cultural prestige far higher than in Britain and America: poets and novelists have turned with enthusiasm to the medium, and with the help of the government-subsidized film school, a group of directors has grown up who see films as a means of expressing their private thoughts and fantasies, without compromise: the 'new wave' which appeared in the late fifties, showed their own ideas on the medium. In films, the contrast between French and British styles is specially extreme; as one British critic, John Ardagh, has described it; 'The French are not obsessed like us by the problems of community; but they are by individual solitude within community, by romantic love as a way out of solitude, by the chaos on the fringes of modern life, by the struggle for self-identity. French films today are about love, the British ones about sex; French films are about despair, and British ones about social climbing.'[1]

The privacy and seclusion of French films has obvious dangers; the directors belong to a privileged Paris world, are

1. John Ardagh: *The New French Revolution*, Harper & Row, 1969.

not much concerned with social problems, and are tempted towards snobberies, cults and obscurity for its own sake. French film criticism, in its anxiety to become a fine art, is capable of absurd flights of pretensions. But the sheltered conditions of the French directors have, up till recently, enabled them to experiment and explore without worrying too much about the big-business pressures. Now the French cinema, too, is in financial crisis; costs are growing, audiences are falling, and becoming less adventurous and more conformist, preferring action to fantasy. With a more commercialized and uniform home market, with growing costs and more expensive ambitions, the French directors, too, are turning towards America for their backing, and trying for the world market. Louis Malle's *Viva Maria* and François Truffaut's *Fahrenheit 451*, both with American backing, showed the uneasy influence of American backing, while the all-star epic of the Liberation, *Paris Brûle-t-il?* with its flagrant falsifications of history, showed the kind of corruption that the French cinema had seem fortified against.

The European film-makers are embarrassed both by the American invasion and by the dwindling box-offices. Eitel Monaco wrote[1] that '1967 was a continuation of the uninterrupted and insidious deterioration of Europe's film market – Europe last year lost another one hundred and twenty million admissions. . . . I find myself compelled once more to point out that economic integration and common market unification for motion pictures is advancing rather slowly and with considerable difficulty.' Monaco wants to standardize European methods of subsidy, and, to build up a fund – a kind of European 'Eady Money' – which would subsidize productions. But as with other industries, each film business had grown up leaning on its own government; and for them to lean instead on a European prop requires a new confidence in supranational authority. In the meantime, the film-makers prefer to find their money where it is easiest – in America. We are back at the familiar dilemma of Europeans who want to unite, but prefer to collaborate with Americans. Monaco, while insisting that the film industries must acquire 'a clearer and more precise European mentality', wants to increase still further the Italian co-participation with America.

1. *Variety*, 18th May, 1968.

Nowadays American film tycoons maintain that 'this is the most international industry in the world'. It is certainly remarkable that the same films and the same fantasies should be acceptable to half the world, scooping up talent, writers and directors from half a dozen countries. The big films can no longer simply propagate the American way of life; they have been forced to mix up the nationalities. It is fitting that Zeffirelli's production of *The Taming of the Shrew* should Italianize Shakespeare, as Shakespeare four hundred years before anglicized his Italian plots and characters. The old play re-emerges as a kind of slapstick opera, led by the Burtons, the Tsar and Tsarina of Internationalia.

Yet it is an irony that the film industry which is one of the most internationalized should also be most easily damaged by the process. For razor blades, motor-cars or tape recorders, the bigger the market, the better the product should become; but with films, sheer size constantly threatens to extinguish originality. Most of the innovating directors have begun outside the big markets, presenting a more private and local world without looking over their shoulders: it is no accident that so much creative work should come from Sweden, Poland or Czechoslovakia, protected from the multimillion market with the help of nationalized film industries. Films, unlike television and the press, have by their nature a power to communicate internationally. The emotions to which they appeal are universal. But the search for international stars and settings can easily end up in a featureless and characterless no-man's-land.

'MORGAN' AND OTHERS

Among the many new factors over the past ten years there has been one of special importance: the audiences have become very much younger. While television is a medium for the middle-aged, who like to sit at home, the young like to get out, to escape from their parents or to snog in the dark: the average age of cinema-goers is around twenty-two. The youth of audiences has helped to demoralize the old Hollywood tycoons. They no longer know what their audiences like; the young have inexplicable tastes; and trying desperately to keep up with them, they have to hire foreign directors who seem to understand, and to leave them to it.

The preponderance of youth accounts for the succession of off-beat films, particularly English ones, which have had unpredictable successes in America and Europe. *The Knack*, the Beatles films, *Morgan*, and many others all project the same kind of alienation from a middle-aged bourgeois society, the sense of floating above material things; there is a mix-up of fantasy and fact, implying that concrete is cardboard; there is a background of shocked old people. The same kind of alienation, with different forms, appears in some of Godard's films, or in Antonioni who hit the world jack-pot with *Blow-Up*. The story of *Morgan* might be taken as an odd example of the idiom: Morgan is the mixed-up son of a communist café-owner, who lives in a world of fantasies about big game and revolutions, and has had a hopeless marriage with an upper-class girl, which is wrecked by his wild practical jokes. When his ex-wife marries a conventional capitalist, he dresses up as a gorilla and invades the wedding party, scattering the horrified guests. He is last seen at an asylum, bedding out the plants in the shape of a hammer and sickle.

It is these films of alienated youth which have spread so successfully through the capitals, to the bewilderment of the Hollywood financiers. Fantasy, as we have seen, travels across frontiers more easily than fact. But this kind of fantasy has a special significance; for it gives a hint of the mood which unites the young inside western society, and unites them against it.

INTERNATIONALIA

I asked an American film tycoon: 'are tastes in films, in America and Europe, converging or diverging?' He looked at me hard, and said, 'Off the record – diverging.' He went on: 'Nowadays Europeans don't go for the American comedies, the Doris Day kind of thing: even *Barefoot in the Park* was a flop. You used to be able to sell most things American; now they're more choosy, and they don't laugh at our jokes.'

The film industry is the most public example of the interaction of America and Europe, and it provides a kind of caricature of the problems of big corporations and local communities. On the one hand European film industries are becoming still more dependent on American finance and distribution. On the other hand, European talents are, if anything, still more important to the industry, not only in Europe but in America. The film business can never be seen entirely in terms of money; because it is in the nature of the commercial machine to grind down its talent, and to turn in on itself, it has to be constantly revived and refreshed from outside itself, and to look further and further afield for original talent – to Poland, Czechoslovakia, Japan. The vast international spectacles, belonging to no place, will doubtless continue to be the real money-spinners; but what matters in the end to the cinema is the infusion of original observation, which comes not from Internationalia, but from the private personalities of directors, operating often in very local surroundings. The conflict and tension between the integrity of the director and the tempting, corrupting opportunities of big finance has been in the nature of the medium, from the beginning; it exists in every encounter between director and producer. Though the American involvement in Europe is now greater, and the financial stakes much higher, it remains quite possible – because of the desperate shortage of talent – for strong-minded directors to retain their independence. The formation of a European film industry, though it may make the cinema more prosperous, will not resolve the basic conflict; there is no reason why European tycoons in search of the American market should be any less philistine than the American ones; and the American companies are themselves striving, like IBM, to become more 'geo-centric'. What is ultimately important is that the European cinema retains its element of privacy and local involvement – whether based on individuals, regions or nations – and keeps up the conflict with big business.

In the last seven chapters we have looked at part of the machinery and the décor of a cosmopolitan Europe, and touched on some of the bleaker symbols which spring to many people's minds when the word 'international' is mentioned. Airports full of glazed-eyed tourists, flying from one big hotel to the next, or eating fish fingers in six countries to the juke-box sounds of 'La-La-La'. Translators intoning their own lifeless American-English, with strings of meaningless nouns. Magazines recounting the same stories of Jane

Fonda, the Burtons or Brigitte Bardot. Colour advertisements showing lean, supercilious escorts smoking Peter Stuyvesant in opera foyers. Glossy shop-windows full of international gadgetry, Grundig tape-recorders, Ignis refrigerators, Instamatic cameras, displayed on Scandinavian furniture against chaste white walls. Swinging people racing in Hertz cars across frontiers, from Hilton to Hilton. Such clichés are familiar from advertisements, and from the most escapist films, which express well enough the ultimate nightmare of Internationalia – that its inhabitants in the end have nowhere to go to, and nothing to say, and that if they ever stop still they will cease to exist. But the great films can also express the realities of Europe; the small, subtle communities of people with complex relationships, whose approach to intruders is wary and sceptical; the individual constantly in search of his identity, escaping from the harshness and inhumanity of the city into private discovery and love. The cinema is at its most truly universal not when it parades international stars, but when, from within its own local setting, it reveals human emotions and predicaments with such honesty and perception that it can cross frontiers and iron curtains and language barriers and still produce the same reactions among audiences at the other side of the world.

The cinema, like other media, reflects the political climate of Europe. In the present state of western European unity, it is not surprising that 'internationalism' should be readily associated with glitter, speed, money and rootlessness; for that unity is essentially hollow: the casing is there, the communications, the capital, the goods – all the apparatus of a banker's Europe. What is missing is the political substance, the community of ideas and ambitions, the common way of life of ordinary people, who can react to the machinery and superstructures with a sense of belonging to a genuine European community. It is the political content – which forms the matter of the next section – by which the unity of Europe will stand or fall.

Part Four

Chapter Eighteen

Technocrats

> In what modern nation has not one already noticed the astonishing contradiction between these solemn assemblies, composed of men elected after the show of popular passions, meeting in historic and sumptuous palaces, and these unknown dusty offices, where people rule whose names are not heard outside a narrow circle of initiates?
>
> *Michel Debré, 1950*

With governments preoccupied by industrial growth, with voters engrossed by material improvements, with the old distinctions between left and right becoming still more muddled, it is not surprising that the bogy of the technocrat should again be stalking through Europe. The notion of 'depoliticization' implies that decisions can be taken at the top which are based on rational, not political considerations; and the current trends of European unity, more concerned with integrating things than people, encourage the belief that the technocrat is a more sensible substitute for the politician. The word technocrat is given many meanings, and is often used to attack anyone who knows his job properly. But the only important meaning is someone who is able to wield great power through his special expertise without being accountable to any political process.

The physical transformations of Europe that we have seen in earlier chapters – motorways, airports, nuclear power stations, tourist centres and the whole apparatus of the industrial corporations – have all increased the need for strong centralized planning, run by committees of experts interlocking with the state. Their decisions superimpose themselves on the local communities as suddenly as foreign armies – a steelworks at Taranto, hotels and harbours in Languedoc, a motorway to Calabria. Only in rare cases, when the technocrats come up against a powerful bourgeois lobby, are they openly challenged or reversed; but these cases, frustrated by influential minorities, only show how many other cases go unchallenged. As the crowded continent undergoes the next stage of industrialization, based on the massive centralized resources of the computer, so the conflict between the central planners and the regions will, I believe, become an increasingly fierce issue on the continent, a new version of the old struggles between absolute monarchs and their disaffected provinces.

The idea of government by technocrats is a very old one. The word itself came from America after the First World War, but the concept goes back to early nineteenth-century France. The first prophet of the technocrats was the eccentric Comte de Saint-Simon, who took some of his inspiration from the École Polytechnique, which has ever since been a breeding-ground for technocrats and prophets of technocracy.[1] Saint-Simon visualized a great new age in which life could be measured and controlled in scientific rather than metaphysical terms. He believed in 'the government of things, not men', and advocated that the state should be run and planned by experts – scientists, industrialists, bankers. On this basis he even visualized a United Europe, run by the sages of France, Britain, Germany and Italy, and dominating the rest of the world. Saint-Simon foresaw the vastly growing role of industrial power; though the nineteenth century success of *laissez-faire* seemed to deny the need for central planning. But with the breakdown of the capitalist system in the 1920s, and the apparent incapacity of political parties to do anything about it, the notion of planning, in France, Britain and elsewhere, came back into favour with intellectuals: in France, the Polytechnique was once again the centre of it. But it was not till after the war that the planners, first in France and then in Britain, began finally to enter their kingdom; the economy had become so intricate, and the technological industries so vast, that they depended more and more on the state; and the dreams of Saint-Simon seemed, after nearly two centuries, to be coming partially true. De Gaulle's cabinet, with its array of ex-civil servants,

1. See pp. 359–63.

began to look like a planning council, and the French five-year plans acquired, each time, a more confident moral tone. Planning brings with it a new scope for the technocrats, for by dealing with the distant future they can more easily escape the control of parliament and politicians. British governments, first under Macmillan then under Wilson, looked with some envy towards French technocracy; and industrialists and journalists complained more and more about the muddles of parliament; in 1968 there was even a brief campaign, led by Lord Robens and Cecil King, to build a 'technocrats' cabinet'. In Italy there were attempts to adapt French planning, and even in Germany, particularly after the Ruhr crisis in 1967, the word planning ceased to be suspect. In the common market, the technocrat became a special bogy, and De Gaulle, while making full use of the French mandarins, was able to warn against the *technocrates apatrides* who stalked the corridors of Brussels.

The danger from the technocrats is a real one. All kinds of fields which used to be regarded as subject to political argument – not only in technology itself, but in education, agriculture, transport, welfare and above all defence – have become obscured and apparently 'depoliticized' by their very intricacy; where efficiency and growth are the universal cries, it is often hard to say which policy favours left or right, rich or poor, weak or strong. But the idea that there can be technocratic solutions independent of politics is usually a fallacy. The political implications remain, however much they may be concealed.

BUREAUCRATS

Of the continental nuisance called 'Bureaucracy' I can see no risk or possibility in England. Democracy is hot enough here, fierce enough, it is perennial, universal, clearly invincible among us henceforth. No danger it should let itself be flung in chains by sham-secretaries of the Pedant species and accept their vile Age of Pinchbeck for its Golden Age!

Thomas Carlyle

The tradition of bureaucracy, as Carlyle complained, is stronger on the continent, where strong administrations came before parliaments. The continental civil services stemmed from the absolute monarchies of the seventeenth and eighteenth centuries, who built up a professional caste to administer taxes and public works, and to protect them from the nobility; they were strengthened by the Napoleonic system, which spread through most of western Europe, and stopped at the Channel. Behind the strength of bureaucracies lies the special status of 'the state' and its servants after revolution. The first modern administration was built up by Frederick William I of Prussia, father of Frederick the Great, in the early eighteenth century; he insisted on university degrees for higher civil servants, gave them a period of training, and promoted them on merit, thus building up a new profession. But the Prussian standards declined, and Europe was soon to be overwhelmed by France. Napoleon took over the old corps and institutions of France and formed them into a precise hierarchy of administrators and experts, reinforced by a strict code of law and with clear personal responsibilities. Most continental countries – notably Germany, Italy and Spain – adopted the Napoleonic system; only a few smaller, newer countries like Belgium, were influenced by England.

Bureaucracy, having developed more openly on the continent, has also been more thoroughly studied. The German sociologist Max Weber outlined his theory of bureaucracy before the First World War. Tracing its development through ancient Egypt and Rome to its paramountcy in modern Europe, he regarded the characteristic principle of bureaucracy as 'the abstract regularity of the execution of authority, which is a result of the demand for equality before the law'. He observed the growing independence of German bureaucracy, particularly after Bismarck, and saw it emerging ever more strongly as the enemy of parliament. 'In facing a parliament, the bureaucracy, out of a sure power instinct, fights every attempt of the parliament to gain knowledge by means of its own experts or from interest groups.' Critics since Weber have become concerned by the discrepancy between the theory and practice of bureaucracy. 'On the one hand, most authors consider the bureaucratic organization to be the embodiment of rationality in the modern world, and, as such, to be intrinsically superior to all other possible forms of organization. On the other hand, many authors – often the same ones – consider it a sort of Leviathan, preparing the enslavement of the human race.'[1]

1. Michael Crozier: *The Bureaucratic Phenomenon*, p. 176.

The discrepancy has never been more evident than in Europe today, where the student rebels from West and East are united in their hatred for the bureaucratic machine.

The recent power of bureaucracies has been limited by their discontinuity. The German and Italian civil services were both demoralized and broken up by dictatorship, and are only now recovering. In Germany the stern Prussian tradition was undermined first by the inflationary chaos after 1919, then by Hitler, who distrusted the old bureaucrats; then by the Allies, who sacked fifty thousand officials for their Nazi record, and vainly tried to liberalize the training. Since the last war, the West German civil service has found it hard to compete with big business and bankers for the cleverest men; bureaucracy, even more in Germany than elsewhere, has been an unpopular word, and promotion has been complicated by the system, which provides eleven separate civil services, each with its own selection and salaries. The guilt of the past has helped to make senior German civil servants seem unsure of themselves and cautious in international gatherings; only among under-forties are there signs of a more coherent and confident class.

In Italy, a special chaos prevails. I remember in Rome a few years ago, a mysterious intruder used to clamber into civil service offices, muddle up the files and reduce them to chaos, leaving behind a message signed 'enemy of bureaucracy': he became a kind of national hero. The Italian bureaucracy has never really caught up with the problems of unification a hundred years ago; the strong administration of Piedmont was invaded by highly-political southerners, and the numbers swelled to unmanageable size, made greater by Mussolini's policy of using a huge civil service as a cure for unemployment: even today the citadels of officialdom in Rome have flunkeys lurking in every corner. The labyrinthine confusion of officialdom is a theme which Italians describe, with a special passion: 'Bureaucracy (like handicrafts)' writes Luigi Barzini, 'belongs to a world where time doesn't count: time is an element which does not cost anything, like the air, and which one can consume at will . . .'[1] The need to reform the bureaucracy is obvious to all Italians; there is even a special Ministry for the Reform of the

1. Luigi Barzini: 'The Italian Bureaucracy', *Encounter*, June 1956.

Bureaucracy, with its own large bureaucracy. But nothing much happens.

LAWYERS

Since the French Revolution, the modern lawyer and modern democracy belong absolutely together.

Max Weber

To the English visitor, the most striking characteristic of continental government is the influence of lawyers. It is hard to get away from them. In parliaments they are less evident than they were (in the French assembly in 1871 two-fifths of the members were lawyers; in 1956, only one-tenth: as in Britain, lawyers have been superseded by teachers as the biggest profession in parliament).[1] But in the bureaucracies the lawyer remains paramount, giving them their sense of legitimacy. He inherits the confidence and splendour of Roman and Napoleonic Law.

The difference in the position of lawyers is significant. In Britain, the lawyers – particularly the barristers – have remained since the Middle Ages a separate caste, privileged, isolated and predominantly upper-middle-class. But in continental countries magistrates and judges are part of the civil service, inside the bureaucratic machine.[2] The word 'judge' has little of the sense of awe and isolation that it has in England (perhaps the German 'professor' is the only title that strikes the same dread as an English judge). There are said to be 35,000 judges in Germany, including all kinds of administrative ones, most of them without any kind of grandeur; some share an office with three others.

The integration of the judicial system into the civil service has important advantages. While British judges love to fulminate against the inhumanity of bureaucracy, they know little and do little about it; most cases never come near the courts. Continental bureaucracies have, in normal times, been better able to control citizens' rights with administrative courts. On the other hand, the prevalence of lawyers has tended to lead to an extreme rigidity in administration. In times of crisis and impending dictatorship the judiciary

1. See Mattei Dogan: 'Political Ascent in a Class Society', in *Political Decision Makers*, ed. Marwick, Free Press of Glencoe, 1961, p. 69.
2. See Brian Chapman: *The Profession of Government*, p. 192.

lacks that proud aloofness which can make it in Britain the ultimate safeguard.

The paradise for lawyers is Germany, where their monopoly, the '*Juristenmonopol*', has become notorious. Most familiar German politicians have graduated in law – Kiesinger, Strauss, Schroeder, Hallstein – and most heads of civil service departments are lawyers: recently it was found that of the eleven ministers of education in the Länder, ten were lawyers. Professor Dahrendorf, the sociologist, maintains that law faculties are 'the functional equivalent of the public schools in English society,'[1] and that law students are subtly selected from the more prosperous families, being better dressed, more likely to own a car, or belong to a fraternity: he concludes that 'in the interests of a spreading of liberal ideas, almost any other subject would be a better medium of élite education than law'.

Back in 1949 the Allied occupation tried to liberalize German civil servants by broadening their educational base, to include economics, finance, political science or sociology; the French occupation even set up a special civil servants' college at Speyer. But after the Allies' departure, the Federal Civil Service Act of 1953 went back to insist on legal training. More recently the civil service selectors have tried to bring in more arts graduates, but the legal tradition dies hard.

In the shaping of Europe, lawyers have had a role out of proportion to other professions; out of the fourteen Commissioners of the common market nine are law graduates. and legal advisers (predominantly German) play a central part. The Commission, frustrated in its political progress, rests still more of its authority on the legal interpretations of the Treaty of Rome. The greater the movements to federation (as in America) the more likely are lawyers to be in the forefront. In Europe, their strength stems not just from the complexities, but from the sense that the law and lawyers are the most stable element in an unstable world.

1. Ralf Dahrendorf: *The Education of an Élite: Law Faculty and the German Upper Class*, 5th World Congress of Sociology, 1962.

FRENCH CIVIL SERVANTS

Republican France has in reality two constitutions. One, that of 1875, is official, visible, and fills the newspapers; it is parliamentary. The other, that of the year VIII, is secret, silent – the Napoleonic constitution which hands over the direction of the country to the administrative corps.

Elie Halévy, 1931

Two countries in the world, Britain and France, have over the past century built up a strong group of senior civil servants, sophisticated 'mandarins'. Both administrations, up till the mid-nineteenth century, were riddled with patronage and corruption; and both then set up systems of competitive examinations. While Britain was setting up her Civil Service Commission in 1855, followed by the first examination in 1870, France had begun to set examinations in 1847. Since then, in both countries the higher civil service has been a respected profession, served by some of the ablest men, and rewarded not with high salaries but with social prestige. Both groups have traditionally been preserves of the *haute bourgeoisie*. Both professions, since the war, have become more powerful, extending their sway to the nationalized industries and the welfare state. If there is such a thing as a power élite, then they are in the middle of it.

Yet the differences are equally striking, and it is astonishing (as in so many other fields) that two countries so close together could acquire such opposite systems. The British mandarins were intended to be non-political, carefully separated from the politicians, studiously anonymous, terrified of publicity. They were regarded as umpires, to maintain fair play in a country of *laissez-faire,* with the least possible interference.

But the French civil servants have been accustomed to take bold political decisions. They belong to a strong centralized administration which goes right back to Richelieu and Colbert: beside it, the French parliament is a *parvenu.* The hand of bureaucracy was heavy, and in the nineteenth century, when Britain was romping ahead in a liberal economy, France was held back in many sectors by its slow-moving bureaucratic controls. But the years since 1945 in some fields brought a reversal; while the British civil service has been reluctant to face up to its new responsibilities for nationalized industries and planning, the French have extended their scope with enthusiasm. The post-war years of the Fourth Republic were full of secret achievements which only emerged publicly years later; the first Plan, run by Jean Monnet, which laid the basis for French industrial recovery, was never formally approved by the French parliament. De Gaulle, with his apparent contempt for experts and economics, might seem to be a setback for the mandarins. But in fact he has given rein to the top administrators, and has provided the stability and sense of direction that they always look for.

Like other opposite poles, the British and French civil services are attracted to each other. Some French civil servants, I found, look with envy at the more democratic British system, while the British envy the scope that the French give to the best brains. The Fulton Committee, who proposed the reform of the British civil service in 1968, were clearly influenced by the French civil service; while granting that it was 'extremely élitist', they were impressed by the opportunities for young men, and the quality of the men in top jobs: 'they were lucid, expert and possessed of that confidence which comes from the achievement of high responsibility combined with a certainty that one knows one's own subject as well or better than anyone else'.[1]

The French civil servants have become a legend in modern Europe, and the British have been sometimes too easily awed. As Raymond Aron has remarked: 'I cannot help being somewhat suspicious of too heavily sociological explanations for changes in the economic sphere. Yesterday the graduates of the École Polytechnique and the *inspecteurs des finances* were held responsible for France's stagnation; today *Encounter* sees in them the builders of France's economic renewal.'[2] I share those doubts. The French advantage rests on much more than these top layers; it stems from the whole public attitude to government and the state, and it brings with it massive disadvantages and dangers. But there can be no doubt of the achievements of the system, and the advantages of the French mandarins over others. They rep-

1. Fulton Report, Appendix C, p. 133.
2. Raymond Aron: 'Old Nations, New Europe', *Daedalus*, Winter 1964, p. 61.

resent the nearest thing we have seen to a complete system of technocracy exemplifying its strength and its weakness.

The bulk of the French bureaucracy, like others, has been the despair of governments and the public. But above this inert mass, the French Civil Service has a separate breed of super-administrators, untrammelled by the internal hierarchies, and operating freely on the frontier between politicians and administrators. They move easily from one office to another, their views are definite, and they can – against the French tradition – be quite pragmatic: to quote M. Crozier, 'They have become empiricists, more devoted to economic growth than to purity of style, and, especially, financial purity. Their heroes are no longer the perfectionists but the doers.' They are liberated from the laws of bureaucracy, which tend always towards caution and conservatism: as one *Inspecteur des Finances* put it: 'Our métier is change.' The French élite are the arch-technocrats of Europe, and as such deserve special study.

'X'

No Frenchman, except a very few at Paris who know more than anybody in the world, knows anything about anything.

Matthew Arnold, 1864

The basis of the French technocratic system lies in its tradition of efficient élitist education, by which the Grandes Écoles, dating back to before the Revolution, have provided an unbroken supply of graduates, from the high bourgeois families, for the service of the state. These schools have on the one hand been the envy of other nations, and have inspired imitations; on the other hand they exemplify the dangers of the arrogant technocratic tradition, which is now increasingly challenged. The most influential of the Grandes Écoles, has been the École Polytechnique, the 'school of many skills,' which for nearly two hundred years has provided the top French engineers, and which has had such an influence that it deserves special treatment. From its earliest years, when Saint-Simon was its fervent admirer, the Polytechnique has been the centre of ideas about 'technocracy', and the word and the idea – in a watered-down form – spread to Germany, England and through Europe: it impressed President Jefferson so much that he set up West Point in imitation of it.

Every November, in the gilded foyers of the Opera House, Paris holds its grandest ball. The Garde Républicaine, in shiny gold helmets trailing long horsetails, stand immobile: there is a flourish of trumpets, and then the Minister of the Armies slowly mounts the grand staircase, escorted by seven young men in full-dress uniforms – high-necked black jackets with gold buttons, red-striped trousers, and extraordinary curly hats. It is the annual binge of the École Polytechnique, cryptically known by all France as the 'X', and these young men are its proud alumni. They combine assurance and mental agility with a rigorous training – above all in engineering and mathematics. To anyone who is astonished by the industrial recovery of France, by her ability in the midst of nostalgia and pomp to build daring new jets, mono-rails, airports, tunnels or dams, the Polytechnique provides part of the answer.

The Polytechnique was invented to train engineers for the revolutionary armies. It is still a military school, with military uniforms, and the Minister of the Armies is its boss. But nowadays the polytechnicians do not run the army, they run much of France. At the head of Civil Service departments, in the boardrooms of industrial corporations, at the head of banks, nationalized industries, in politics or in teaching, you find 'les X'. The Channel tunnel idea came from the 'X', sponsored by Louis Armand, ex-boss of Euratom and of the French National Railroads; and it was another 'X', Jules Moch, ex-cabinet minister, who led a rival scheme for a Channel bridge. Monuments to the 'X' are all over France, and their inventions include the Paris Metro; pre-stressed concrete; and the ingenious French tax system, the added value tax (TVA), now adopted by the whole common market.

There are a dozen national engineering schools which are the nurseries of higher civil servants and industrialists, politicians, professors and research scientists. But it is the polytechnicians who are the most formidable products for they are at the meeting point of science, culture and power; they are, in American terms, a cross between the graduates of MIT and Harvard, or, in English terms, between Oxford and Imperial College. They know from the moment they arrive at the school at the age of twenty that they are a race apart, that doors will be opened to them and that they need only mutter the syllable 'X' for respect to be shown.

You can see the young polytechnicians milling round the entrance to the school itself, in the heart of Paris, beside part of the walls of the medieval city (it is planning to move outside Paris in 1970, in order to expand). The school has an extraordinary mixture of the military and intellectual. The students spend all day wearing khaki tunics, with black flaps. Their dormitories contain a bizarre collection of trappings from different worlds – tin hats, kit-bags and military great-coats; blackboards, chemical diagrams and advanced math-ematical symbols; *tachiste* paintings and the latest novels. All over the school there are symbols of the army and of science: in one hall Foch and Joffre, two great generals of the First World War, glare at each other; in another there are long lists of famous professors of mechanics and cal-culus.

You might expect an unbearable hothouse atmosphere. The students are allowed out only two and three-quarter hours a night and for weekends, and from the beginning each 'promotion' of three hundred is ruthlessly graded by marks which will count in the final passing-out order. But in fact polytechnics are not too worried, for both the state and private industry are clamouring for their services, what-ever their marks.

The studies at the 'X' are designed, boldly, to produce something like Renaissance universal men, who can turn their hands to running anything. This bold assumption, not surprisingly, has its critics: 'That man knows everything,' Marshal Pétain once said of a polytechnician, 'but he knows nothing else'; and many others before and since have pro-tested about the 'X's' mixture of confidence and ignorance. They certainly have an extraordinary range of knowledge and interests. The network of the 'X's' gives them inside knowledge of all kinds of things, from the best makes of cigarettes (the state tobacco industry is run by poly-technicians), to the secrets of the French Plan (also run by 'X's'). 'But it's all quite rational' is a recurring phrase. They withstand the strain of their schooling with surprising stabil-ity. One recent polytechnician, it is true, thought he was a motor-car, though his colleagues were glad to note that, when he got into bed, he went into reverse so he could get out faster next morning – rational to the last. But polytechnicians in later life are sometimes apt to take their brilliance too far: two rebel officers who tried to assassinate De Gaulle – Colonel Argoud and Colonel Bastien-Thiry – were both polytechnicians who believed that they had found the final solution to saving France.

In Paris society the polytechnicians constitute almost a separate caste of their own: fifteen per cent of 'X's' are sons of 'X's', and one family has had a continuous succession of 'X's', father to son, from 1794 to the present day. Although the school was an indirect product of the French Revolution, it is not at all democratic in its recruitment: only about two per cent of the 'X's' are sons of working-class parents, and the great bulk come from the professional classes and the more prosperous bourgeois society. Most 'X's', too, marry into the most respectable ranks of the bourgeoisie. ('The trouble with *polytechniciennes*', said one 'X' looking round the annual ball, 'is they never go in for *décolleté*.') People like to have an 'X' as son-in-law, to run the business or look after the family fortune.

Since the advent of ENA[1] the influence of the 'X' on the Civil Service has been slightly less; but the Polytechnique still provides the open sesame to technical jobs. In theory, because the state pays for their expensive education, all polytechnicians are supposed to spend at least ten years in state service, but in fact many of them are 'bought out' by private firms, who can pay 36,000 francs – the cost of their schooling – to rescue them. Moreover, a number of the polytechnicians, having reached high positions in the Civil Service in their forties, decide to 'parachute' into private industry or banking for double the salary. An 'X' in almost any situation can always find another anywhere in the world; he just looks up the relevant section of the school's fat brown annual or 'bible', which lists every 'X' four times over, by classes, towns, jobs and alphabetically. If an 'X' in Renault has to deal with IBM, he just looks up IBM France in the bible and decides which of the thirty-two 'X's' employed there to write to. If a young 'X' wants a job, he looks up which high-ups are 'X's', knowing he will receive special consideration. However important the boss, he will begin the

1. See following pages.

letter *Cher camarade*, and if he is within six years of the other he will use *tu*. Young polytechnicians love to roll off lists of distinguished alumni, and if you mention a big name, they will mutter 'X' with the year of his class. Servan-Schreiber, the editor of *L'Express*, and author of *Le Défi Américain*? He's 'X43'. Jacques Rueff, the financial expert who has advised everyone from De Gaulle to Salazar? He is 'Z19' *spécial* (entering after the Army).

The advantages to France of this close-knit group are obvious. It encourages the flow of men and ideas between the professions, and in the development of national planning which France pioneered after the war it was specially valuable. 'How do you imagine the Plan could have worked,' asked one *ancien* 'X' without the old-boy net of the Polytechnique?' For the British, who have administrators who know nothing of engineering, and engineers who know nothing of administration, the example of the Polytechnique is specially tempting. But the confidence of the Polytechnique rests on its least attractive characteristic – the segregation of a small group from the rest of the university population, and their assurance of key jobs in the state. The enclosed privilege of the school has worried many of the polytechnicians themselves, and in the revolt of May 1968 they put forward projects for reform to turn the Grandes Écoles into specialized colleges for post-graduate scholars. But the association of old boys replied that the Grandes Écoles must maintain their fundamental characteristics, to provide a 'way of life favouring both team spirit and a sense of responsibility'.

As many historians have pointed out, the Revolution that produced the idea of liberty, equality and fraternity also produced one of the most self-contained ruling élites in the world, which has survived all the revolutions, republics and empires since. Napoleon may have believed in the ideal of a 'career open to the talents'; but to become one of these rarefied mandarins requires a very special background and training, if not a special parentage; and the chances of the son of a working man reaching a position of power are almost – but not quite – as remote as they were in 1789.

ENA

The graduates of the Polytechnique, though equipped with all-round knowledge and confidence, are destined for the most part for technical posts, based on their engineering skills, from which they can develop into administrators, politicians or industrialists. But alongside this ancient élite there is also a newer one, more directly geared to government administration. It is this dual system which specially aroused the envy of the British commissioners: 'It is a remarkable achievement', said the Fulton report, 'to have created two complementary élites on the technical and administrative sides. ... Each is a highly selected and highly trained breed. Yet because the polytechnician's training is widened so as to include economics and managerial disciplines, the two élites have common ground on which they can both meet.'[1]

Just off the Boulevard St Germain in Paris, in the Rue des Saints Pères, is a grey, pillared archway leading into the courtyard of an eighteenth-century mansion, looking much like many of the Napoleonic 'great schools' in its architecture. Above the entrance, in gold classical letters, are the words ÉCOLE NATIONALE D'ADMINISTRATION; and these words, or ENA for short, have become a very special object of awe or anger in contemporary France. From this building, each year, will emerge seventy-odd young men who will take up key positions in the French senior civil service.

It has become an object of pilgrimage for foreign administrators. The Director, François Gazier, a voluble academic, enjoys explaining its special benefits. He told me in 1967 how he had been visited by a delegation of German industrialists from Düsseldorf, who had been infuriated by how often in common market negotiations the French had got the better of the Germans. They had been told that the reason was ENA, so they had called on M. Gazier to invite him to come to Germany to explain how it was done (which he did). The example of ENA has specially fascinated the Germans, who with their decentralized state feel the lack of a single technocratic élite. Kiesinger himself tried to set up a German ENA in 1967, and his cabinet approved; but the pro-

1. Fulton Report, p. 133.

ject was conveniently frustrated by a civil servants' committee.[1]

ENA is only twenty-three years old, and the oldest graduates are only now coming into their fifties. There are only 1500 of them altogether, but they crop up everywhere. In 1967 they held seven out of the eleven top jobs in the Ministry of Finance, and headed sixteen out of the twenty-nine *cabinets* of ministers.[2] It is an old-boy net or a 'Mafia' which makes others – the Harvard Business School, Balliol or even the Polytechnique – seem amateurish. It was set up after the war in a mood of high democratic idealism, and the lecture rooms are called after resistance helpers. It was designed by Michel Debré, later De Gaulle's prime minister, to make the top civil service both more efficient and more democratic. The old élites of the Grands Corps[3] would no longer be recruited separately; all senior administrators would take the same examination, then spend two years training in the new ENA, then pass into the top posts. Debré was (as he told me) much influenced by the British civil service, but he did not believe that they should go into administration without previous training. As the official booklet explains (everything is explained) 'the system is the result of the opposite choice, since it gives preference to training of a technical, if not entirely specialized, nature over training solely based on general culture and academic knowledge.'[4]

But the biggest difference between ENA and the British system lay in its emphasis on service to the state, perpetuating and reinforcing the Napoleonic concepts. In an extraordinary passage, Debré outlined its aims in 1945:

The school must teach its future civil servants the sense of the state; it must make them understand the responsibilities of the Administration, make them taste the grandeurs and appreciate the service of the profession. It must do more. By a sustained effort of its best teachers, by recalling the great examples and great men of history, it must give to its pupils the awareness of some master qualities; the sense of humanity which gives life to all work; the sense of decision which allows them to take risks,

1. See *L'Express*, 11–17th December , 1967.
2. Jacques Mandrin: *L'Enarchie*, p.100.
3. See p. 368.
4. *ENA: Recruitment and Training for the Higher Civil Service in France*, by H. Bourdeau de Fontenay.

having weighed them; the sense of imagination, which is not afraid of any boldness, or any grandeur.[1]

In its two-year course ENA gives its students more practical experience of administrative problems than the British civil service. In the first year they have 'training in the field', attached to a Prefect or an overseas department. In the second year they have seminars, study-groups and lectures, about administration, finance or economics. Some idea of the end product can be seen from the final examination: here are the first three questions in one paper:

1. Is it conceivable under our present system for a law to stimulate the division between the legislator and the authorities responsible for drafting regulations? If your conclusion is in the affirmative, do you consider such a law to be opportune?
2. Personnel management services: their importance.
3. The division of investments between productive equipment and social equipment in the second Modernization and Equipment Plans. Is it satisfactory, in your opinion?

ENA certainly made the selection of civil servants more efficient, but it did not make it much broader. To an extraordinary degree, the school perpetuates the old Napoleonic tradition of a high bourgeois élite, firmly based on Paris. The French system has a far narrower entry, even, than the British. Out of sixty-seven successful candidates in the main examination in 1966, fifty-five came from Paris, and no fewer than fifty came from a single college, the celebrated Institute des Études Politiques, or 'Sciences-Po'.

The Sciences-Po is the most crucial sector of the ambitious young Frenchman's road to power; in spite of having been nationalized after the war, it remains a bastion of the bourgeoisie. It was set up after the defeat of France in 1870 by a group of high-minded Protestants who believed that the regeneration of France could be achieved by copying English liberal institutions. It has some resemblances with the London School of Economics, but while the LSE is a mix-up of all races and classes and inhabits an over-crowded slum, Sciences-Po is visibly a haven of privilege. Its building, library and lecture-halls, full of sport-coated young men and well-tailored girls, are a world away from the turmoil of the Sorbonne. (Its students are noticeably more at home with economics than with politics. In March 1968 I took part in a

1. Michel Debré: *Réforme de la Fonction Publique*, Paris, 1945.

debate on the question, 'Can Britain make a come-back?' at the Anglophile club of Sciences-Po, called 'La Debating Society': the speakers ruthlessly analysed Britain's economic weakness, with scarcely a word about her political state.) Though not technically a Grandes Écoles, Sciences-Po is really the grandest of them. It takes the sons and daughters of the bourgeoisie, and prepares them for administration. The building itself, appropriately enough, backs on to the building of ENA; and it is to ENA that the most successful graduates of Sciences-Po pass on.

Thus linked with the middle-class tradition, it is not surprising that the social base of ENA is restricted. Out of the same sixty-seven who joined in 1966:[1]

17 were sons of higher civil servants (A1 or A2).
12 were sons of professional men.
10 were sons of artisans or tradesmen (*commerçants*).
1 was the son of a worker (*ouvrier*).

ENA now brings in more top civil servants from inside the civil service itself; a second examination is held each year to admit about thirty older men. But it is hard for them to reach the academic standard; and often they do not fill all the vacancies. 'It usually takes two generations to make a senior civil servant,' M. Gazier told me. 'We have several grandsons of workers, but not many sons of workers. It's difficult to break the monopoly of the Sciences-Po: we're giving more marks for mathematics and engineering, to encourage engineering schools – but then Sciences-Po will adapt itself to that.' I asked one of the first graduates of ENA, who now lectures there: 'ENA isn't really much more democratic. It hasn't much changed who goes in, or – more important – who comes out. There are more men from the petite bourgeoisie, but they're more conformist and less eccentric than the old lot. After the war people were more independent and more political; but now there's a kind of technocratic conformism.'

In spite of their various backgrounds, I found that ENA people all radiate an intellectual assurance, which distinguishes them clearly from their British equivalents. It is partly the verbal confidence that they acquired, no doubt, at the Sciences-Po, where oral exposition is part of their training (in contrast again to the London School of Econ-

1. *ENA: Statistics for Entrance Examination*, September 1966.

omics). But it is partly, I think, the superiority which comes from their isolation from any kind of political struggle, which allows them to reduce every problem, at least apparently, to an intellectual exercise. The British civil servants are constantly coming up against values which are not intellectual, and are often squashed by them. The Oxbridge Treasury man, face-to-face with a big booming politician who has been through the hustings, can still feel himself at an acute disadvantage, and learn that 'bullshit baffles brains'. But the men from ENA do not have much occasion to defer to other influences; even towards older mandarins (one of them complained to me) they can be maddeningly patronizing. (Perhaps the nearest British comparison would be an administration composed entirely of Wykehamists.) They have been taught in the tradition of French administration that all problems have a single rational solution: 'the fundamental assumption is that disagreements occur not because people are bound to differ but because they are misinformed'.[1]

INSPECTEURS DES FINANCES

A young civil servant once inside ENA finds the tension still there; for the ultimate test is the passing-out, where the top students can choose one of the Grands Corps. Those who pass into the Grands Corps can afford at last to relax, for their future is assured, and they are now part of a Napoleonic élite which has survived revolutions, republics and empires. But the others feel very left out. 'This is one of our problems,' Gazier explained to me. 'Most people go into ENA with the ambition to reach the Grands Corps; but eighty per cent don't manage it, and go into the rest of the Civil Service: they often feel a bit bitter, and some of them get their revenge with *arrivisme*, throw themselves into *carriérisme*.'

Four corps stand out which are nearly always preferred by the top graduates – the *Inspection Générale des Finances*, the *Conseil d'État*, the *Cour des Comptes* and the *Corps Diplomatique*. The most prestigious and most powerful is the first. The *Inspecteurs* – only three hundred and fifty altogether – are the intellectual shock-troops of the French administration; they have similarities with the two hundred

1. F. Ridley and J. Blondel: *Public Administration in France*, p. 322.

British Treasury men, likewise picked out from the top entrants, but they are more mobile, more privileged, more political and much more arrogant. 'We could not only think deeply,' one veteran *Inspecteur,* Jacques Rueff assured me, 'we could also *speak* about everything whether we knew about it or not.' They are nearly always stimulating to talk to – full of generalizations, paradoxes and odd facts, and they are especially proud of their writing style – which enables them to describe complex problems simply, without socio-economic jargon.

The first job of the *Inspecteurs,* as their name implies, is to look at accounts: they travel around the country examining the books of government departments and writing reports, which gives them a super-accountant's knowledge of the skeletons in other people's cupboards. But they soon turn to other jobs. Only half of them are actually looking at books: others work in ministers' cabinets, become diplomats, turn to business, write books, go into politics (in banking, as we have seen, they are almost inescapable). They are given (like Fellows of All Souls) wide freedom; one of them, Michel Rocard (who has all the confident articulation of the Corps) is currently secretary of the left-wing socialist party, the PSU: another is said to be an explorer. I asked one *Inspecteur* whether any of his colleagues had been sacked. 'It's very difficult,' he said, 'but there was one. It was because he seduced an official whom he was supposed to be interviewing.' These are some well-known current *Inspecteurs:*

Maurice Couve de Murville – Prime Minister
François-Xavier Ortoli – Finance Minister
Valéry Giscard d'Estaing – ex-Finance Minister
Hervé Alphand – Head of the Foreign Office
Jacques Brunet – Governor of the Bank of France
Bernard Clappier – his Deputy
Pierre-Paul Schweitzer – Chairman of International Monetary Fund
Jean-François Deniau – Commissioner of the European Community.

The relationships between the *Inspecteurs* are close. They not only talk the same language, but live in the same places. In 1967 one of them, Claude Lachaux, analysed their changing habitat in a pamphlet 'Where Do We Live?'[1] Of the 347

1. *Ou habitons-nous? Syndicat CFDT de l'Inspection Générale des Finances,* 1967.

names listed in the annual, 336 gave addresses in Paris. He found that there had been some dispersal of the *Inspecteurs* to the suburbs since 1939 (particularly to the departments Yvelines and Essonne) and that within Paris they had become slightly more adventurous; but that nevertheless, 103 lived in the leafy streets of the XVI arrondissement (Passy) (with sixteen of them in two streets, Rue de Rémusat and Rue de Civry): fifty-two lived in the VII arrondissement (Invalides, etc.) and forty-two in the plush suburb of Neuilly. The map

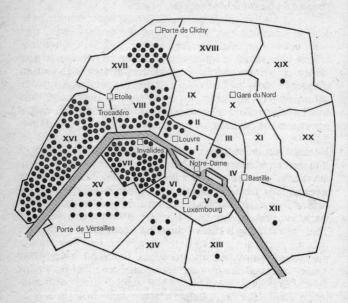

Where the *Inspecteurs* live in Paris

shows their intense concentration in the 'arrondissements bourgeois' of Paris.

(A similarly detailed study of senior British civil servants is not possible, since many do not give their addresses; but a brief inspection of *Who's Who* shows a much greater dispersal, with over half in the suburbs, and a wide spread of London addresses, from Finchley to Twickenham.)

The scope of the *Inspecteurs* increases as they get older: in their fifties, like polytechnicians, they often 'parachute' into lucrative jobs in industry – as Treasury men in Britain have begun to, but on a much larger scale. This exodus clears the field for the younger ones, who can thus often sail into very big jobs. Their certainty of power and respect gives them a relaxed arrogance that out-Balliols Balliol. 'I think you would be wrong to say that we're an *isolated* group,' the head of the *Inspection* told me, 'but if you were to say that *Inspecteurs* believe that 'they're exceptionally intelligent people – you would be correct.'

COUVE

The whole spirit and confidence of the French mandarins might be summed up in the single personality of Maurice Jacques Couve de Murville. For ten years he was Foreign Minister – (longer than any counterpart), casting his cold spell over the Chancelleries of the west: and in 1968, after a short spell as Minister of Finance, he became Prime Minister.

Couve wears, with perfect ease, the dispassionate mask of the perfect diplomat. He looks like the example of Talleyrand's '*pas trop de zèle*': his wavy silver hair, his weary eyes and his sceptical mouth all fit together to give a whole which is severely classical. Behind the bored exterior, he is capable of relentlessly hard work. Jean Daniel has described him: 'His bearing is that of the great European diplomats of whom Stendhal speaks in *Le Rouge et Le Noir*: a distinguished ennui and an attitude a thousand miles away from the actual situation. The recipe of Stendhal is roughly this; if there is occasion to laugh, content yourself with smiling a little after the others; become serious again a little before them. But if it is advisable to be moved, then smile openly, and for a long time. Vigilance must be an obsession and relaxation a phobia.'

He began, of course, as an *Inspecteur des Finances*. His background was modest; he was the son of a public prosecutor, Édouard Couve, from unassuming Huguenot stock. As a young man he went as a tutor to the children of Sir Harold Nicolson at Sissinghurst; he seemed to them (as one of them told me), shy and intense and he clearly did not enjoy England – an experience which may have reinforced

Couve's later lack of sympathy towards the British. To many Frenchmen Couve looks Anglophile: there is a joke which says 'if he's not carrying an umbrella, that's because he's swallowed it'. Couve insists that he only *looks* English, and explains that one great-grandmother was Irish-Scottish.

Couve excelled as an *Inspecteur* and in the meantime had married a girl from 'high Protestant society'. In the war he worked for a time for Pétain, negotiating with the Germans on financial questions. Then he got out to Algeria, where he first served Giraud and then switched to De Gaulle, which began his long service for the General, from which he never then wavered. After the war he rose to be ambassador in Cairo, Washington and Bonn, and in 1958 became De Gaulle's Foreign Minister. The two men agreed on most things, including dislike of America, wariness of England, belief in authority. Couve became the archetype of the new breed of Gaullist super-administrators, a neo-courtier in the neo-monarchy, appearing to be apolitical, wholly rational, while following all his master's swerving foreign policies. 'I don't recall ever having disagreed with De Gaulle on anything that was really important,' he told Raymond Tournoux in July 1968. He did not conceal his contempt for his own diplomats and preferred economists: he himself was able to mix diplomacy and monetary affairs with great ease. He liked to have aristocrats around him, and saw no reason to curry favour with anyone. In 1967 De Gaulle insisted that all his ministers should stand for parliament, and Couve was forced into the market-place. He hopefully stood for the 7th arrondissement of Paris, a district noted for its concierges, and provoked much amusement with his pained and formal replies to questioners. He lost the seat to his rival, and was said to be very bitter about his defeat; but (since French ministers are not MPs) this did not prevent his being re-appointed. In 1968 he stood for a safer arrondissement, the 8th, and was returned.

After the crisis of 1968, when De Gaulle reconstructed his government, it was not perhaps surprising that he should turn to his most trusted lieutenant as prime minister; Couve had the firmness, the 'sense of the state' and the respect for authority that De Gaulle valued above all. Yet the idea of Couve as the agent of 'participation' was breathtaking in its novelty; even at the Foreign office, he had been reluctant to consult anyone, and he had never bothered to disguise his contempt for inferiors. He had none of the cosy, avuncular manner of Pompidou, who could at least appear to talk as man-to-man on television. His whole style depended on the assumption of the dignity of the state, and the direction of a single master. Without that, he would be nothing. He had all the strength of the French technocrats, and also their ultimate weakness – that their confidence comes from the state, and not from the people.

ANTI-TECHNOCRATS

The senior French civil servants are the most co-ordinated and formidable group of administrators in Europe: they are broadminded and far-sighted; they are sensitive to international implications. But they revolve essentially round the nation-state; when the state is strong, they are strong. Their profession is power, and the game that they play, year in year out, is the game of defending the extending power of the nation. They need strong leadership and purpose, to make sense of their planning, and give shape to their future: they inevitably resent the muddles of parliament and the compromises of party politics. They are not, for the most part, dedicated Gaullists; but most of them, probably secretly, welcome the bold leadership of De Gaulle; for he gives dignity to their profession and embodies, in the most romantic way, the conception of bureaucratic power, by which they live and die. Their confidence rests not only on the state, but on their language: as one of them said: 'We express ourselves extremely well – provided it's in French.' Nuances, faint doubts, 'mmm's and 'er's, do not translate; and the defence of the national language is part of the defence of national interest. All bureaucracies revolve round the hub of the nation: the French are the European masters of the national game.

In the first years of Gaullism, the sway of the French technocrats did not arouse much resentment; they were associated with the spectacular prosperity, and they were bringing new dignity and glory to France abroad. Efficiency was what France craved for, and efficiency, after all, was the god of ENA. The rigorous selection and conformism of the young technocrats seemed a reasonable price to pay;

the more strained and incompetent the rest of the French established system, the more important it seemed to keep this spearhead, which really worked. When I first became interested in ENA, in 1962, there seemed to be not much public interest or resentment against the system: indeed other countries were looking towards it, as a model of enlightened technocracy.

But as the authoritarianism of the French state became more questioned, and as the ENA men became older and more powerful, so the building in the Rue des Saints Pères began to seem more sinister. A sharp attack on the '*Jeunes Messieurs*' of ENA came in 1965, from Mendès-France's journal, *le Courrier de la République*, which sums up (it seems to me) the dangers of such technocracy:

Instead of a homogeneous administration equally open to everyone, one sees established an aristocracy of a few thousand young men produced through privileged channels; the isolation of their education easily persuades them that they are destined to retain among themselves (and for themselves) the administration of the state, and above all of its best jobs. Less and less are they touched by doubts; the assurance of their elders and their own success convinces them that it is enough to advance confidently under cover of their technique to make obstacles disappear. The sharing of a certain exoticism of language or of modern administrative techniques or of economics; the sense of making up a kind of network between the bosses and dauphins of the great public and private businesses; the exhilaration, still hardly acknowledged, of feeling in their hands such means of action, and such docile underlings; all these make up the psychology of a senior civil servant, young and ardent, certainly devoted to what he considers the public good, but more inclined to define it himself, or to let it be defined by the boss, than to listen on this subject to the aspirations of the country.[1]

In 1967 there was a more treacherous blow, from inside ENA itself; under the pseudonym Jacques Mandrin, a young left-wing graduate of the college, published a book called *L'Enarchie* or 'The Mandarins of the Bourgeois Society'. In it he protrayed the narrow competitiveness of the 'Enarchs', their arrogance and insulation, with the authenticity of one who had been through it; a few quotations convey both the lines of his attack, and the style, itself redolent of ENA and Sciences-Po:

1. *Courrier de la République*, November 1965. 'Le Régime des "Jeunes Messieurs".'

The ambiguity of the school was that of the resistance, which wanted to restore France more than to reconstruct it.

The examination is nothing else but the means by which older people make sure that the young are like them; hence the importance of the orals in which, from small details, the family can recognize its own kind.

The Grands Corps dominate the scholars of ENA as eternal salvation dominated the worldly life of the early Christians.

The future civil servant learns at this time that an administrative circuit works like an electric circuit.

Like the eunuchs from whom the Emperor of China recruited his counsellors, the Enarchs appointed to the service of the bourgeoisie have scarcely more than passive virtues.

The catch-phrase of ENA reasoning is: 'All things being equal,' which means 'All things must remain unequal.'

Many ENA students themselves, however privileged their position, kicked against their conformist training. The group of 1967–8 seem to show special spirit; they even wanted to adopt the name of Jean Jaurés, the late leader of the French socialists, but this was not allowed, so they had to adopt Turgot (Louis XVI's finance minister) instead. I talked with three of the more rebellious of them in March 1968; they complained passionately about the narrowness of the course, how they were forced to disguise their feelings and to wear a mask; how they were taught to see the future as a simple extrapolation from the present, of a mathematical kind; how people of character were ground down, or excluded. One of them talked with envy of his visits to Cambridge, where he saw individuality positively encouraged. Half of the ENA students, they said, were left-wing in theory; but they were sucked into the system, and they could only try to reform it ineffectually from inside. In the Paris revolt of May 1968, ENA was not surprisingly more cautious than the other students and they refused to go on strike. But they did make a public statement (by forty-eight votes out of sixty-three present) condemning the brutal methods of repression, and they later debated proposals for reforming their own school, to democratize it and give less emphasis to the top Grands Corps.

The question of how to reform ENA goes to the heart of the problem of technocrats in a democratic society. On the one hand a group of high-fliers with exceptional powers are the essential instruments of change. The more resistant the rest of the bureaucracy, the more important these shock-

troops; and intelligent planning must require men who can
see above the trees. If France or other European countries
are to be changed, in whatever direction, then technocrats
are needed to change them. Yet left to themselves, they will
always tend towards solutions which favour efficiency, centralization, profitability at the expense of individual rights;
they cannot be expected to control themselves, for they have
long ago grown out of touch with ordinary people.

ESTABLISHMENTS

The specific dread of a closed circle of technocrats is
linked with a vaguer but more evocative nightmare, of an
Establishment, united as much by social background as by
technical knowledge. The word is impossible to define, for it
represents less a fact than a mood of people outside it. It
sums up the sense of exclusion and separation, that has
become something of an obsession in contemporary Europe.
The word first gained currency in Britain in the late fifties,
describing the secretive influences behind the Macmillan
government, associated with country-houses and the old aristocracy: the attack on the Britsh Establishment was mixed
up with a good deal of nostalgia, and – as with other studies
of power – coincided with a time when its influence was
visibly crumbling. The lack of national purposes encouraged
curiosity about the workings of power rather than its aims,
leading to a boom in what Malcolm Muggeridge has called
the 'pornography of power'.

The obsession was echoed in the United States, much
stimulated by C. Wright Mills in his book *The Power Élite*,
which presented an exciting conspiratorial view of the sinister American triangle of power – politicians, industrialists
and military leaders. Later American writers attacked the
conspiratorial view, but remained fascinated by the social
origins and links of the ruling class.

The preoccupation crossed to the continent, particularly
to Germany, where the vibration was quite different from
England's but where in a sense the word was more useful.
Germany has no real social élite. There are no particular
families, schools or universities which unite top people; they
are held together (as Professor Dahrendorf describes it) 'by a
cartel of anxiety'. 'The "élite cartel" is the result of a gen-

erally defensive attitude on the part of its members. The plurality of German leadership groups has proved to be a plurality of men who awoke one day with a shock to the awareness that they were at the top, and that there was nobody above them. The shock was more than their self-confidence could stand. ... The traditional monopoly has been replaced by a cartel of anxiety.'[1]

Dahrendorf and other German observers look with some envy at the tradition of the British Establishment which (they believe) carries with it a sense of responsibility and liberal broadmindedness: they find a greater danger in their own loose-knit unconfident élite. But the Germans talk about their own Establishment in a different sense, of being a concentration of political power in a one-party system. The word really became popular after the Grand Coalition in 1966, when Socialists and Christian Democrats presented a solid front with virtually no other opposition than parliament. The complacency of the coalition, the authoritarian structure of society, the Springer monopoly of newspapers and the absence of extreme parties from the Bundestag, all made young Germans feel that there was a single impregnable citadel with which they had no connection, which they did not like, and which they could not change. '*Das Establishment*' soon came to be used to describe any kind of orthodox behaviour:

> Wer zweimal mit derselben pennt
> Gehört schon zum Establishment
>
> Whoever sleeps with the same girl twice
> Belongs already to the Establishment.

It is in France where the idea of an 'Establishment' or a 'power élite' is most relevant: for here the tradition of strong centralized government, run by a homogenous and sophisticated group, has been unbroken. Through all its revolutions, as De Tocqueville and many others have pointed out, French administration has kept its continuity and strength. The argument for decentralizing authority in France has been kept up over two hundred years, but in the last decade – in spite of gestures in the other direction – still more power has gone to the centre. The French Establish-

1. Ralf Dahrendorf: *Society and Democracy in Germany*, Doubleday, 1967, p. 269.

ment has not been closely linked with hereditary privilege as
the British one; it is largely separate from the old aristocracy. It is more meritocratic, more up-to-date, and thus
more formidable. It has been enormously admired by its
neighbours for its ability to plan for industrial growth.

But its weakness, and its danger as a model for Europe, is
that it has grown up without an effective opposition to curb
it, either from parliament or from trade unions. The problem of all these Establishments is how to combine the advantages of close-knit planning from above, with the
collaboration and support of the workers from below, and
that problem will grow much harder with the technological
developments in the next decade, and with planning on a
continental scale. In France there is now much talk about
schemes for 'participation', for joint planning with workers
at different levels. But the only effective basis for participation is a strong and disciplined trade union movement,
which can counter a centralized technocracy with its own
central power. That is something – as we will note in the next
chapter – which most European countries are lacking, and
which is the glaring lack in the components of a united
Europe.

Chapter Nineteen

Workers

Travailleur: tu as 25 ans mais ton syndicat est de l'autre siècle. Pour changer cela, viens nous voir.

Students' slogan, Paris, 1968

In the centre of the European capitals you can see, if you know where to look, the darker side of their prosperity – the troops of foreign workers from the periphery of the continent. You can find them at those baroque German railway stations at weekends, standing and waiting, munching buns and drinking cheap beer, taking over the station as their meeting-place, as a kind of temporary village square: (it is said that you can gauge the state of the German economy by the number of foreign workers at the stations). Greeks, Turks or Italians queue for their home papers, tense with expectation, seizing their copies of *Grand Hotel* or *Hurriyet*, devouring the romantic comic-strips or the adventures of Tarzan sitting on their battered suitcases. With their open collars and huge shoes, their tanned faces and glazed eyes, they sit in their own strong separate world, cut off by time and place from the commuters hurrying past.

In Paris the contrast is more extreme. Only a few minutes' drive from the Bois de Boulogne, in the suburb of Nanterre, you can emerge suddenly into the midst of a quarter which, on a hot day, looks a replica of an African slum. The homes are tiny shacks, built of breeze-blocks, bits of door or old placards, with tin roofs held down with old machinery or stoves; you can walk between them, round sudden corners as if in the centre of the Casbah, down narrow stony lanes reeking with the smell of stale beer and piss. In the gaps between the houses, the shopkeepers sit crouched in front of tiny piles of peanuts or cheap jewellery, or Moroccan rugs, or small skewers of shish-kebab. Walls are scrawled with Arabic, and from a hut comes the wail of Arab music. North

Africans of all shades – dark Algerians, brown Tunisians, pale Moroccans – sit in small cafés sipping Coca-Cola, or walk desultorily round the township. It has the squalor of a slum, but still the charm of a village, with small children playing in the lanes, a dog gnawing at the rubbish, and a man carrying wood in an improvised wheelbarrow. In the middle of it, the illusion of Africa is complete – except for a skyline of high new Paris flats rising above the Arab roofs as if they belonged to a next-door film set.

As the core of western Europe has grown richer, so its citizens have had to look always further afield for labour to fill their factories and do their dirty work, as in nineteenth-century America. In the first years after the war there was no problem. Germany, the biggest consumer of labour, had its own vast internal migration – thirteen million refugees from East Germany, who poured into the factories of Munich, Hamburg or Stuttgart, and helped to give the German economy its miracle. The Italians, with unemployment at home, crossed over to the Swiss hotels, the German factories or the Belgian coal-mines, to fill the gaps in other countries.

But the Italians were soon enjoying their own boom and were less ready to emigrate. In 1958 (officially) 240,000 foreign workers arrived in the Six, of whom 85,000 came from outside the common market. By 1966 the total number of arrivals had risen to 806,000, of whom 546,000 came from outside (there was a fall in numbers after the recession of 1967, but a recovery in 1968). The map opposite indicates the convergence on Germany, which accounted for more than half the total in the common market. There were 472,000 arrivals in 1966 including:

184,138	Italian
17,377	Dutch
43,412	Spanish
46,184	Greek
48,714	Turkish
9,724	Portuguese
55,071	Yugoslav
19,488	Austrian

Britain and France, both with large ex-Empires, have special problems. Both of them have until recently allowed free entry to immigrants from their ex-colonies, who have

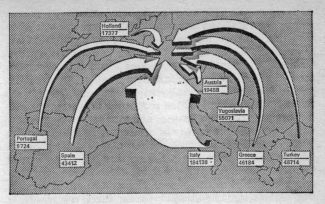

Holland
17377

Austria
19488

Yugoslavia
55071

Portugal
9724

Spain
43412

Italy
184138

Greece
46184

Turkey
48714

Workers' migrations to West Germany, 1966

streamed into the big cities, trying to establish their tropical way of life in wintry streets. With both countries, it is hard to guess the numbers of immigrants, because they have moved in so easily: there are thought to be about 450,000 Algerians in France, and about 700,000 West Indians, Indians and Pakistanis in Britain. The integration of these peoples from outside Europe involves racial questions which are beyond the scope of this book. Their treatment by their host countries, which make use of their cheap labour, leave them in wretched housing conditions, and try to ignore their predicament, illustrates as clearly as anything the current worries about the 'Rich Man's Club'.

The biggest proportion of European immigrants is in Switzerland, with angriest results. In 1968 it was reckoned that the proportion of foreigners in the labour force had gone up in ten years from sixteen per cent to thirty-seven per cent – concentrated in the manual industries, building, stone or cement.[1] The Swiss owe much of their industrial boom to this hard-working influx; but they became more and more anxious about the *überfremdung* or foreign infiltration, particularly because of the large proportion of catholics from Italy and Spain: Geneva, the city of Calvin, now has more Catholics than Protestants. They have tried to keep the

1. *Neue Zürcher Zeitung*, 3rd May, 1968.

labour force as temporary as possible, without permanent lodgings. The more reactionary businessmen have tried to ban Italian labour altogether, with a special campaign and slogans like 'Would you like to share a hospital room with a Sicilian?' The hostility between the Swiss and (particularly) the Italians has come close to boiling point.

There is nothing new about this migration towards the centre of Europe: in 1907 the proportion of foreign workers in Germany was between three and four per cent – the same as in 1964: the proportion of foreigners in Switzerland in 1910 was as high as in 1966. Before 1914, in the age before passports and work permits, the workers of Europe were in fact far more mobile, most notably in the direction of America; before 1914 the annual emigration out of western Europe was eight hundred thousand. There was almost as much migration *inside* Europe. More than half the increase in population in France between 1891 and 1901 came from immigration, and nearly as many Italians before 1925 emigrated within Europe as went to America. Within Europe, the international brotherhood of waiters (much more cosmopolitan or mobile than diplomats or Eurocrats) dated back to the first founding of the Grand Hotels; and the Italian cafés of London or Paris are monuments to those early wanderings.

But today the migrant workers are scarcer, and come from further afield, for shorter times; 'In terms of net emigration, central and north-west Europe shows itself as a rival to North America; these two regions, like Oceania, are in competition to bid in the same diminishing market for emigrants, in southern and eastern Europe.'[1] And the migrations are increasingly short-term. 'The concrete experience of industrialists shows that migratory movements are today above all temporary. If one takes away the frontier workers and seasonal workers, the stable workers living in the country where they work do not envisage staying there permanently, and their length of stay tends to diminish.'

Most of the foreign workers are preoccupied with one ambition – to save enough money to buy a house, or a car, or some land in their home country. To do that, they are prepared to work harder, and to live more harshly, than most western Europeans would now contemplate. Many men

1. M. W. D. Barrie: *World Congress on Populations*, Belgrade, 1965.

come without their wives, and many (apparently) live without women: they are what is rudely called a 'sub-proletariat'.
Many are prepared to work overtime and to do rough jobs —
in the mines, in the undergrounds, in the quarries, and above
all in buildings. Many of them prefer not to join trade
unions, or to get mixed up in any agitation: they can be
carefully watched by the embassies of their home countries.
The women who come often leave their children behind, so
that they too can work long hours and live in a small space.
The sheer toughness and sacrifice of the migrant workers are
a reminder of an austere earlier age, before luxuries became
necessities.

The co-existence of these two worlds, living in two ages, is
full of new problems, and a succession of seminars, colloquies, conferences and sociological suicides have been devoted to them. Do the migrant workers benefit, or not? On
the one hand, their conditions are visibly miserable and unstable. The host countries – though not all as irresponsible as
Switzerland – regard migrant workers as expendable, ready
to be sacked (as in 1967) at the first sign of recession. And
the pool of cheap, willing labour has (it has been argued)
diverted employers from making use of automation, while
the foreign workers underpin some of the most backward
and unnecessary industries – particularly coal-mining. The
notoriously inefficient Belgian coal-mines depend on
foreigners for much of their labour. The migrants are regarded in most countries as second-class citizens; the whole
system has a nasty similarity to the contract-labour system in
South Africa, which exploits and demoralizes the surrounding countries, and provides cheap labour for antiquated gold-mines.

But, it is argued, the migrations help the poor countries;
they relieve unemployment, they provide skills and experience in industry, they provide savings and foreign currency.
If the workers go back to a rapidly-developing country, like
Spain, they can get work more easily if they have been
trained in a German factory; and the new industries of
southern Italy (I was told in Taranto) are much helped by
Italian workers who have done stints in Germany. Some
workers go back, too, with more political education; many
of the more militant young trade unionists in Spain are returned workers from France or Germany, who have been

awakened by their glimpse of a freer system. Greek workers in Germany have demonstrated quite boldly against the new Greek regime.

The host countries constantly complain about their foreign workers, but migrants in the past have often helped to stimulate activity and growth. 'Under the Renaissance, already, the influence and radiance of the Italian city-states was not unconnected with the fact that they welcomed a great number of refugees, and were pools of development. In the nineteenth century the United States welcomed a great number of immigrants who, far from leading the country to chaos, pushed it on the way to a dynamic economy.'[1]

Whatever the other benefits, the migrant workers add little to the social integration of Europe. The American idea of the 'melting pot' is not really applicable, for these are people who have not abandoned their roots. The Spanish in Paris walk up and down the Avenue Wagram on Sunday afternoons, meeting their friends and chatting as if in their home town; or, just beyond the Étoile, wait for the buses which take them, in twenty-six hours, back to Valencia. The Italians at Wolfsburg, the Volkswagen town, live in their own suburb called Castel del Luppa, which is described as a village, with its own cinema and church, but which turns out to be more like a compound, with a high fence all round it and a guard at the gate to keep out visitors. (There had been trouble in the town, I was told, between Italians and German girls, and communist agitators had been getting in among the Italian hostels.) I heard a Turk at Düsseldorf station repeating the incomprehensible name of a town to the man in the ticket-office, knowing no word of the language to explain himself further. In the old cosmopolitan cities of Europe, like Paris and Brussels and London, there are settled foreign communities which can absorb and understand newcomers; but in the newer German cities the 'guest-workers' leave hardly a trace on the permanent life, and German food, habits or music are not much affected. According to a survey made in Ankara University, more than half the Turks in Germany don't speak German, and 'more than three-quarters of the Turkish workers have gen-

1. P. Grandjeat: *Les Migrations des Travailleurs en Europe*, Paris, 1966, p. 38.

erally no contact with a German or a German family. The German worker shuts himself up jealously in his own home, from which foreigners are banished.' The insensitivity of Germans to their 'guest-workers' is distressing to German liberals: Professor Dahrendorf, one of the severest critics, comments: 'the number of accidents in which foreign workers are injured for life and not seldom killed while their work helps to establish the prosperity of Germany, provides hardly a notice in the German press. There are after all "only" Italians, Spaniards, Turks involved.'[1]

To watch these bewildered processions of foreigners wandering like ghosts through the rich cities, is to be reminded of how far the centre of Europe is cut off from its poorer edges, and the problems of the rest of the world. And the strangeness of this sub-proletariat spotlights the fact that the Western European workers, for their part, are gradually joining a more comfortable existence, for which migration and hard manual work are no longer necessary.

BOURGEOIS WORKERS

That the simple fact of a change of residence is among the most effective means of intensifying labour is thoroughly established.

Max Weber, 1904.

Once the Western European workers have become settled in the towns, they become very reluctant to move. You can hear the same complaints from industrialists or economists about South Wales, the Ruhr, or Lorraine. In each the coal-miners have settled into a way of life which, however exacting or unnecessary, they do not wish to leave; and even the inducements of cheap housing and free transport, away from old smoky towns to sunny suburbs, will not easily lure them away. The British have been used to the special problem of their settled mining communities. It comes as a surprise to find the Ruhr workers are almost equally immovable. All over Europe there are pockets of workers whose industries have collapsed but who refuse to be moved – the textile workers of northern France, the dockyard

1. Ralf Dahrendorf; *Society and Democracy in Germany*, Doubleday, 1967, p. 348.

workers of Trieste, the coal-miners of Marseilles, the ship-builders of Dunkirk. In July 1968 the last technical obstacles were lifted by the common market against the free movement of workers among the Six: but that was not likely to make much difference, for the obstacles of language, customs and climate remained.

Even the Italians, the most enterprising travellers of the past, are losing their restlessness. In the post-war upheaval, the willingness to move was a huge factor in Italy's growth, particularly in her capacity to survive her recession of 1964. Unemployment in some areas could be quickly taken up by industries elsewhere, and by contracts abroad. But as the Italians became more prosperous, so they, too, became more settled: in the northern cities of the 'industrial triangle' they are no longer prepared to pack their bags. The spurs to mobility in Europe in the past have been poverty and starvation: as those vanish, Europeans settle into their provinces and towns.

All this is a recurring contrast with America. America never settles down; there is no recent European parallel for the voluntary migration of millions of Americans from east to west in a single post-war decade. Ambitious French or German industrialists dream of a new, mobile worker, for so much of American enterprise comes from this restless wandering. How easy to shut down a factory if workers will just move somewhere else! But how impossibly ruthless, if the factory is regarded as a kind of estate, as settled as the trees and the hills, and the workers as part of the family. How hopeless, in an age of unprecedented change, when factories or materials can be outdated in ten years, to be saddled with these static dependants. 'The transatlantic bosses do not shrink, like ours, from surgical remedies,' said *Le Monde* in 1967, after General Electric had ruthlessly shut down a computer factory of Machines Bull: 'Shutting a factory, disbanding personnel, opening another one, re-engaging – that is life, economic life, with risks but also with chances of a better share on new ground. In France we have got used to prolonging the invalid, and even to sustaining the dying with subsidies.'

Mobility goes to the heart of the differences between American and European attitudes: after all, what transforms a European into an American is the uprooting. The Europeans have been quite willing to dislodge themselves from the farms – as we have seen in Chapter 3 – in pursuit of higher wages in industry; but once in the cities, they are very reluctant to move again. The immobility of Europeans may be deplored by economists, and condemned as a peasant legacy from a feudal past. But the desire of the worker to stay in his own house among his own friends is something more than stubborn conservatism. If the price for faster growth is wholesale uprooting, it is hard to imagine that Europeans will ever pay it.

Most workers have less incentive to move, partly because they have experienced an unparalleled rise in their standard of living. Of course there remain vast discrepancies even within the rich countries, and unemployment has grown throughout western Europe in the past two years. But for those with good jobs in new industries, the change has been steep. This is the increase in the wages of metal-workers between 1960 and 1966:

Britain	+44.3%	W. Germany	+70.6%
Holland	+80.3%	Belgium	+58.5%
Italy	+72.8%	France	+54.1%

The laggards are the British workers; in ten years, from having had a much higher standard of living than the continent, they have slipped right back. Taking the national income per head (a rough yardstick), the British by 1967 had sunk to eighth place among OECD countries, with an annual income of $1,910 compared with $2,010 for Germany, $2,060 for France and $2,480 for Switzerland:[1] and Britain's falling position already shows itself in the lower proportion of new cars and new houses (though still leading with TV sets and washing machines).

The British still get more money in actual wages; and this reflects a central difference in individual attitudes. In the common market countries, a large proportion of the earnings are paid out in other benefits – pensions, insurance, free meals, even free travel. In Italy an average of only forty-nine per cent of a worker's earnings are paid in wages: in the common market generally it is sixty-three per cent, com-

1. *Financial Times*, 23rd February, 1968.

pared to eighty-four per cent in Britain.[1] The high proportion paid in 'fringe benefits' dates back to the old
traditions of paternalism on the continent; and often the
social security payments are enforced by law. The common
market countries are closer in this to each other than any of
them are to the British. The British, while still regarding
themselves as the model welfare state, are less well provided
for. This might be expected, at least, to make the continental
worker less prepared to move, bound as he is by chains of
benevolence to his company. But the British workers show no
signs, even without company benevolence, of being more
mobile.

The growing prosperity of the European workers, the fact
that they are committed to all the benefits of the consumer
society – houses, cars, durables, holidays – have all led politicians and political scientists to decide that they are losing
their class consciousness, becoming identified with the bourgeoisie, and lacking incentive for revolutionary movements;
that the word 'worker' in fact is losing its old meaning. The
socialist parties have recognized the fact, and adjusted their
policies accordingly; and many Marxists have reached the
same conclusion. The German-American philosopher Herbert Marcuse, the early prophet of some of the Marxist students, while condemning the totalitarian nature of modern
industrial society, believes that the workers have become too
involved in the manipulations and persuasions of that
system to provide an effective resistance to it. But the young
student revolutionaries, while accepting Marcuse's attack on
society, reject his contention that the workers have lost their
class consciousness, and still look for an alliance with
workers to bring about their new world.

Watching the new armies of car workers arriving in their
factories, driving up in their Renaults, Volkswagens and
Fiats, well-dressed, well-fed, well-disciplined, to make more
Renaults, Volkswagens and Fiats, I found it difficult to imagine them as a revolutionary force: so much has changed in
their lives in the past twenty years, to envelop them in new
incentives and commitments. I remember, touring the Renault factories along the Seine in 1966, thinking how totally
different their atmosphere seemed from any traditional pic-

1. Survey in *Management Today*, March 1968.

ture of the French workers; with their four-week holidays, their rising wages, their delicious lunches, their shining Renault 16s outside, what had they to worry about? Yet it was at Renault that the strike of 1968 began, in a way that the company still does not understand, when a group of young anarchists at Cléon locked their manager into his office. The extraordinary events in France of that summer make it hard for anyone now to generalize so confidently about the conformism of the European worker. The old patterns of French syndicalism, the pockets of anarchy in Germany, the bursts of wildcat strikes in Britain, still recur against the comfortable background. Under the surface of calm, monotonous employment there are still the old undercurrents of resentment and individuality, which can still defy the rules of security and self-interest.

A WORKERS' EUROPE?

A moment could come when the trade unions would have to throw all their weight – in the literal sense of the word – in the balance to prevent part of European democracy sinking in the corridors of negotiations between technocrats and diplomats.

Harm Buiter, Rome, November 1966

While technocrats, bankers and tycoons are beginning to operate increasingly on a European scale, and the international corporations are co-ordinating their factories and markets across frontiers, the workers and their trade unions remain much more deeply divided. They have inherited all kinds of rivalries and suspicions – political, religious and class divisions, and divisions between trade unionists and the rest. Their ineffectiveness is alarming, for without the countervailing force of organized labour, the creation of huge new continental industries and institutions can still threaten democracy. No plans by the technocrats for 'participation' can add up to much without strong trade unions.

The European unions, like the European left, have suffered much more than the bosses from religious and ideological wars, culminating in the cold war; and they perpetuate schisms and dogmas long after the first cause has subsided. Their philosophies vary accordingly to their national political background. Harm Buiter of the ICFTU has said: 'In the Latin countries trade unionism is a movement and not an organization. In the well-established democracies there needs to be a little more of a movement, as there needs to be a little more organization elsewhere.' In the northern countries the unions have become virtually part of the fabric of government. In Britain the Trades Union Congress – the first organized movement, founded in 1868 – helped to give birth to the Labour Party, and soon worked cautiously in the framework of parliamentary democracy. In Germany after 1890 the unions built up a solid bureaucracy, with great respect for the new state. In Sweden the Workers's Confederation, taking the advantages of later industrialization, provided a disciplined hard-bargaining front which is now the envy of Europe.

Further south, the lures of extremism, or of a trade-union revolution, or of communism, were much more attractive. The French unions were fascinated by anarchism or syndicalism, and the Confédération Génerale du Travail (CGT), founded in 1895, developed a hatred of the state and of political parties which it still keeps. The Italian federation, the CGL, adopted a fiery political policy after the First World War, but failed to strike effectively against Fascism. In Spain the anarchists became most famous, and the Spanish CNT, founded in 1910, built up a strong revolutionary base in Barcelona; in the Civil War their workers' committees took over banks, railways and factories, and ran them with some success, until they were suppressed by the government in Madrid. Anarchism has lost much of its attraction in Spain, but elsewhere in Europe and particularly in France, it is still liable to burst out again. In the new computer age it is quite possible that anarchism will achieve a new importance.

After the last war there were new hopes for united trade unions in Italy and France, but the cold war soon caused the biggest rift of all. The complexities are very confusing, but they must be briefly summed up. In Italy the Allies hopefully encouraged a non-political federation, the CGIL; but it had three separate secretaries-general (communist, socialist and Christian Democrat) and they could not stay together. In 1948 a Catholic group split away, with encouragement from Washington and the Vatican, and soon afterwards a socialist group, which eventually settled into two new federations, the CISL (Catholic) and the UIL (socialist), leaving the CGIL predominantly communist. The intricate politicking which followed made many workers leave the unions altogether.

In France after the liberation the communist and Catholic unions worked together quite closely for a time; but by the end of 1947, when the cost of living had shot up, the communists organized a succession of strikes, in Paris, the coalmines and Marseilles. The socialists had misgivings, and the government, under Robert Schuman, broke the strikes with ruthless police action. Soon afterwards the socialists, led by their veteran Louis Jouhaux, split off to form the '*Force Ouvrière*' – smaller than the CGT, predominantly white-collar, and openly supported by American funds. The splits still remain, and the alphabetical chaos of names still muddles Europe. Over the page are the main federations, and their affiliates in Britain and the common market, with their approximate memberships early in 1968 (the French figures shot up after the May strike).

The rivalries are crippling. The total French trade union membership is not more than two and a half million – less than a third of the British. There is no real middle ground between communists and catholics in spite of the hopes of the Socialist *Force Ouvrière*. In Italy the membership *looks* higher, but the numbers certainly include, according to local custom, tens of thousands who are dead, retired or who have joined a rival union. Even in Holland, which has no communist union, employers may still have to negotiate with three unions – catholic, protestant and socialist – in the same factory. In the common market the highest proportion of unionization is among Belgians, but they are hampered by the bitterness between the Flemish and Walloons, and by a militant communist movement.

The splinters make an obstacle-race to continental integration. The three sets of unions each have their own international confederation, with their separate headquarters. The socialist group (ICFTU) and the Christian (CISC) both have their offices in Brussels, and they are be-

Trade Unions in Seven Countries

	Members	Leaders	Affiliations
BRITAIN:			
TUC	8,000,000	Feather	Socialist
GERMANY:			
DGB	6,000,000	Rosenberg	Socialist
CGB	200,000	Seiler	Christian
FRANCE:			
CGT	1,300,000	Seguy	Communist
CFDT	800,000	Descamps	Christian
CGT (FO)	500,000	Bergeron	Socialist
ITALY			
CGIL	2,000,000	Novella	Communist-Socialist
CISL	1,500,000	Storti	
UIL	600,000	Viglianesi	
CSC	?	Rapelli	Christian
HOLLAND:			
NVV	527,000	Kloos	Socialist
KAB	408,000	Mertens	Christian (Catholic)
CNV	230,000	Van Eibergen	Christian (Protestant)
BELGIUM:			
FGTB	713,000	De Bunne	Socialist
CSC	700,000	Cool	Christian
LUXEMBOURG:			
CGT	30,000	Hinterscheid	Free
LCGB	18,000	Wagner	Christian

ginning to co-operate. But the communist group (WFTU) has scarcely any contact, and they each discuss the world as if the other didn't exist. And as the cold war apparently thawed, a good deal of the fire has gone out of the confederations: the ICFTU has become disillusioned about its international crusades, and its members have sunk back into national scepticism.

UNIONS AND THE COMMON MARKET

The common market posed new problems. The communist unions opposed it from the beginning, as a super-monopoly of capitalists, which would lead to warmongering and the ruin of the working class. When this didn't happen the Italian communist union, the CGIL (which includes socialists), began to come to terms with it, and has now even opened an office in Brussels; but the French have stood out against it.

Among non-communist unions many leaders, particularly the Germans and Dutch, were enthusiastic for the common market, and became key members of Jean Monnet's committee which pressed for further European unity.[1] They saw it not just as a great reconciliation, but as an opportunity for the workers – provided they could be strong enough. These unions maintained their support; but as the years passed, and political Europe failed to develop, their misgivings increased. They had an uneasy, undefined feeling that the boom would soon turn against them. In particular they worried about the exclusion of Britain and the British TUC, which they regarded as a pillar of unity. Just before the tenth anniversary of the Treaty of Rome, in 1967, the non-communist trade unions had their own meeting in Rome, where they voiced their worries. 'We don't in the least believe that social phenomena automatically derive from economic ones,' said Auguste Cool, the chairman of the Belgian CSC: 'If the European community is ever to become genuinely social in character, it will need to develop a drive it has certainly not shown in the past ten years.' 'The common market must admit other democracies – first and foremost Great Britain,' said Eugène Descamps, secretary-general of the French CFDT: 'It must develop a more effective solidarity with the third world. As trade unionists we cannot in decency allow Europe to develop into an affluent countries' club.' 'National emotions are almost stifling the true European fire,' said Van Eibergen, chairman of the Dutch CNV. One trade union observer summed it up afterwards: 'Whatever kind of Europe they're making, it certainly isn't a workers' Europe.'

Part of their worry is that they never know quite how to grapple with the common market; without a proper parliament, and with its mysterious 'dialogue' between bureaucrats and politicians,[2] the trade unionists have to put in a wedge as best they can. The central figure among inter-

1. See p. 31.
2. See p. 58.

national unionists is a Dutchman, Harm Buiter, now secretary of the world confederation, the ICFTU; before that he was secretary of the European trade union secretariat (ECTUS). He is the son of a socialist trade unionist, worked in the Dutch resistance, took a degree in economics and became adviser to the Dutch metal workers; he was soon in the middle of the European movement, and when the common market began he opened the union office in Brussels. He talks with frankness about the problems of the common market. 'It's like dealing with an amoeba. You have to work underground, to find out what's really happening before it happens. The telephone is what's really important – and there is nothing about that in the Treaty of Rome. If you can't find out who's responsible for a decision, you're lost. We often think – "let's have a debate. If necessary let's be defeated – that's what's built the trade unions". But with this system, you can't even be defeated. A commissioner thinks that because he calls me by my Christian name, and shows me his speeches, that's a substitute for democracy. But it isn't.'

Buiter is worried about the weakness of European unions, though he believes that strong leaders can often make up for weak unions. He thinks that if they are really threatened, the trade unions can unite: 'There's not really much of a gap between the integration of Europe and the integration of the unions – they've neither gone very far. If they have to, the unions will work together.'

Like most other socialist trade unionists, Buiter sees the main hope of unity as Britain. The arrival of the TUC in the common market, they believe, would step up the democratic pressure, diminish the importance of the communists, and provide a counter-weight to the Germans. Buiter says: 'We would like to have two elephants, rather than one.'

GERMAN UNIONS

The European unions look with a wary admiration towards the German trade unions and their federation, the DGB. They are so huge – as big in membership as all the other non-communist unions in the Six, with over six million members, all properly paid up. Only the British TUC (with

eight million members) beats them. They are the richest in
Europe, they actually subsidize French and Italian unions,
and in the French strikes in May 1968 they gave substantial
help to the French workers. They appear so rational, so far-
sighted, so intelligent, so praised both by employers and
workers – altogether too good to be true. Their federation is
so neatly made up of sixteen unions, in sixteen different industries; no demarcation disputes, no unnecessary strikes.
They have their retraining schemes, arts festivals, banks, staff
of economists. They are constantly driving hard bargains;
yet with a record of strikes lower than most other countries
in Europe. This table shows the number of days lost per
thousand workers in strikes in 1966, in mining, manufacturing and transport, according to the International Labour
Office:

Italy	1,700
Belgium	310
France	240
UK	180
Finland	150
Sweden	110
Holland	10
Switzerland	⎫
Norway	⎬ Negligible
W. Germany	⎭

The reasonableness of the German trade unions had its
roots in the industrial revolution. While the English workers
had to battle for human working conditions for decades, the
German workers on the Ruhr and elsewhere had a much
easier time; Bismarck in the 1870s realized that bold government intervention could prevent a class rift, and he pushed
through welfare legislation ahead of the rest of Europe.
German workers felt a much greater loyalty and involvement with their companies and today, while British
workers are still refighting old class battles, the Germans are
quite prepared to co-operate in innovation and management.
They have the extra advantage (as for so many German
institutions) of starting again after the war from 'point zero',
allowing a reorganization and rationalization which other
countries dream of.

The DGB headquarters, a big rugged building with its

initials on the skyline, stands in the heart of Düsseldorf, the industrialists' city, not far from the steel palaces of Mannesmann or Thyssen. Inside in a homely office, their president, Dr. Ludwig Rosenberg (like other German socialists), sits below a portrait of John F. Kennedy. He is a fine-looking man of sixty-four, tall with a beak nose, brushed-up eyebrows. He speaks enthusiastically, raising his finger, chopping his hand, and making everything simple. His own record is impeccable; a Jew, he spent the thirteen Nazi years in England, lived in the London suburb of Petts Wood, and worked as a temporary civil servant in the Ministry of Labour. He made friends with English trade unionists, and dreamt of rebuilding the German movement. Then he went back to Germany and helped to do it. In 1962 he was elected president. He has been an active 'European' and a member of Monnet's Action Committee, and keeps a qualified optimism: 'In the end, we'll have a Confederation of European Trade Unions,' he said to me in 1966. 'It may take twenty years, but it will come.'

Rosenberg talks about the splendours of the German trade unions, and their contribution to industrial progress: 'You can't stop progress – our job is to see that workers get the benefit of it. We believe that in the modern economy it is possible to give everyone a job, but we don't believe that we can necessarily give him the same job all his life; that's why we spend so much money on trade union schools, to retrain people from dying industries; we train people for all kinds of new trades – computers or time-and-motion study. Men who only sell their physical power are lost in the modern world.' He sounds quite American, but he disagrees with American unions on, for instance, their callousness towards unemployment, and their willingness to sabotage employers: 'Our attitude is quite different from America,' he insisted, 'we believe it's the most idiotic thing to pay someone to do a job that doesn't exist any more.'

He is quite satisfied with the trade unions' detachment from politics. 'We never say vote for the Social Democrats, or vote for the Christian Democrats: most of us are socialists, but we have close contacts with the Christian Democrats. Our leaders are elected for their trade union qualities, not for their political following. We don't take part in local elections; we know that whichever side wins, the bürgermeister will be a trade unionist. We believe that a democratic state is only stable if it can rely on one big workers' organization. Division is always dangerous – look at France: everyone has to prove constantly that he is the most radical.'

Rosenberg's moderation and detachment are not unchallenged; he is the chairman and the conciliator for sixteen heads of unions, some of them formidable; he denies that he is any kind of 'pope' of the German unions, and he said in 1967, 'I would be proud, if I am included in the history of the trade-union movement, to be described as someone who constantly, and under the greatest difficulties, has tried to reach a compromise.' His greatest difficulty takes the shape of Otto Brenner, one of the toughest trade unionists in Europe. Brenner is head of the biggest single union – the IG Metall or metal workers, with two million members and a record, like many metal workers, of unrelenting militancy. (They struck for 117 days in Schleswig-Holstein in 1956.) Brenner had a tough political education in Nazi Germany, when he spent two years in prison before going abroad as a journalist. He rose quickly after the war and became head of the metal workers in 1951. Now he sits on the board of (among other companies) Volkswagen and the remodelled Krupp. Like Frank Cousins in England he has not been afraid of putting his whole weight into politics; he is in favour of the nationalization of key industries – a rare policy on the German left – and he fiercely opposed the 'Emergency Laws', though he became more wary after the students joined in the protest.

Brenner's bold stands gain him much support, and his authority inside his union is unquestioned. But it is Rosenberg's political neutrality, and his preoccupation with industrial progress that represents still the prevailing spirit of German trade unionism.

Is it too good to be true? Compared to the English, the German attitude has certainly had huge advantages in productivity. By helping to educate and retrain their workers, the unions have allowed industrialists to be much more flexible. They can be criticized for not getting as great a share of the national product as the British. But much of the balance goes towards investment which will benefit the workers later, and they have played their part in pushing up

hourly earnings by 130 per cent in the ten years up to 1965 –
compared to eighty per cent in Britain. The German worker
feels involved in the progress of his industry and knows that
he will have his share in it. Yet the industrial strength can still
be a political weakness. For in their enthusiasm to become
part of the economy, and of the state, the German workers
are apt to lose sight of the ultimate political safeguard of the
unions, to be able if necessary to detach themselves from the
assumptions of the state. This adds to the worries of other
Europeans, about having only one elephant.

IRON INTERNATIONAL

While the common market unions are gradually coming
to co-operate, the real challenge to workers' solidarity is on a
much wider front. The growth of the international corporations, which we looked at in Chapters 5 and 6, has
forced unions to work together more closely; but since most
of the international corporations are based on America, the
main impulse for the countervailing force comes from the
American unions, who are concerned to stop the companies
from exploiting low wages and weak unions abroad. Here
we are back at the familiar situation, that European industry
cannot be treated separately from American industry.

The growth of international federations is an important
world development, which will have a growing influence on
social and industrial patterns in Europe. They are organized
by trades, and the most effective and well-organized of them
is, not surprisingly, the international metal workers' federation, the IMF, which revolves round the car industry: the
car, once again, is the heart of the matter. Their president is
the omnipresent Otto Brenner, who has ominously described
the federation as the 'iron international'. I visited their
European headquarters, in a big modern block in Geneva,
redolent of business efficiency; an enthusiastic American or-
ganizer, Daniel Benedict, showed me the files of statistics
comparing detailed wages for car-making jobs, from
sweepers to headlight-installers, in Ford factories all over
the world.

The federation goes back to 1893, when ship-builders and
steel-workers were first trying to get together, but it is only in
the last few years, with the massive expansion of American

industry, that it has become highly organized. In 1966, the federation decided to set up 'world company councils' to counteract the power of the big companies, and they held two inaugural conferences, one in Detroit and one at Wolfsburg: at Detroit a declaration was signed proclaiming 'we, autoworkers from 14 countries, representing 1,440,000 wage-earners in the world-wide manufacturing, assembling, and distributing operations of the three giant corporations that dominate the international industry where we earn our living . . . have laid the groundwork for a solidarity structure capable of defending the rights and interests of automobile workers in the new transnational automobile economy'. At Wolfsburg the Volkswagen-Daimler Benz Council was launched to co-ordinate the workers in the German companies all over the world. 'The fact that in the automobile industry we have to deal with international corporations and their ramifications', Otto Brenner told the council, 'renders trade union resistance imperative. But this alone does not solve our trade union problems. Our activity, as ever, carries weight primarily within each nation. Unless there are powerful unions, capable of taking action in various countries, international trade union co-operation would be largely void of meaning'.[1]

This, of course, is the rub. The international federations are no substitute for strong national organizations, and the weakness of the French and Italian unions cannot be cured by the Germans, Americans or British. The French strike of May 1968 revealed the militancy of the French workers, particularly car workers, but also the lack of disciplined trades unions. The German car workers were sympathetic to the workers in Renault and Citroën, whose wages are much lower than theirs, and their union (they told me) subsidized their strike with quite large sums; but the suddenness and uncontrollability of the strikes gave an indication of how far the car unions have to go, before they can plan concerted action across the continent.

TUC AND EUROPE

By comparison with the Germans or Swedes, the British trade unions belong to a different century. They remain il-

1. *World Company Councils*: IMF, Geneva, 1967.

logically suspicious of management. They have one hundred and sixty-three separate unions in the Trades Union Congress, which squabble and strike against each other, and obstinately refuse to amalgamate. They spend a great deal of time discussing issues like Vietnam over which they can have no influence. They are increasingly weakened by unofficial strikes which in Britain are not (as they are in most of the continent) illegal. They are certainly responsible for much of Britain's industrial backwardness. Managers on the continent, I found, speak of them with a mixture of mockery and dread.

Yet the role of the British TUC in Europe may become more, not less important. No sector of opinion on the continent has been more consistently pro-British than the trade unionists, and slowly the British have responded. After a long period of parochialism, several leading British unionists, including George Woodcock, Lord Carron and Fred Heyday, have begun to look towards Europe. As the American unions have become more exasperated with Europe, so the British have become closer. A new rift appeared when the German DGB set up an office in Moscow; George Meany, the American union leader, was furious, while the British unions were delighted. The British and Scandinavians have tried to ignore the political divisions of Europe between the 'Six' and the 'Seven', and in 1968 the EFTA countries, led by Britain and Sweden, set up their own 'EFTATUC' offices in Brussels – in the same building as the common market unions.

With all its absurdities, the British movement still enjoys a special reputation on the continent, and with some justification. It is not just the founder of the trade union movement, with a romantic and often heroic past. It is a genuine independent force, neither capitalist nor communist, detached from the managements and remaining stubbornly independent. Its independence is usually irrational, obstinate and sometimes (as when the dockers supported Enoch Powell) unashamedly reactionary. But the bloody-mindedness and outspokenness which is so exasperating to managers and politicians and so damaging to the British balance of payments, is still in the end a massive safeguard against political coercion. If Europe were ever again to move towards dictatorship, the British union movement – if it were inside the European structure – would be a formidable obstacle. And in the future shape of a continent made up of giant corporations and international managers, it will be difficult for Europe to build an effective counterweight without the help of the British trade unions.

Chapter Twenty

Decline of the Left

One can no longer doubt it. The battle against ideology
has become a new ideology.

Bertold Brecht, July 1938

All the isms are wasms.

Anon

With the massive changes that we have so far looked at – the
flight from the land, the spread of the consumer society, the
scope of communications and media, the growth of international corporations and technology – all of them bringing
uniformity and prosperity – it has frequently been assumed
and stated that Europe is becoming 'de-politicized'; and that
the great rifts that have split the continent over the past
decades are at last disappearing. By the middle of the sixties
it had become a commonplace among political scientists and
sociologists that the European class struggle was subsiding
and that ideologies had lost their hold. The workers were
becoming bourgeois, their solidarity was dissolving and the
new voters were being influenced by more private and frag-
mented interests. Europe was gravitating towards a new kind
of society, a consumer society, a post-bourgeois society, a
service-class society, a technical society, a classless society. In
these circumstances, a 'consensus government' would
emerge, and Europe would begin to follow the two-party
system habitual in America or Britain, with each party representing less a solid class than a loose coalition of interests.
There were persuasive generalizations:

The dominant structural trend in Europe involves the final triumph of the values of industrial society, the end of rigid status
classes derivative from a pre-industrial world. . . .

Seymour Martin Lipset.[1]

1. 'Class Structure and Politics', in *Daedalus*, Winter 1964, p. 287.

Out of all this history, one simple fact emerges: for the radical intelligentsia, the old ideologies have lost their 'truth' and their power to persuade. Few serious minds believe any longer that one can set down blueprints and through 'social engineering' bring about a new utopia of social harmony.

Daniel Bell.[1]

Throughout western Europe the type of society some call technical and others scientific has come into existence and it disrupts the system of human relations inherited from the *ancien régime* or even from the bourgeois property-oriented society of the last century.

Raymond Aron.[2]

To sum up, western Europe is belatedly 'Americanizing' itself and in the process acquiring some of the characteristic strains, as well as the familiar material appearances, of a fully industrialized society. 'Mass culture', democratic pluralism, the impact of piecemeal socialization, and the retreat from overseas empire and unrestricted national sovereignty, are all making their impact more or less simultaneously.

George Lichtheim.[3]

These interpretations are based on the central assumption, that since industrial development conditions political development, Europe will belatedly follow America. But in the dark forests of European politics, it is hard to be so sure of the common characteristics of industrial or post-industrial society. In the early nineteenth century, when the French and the Germans borrowed British industrial technology and moulded it into their own state, they showed how effectively industry can be subjugated to political systems; the same industry that was held to encourage liberalism in Britain, was used to strengthen the authoritarian state in Germany. Today, the outward likenesses of factories and suburbs still conceal fundamental national differences in structures which can be traced back to the pre-industrial ages.

Behind the production of the Fiat and the Renault, however alike they may look, lie contrasted assumptions going back to early centuries; even the two Concordes, identical in substance, are the results of almost opposite industrial philosophies. Europe has always managed to press new materials into old shapes; and however much she may borrow tech-

1. *End of Ideology*, pp. 402, 403.
2. 'Old Nations, New Europe', in *Daedalus*, Winter 1964, p. 44.
3. George Lichtheim, *Europe and America*, p. 237.

nology, management, or suburban houses from America, she is still able to fill them with old ways of living and working.

RIGHT AND LEFT

The apparent dwindling of ideological differences has added to the old European problem, of how to make effective oppositions. The machinery of modern capitalism and the universal lures of consumer society all seem to favour some kind of consensus government, which can maintain industrial growth without too much unemployment; without a convincing single alternative system it is hard for an opposition group to mobilize equal support. In this chapter I will not describe the whole jungle of European political parties; I will not try to explain the problems of the conservative ruling parties in Europe, which each have quite different national roots. I will restrict myself to the main question of the state of the oppositions, and specially of the left, as they stood in the Autumn of 1968.

In the northernmost Protestant countries, Britain and Scandinavia, socialist governments had been in office, but had suffered heavy losses. In Norway the Social Democrats were defeated in 1965 after thirty years in power, after they had tried to extend nationalization. In Denmark the Social Democrats fell in 1968, after trying to introduce an incomes policy. In Sweden the Social Democrats, under heavy attack over the housing shortage, recovered support after the Czechoslovakia crisis, and romped back into power in the September general election.

In Germany, Italy, and Austria, the socialists had been in coalition with the Christian Democrats, with disastrous results, losing votes while strengthening the right.

In most countries the left had been in retreat while the right had made substantial gains in the last two years. The eclipse of the left seemed to arise out of specifically national difficulties and mistakes, and was clearly much affected by the shadows of the communist parties (which I deal with at the end of this chapter). Yet there were some resemblances in the socialist predicaments. In the next pages I look at the cases of the four biggest countries in western Europe, to try to see what is common, what is different.

GERMANY AND THE GRAND COALITION

Wer hat uns verraten? Sozialdemokraten!
(Who has betrayed us? The Social Democrats!)
Students slogan, 1968.

It is in Germany that the condition of the opposition is
most anxiously watched; for here the very notion of opposition is so new. The problem is, of course, deeply affected
by the division of Germany and the existence of a menacing
opposition in the east. But the troubles of the German left
also stem from its past history and from the very different
associations of the word 'opposition'.

The Social Democratic Party (SPD) is one of the oldest in
Europe, founded by Ferdinand Lassalle in 1863, in the midst
of the headlong industrialization. It has been through banning by Bismarck, schisms since the First World War, and
banning again by Hitler. Its turbulent history is full of courageous men, but it has a congenital weakness, which showed
itself under Bismarck, under Weimar and under Adenauer;
that it dreads to be branded as an enemy of the state, and
longs for political respectability.

The predicament of the German socialists might be described through the position of their leader, Willy Brandt,
whose career has spanned the post-war years, and whose
dilemma is both personal and political. When I saw him in
1967, I found him a sympathetic, melancholy figure: his
boyish appearance, so much part of the Berlin of the fifties,
now has a defeated look: he talks softly and pensively, as if
looking at himself from some way off. Having been an exile,
and very much an international man, he can still look at
Germany in a larger perspective.

In his career, his private and public battles have been
mixed up. He was born an illegitimate child in Schleswig-
Holstein, joined the socialist youth organization at school in
the twenties. In the battles with the Nazis he felt that the
SPD had become too respectable and joined a left-wing
party, the SAP. When the Nazis came to power in 1933 he
fled to Norway, where he changed his name to Brandt,
worked as a journalist, and married a Norwegian girl. He
was impressed by the Scandinavian social democrats who
were in power, and became less radical in his politics. When

Hitler invaded Norway he fled to Sweden; and only after the war returned to Norway. He was torn between his Norwegian citizenship and his German background, and went to Berlin as Norwegian press attaché; there he was persuaded by Kurt Schumacher, the SPD leader, to come back to German politics; he became a member of the federal parliament in 1949, and inspired by the Scandinavian parties he helped to moderate the SPD. He was much attacked for his nomadic past, as one of the 'vaterlandslosen Gesellen' (men with no country) but his undoctrinaire approach and his glamour fitted well with the socialist mood of the fifties. In 1957 he became Mayor of West Berlin, and through the succession of crises became a world figure; the peak of his prestige was when President Kennedy came to Berlin and proclaimed '*Ich bin ein Berliner*'. Three years later he took over from Erich Ollenhauer as leader of the party.

The party which Brandt took over had renewed hopes of power. Adenauer had been Chancellor since 1949, ruling over the coalition of Christian Democrats and Free Democrats – the so-called 'burgher-bloc' – but he was at last losing support. The general and provincial elections were showing an unmistakable movement towards the left, charmingly known as 'Comrade Trend'. The Social Democrats had refurbished their image more drastically than the British Labour Party, to cope with the success of the 'social market economy' preached by Dr. Erhard, and had virtually ceased to be an 'ideology party'. At their Bad Godesberg conference in 1959 they excised all mention of nationalization, and devised a policy hardly distinguishable from their rivals', which so disgusted the student socialists, the SDS, that they left. The new programme stressed that 'Democratic socialism, which in Europe is rooted in Christian ethics, humanism and classical philosophy, does not proclaim ultimate truths . . .' They were very apologetic about planning: 'The SPD does not desire more planning within the framework of our country and our economy than is practised in other western democratic countries, including the USA,' said Brandt at the 1966 congress; 'but we simply cannot get by with any less.'

Visiting the SPD headquarters in Bonn I had at first a vision of Spartan idealism: it is a low hut-like building known as 'the barracks', with shabby lino and grubby-looking offices. But I found no revolution in the air. 'The classic division between left and right is no longer valid in this country,' explained their international secretary, Herr Dingels, in 1967. 'If you ask a party member whether he's left-wing he won't understand. Since 1945 the divided Germany has made the word "left" meaningless: people who've been in the east don't consider communism left-wing. Nobody wants communism legalized in West Germany. There's no international ideology now – every party is working in national circumstances. You can't force internationalism – variety is better than the shadow of coherence.'

A young generation of socialists had emerged, looking towards John Kennedy rather than Marx: one example is Helmut Schmidt, a party manager with a shock of Kennedy-type hair and an armoury of technocratic phrases; he made his name in Hamburg, dealing with the flood disaster, and in 1967 became leader of the parliamentary party in Bonn. Another is Klaus Schütz, now the young mayor of Berlin, an Americanized political scientist who became an expert on American election techniques.

'Comrade Trend' was even more helpful when Adenauer at last resigned. Erhard's indecision, the recession of 1966, unemployment on the Ruhr and the crashes of Starfighters brought out open recriminations. In the autumn of 1966 I found the Socialists quietly confident, while the Christian Democrats seemed bent on fratricide. A few weeks later the Free Democrats (FDP) resigned from the coalition thus bringing down Erhard. A near panic ensued, while secret talks were held with Brandt and other leaders to establish an alternative coalition; there was talk of a 'small coalition' between Socialists and Free Democrats, or of the Socialists governing alone. The Christian Democrats cast round frantically for a new leader, and found one, Kurt-Georg Kiesinger, a suave conservative who had been a Nazi in the pre-war foreign office. Eventually Kiesinger produced a solution. There would be a 'grand coalition', the Social Democrats would join the government, with their old enemy Strauss back inside it as Minister of Finance.

For socialists elsewhere the news was unbelievable, for the SPD seemed so close to gaining power alone, and Brandt was

known to be against coalition. But behind the scenes the idea
had long been favoured, particularly by the Socialist deputy-
chairman, Herbert Wehner; he was a tougher and more persuasive man than Brandt, had been a leading communist
before the war and had then switched to become a right-
wing socialist. Wehner argued that the Socialists needed experience of power to give them respectability with the voters
(a doubtful argument, since they already held power in
many of the provinces); and that only a coalition could
enable West Germany to deal with the east. Brandt argued
against and wanted himself to stay out of the cabinet; but
Wehner persuaded him to become Foreign Secretary.

Germany was now virtually without an opposition; ninety
per cent of the Bundestag supported the government, and the
only critics were the small and confused Free Democrats
(whose leader, Erich Mende, soon left them to join Mr. Cornfeld).[1] A few socialists resigned, and the left-wing students'
party, the SDS, gained support; Günter Grass, who had
helped to write Brandt's speeches, wrote to attack this
'wretched marriage', and to warn that the SPD would pass
into a 'vague state of limbo'. Augstein and his *Spiegel* pro-
phesied disaster not just for socialists, but for parliament.
'This is the dilemma of the Grand Coalition in Bonn,' said
Augstein in 1967: 'If it separates in 1969, it can have re-
formed hardly anything. If it stays together into 1973 or
longer, the damage to the democratic conscience may be
irreparable.'[2]

Yet most Socialists were clearly relieved to be seen as part
of the government, and no longer its enemies; in Bonn,
where power is the only profession, the elation was obvious.
The Socialists knew that they had rescued the Christian
Democrats from collapse, and they confidently awaited their
reward. But Kiesinger behaved as if he had not been rescued
by the Socialists, but had rescued them. There were a few
shifts of policy, a bolder approach to eastern Europe, the
beginning of an incomes policy, planning on the Ruhr: but
these would probably have happened anyway. At the next
Länder elections, the Socialist vote showed a calamitous
drop: 'Comrade Trend' had finally turned against them. The

1. See p. 211.
2. Speech in London, 3rd May, 1967.

CDU seemed to be taking credit for successes, while the SPD took the blame for the failures: their disrepute had followed them into the cabinet room. Yet they could not now break up the coalition without losing still more votes.

The left-wing students turned against the Social Democrats with special venom, and Willy Brandt was personally in the thick of it. His two sons were both on the left, and took part in demonstrations in Berlin. His elder son Peter, in a television interview, accused the Social Democrats of always coming to the rescue of the right-wing parties when they were collapsing: in 1968 he was sentenced to detention for taking part in an illegal demonstration. Brandt had always suffered from personal attacks – for his illegitimacy, his self-exile, his Norwegian loyalties – and now he was under fire as a permissive father. But his tolerance of his sons gained him credit with the students. He made a speech in which he said that it was not enough for fathers to understand their sons: the sons must also understand their fathers.

Perhaps the most serious outcome of the Grand Coalition was the fact that a new kind of opposition was emerging; in a succession of provincial elections, there were gains for the new right-wing faction, the National Democratic Party (every party in Germany includes the word democratic), loosely called the 'Neo-Nazis'. It would be wrong to put the main blame on the Grand Coalition. The confident mood of the mid-sixties encouraged a new right which would champion the cause of refugees, attack the dependence on America, and foster a militant national pride; it would be more surprising if it had not emerged, and the fact that the new party has a fairly broad cross-section of classes, ages and regions suggests that it reflects a national reaction. The continued division of Germany was bound to encourage unrest and extremism. But the lack of any serious opposition in parliament, and the two-faced policies of the Grand Coalition gave the new party much greater scope, to appear as the only outspoken critics of *das Establishment*. After the next general election, when NDP members come into the federal parliament, the Christian Democrats – particularly Strauss – may be tempted to make a coalition with them;

and for this ugly alliance the SPD would be at least partly to blame.[1]

ITALY'S 'OPENING TO THE LEFT'

The division between progressive and conservative is the only true great divide of politics. To the extent that Italian political forces do not recognize this fact by trying to differentiate themselves on a different basis, they, for all practical purposes, help the conservative cause.

Pietro Bassetti.[2]

The zig-zag course of Italian socialism, swerving between the rocks of capitalism and communism, can be traced through the extraordinary career of its leader, Pietro Nenni, who has been involved in most of the European cataclysms of the twentieth century. He is now 77, a generation older than Brandt, Wilson or Mitterand, and looks back to a more romantic and ideological age. He came from a peasant family in the Romagna, and spent his childhood in an orphanage. He became a socialist before the first war, when Mussolini was one, and was in prison with him in 1912. Then he briefly became a fascist (when all kinds of people, including Toscanini and Puccini, were fascists), but soon broke with Mussolini; in 1925, when he was editing the socialist *Avanti*, he was arrested and his paper shut down. He fled to France, and spent seventeen years in exile; he fought in Spain, was captured by the Nazis in France during the war, turned over to the Italians and deported to Ponza. His daughter died in a concentration camp. He was liberated in 1943, and organized partisan fighting. After the war he came back to Rome as a hero, and during the brief coalition government he was Foreign Minister: but he supported unity with the communists, and as the cold war blew colder the socialists split. Giuseppe Saragat led the anti-communist wing, who called themselves Social Democrats (PSDI), while Nenni stayed leader of the 'pure' socialists (PSI). After the 1948 elections Saragat was in the government and Nenni was out of it – a bitter division. Nenni continued pro-communist,

1. This fear, of course, turned out to be unfounded: the election enabled the Social Democrats to make a coalition government, frail but effective, with the Liberals (FDP).
2. *Tempi Moderni*, No. 26, Autumn 1966.

and anti-NATO, and even received the Stalin peace prize (£10,000). Then came Hungary, Nenni denounced the Russian intervention, condemned the whole Soviet system, gave away the £10,000, and broke with the Italian communists. He soon softened towards the ruling Christian Democrats and obviously looked for a share in the power.

The Christian Democrats in the meantime had no absolute majority, and needed to make awkward alliances with either Saragat or the extreme right; after the 1958 elections Italy seemed to be moving leftwards, and a group of moderate Catholics called the 'Dorotei' (after a convent where they first met), favoured a move to the left. They included Aldo Moro, Mariano Rumor and Emilio Colombo. At first the party swung to the right; a provisional government under Fernando Tambroni ruled for a few months with the support of the Neo-Fascists, and with hints of police-state methods. But Tambroni eventually discredited this 'Opening to the Right' and after an outbreak of rioting he was followed by the more flexible Fanfani, who saw better prospects with the left; the *détente*, and Pope John, made the left seem less alarming. After devious manoeuvres, Fanfani put together a policy, including nationalizing electricity, which Nenni could accept. In April 1963 the general elections showed a further swing to the left; and at last a coalition was agreed between the Christian Democrats and the Socialists, with Moro as prime minister and Nenni as deputy.

Nenni was delighted that the socialists were out of 'the ghetto of isolation', and Senator Bo, one of the left-wing Christian democrats, said that the 'old ideological barrier between Catholic and socialist masses' was crumbling. There were loud protests. The 'pure' socialists formed a new party called PSUIP, the right wing remained dangerous, and in 1964 the country came close to a *coup d'état,* when President Segni resigned and twenty-one ballots were needed before the parties could agree to a successor – Saragat. But Moro held the coalition together; a dry, pedestrian figure, an ex-professor of law, his dullness was often to reduce the explosive idea of a centre-left government to plain tedium.

To many Italian socialists the coalition seemed a betrayal; with the power, and the spoils, Nennie and his fellows seemed to lose their political fire. Even the reunion of Saragat and Nenni (the PSI and the PSDI), after twenty years was unproductive. The two parties merged with a fanfare of celebration at the Sports Palace in Rome, and Nenni promised they would model themselves on the British Labour Party; they would launch new initiatives, give up useless rhetoric and be a barrier to communism, 'We have moved from a position of protest to one of responsibility.' But the two parties did not really merge, and each kept its own secretariat. Inside the coalition, the socialists could not point to much achievement. The nationalization of electricity, not surprisingly, turned out to be a bonus for the owners, and a burden for the government; the Christian Democrats, as in Germany, were able to take credit for the few reforms, while the real problems – the modernization of the Italian state and the removal of corruption – had scarcely been broached; the most pressing reform, of the university system, was still not achieved.

The result, in the elections of April 1968, was a disaster for Nenni. The communists and the Christian Democrats both gained votes, and the far-left PSIUP, which attracted many of the students, took twenty-three seats. But the socialists lost twenty-nine seats. The Christian Democrats carried on with a caretaker government, led by Giovanni Leone, while the socialists decided what to do. They were faced once again with their old divisive dilemma – whether to ally with the communists or with the Catholics: their two parts seemed unlikely to hold together. Nenni, having tasted power after his forty years in the wilderness, was determined not to give it up. As in Germany, the opening to the left had only served to strengthen the ruling party, and to weaken the special identity of the socialists. But the Italian socialists were also overshadowed more darkly on the left side, by the still-growing presence of the communist party.

FRANCE AND THE UNPOPULAR FRONT

Can the left attract our sons – the left, that great corpse lying on its back riddled with worms?

Jean-Paul Sartre, 1960

Nouse avons une gauche préhistorique.

Students' slogan at Sciences-Po, Paris, 1968

The word 'left' had its origin in France (from the seating arrangement in the Assembly after the Revolution), but its history there has been specially confused; it has had intricate divisions from the beginning, and a succession of rival splinters between revolution and reformism. The official socialist party was born in 1904, with the hopeful name '*Section Française de l'Internationale Ouvrière*' (SFIO) which it still bears. It was never very united, but it was at first held together partly by the poetic personality of Jean Jaurès, who combined intellectual and popular appeal. Since the twenties, when the socialists lost much of their glamour to the communists, they have had a drab image as the party of teachers, functionaries or postmen, run by a leaden bureaucracy. Their revolutionary fire was dimmed by their brief periods of compromised power.

The beginning of the cold war faced the French left with the same kind of contortions as the Italians: the SFIO accepted the Atlantic alliance, the communists went into permanent opposition, and a cluster of small and sophisticated parties grew up in between, with varying degrees of Marxism. For much of the post-war time the socialists were in coalition governments, and their ill-repute reached a climax in the 1956 government of Guy Mollet, who changed his policy in Algeria after being pelted with tomatoes, and helped to launch the Suez campaign. Mollet, who has now been leader of the SFIO for twenty-two years, epitomizes the image of the party – a bespectacled schoolmaster, always with a cigarette hanging dejectedly from his mouth. But he controls the party machine, and no alliance of the left has been able to do without him.

When De Gaulle came to power in 1958, he demoralized the socialists still further; he lured left voters, and stole some socialist clothes. It became obvious that the opposition could only remove De Gaulle by uniting: the new presidential system, the government majority, television and the 'personalization' of elections all seemed at last to be simplifying French politics towards some kind of two-party system. By the 1965 presidential election the non-communist left had at last formed a loose federation headed by François Mitterrand, who was supported by the communists in a tacit alliance against De Gaulle. Mitterrand is not a self-evident socialist; he is every inch a professional, and he has been in and out of governments since 1944, when he was only twenty-nine. He had a spectacular early career; he was the son of a railway-worker who turned to making vinegar. François had a brilliant school and university record, became a sergeant in the war, was captured and escaped and then joined the resistance; after that he worked in Algiers, London and France. De Gaulle admired him, and brought him into his first government to deal with returning deportees. He was a minister in successive governments, and was implicated in embarrassing policies with North Africa. Since De Gaulle's return he was in the wilderness. In 1965 the two Socialist leaders, Mollet and Defferre, were at logger-heads, and to many people's astonishment, Mitterrand was chosen as a compromise for the presidential candidacy. From this uneasy beginning, Mitterrand became the indispensable buckle of the left-wing alliance.

I went to see Mitterrand in February 1968 at his flat in Paris, which looks over the Luxembourg Gardens, but has an atmosphere even gloomier than most French flats – harsh lights, uncomfortable chairs, dour family portraits, and bound volumes of French classics; only relieved by photographs of a very pretty wife. Mitterrand has a reputation for unpunctuality: I waited for three-quarters of an hour before being shown into his study. I kept on remembering what a French friend had told me, that she liked the top half of his face, but couldn't stand the bottom half. He talked about his hopes of a European defence system; he said that the majority of French voters were against America staying in Europe indefinitely, but wanted them to stay for the time being. He stressed the importance of the common market as giving independence from America. He thought that the French communists were coming round to the common market, which could transform the common market parliament (he is a member of it, and not impressed). He thought that the Vietnam war had pulled Europe much farther away from America. He was not hopeful about French links with other socialists: the British left were much their closest connections, then the Italians. With Germany there was little contact, partly because they were so busy with reunification and government. He had recently begun to write and talk more about Europe: 'The mission of the French left is to make our economy a fulcrum for European independence,' he wrote in *Le Monde* in February 1968.

The first test of the left-wing alliance with the communists was in 1965, when the socialists and the communists went to the polls in a wary alliance, for the first time for twenty-one years. Many socialists were nervous that the communists would frighten voters away, but the result was a triumph for Mitterrand's policy; both socialists and communists gained, and the Gaullists were left with a majority of only one. By the time of the students' revolt in May 1968, Mitterrand's position appeared still stronger; when De Gaulle seemed about to fall, he offered himself as president. But when De Gaulle counterattacked, Mitterrand was made to look like one of the forces of disorder, and in the prevailing panic the alliance with the communists could now be used as an effective smear. The communists and socialists went to the polls in June 1968 in a much looser alliance, and they both suffered an ignominious defeat; the federation of the left went down from 118 deputies to 57 while the Gaullists went up from 197 to 294. The socialists had obviously suffered from being blamed for the outburst of anarchy, but what was more serious was that the young voters had shown so little interest in their ageing and cautious candidates. Even the independent party of left-wing socialists, the PSU, had lost its only four deputies in the landslide; and their most prominent member, Pierre Mendès-France – who a month before had seemed close to taking over – lost his seat.

The elections, as in Italy, had polarized the parliament, leaving the centre even less effective; but the predicament of the French socialists was much worse. The victory of the right was more complete, the socialists' road to power, via the communists, had proved a dead-end, and new radical movements have burst out, with which they have scarcely any contact.

WILSONISMUS

To govern is to choose.

Pierre Mendès-France

Seen from the continent, the British Labour Party has obvious advantages. It has not had religions to divide it; it has only a tiny communist party to embarrass it; it has strong trade unions to finance it and usually to vote for it; it has no need to prove its patriotism or respectability. The whole tradition of British socialism is less revolutionary, less linked with Marx, than that of the continental parties. All these factors have given the Labour Party a much more solid and enduring support than the continental socialist parties.

I need not recount here the very different post-war development of British socialists, who avoided most of the convulsions which split the European left during the cold war. The conservatism of the British working-class and the moderation of the Labour intellectuals held the party together as a single opposition; but it also led to a complacent belief that British socialism would have a special splendour, and could triumph on its own. When the Labour Party returned to power in October 1964, its hopes were echoed by many on the continent. But in the following years, Wilsonisme or Wilsonismus came to stand for the reversal and betrayal of socialist policies, and a compromise socialism conducted with characteristic British humbug.

Many of these reversals were forced on the government by the economic crisis. But it is important to remember that the most bitter attacks on Wilsonismus have been over a policy which was not forced on him – the condoning of the Vietnam war. The explanations which may have been accepted in Britain – that the British have more influence on Americans by protesting privately, not publicly – cut no ice on the continent. Nothing in my experience has done more to discredit British socialism in the last four years than this refusal to make public protest against the Vietnam war.

The British Labour Party, by its experiences of the past fifty years, has inevitably been separated from the continental parties, and its leaders' lives have been comparatively sheltered and insular. Harold Wilson, the same age as Mitterrand and three years younger than Brandt, had no ordeal as drastic as exile or resistance. He was grounded in the non-conformist tradition of British socialism, with only a flavouring of Marx (he claims that he has never even read *Das Kapital*); he spent the war years in Whitehall, and after the war showed little interest in the continent; like most other Labour ministers at that time, he was profoundly sceptical of the European socialists, divided and confused by the cold war. In the years of opposition he put his faith in the Commonwealth rather than the common market, and when

Gaitskell came out against joining the common market in 1962, Wilson agreed with him, and continued to steer clear of the continent after he became prime minister. Only as the economic crisis deepened after 1965 did Wilson, pushed by George Brown, move gradually towards Europe; and his conversion was much more calculated than emotional. He toured the capitals of the Six to lobby for Britain's entry, but made little contact with socialist parties. After the second veto by De Gaulle in 1967, the enthusiasm for Europe inevitably waned; George Brown left the government, and after the French crisis of May 1968 there were recriminations of 'I told you so' while the old fear of the instability and right-wing reaction from the continent came up again. In spite of protestations about European technology, the Labour government backed out of two projects, ELDO and the new giant accelerator for CERN. The cabinet, without George Brown, did not show a very European face; the Foreign Secretary, Michael Stewart, was lukewarm; the Minister of Technology, Wedgwood Benn, had been suspicious of Europe; the two men who knew Europe best, Richard Crossman and Denis Healey, had been the two who most disliked it. Of the senior ministers, only Roy Jenkins and Anthony Crosland had been consistently staunch for Britain-in-Europe. Yet the Labour Party, even after the come-back of De Gaulle, stood firm on its European policy, and showed no signs of a serious revulsion against the continent. The schemes for an Atlantic Free Trade Area attracted little support, and even the more distrustful ministers, like Healey, now accepted that Britain's future lay with the continent, for the economic reasons for Britain's involvement were pressing. The conversions had not been very heart-felt or dramatic, but they made up a striking contrast with the Labour Party's attitudes of five years before.

In the meantime Labour's popularity, as shown by the by-elections, was falling so fast that it seemed unlikely to survive the next general election. There was a burst of debate about a coalition government, or even a technocrats' government (proposed by Lord Robens) which could run the country as 'Great Britain Limited'. Professor Beloff of Oxford advocated a coalition as not just desirable but inevitable: 'The fact that most of our friends and competitors in western Europe regard coalition as normal should make us wonder whether we do not pay too high a price for our fidelity to the Gladstone-Disraeli Syndrome.'[1]

Certainly the British experience seemed to show, more poignantly than the coalitions in Germany and Italy, how little room for manoeuvre was left to a left-wing government; as long as the country was in debt, the conditions of international loans dictated economic policy; while the weakness of the pound dictated most foreign policy. There was little difference between Tory and Labour. But this was no argument for coalition. The tragedy of the continental coalitions is that they are in effect one single party, fortified by all the machinery of consensus government, which absorbs its lesser partners and destroys their individuality; while the radical opposition is forced to operate outside parliament, with dark thoughts of revolution. The strength of the British two-party system is that at least there is always a possible alternative government, which can make room for a wide range of discontent, and that the continuity of parliament is assured: there is never any serious worry about where the next government might come from – as there was in France in May 1968.

The experience of the Labour Party, alongside the setbacks of the Scandinavian socialists, has been held to show that social democracy is not viable in the conditions of postwar capitalism. But it is important to remember that the devaluation of 1967 was at least partly a legacy of an earlier government; and that if Wilson had dared to devalue and withdraw from the Far East two years earlier, the crisis might have been avoided. What the British experience seems to show most clearly – as the German has shown – is that a socialist party can only retain its right to rule if it is prepared to make bold choices based on its beliefs; and that the policy of 'keeping the options open' leads inevitably towards the loss of prestige abroad and the loss of votes at home.

In spite of the disillusion with Wilsonismus, much of it justified, I believe that the British Labour Party has a central, and even indispensable role, to play in the future of Europe. Between the two extremes of total assimilation into the consensus system and total rejection it is still able to steer

1. 'The Case for a Coalition Government', *The Times*, 7th December, 1967.

a middle course. Its deep roots in society, its link with strong trade unions, its unbroken continuity and its moderation all help to make it a more reliable countervailing force than its continental counterparts. In the mounting prosperity of the fifties and sixties, that force has not seemed very necessary; but in the restlessness that seems likely in the seventies, and with the danger of a resurgence of a new Right, it will be an imperative for real stability. If there is to be a European socialist movement, then the Labour Party is the solid core that it needs.

A SOCIALIST EUROPE?

Our socialism will be European, or nothing.

Club Jean Moulin, 1965.[2]

There is nothing socialists nationalize so well as socialism.

Ignazia Silone

There are some common difficulties in these socialist parties. However much their difficulties grow out of national predicaments, one common attribute is apparent in Germany, Italy, Britain and Scandinavia; that once in power, the parties lose their special identity, and find themselves having to compete on equal terms with capitalist parties on capitalist lines. In this situation they can hardly win; so long as the yardsticks of success remain the current ones – gross national products, growth rates, consumer durables, balance of payments – the other side will always command more confidence. Even the socialist countries in eastern Europe, with their new fascination with the machines and the comforts of the west, are showing their weakness: they have to get Fiat and Renault to build their cars for them.

Yet it is not certain that these will always be the yardsticks. The preoccupation with growth rates over the past twenty years may diminish in the seventies. We have seen plenty of evidence of the coming dangers of a European free-for-all – whether in cars, land, suburbs or the blind keeping up with American competition. The problem of what is vaguely called 'the quality of life', of maintaining

1. The role for the Labour Party in Europe could be more important in opposition than it was in power, since its leaders have the opportunity to make really close contacts with left-wing oppositions on the continent.
2. Claude Bruclain (pseudonym): *Le Socialisme et L'Europe*, p. 14.

individuality in the midst of the consumer society, of making use of leisure, of balancing private wealth with public services – all these new factors are likely to condition the affluent Europe of the seventies. It cannot be assumed that a *détente* between east and west, if it reoccurs, would show an automatic advantage to the western capitalists: their sense of purpose, their broader access to education, and the seriousness and austerity of their youth, may all serve to give the east a special attraction. The car itself may yet come to be not the main trophy of a free economy, but the most pressing reason for its control. Future problems may present a challenge to socialism, not of the familiar monolothic pattern, but of a more imaginative kind, to provide a balance between the central engines of industrial growth, the patronage of the state, and the essential liberties of individuals and communities.

But the problem of the socialist parties has been not only their lack of a convincing alternative system to capitalism; it is also that, by operating on a purely national level in an economy which is becoming increasingly international, they have been constantly at the mercy of forces outside – a situation of which Britain has the most painful experience.

We have seen earlier that socialists and some trade unionists have had mixed feelings about a united Europe.[1] They believed in Franco-German reconciliation and (in theory) in abandoning nationalism; but they dreaded a 'Bankers' Europe', a capitalists' free-for-all, that would obstruct national planning. The two strongest socialist parties, the British and the German, were both very suspicious: Kurt Schumacher, the German socialist patriot, was against Monnet's schemes and when the treaty for a European Army came up, he insisted that 'whoever approves this treaty ceases to be a German'. The British Labour Party was absorbed in its own country and pessimistic about the future of the continent. The French socialists were divided. When the Council of Europe first met at Strasbourg, Guy Mollet said:

Europe has been born. We shall also create the United States of Europe. A socialist might wonder whether he should rejoice,

1. *See* Workers, p. 393.

since the socialists are in the minority. Still, without hesitation, I say: yes, we are glad. . . . We know that events will rapidly sweep Europe along the road to socialism.[1]

But many other socialists were worried. They had all been accustomed to think of planning and welfare on a neat national scale. The whole concept of the welfare state and social security evolved round the nation-state and provided a real obstacle to international attitudes.[2] When the idea of the common market came up, it looked as if the continental market could wreck socialist plans, and the enthusiasm of big business was ominous. In Italy the '*Confindustria*' made no secret of the advantage of the common market as an escape from the socialist threat; they much preferred moving into the rich markets north of the Alps to the thankless task of developing the south. The common market, to many socialist eyes, was in danger of creating a Rich Man's Club, cutting off Europe from Africa and Asia, and also of perpetuating the divisions of Europe and of Germany.

The common market boomed ahead, and all socialists, including finally the British, accepted its bounty. Even the French PSU, which at first had opposed the common market as being part of the western alignment, came round in 1963 to supporting it, as being essential to European independence from America. The new Europe was achieving its growth without obvious damage to democracy or full employment, and during the late fifties the Germans and the British were rethinking their dogmas and abandoning the extension of public ownership. The mission of European socialism required new definition. In 1965 the Club Jean Moulin, the group of French left-wing intellectuals and managers (roughly equivalent to the British Fabian Society), produced a frank study of socialism and Europe, with which I find myself very much in agreement.[3] It began by saying: 'Nobody knows any more what socialism is, and nobody yet knows what Europe is.' It admitted that the 'neo-capitalism' of western Europe had raised living standards more effectively than the socialism of eastern Europe. It argued that a properly united Europe, far from being the obstacle to

1. Quoted in Alexander Werth: *France 1940–55*, p. 432.
2. For an exposition of this problem, see Gunnar Myrdal: *Beyond the Welfare State*, 1961.
3. Claude Bruclain: *Le Socialisme et L'Europe*, 1965.

socialism, was the only means to achieve it, since the individual countries were no longer masters of their own future; and that European planning could provide a society much richer than Russia's and much more humane than America's. It insisted that the common market, in its existing half-way state, was an obstacle to planning, but that the solution was to develop it further: 'The compatibility between socialism and Europe can only establish itself on a higher level – of political unity.'

COMMUNISTS

Communism is a factor, sometimes serious, sometimes vestigial, in western Europe today; but 'western European communism' does not exist.

Joseph Starobin, 1965.[1]

Part of the socialists' difficulty has been that they have been caught between the extremes of respectability and revolution, and that at either end they are outbid by their rivals. The right-wing parties have been more respectable, the communists more vocal about overthrowing the whole system. Yet even the communists, after fifty years, are becoming far less convincing as agents of revolution, and show signs of settling down to a muddled middle age.

The Italian and French communist parties, with their stormy common past, might be expected to be the twin pillars of European communism: but in fact they might almost belong to separate continents. The Italian party, the biggest in the west, has an exotic variety. Crossing over from Germany, where the communist party is (absurdly) banned, I was bewildered to find myself seeing Catholic communists, millionaire communists, artist communists, intellectual communists, Chinese communists or Cuban communists, all within the ample folds of the party; only the most deviationist (like Feltrinelli, the publisher of *Doctor Zhivago*) are actually expelled. Much of the tolerance stems from Togliatti, who led the party for thirty-eight years, and invented the idea of 'polycentrism': he could be all things to all men, loudly proclaiming 'the Italian road to socialism',

1. 'Communism in Western Europe', *Foreign Affairs*, N.Y., October 1965.

while still accepted by Moscow. His successor since 1964, Luigi Longo, a much duller man, has allowed the toleration to develop into two factions, between which he holds a tricky balance. One, led by Giorgio Amendola, advocates a co-alition of the left, to prepare for a coming clash with the right. The other, led by Pietro Ingrao, insists that the communists must maintain their purity, while having a 'dialogue' direct with the Catholics. The argument reflects the recurring dilemma of communists in western Europe – how to manoeuvre towards power, without losing their basic faith. Most of them, growing impatient for power, have gradually come round to some form of 'popular frontism'.

After twenty years of European prosperity, the Italian communists might be expected to lose much of their ground. But they have gained. In the 1968 general election in Italy, the communists polled thirty-nine per cent of the votes, against thirty-eight per cent in 1964, and held 177 seats in the assembly of 630 members. The communists have long ago ceased to depend on poverty: the Italian communist party still keeps its popularity in very prosperous provinces, such as Emilia and Tuscany. Bologna, a boom town, is efficiently run by a communist municipality and a communist mayor. It is this regional loyalty, united in its resentment of the government in Rome, which the Christian Democrats have been unable to shake. As one authority, Giorgio Galli, has described it: 'In those regions the communist party is far more than a party to which one might belong or for which one might vote. It is a true instrument of social organization and integration. A network of co-operatives, of labour unions, of cultural and athletic associations, together with control of movie houses and the systematic listening to broadcasts from behind the Iron Curtain (spoken of as our radio) contributes a social, economic and political universe.'

The success of the Italian communists in capturing and keeping local citadels gives them a strength which can outlive the alliance with Moscow and the unity of the cold war. If, as I believe, the conflict between regions and the central states becomes an increasingly fiery issue in Europe, then the Italian communists are well equipped to exploit it.

The French communists have a much more disciplined hierarchy, forged by their history of militant pre-war strikes and wartime resistance, and a stolid predictability which

Italian communists describe with contempt. For thirty-four years they had the same autocratic leader, Maurice Thorez, who remained loyal to Stalin: his successor, Waldeck Rochet, a bald, phlegmatic Burgundian, does not have the same panache; but he still has the rigid bureaucrats. The French party has a solid proletarian backbone, and even the debunking of Stalin had little effect. The left-wing intellectuals have been infuriated by its stiffness and lack of imagination: of the array of artists and writers who used to adorn it, only a few eccentrics (like Picasso or Aragon) remain loyal. But its strength (as in Italy) is in its local roots. In the north of France and in the 'Red belt' of Paris (which includes the Renault works) there is a communist tradition now spanning three generations.

For years now, the French communist party has been trying to get rid of its revolutionary image, and since it joined with the socialists in 1966 it has been determined to show itself respectable. Apart from the occasional one-day token strikes, it has not seriously threatened the Gaullist regime, and it has co-existed uneasily with De Gaulle, as eastern Europe has co-existed with the west. De Gaulle's alliance with Moscow helped to neutralize the French communists, and effectively stole the main plank of their foreign policy.

Then came the 'May days' of 1968: the young workers, set off by the students, decided to occupy their factories, against the will of the French communists and their union, the CGT. The CGT were then forced to order a general strike, to avoid losing all their authority. As De Gaulle seemed to be toppling, and agitation pressed up from students and workers, the communists were reluctantly forced to politicize the strike, demanding De Gaulle's removal. And at this point De Gaulle had his chance, for the communists had abandoned their respectable image, and appeared (though pushed into it) as once again a revolutionary party. De Gaulle lashed back, denounced the 'totalitarian' menace of the communists, made a pact with the army leaders and called for a general election. The communists were hopelessly vulnerable from both sides: they had lost their respectability, and annoyed their more sedate members (and more particularly their wives) by the long strike, but they had also shown their reluctance to be revolutionary, and had thus lost radical support. In the election, the number of communist deputies went down from 73 to 34.

The Russian invasion of Czechoslovakia in August 1968 provoked a new, perhaps final, crisis for international communism. The Italian party considered 'the decision unjustified and irreconcilable with the principles of autonomy and independence of every communist party and socialist state'. The British party condemned the invasion as 'completely unjustified'. The French party, for the first time in its history, emphatically condemned Moscow policy, and the CGT announced that 'French workers can only deplore the present military intervention'. The breaks seemed to mark the tail-end of the long-lasting equation between Moscow and world communism; as one Sovietologist, Robert Conquest, described it (*The Times*, 24th August, 1968): 'We are back in something like the position immediately following the First World War, with dozens of socialist and revolutionary sects, with a wide variety of tenets'.

Of the ninety communist parties in the world, only twelve – including the five countries that took part in the invasion – supported the Soviet action. The final collapse of the leadership of Moscow may leave the Western communist parties in still greater disarray, each subject to their own national pressures and bureaucracies; but it may also leave the way open for their closer participation in the institutions of western Europe (particularly in the common market and its parliament) and a closer alliance between the French and Italian parties.

For young European revolutionaries, the communist parties no longer offer any encouragement, but rather a series of warnings. The French students' revolt served to reveal the basic contradiction of the French communists; that while still invoking the Marxist and revolutionary mystique, they had long since become cautious and bureaucratic, and had no wish to disturb the regime until they were strong enough to out-vote it. The Italian communists, though much more adaptable and many-sided, were likewise deeply involved in the parliamentary game and the fruits of local power, and they reacted to the students by closing their ranks. As for Germany, the Ulbricht regime provided the most depressing example of the hardening of communism into a rigid and stifling bureaucracy.

For the younger generation of intellectuals (who are the subject of the next chapter), the communist parties, with their humbug, their autocracy and their gerontocracy, are as exasperating as the conservatives. For their new heroes and models they look further afield, to the battlegrounds where distance lends enchantment – to Cuba, Bolivia or China. They reject Stalinism, Kosyginism, Ulbrichtism, Waldeck-Rochetism; but they turn back to the original Marxism – the early Marx of the eighteen-forties. After a hundred and thirty years, the intellectual appeal of Marx appears as strong as ever.

Ideology, whose death has been so widely reported, has refused to lie down. The world systems of Lenin or Hitler have been discredited; and for the first twenty years after the war there was little sign of new inspiration. But the past two years have shown that the new educated generation cannot tolerate a continent which rests on purely mechanical assumptions, and which has cut itself off from the rest of the world. However partial, unformed and old-fashioned their ideas may appear, they are still able to move people against their own material interests. There may be some relevance in the words of one of the earlier generation, the Yugoslav rebel Milovan Djilas: ' "The tree of life is always green, and all theory is grey" . . . Yes, all ideologies are undergoing a process of disintegration – in the west as well as in the east. . . . But we are also living in an age in which new ideologies still unknown to us are being formed.'[1]

1. H. J. Stehle: 'A Talk with Milovan Djilas', *Encounter*, 1967.

Chapter Twenty-one

Students

> We are never completely contemporaneous with our present. History advances in disguise; it appears on stage wearing the mask of the preceding scene, and we tend to lose the meaning of the play. Each time the curtain rises, continuity has to be re-established. The blame, of course, is not history's, but lies in our vision, encumbered with memory and images learned in the past. We see the past superimposed on the present, even when the present is a revolution.
>
> *Régis Debray, Revolution in the Revolution?*

Passing from the Europe of technocrats and politicians to the Europe of students seemed like going backstage in a theatre. The buildings and rooms which looked so solid and convincing suddenly appear to be just tricks of lighting and façades hung from the roof, with nothing behind them. The furniture is made of paper and the stone walls flap when you touch them. The speeches and crowd scenes, seen from these wings, are ridiculous. Whenever I have passed from one side to the other I have had the same sense of not just going from one stage to another, but of going offstage. The student leaders make the point often enough, with their vocabulary of contestation, manipulation, their obsession against the Establishment and Authority, their reiteration of 'you're asking the wrong question', 'that's not meaningful'. But to isolate them from other students is misleading; they are not expressing or whipping-up surprising ideas, but only re-stating what to other students is self-evident; that the whole world they are being invited to join – of technology, technocracy, political parties and corporations – is completely irrelevant and hostile to their own ambitions and desires.

The earlier generations have tried to explain the phenomenon in their own technological terms, with expressions like 'generation gap', 'failure of communication' or 'margin of tolerance', as if the problem was one of engineering or electronics. The student protesters can be categorized and explained away; they come from a thin layer of society; many are fatherless, or from difficult homes; they nearly all have bourgeois backgrounds, and a large proportion are sociologists, philosophers or political scientists. Their ideas are not original, but come from America, from Marx, Marcuse, or Mao. They talk a great deal about the third world, but few have ever been there, or done anything about it; they prefer dead or distant heroes, like Guevara or Giap, and they look at China (as French intellectuals have so often looked at China) as a convenient Utopia in which to deposit their own cultural baggage. They follow the ideas of old anarchists without bothering to study why they failed, and how they induced counter-revolutions. With this kind of self-deception and ignorance it is hardly surprising that the students have achieved the precise opposite of what they intended – the closing of the ranks on the right and a strengthening of all authority.

Yet all this could have been said of earlier revolutionary groups: the Romantic movement, with its immense impact on Europe, likewise stemmed from a small clique of maladjusted bourgeois. What matters in the end is not the class or psychological origins, but the strength of the ideas and their capacity to influence other people. The students' ideas are not, it is true, at all original: but their obviousness (like the Romantics') does not necessarily disqualify them. What is hard to deny is that ideas have power. It is impossible now to be so confident about the 'End of Ideologies'. The students have, however briefly, made all Europe look different; they have managed to break through the machinery, the complexity, the routine and the smoothness to convey something which has excited not only themselves but their elders. As Edgar Morin described it in *Le Monde*, during the height of the 1968 crisis:[1]

It is the sudden crisis of a fine consumers' society which turns, rolls, purrs, peacefully and busily; of a society which the most furious political assaults or the most dangerous backwash of decolonization have never shaken; of a society still climbing, whose income per head, already one of the highest in Europe, must still grow; of a society where miseries and archaisms are becoming exceptions, while fifteen years ago they were the back-cloth. ... And here in this society which is on the way to

1. 5th June, 1968.

American harmonies – and real harmonies because without the cancer of the Negro problem or Vietnam – here everything seizes up, everything cracks, everything is immobilized and the whole prodigious cybernetic machine comes apart to produce millions of discontents who stop, protest and contest.

It is not easy to see why this crack-up should happen – in varying degrees, all over Europe – at this point of time, and why a new generation should so suddenly break out. After all, earlier generations have had greater grievances, fewer opportunities. Many explanations have been offered, but there is one obvious one, which is valid everywhere. The new generation have no memory of the war; they take the prosperity and recovery of Europe for granted, and are bored by the obsession with money and the absence of ideas. They are the first intellectual generation for over half a century who have not been preoccupied by the horrors of the previous war, or preparing for the next. The war which influenced so many of the new institutions, centring round NATO and the common market, finished a quarter of a century ago, when many of the student leaders were born. The weight of it is no longer the same; the pessimism it induced has evaporated; the sense of Europe having defeated itself, of having passed out of history, is no longer there. For young Germans, the break has a special significance. For better or for worse, the period is now drawing to an end in which Germany was grappling with her war guilt – a sense of guilt which played a crucial role in the European movement. As one of the students put it: 'My parents' generation only think of the *Bewältigung der Vergangenheit* – the overcoming of the past. We are only interested in the future.'

In writing about the students' revolts, it is impossible not to be subjective, not to see them through one's own experience. I belong to a generation that went to university, just after the war, when Europe seemed chaotic, jobs were scarce, and Oxford colleges were full of beery captains and majors. Hardly anyone dreamt of questioning the absurd rules by which the college was run, the superfluity of professors of theology and the absence of professors of engineering. After all, it was no more absurd than the Army or the Navy. One American in my college who submitted a list of thirty-five sensible improvements to the bursar was laughed out of court. A song at that time, 'Baby, It's Cold Outside', expressed most people's thoughts about the rest of the country, and when they left university, quite radical-minded men were thankful to throw themselves into the arms of Lloyds Bank, the *Daily Express* or an advertising agency. It seemed astonishing that England was reviving at all from the ruins of the war. As for the continent, it might any day go communist. Looking back at that time, it seems to me now that the mood of the time was far too uncritical, that most of us were too unquestioning, that the place was too lacking in new political ideas. The universities were full of gloomy economists and disillusioned Marxists, and even the Labour Party's reshaping of Britain was being undertaken by old men with pre-war notions. British universities – particularly Oxford and Cambridge – were no doubt unusual in their capacity to look backwards; but all western Europe shared the pessimism, and even the European movement (in spite of the brave talk at the Congress of The Hague) seemed more influenced by the fear of war than the hopes of a great new society.

With this recollection of gloom I find myself listening to the new students with a mixture of envy and alarm. In spite of their ferocity, they seem to have a far greater optimism, a much more vivid sense of the future, than their predecessors; and they have a faith that they can actually change it. As they push the boats out again, laden with old Utopias and manifestos, still furnished with Marx and even Rousseau, it is hard for men of the forties and fifties not to say 'if only they'd learn'; the middle-aged criticisms are heavy with *déjà vu*. But when they reply, as they do, that the sixties are quite different from the forties and that it's better to have a second-hand Utopia than none at all, then I feel bound to agree. Utopias are necessary (as Professor Havemann, the East German rebel, remarked) not because they'll ever come true, but because they show up the barbarity of the actual society. The importance of the students' revolt is that it has reopened a serious debate on the nature of western society, for the first time for twenty years.

UNIVERSITIES

An investment in knowledge pays the best interests.
Benjamin Franklin

It is important to remember that the first cause of the discontent through all western Europe has been the ineptness of the universities themselves. The students all began by attacking their own universities, and many of them still confine their protest to that; without the political ingredients – Vietnam, De Gaulle or the Grand Coalition – there would still have been a revolt against the closer enemy, the professors.

It is the universities which show the greatest strains between the old Europe and the new. Yet in some ways the newest students are attempting to get back to the position of the oldest; here, as in other fields, Europe looks forward to the Middle Ages. In the fourteenth century the universities were supranational; held together by a common language and religion, the students all understood each other, and could move from one city to another. Bologna and Paris were the models; Oxford was founded by students chucked out from Paris, and Cambridge by rebels from Oxford. Bologna was a model not only for internationalism but for democracy; the students elected the professors, and sacked them if they were inadequate. Not surprisingly, medieval Bologna and Paris are often quoted nostalgically by the students of 1968, as the ideals of independence or democracy. The medieval democracy does not bear too much inspection; many of the students were sons of noblemen and future rulers, to whom the professors were more like tutors. But the internationalism is still relevant today, and the example of the medieval universities is in the minds of common market enthusiasts who have tried, with total failure, to establish a European university which could cut across national divisions.

In the intervening seven centuries, with the break-up of the common language, the religious wars and the rise of nationalism, the universities lost their supranational unity, and became deeply involved in national quarrels; there can be no sadder example than the University of Louvain, one of the greatest medieval universities, now being split in two by linguistic battles. The national universities acquired their own hierarchies and vested interests, and the old notion of academic freedom became an excuse for professors to build their own empires. The more the institutions outside were threatened and transformed, the more the continental universities felt justified in retaining their own traditions, and the inviolability of universities survived democracy.

Faced with the sudden and bewildering increase in students, the professors have tried both to ignore it and to take advantage of it. The corruption and exploitation of the system is a scandal so obvious that few students can fail to notice it. In Italy, where the universities are oldest and the expansion most sudden, the corruption is extreme. In thirty years the number of students has multiplied by seven, while the number of professors has only trebled. The professors relax in their self-perpetuating world, often taking two jobs at once, adapting courses and examinations to the convenience of their own careers, selling cyclostyled lectures for their own profit. In a vast university like Rome, with seventy thousand students, a student may never see a professor.

In Germany the universities retain the pomp and grandeur which other institutions have lost, and professors, having struggled to reach their eminence, revel in their powers. They have the grandeur of an English judge, but without the detachment: they can make or break junior teachers, appropriate the work of their assistants, and run their departments as private offices. In Law faculties, professors make money by giving private lectures which are almost essential to pass the examinations; in Medicine, they take the most lucrative private practice. Some rectors still insist on being addressed by the old title of 'Magnificence', and the hierarchy of titles, though much mocked, remains a reality. The influx of a new generation of professors, and the post-war exchange with America, have done something to loosen up and de-mystify the hierarchy; but even liberal young professors, when threatened, can seek refuge in the assumption of authority. The universities, far from being a model society, are caricatures of some of the worst aspects of what goes on outside.

Everywhere the flow of students has massively increased since the war – straining old universities to their limits. Only one country, Austria (with a specially low birth-rate after the war), has shown a decrease in intakes. Since 1960 the

average growth in numbers of European students has been
nine per cent a year. In fifteen years the numbers in West

	1950	1965
Belgium	3·7	14·1
Denmark	4·5	8·5
Finland	4·2	11·4
France	4·1	14·1
W. Germany	3·4	8·9
Hungary	3·3	6·8
Italy	3·7	7·7
Netherlands	7·4	14·3
Norway	3·3	7·8
Poland	5·9	13·2
Sweden	3·7	11·1
United Kingdom	4·0[1]	8·5

Germany have almost trebled; in France, they have more
than trebled. The proportions of populations in the age
group 20–24 who had enrolled in higher education in 1950
and 1965 (according to the UNESCO report of November
1967[2]) are shown above.

But to be a student doesn't necessarily mean very much.
The French boast that their numbers are growing faster
(fourteen per cent a year) than any other European country:
and that they have more students than Britain and Germany
together. But on the continent, and particularly in France,
there is little relation between the numbers of students and
graduates. Vast numbers drop out after a year or more, and
some 'ghost students' enrol to take advantage of benefits
and never turn up again. In some ways the first year at a
French or German university (as at an American one) is
more like the last year in a British sixth form: the real weed-
ing-out happens after that.

The differences in the meaning of 'student' are fundamental. Russia and eastern Europe, like Britain, weed out
their students before they come up to university (in Britain,
many students, without university ambitions, weed out
themselves). But the rest of Europe has promised entry to
universities for anyone who passes the *baccalauréat* or its
equivalent – which has left the floodgates open. As the flood
has swelled a heated debate has waged between the two

1. 1955 figure.
2. *Factual background on access to higher education*, UNESCO,
November 1967, Vol. 3, p. 370.

systems, *laissez-passer* and *numerus clausus*. Restrictions have crept in: Germany, whose constitution requires free access to universities, has a 'provisional' limitation on medical students. In France, where the universities are most crowded and where the tradition of *laissez-passer* is defended as a fundamental right, the debate has been specially intense.

France and Britain, as in so many fields, are at opposite extremes. France has more than twice as many students as Britain. Yet France has slightly *fewer* university teachers. The difference can be guessed by looking at the new universities; compared to the new British ones, with their expensive architecture, their open spaces and their controlled flow of students, the new French ones are like austere office blocks. The luxury of Oxford or Cambridge, with their private suites, bedmakers, waiters, and personal tutorials, is scarcely credible to the harassed students of the Sorbonne. It is tempting for the British to congratulate themselves on having avoided the continental chaos; yet the danger is that in Britain, where privilege still hangs over the universities, there will be no political pressure inside for expansion, and that she will be left further behind in the education race.

The student boom on the continent was not planned or prepared for; it happened because of the bulge in the birth rate, and because more students were passing their *baccalauréat*, and wanted to stay on. But governments are pressed to make room for them, not so much for egalitarian motives (which are curiously scarce) as because higher education is coming to be regarded as a key factor in national status and industrial growth. The comparisons of educational achievements and of numbers of students has become more important than comparisons between armies. In November 1967 delegates from every European country except Albania gathered in Vienna, under the wing of UNESCO, to discuss access to higher education: 'You are distinguished more by your resemblance than by your contrasts,' said the director-general of UNESCO, René Maheu, and with some reason. While eastern Europeans were trying to liberalize their plans, many western countries, like France, were worrying about controlling admissions. But everywhere it is becoming accepted that students or graduates are a measure of the country's future strength.

And here, as in so many other fields, the example of America is dominating. Of all transatlantic comparisons, one of the most devastating is that in 1966 the proportion of western Europeans in the age-group 20–24 at university ranged between eight and fourteen per cent, while that of Americans was forty-three per cent. Europeans may console themselves with the assurance that American universities are inferior, but even the ratio of teachers to students (one to thirteen) is twice that of France's. The American superiority is a refutation of the traditional European pride (encouraged by the post-war invasion of GIs) that the Americans might have the money, but Europe has the culture.

Many theorists, from Adam Smith onwards, have recognized the importance of education as a national asset, but it is only in the last few years that mass education has been linked with industrial growth. In Europe the economic miracles happened without much help from university graduates. The new tycoons, like the old ones, were often men who had come up from nothing; and in Italy, where the growth was most spectacular, many of the 'neo-capitalisti' were scarcely literate, and very sceptical when economists talked about the role of education.

But in America the new boom from automation and computers has shown the economic importance of education. In a much-quoted calculation, Professor Edward Denison reckoned in 1962 that education had been responsible for forty-two per cent of the increase in real income in America. His findings have been much debated, and in Europe it seems difficult to make such a close correlation: Britain's post-war advantage in education over the rest of Europe did not seem to help her to innovate.[1] There are some critics, like Enoch Powell in Britain, who insist that education is no more than a sacred cow of leftish liberals. But the example of America is very powerful. Robert McNamara said in February 1967: 'How then can the technological gap be closed? Ultimately it can be closed only at its origin: education. Europe is weak educationally. And that weakness is seriously crippling its growth. It is weak in general education; it is weak in its technical education; and it is particularly weak in its managerial education.'

1. *See* Michael Postan: *An Economic History of Western Europe*, p. 156.

The expansion of universities to provide more managers or technologists, according to the gospel of McNamara, is a need that most governments will probably accept. For the great majority of students it is the most desirable kind of expansion, leading the way to opportunities and salaries: and for all students the sense of their importance to the nation has contributed to the idea of 'student power'. But it brings to a head the question: what is a university for? And it challenges the ancient insistence of European universities, that they should pursue their scholarship undisturbed by political requirements. The conflict is a familiar one, and both traditions have for long co-existed. But for the new generation of militant students, nothing is more hateful than the idea that universities should become nurseries for the new managerial society. They wish to get rid of the authoritarianism of the old universities, and the pomp and privilege of the professors. But they want at all costs to retain, or regain, the academic freedom which allows universities to study society from outside it, without preconceptions. It is a central thesis of the student revolutionaries that the universities should not be the tools of the existing capitalist system, but the main agents for its overthrow.

The new demand for education may soon challenge one of the basic traditions of continental universities – that they are reserved for the bourgeoisie. In spite of the democratic convulsions over the past century, higher education remains a middle-class preserve, and subsidies and grants have made little difference. In West Germany the tiny percentage of working-class students (five per cent) compares embarrassingly with East Germany; for young Germans from workers' families, the idea of five years on a small allowance at university seems unattractive compared to business; and the whole German academic rigmarole is severely high-bourgeois. Eastern Europe, as the table below shows, has a far greater proportion of working-class students. As the UNESCO report comments:[1]

There is substantial disparity between the social and economic structure of the active population and the student population in the highly industrialized countries of western Europe, where the average percentage of workmen in the active population is

1. *Comparative Statistical Data*, UNESCO, Vienna, November 1967, p. 18.

40 per cent to 50 per cent. For example, in Belgium the proportion of workers in the active population is 47.9 per cent and the proportion of working-class students 11.2 per cent of the total student population. There is, however, one striking exception, namely the United Kingdom, where the proportion of working-class children who have access to higher education is considerable.

Percentage of manual workers' sons in student body[1]

Country	Around 1960	Around 1964
Yugoslavia	56·0	53·3
Czechoslovakia	39·3	37·9
Rumania	36·6	31·5
Hungary	33·1 (1959)	—
Poland	32·9 (1961)	35·0
Bulgaria	28·0	34·5
United Kingdom	25·0 (1961)	—
Norway	—	20·1 (1964)
Finland	17·6 (1961)	—
Sweden	14·0	—
Italy	13·2	15·3
Belgium	11·2 (1962)	—
Denmark	9·0 (1959)	10·0
Holland	8·0 (1958)	6·0 (1961)
Austria	6·0	5·0
France	5·3	8·3
Ireland	—	5·7 (1963)
W. Germany	5·2	5·3
Spain	—	4·1 (1962)
Switzerland	3·7	—
Greece	1·9	0·1 (1962)

THE INTERNATIONAL TRAIL

All the student revolts have first arisen from discontent within the universities, and there seems to be a rough correlation between the overcrowding – particularly the ratio of teachers to pupils – and the disturbance. Oxford or Cambridge have so far not seen much protest. (A mild anti-proctor demonstration at Oxford was instantaneously countered by the university Conservative club with their slogan: 'Long live proctorial power'.) But at the same time universities which are most 'liberal', which encourage the freedom of students, and the 'modern subjects' of sociology, psychology

1. Data supplied from UNESCO and OECD, published by UNESCO: *Access to Higher Education*, Vol. 4, p. 28. Vienna, November 1967.

or political science (like West Berlin or Essex) often have the most trouble – a fact which is used as a strong argument for stricter discipline. It is not surprising that students in universities where they are encouraged to think for themselves, and to analyse society, take their teaching literally; and that they take action on the discrepancy between the ideals of society and the hierarchy that still governs them.

The protest against the universities has nearly always been mixed with a wider protest; it is the political issues which have given the revolts their international ardour. What lit the fuse between countries was, more than anything, the Vietnam war, and all student movements have a common anti-Americanism. Yet even for their anti-Americanism they depend on America. The American student rebellion – first stirred up in the early sixties by the civil rights movement and then much further provoked by the Vietnam war – provided much of the inspiration, the techniques and even the language for the European movements which followed. The technique of the sit-in, the teach-in, the do-in; the idea of the 'anti-university'; the critique of the consumer society; the strategy of demonstrations and the exploitation of television – all these were borrowed by the Europeans. Many of the student leaders have American connections, particularly in Germany: Rudi Dutschke has an American wife; Ekkehart Krippendorf studied in America and is now in New York; Karl-Dietrich Wolff had his political education in civil rights marches.

While the Vietnam war was the catalyst for all student explosions, the Europeans added their own ingredients of anarchism and Marxism, and each country gave its local colouring. The Provos, who improbably emerged in Holland in 1964 and fizzled out two years later, gave a fillip to anarchism with their imaginative ideas: their policies included having 60,000 white bicycles for the use of everyone in Amsterdam, and transforming car parks into giant chess-boards, and their protests against the 'enslaved students' had great influence among German students. All over western Europe the syndicalist movement had been gaining some ground among students, advocating not only students' control, but workers' control of factories; the French students' union UNEF, part of the German union ASTA, and the small British Radical Students Alliance (started in 1966) were all loosely linked through the syndicalist movement. The far left, unhampered by parties or power, has a special internationalism. The language of Marx, Trotsky or Mao is common to the European movements.

By the new university term of November 1967, the students were beginning to show a new anger. In Paris, when the Sorbonne reopened, two thousand students marched down the Boulevard St. Michel to protest against overcrowding and restrictions. In Milan, two hundred students occupied the hall of the Catholic University all night, to protest against the increase in fees and the autocracy of the professors; they were forced out, singing hymns, by the police and expelled for two years. In Hamburg, when the new rector was being installed with traditional pomp, two student ssuddenly appeared in front of the professors' procession, carrying a banner saying 'under the gowns, the dust of a thousand years'. The political atmosphere was clearly hotting-up, but no one was predicting explosions. The unawareness was itself very significant; for it showed how cut off the mass media had become from the new generation.

THE GERMAN SDS

It was in Germany that the students first showed their teeth. The German students were up against all the traditional authority of the Magnificences and the professors, and beyond that the authority of the German state. They moved from attacking the one to attacking the other.

The German socialist students' federation, the SDS, though it goes back to 1948, derived its real fury from the Grand Coalition in 1966, when it bitterly opposed the Social Democrat leaders and 'das Establishment' of the coalition, and decided to resort to extra-parliamentary activity. The first major explosion was in the summer of 1967, while the Shah of Persia was visiting Germany, when students protested against his political prisoners; when they demonstrated outside the Berlin Opera, the police panicked and fired, killing a young student, Benno Ohnesorg. The police gave a new purpose to the students, and the huge funeral processions in memory of Ohnesorg gave special dignity. The moving spirit of the SDS, Rudi Dutschke, soon became a European phenomenon. With his black thatch of hair, his

big rolling eyes and his football-jerseys, he looked every inch
an extremist; in fact he was one of the more moderate
leaders. His career was impressive; he was brought up in
East Germany, the son of a post office clerk, a Protestant
and pacifist: he refused to serve in the East German army,
moved over to the west, took up sociology, and became a
fierce opponent of the Kiesinger coalition: but he always
held out against provoking violence. He commandèd great
loyalty among his friends, but his more militant colleagues
began to resent both his moderation and the personality cult
that surrounded him – the occupational hazard of all student
leaders.

After the killing of Ohnesorg, the SDS began attacking
the newspaper tycoon Axel Springer, the personification of
the evils of *das Establishment* and the manipulated society,
whose papers were constantly attacking the students. At
Easter 1968 Dutschke was leaving the SDS headquarters on
a bicycle when a man shot him three times. Dutschke survived, but the shooting set off a spontaneous uprising. In the
next two days students all over Germany marched on
Springer offices; in Berlin they invaded the brown skyscrapers, and in Hamburg they stopped copies of *Bild Zeitung* from leaving the building. Kiesinger had to rush back
from holiday to appeal for calm; police put barbed wire
round the Springer buildings. Overnight Springer became an
international bogy, and even in London a thousand students
marched on the Springer office in the *Daily Mirror* building,
chanting 'Axel Springer today, Cecil King tomorrow'. (King
went, Springer stayed.)

The SDS seemed now to be by far the most militant student movement, which might even threaten the government
itself. Yet two weeks later the fury had moved to France
(where the SDS helped to set it off) whereas in Germany the
movement lost its way. While the Paris students were occupying the Sorbonne, the German students debated at length
the proper relationship between theory and action, and the
dangers of '*aktionismus*'. In Frankfurt students briefly occupied the Goethe University, and renamed it the Karl Marx
University; in Berlin they renamed the Technical College the
Rosa Luxemburg Institute; in Bonn they broke into the
Golden Book of the university where the name of President
Lübke was inscribed, and wrote underneath it 'builder of

concentration camps'. But the moves were disorganized and short-lived. The official SDS policy was to campaign against the Emergency Laws about to be introduced in Bonn; a procession of students and workers marched to Bonn, but the police had become more discreet and offered no provocation, and the trade unions, being fearful of the students, were half-hearted in their support. 'It wasn't until we went to Bonn,' said one of the students, 'that we realized that the trade unions belonged to the Establishment.' The Emergency Laws were passed without incident.

The SDS are nothing if not serious. They are probably the best organized movement in Europe; they only have about three thousand paid-up members, but they have offices in the main centres and effective communications. They get half their money (they told me) from subscriptions, a quarter from donations, a quarter from charging money for interviews (a practice which most student movements now follow). Their offices are determinedly bohemian; when I visited their Berlin headquarters, one student was sleeping on the floor, and a schoolboy had just arrived to ask for help, having just been chucked out of school for teaching Maoism. Round the walls were Cuban or Chinese slogans such as 'If you want to understand the theory and methods of revolution, you must take part in revolution.' In Frankfurt in July 1968 I had lunch with the SDS president, Karl-Dietrich Wolff. He is a charming revolutionary of twenty-five, with an impeccably bourgeois background. His grand-father and great-grandfather were Protestant pastors and his father a judge. He learnt some of his radicalism in America, and now studies law at Frankfurt University; he intersperses his radical remarks with a huge disarming smile. He insists that 'we are in the methodical tradition', though he appears sometimes to be living in a dream-world: he says for instance that the outcome of the 1968 French elections was a victory for the students.

The SDS watched the events in France with envy and frustration: as one of them said to me in June: 'It isn't that the French students are stronger; it's just that the public is more sympathetic.' Or another: 'In France the intellectuals have got real power; every student can imagine he's Victor Hugo or Delacroix; but here the intellectuals have always been outsiders – look at Heine, or Goethe.' The SDS arouse little sympathy from the German middle classes. Between the students and their parents' generation there is almost total non-communication; to hear the middle-aged talking about them, one would think they belonged to a quite different race. Long hair, sex habits, political campaigns are all dismissed as the folly of immaturity: while students listen to their elders' small-talk with unconcealed contempt.

As for the German workers, they regard the revolutionary talk against the consumer society, not surprisingly, as an attack on themselves. The suburban German workers are the very models of the modern consumer, and they insist that 'we won't let them knock down what we've built up'. I talked to a Berlin student who worked in one of the 'Basis Groups' who make contact with the workers, plying them with free beer in proletarian cafés; he admitted that progress was very slow, and that the workers couldn't understand a lot of their talk. There are pockets of young workers – at Daimler-Benz in Mannheim, at Hoechst in Frankfurt – who respond to the students, and their numbers are growing, particularly among metal workers. But the students are exasperated by the traditional conservatism of the German worker – much more disciplined than the British. 'Lenin was right,' complained one student, 'when he said that if German workers were going to take over a railway station, they would first buy their tickets.'

There is an element of fantasy or comedy in the eloquent intellectuals of the SDS, talking solemnly about permanent revolution, each other comrade, vainly trying to make contact with some actual workers. They take themselves very seriously as 'professional students', fellow-workers with the same problems; but their teachers like to point out that as soon as German students take their degree and leave university, they shave off their beards or moustaches, and become conservative lawyers or organization men, like everyone else. It is too early to tell whether this will be true of the militant new generation. Wolff said to me, half-jokingly, 'We'll have to go on making revolutions, because no one will employ us; out of fifteen sociology students at Frankfurt who left the University last year, thirteen were in the SDS; only five have got jobs. . . . Anyway the next generation, who are now at school, are much tougher – they just laugh at the idea of authority.' This only applies, of course, to a militant minority; but what is striking in Germany, as in France, is how many quite non-political students, while not agreeing with the militants, share their contempt for society and will not disown them.

It has often been said since May 1968 that the German students' tactics are self-defeating in the brittle and nervous condition of the German state; that their wild talk of violence, and of 'more Vietnams', of bringing guerilla warfare to Europe, only plays into the hands of the Springers and Strausses, and of the NPD, who clearly welcome the student violence and even share some of their attitudes (including anti-Americanism). A young professor told me that some of his colleagues had moved to the right after students' excesses; Professor Golo Mann, the liberal historian, has appealed to the students to stop 'playing at Lenin', to work through democratic channels, and to emulate the students in America who supported Eugene McCarthy.[1] But the liberals do not really offer an alternative outlet, there is no likely German McCarthy, and while the Grand Coalition rules in Bonn the real opposition is likely to be outside parliament. It is undeniable that the students have already achieved something: they will get some university reform, they have shaken Springer's position, and, perhaps most important, they have challenged that unquestioning respect for authority which still pervades German institutions. Behind their exhibitionism, their real weapon is not so much violence as a respect for truth, and a desire to escape from the humbug and covering-up of German society. One of them said: 'We want to make Germany clean. We don't want to have an ex-Nazi as Chancellor. We don't want to pretend that the DDR doesn't exist. I think the East Germans can teach us quite a lot in the next few years; they don't think so much about money – they think more about society.'

Relations with East Germany are important. The students have few illusions about the authoritarianism of Ulbricht, or the deadly conservatism of his bureaucracy; but they look with some fascination towards the earnestness and austerity of the youth, which is the legacy not only of communism but of the old Prussian Protestantism. The East German youth organization, the FDJ, while enjoying the assaults of the SDS against the capitalist bosses, have reprimanded them

1. *Encounter*, July 1968.

for their disrespect for authority, and disavowed any connection. But there have been a few meetings between the two sides, and the FDJ have their own 'SDS wing'; the mutual curiosity is likely to grow, particularly if the two countries recognize each other; each side has a good deal to teach the other.

I heard much discussion of the family backgrounds of the student activists. A number are children of ex-Nazis, which may help to give a special ferocity to their rejection of society; I heard one gentle-looking girl, the daughter of a high-ranking Nazi officer, relentlessly arguing with her husband (who had the same background) about the need to denounce parents publicly. But many others (like Wolff, Dutschke, or Peter Brandt) are sons of high-minded men, whose principles they seek to follow, or rescue (a similar pattern has been found in America). One German professor of sociology suggested that their attitude is not unlike Christians trying to atone for their original sin. Certainly I was conscious of a private moral element, which may account both for the staying power of the movement, and for its political shortcomings (for instance, its lack of serious interest in the third world). The word 'alienation' is frequently used, but it is very ambiguous, and begs the question; who is alienated from whom? Is it the students, still detached from the political machine, who are ill, or the managers and workers, caught up in its cogs?

THE FRENCH MAY DAYS

Imagination has seized power.

Students' slogan

The most extraordinary fact about the French students' revolt was that no one saw it coming; while the Germans and Italians were fighting and occupying, they complained that the French were too obsessed with their exams, and had no grievance more serious than not being allowed into girls' dormitories. The revolt began in the bleak new university buildings of Nanterre, next door to the *bidonville*, in a slum suburb of Paris which few bourgeois ever visited. It seemed quite frivolous. A group of students (including Daniel Cohn-Bendit), after being caught raiding a dormitory, organized a short strike against the grim conditions, and against the presence of plain-clothes police, who served there as everywhere to galvanize the movement. A small group based on the sociology school called themselves the *enragés* (after an anarchist group of 1793) and began turning out pamphlets and slogans. In March 1968 a Vietnam protest meeting was held, students were arrested and police action again served to escalate the movement: a much bigger 'movement of March 22' emerged. The dean tried to close the university, but the *enragés* had virtually taken it over, making political speeches in the lecture halls. Behind the scenes several mysterious left-wing groups were at work, most notably the *Jeunesse Communiste Révolutionnaire*, a Trotskyite movement led by a 27-year-old revolutionary, Alain Krivine, of Russian-Jewish parents, who was later detained for six weeks.

A group of German students in Paris, some from the SDS, stirred things up, and one of them, Cohn-Bendit, emerged as the leader (or 'megaphone' as he put it) of the *enragés*. He had an appropriate international background: his parents were German Jews who had fled to France, and returned to Frankfurt after the war; he moved between France and Germany, and even spent some time at a progressive school in England. Like Wolff, he has a cosy, mother's-boy look; he is short, with red hair and a podgy face. But he has an explosive oratory in three languages, which avoids sociological jargon, and he can argue cheekily with anyone in authority: he has a clownish manner which makes him fascinating to watch, and his special art (it seems to me) is to make his own stage, to argue on his own terms, so that professors, politicians or mass media men are put in their place. In early May, summoned to appear at the Sorbonne, he arrived with an army of students, and walked into the room of the disciplinary committee with some colleagues, singing the Internationale. All the submerged resentments of the Latin Quarter suddenly erupted. In an extraordinary week of battles, marches, counter-marches, culminating in the 'night of the barricades', the police brutality forced the students and teachers into a solid bloc, and the student movement became a national crisis.

The Sorbonne itself was transformed into a kind of political fairground. The vast brown pile had always had a special gloom: you would see pale men and girls, clutching at their books, scurrying down the high cold corridors, disappearing

into the great amphitheatres to be lectured at or to listen to
loudspeakers outside. Visitors would marvel at the dedication to learning, or the lack of protest. Suddenly, by the
middle of May, the whole place was turned upside down.
The stone entrance hall was packed with moving bodies,
beards, jeans, leather jackets, red handkerchieves and jockey
caps. At one end an African was performing *musique
concrète* on an aluminium instrument which twanged
through the hall, at the other end a student was playing
Chopin on a piano. Rows of desks displayed every kind of
revolutionary literature; on ledges behind were draped men
and girls, looking sleepily over the crowd. The curved corridors inside were all covered with slogans, exuberant handwriting to fit the space:

> Plus je fais l'amour, plus j'ai envie da faire la Révolution.
> Plus je fais la Révolution, plus j'ai envie de fair l'amour.
> Les larmes des philistines sont le nectar des dieux.
> Vive l'occupation des usines.
> Il est Interdit d'interdire.
> Ils pensent donc je suis.
> Vous avez le droit de ne pas fumer.
> Fumer c'est être complice de a société de consommation.
> Prenez vos désirs pour la réalité.

In the 'grand amphi', overflowing with students, the
brooding statues of Lavoisier, Descartes and de Sorbon
looked down on an unprecedented scene: a young revolutionary in a khaki shirt, with bloodshot eyes, sat on the
stage, directing the debate about the revolution; men and
girls stood up to suggest tactics for defeating the government
– how to infiltrate the young men in the army, how to make
new approaches to the trade unions, how to demoralize
parents with argument. A few workers spoke, less confidently
and more literally: some clapped, some booed, but all
listened. The atmosphere, thick with smoke and breath,
looked as if it had been there for ten days.

Inside the central courtyard Victor Hugo and Pasteur had
red flags stuck into their arms, and the rectangle had become
a market-place for ideologies, with a stall for each brand and
piles of leaflets. Mao, Trotsky, Lenin, Guevara stared out
from posters. Orators stood in small groups, trying to con-

vince their opponents, while their admirers listened and interjected. Sometimes a loudspeaker would make an announcement of a forthcoming meeting, a news-flash, or an appeal for volunteers – to take food to workers, to occupy a new building, to look after the wounded. The sense of emergency was kept at high pitch.

A short walk away, the Odéon Theatre, which had been taken over by students one night after the ballet, now had a banner across it, saying *L'Odéon est Ouvert*. Crowds queued to get in, patrolled by students with red armbands, and inside the plush seats were packed, day and night. On the stage, in front of a safety-curtain, a student conducted yet another non-stop debate, with the audience making speeches from their seats. When I was there they were discussing how to counter De Gaulle: 'We must prevent him appearing on TV – once he does that, they'll all obey him,' said one. 'He's so clever that even if we declare a cultural revolution, he'll emerge as the leader of it,' said another. It happened so easily and eloquently that the theatre might have been built for it. Away from the Sorbonne and the Odéon, nearly every faculty had its own protest. Even the Sciences-Po, the nursery of technocrats, had a teach-in with young economists giving solemn lectures about reform, and later even displayed a banner saying *Sciences-Po dit non à la dictature gaulliste*, and a slogan at the entrance saying, rather sadly, *le bonheur est une idée neuve à Sciences-Po*.

The whole student scene at that time was so assured and so eloquent that it was not difficult to believe that a real revolution had come; the proletarian clothes, the Che Guevara hair, the Lenin beards and the revolutionary moustaches all conjured up old battles going back to 1917, 1848, 1789. The explosive speeches against repression or fascism had the authentic Marxist or Jacobin ring. It was hard to remember that these people were themselves the very heart of the bourgeoisie, from comfortable homes in Passy – some the sons and daughters of the technocrats and capitalists and politicians that they were so furiously attacking. Parading alongside the workers, outside the Renault factory, they seemed to have swapped clothes: the bourgeois wearing leather coats and jeans, the workers wearing suits and white shirts.

The element of fantasy was powerful, and could be seen above all in the repeated slogans linking revolution and love-making. In spite of many stories about the Sorbonne becoming a brothel, and the spread of veneral diseases, there was not much evidence that it was a very sexy revolt; but the slogans proclaimed the importance of making love *and* war:

> Embrasse ton amour sans lâcher ton fusil
> Faites l'amour et recommencez
> Inventez de nouvelles perversions sexuelles
> Jeunes femmes rouges toujours plus belles
> Eve

For almost a month the French students seemed to hold the future of France: within the universities they joined committees of professors and lecturers to work out reforms, and let loose a stream of ideas, not all wild. With their love of disputation and questioning, they seemed to some radical professors to have rediscovered the medieval idea of the university – a democratic community of students and teachers, arguing among themselves. Outside the universities, their ideas caught fire in a way that none had predicted.[1] Young workers suddenly decided to occupy their factories, against the will of their unions, so that the communists felt compelled to join in the strike. For two weeks the French government seemed to have virtually abdicated. Finally De Gaulle recovered his nerve, consulted the Army, and declared a general election. The student leaders chanted '*élection trahison*', but the game was lost: the bourgeoisie were terrified, and took shelter with De Gaulle. The student movement seemed out of control, rampaging through the streets. Cohn-Bendit (who was now barred from France) explained in London where they had gone wrong. 'Our action went ahead of our theory, and we couldn't keep away from the streets.' The student groups lost direction, split apart and degenerated into chaos. The Sorbonne was torn by rival groups, including a gang of 'Katangais' who claimed (falsely) to be ex-Congo mercenaries; the police moved in to clear the university buildings; and the new government prepared to impose its own style of 'participation'.

In parliamentary terms the students had hopelessly lost, and had merely united the forces against them. To foreigners there seemed something absurd in the sudden explosion of

1. See speech by Jacques Sauvageot at Grenoble, July 1968.

May, with a strike of ten million, suddenly changing into a huge vote of confidence for De Gaulle; it bore out the old clichés about the French always veering between short periods of anarchy and long periods of authoritarian rule.

But the French students had also revealed the traditional power of French politics – the power of ideas. Their ideas, borrowed from America or Germany or from old anarchists, were neither very French nor very original; but they gave them a new sharpness and ferocity, mixing them with the mythology of French revolutions, and reviving memories of the left, of the resistance, of the Algerian war. They expressed themselves with a creative burst which transformed the French cultural scene, and the slogan re-emerged as an art form which could express the basic simplicity of their case. De Gaulle tried to latch on to the ideas, and emerged in his earlier role of the revolutionary, preaching a philosophy mid-way between capitalism and communism (the student at the Odéon, who warned that De Gaulle might emerge as the leader of the cultural revolution, was not so absurd). But De Gaulle's ideas of *participation* were not the same as the students'. As one of their posters summed it up:

> Je participe
> Tu participes
> Il participe
> Nous participons
> Vous participez
> Ils profitent

STUDENTS' EUROPE

By the summer of 1968 the trail of trouble had led to nearly every country in Europe: even in Zürich there was a students' strike. In Belgrade students, inspired by the Paris example, took over a whole suburb, demanding the democratization of the Communist Party, and the relief of unemployment. In Madrid ten thousand students came to a lecture about the French Revolt, and raised a red flag outside the school of economics. In Rome five thousand students protested outside the French embassy, overturning cars and putting up barricades. In Stockholm fifteen hundred students fought all night with the police to try to occupy the parliament and the opera house.

In Britain the response was more phlegmatic, to the despair of some student leaders I spoke to. A possible flashpoint came when the BBC invited student leaders from all over the world to take part in a television programme; the following day the Federation of Socialist Student Revolutionaries was launched at the London School of Economics, as a kind of counterpart to the German SDS. But the British stressed that theirs was a home-grown movement, and there was a striking contrast between the confident oratory of the Sorbonne and the homely speeches at the LSE. I listened to the first speakers at the LSE meeting; they included a long-winded Irish printer, whose breakaway union had promised the students fifty pounds; a girl from the north who was worried because workers were rude to her in pubs; and a poet from Trinity College, Cambridge, who eloquently explained that students were only students. A few, notably from Essex University, were more eloquent and Marxist; but they were all very British and the delegates resented any interference from Cohn-Bendit ('one-arm bandit'). There are obvious explanations for the British climate. The average British student is much younger, with fewer of the ageing 'professional students' who play a big political role on the continent. The British education does not equip students with the arts of disputation and rhetoric. There are more working-class students in Britain, and although many are quite political, they tend to be more practical and less high-flown. British universities are less overcrowded and more sensibly run – partly because there are fewer students. And the British – as their speeches make clear – are still suspicious and uneasy in the presence of continental isms and ideas.

The sudden spread of the students' revolts not surprisingly aroused old suspicions about an international conspiracy. But there is no serious evidence. Certainly there is a small core of anarchists and Trotskyists and a few Castroists, who travel, make contact at international conferences and keep in touch: the heretics are more cosmopolitan than the orthodox socialists..There are quick communications between Germany and France, particularly between Paris and Frankfurt. Technology plays its role: it is not (as Marcuse and his followers insist) altogether on the side of authority. Direct-dialling between countries helps the rebels to keep in touch; television shows one country what another is doing; transistor radios, notably on the night of the barricades in Paris, report news of the battles, telling the students where to go. Karl-Dietrich Wolff was proud of their ease of communications: 'You have these so-called international organizations with huge staffs of bureaucrats and translators; we have no bureaucracy, but we can always get in touch with our foreign comrades. We're getting to know each other: some of the Italian comrades from different cities hadn't met each other before they came to Germany.' German students (who tend to be richer than others) are the most active abroad; but the whole world of radical students is international, and hospitable to foreigners. The huge publicity from the mass media has made it more so: at the BBC television programme in June 1968 many of them met for the first time, and two weeks later transcripts of the programme were being Xeroxed in Berlin.

The international contacts are the result rather than the cause of the real phenomenon: that students in all countries have come to the same general conclusion about industrial society. The influence of prophets such as Marcuse, Guevara or Debray has been much exaggerated. Debray and Guevara were preoccupied with guerilla warfare, which only has metaphorical relevance to Europe. Marcuse was not read by most of the French student leaders, and even in Germany the sales are not spectacular: he is anyway less in favour since his visit to Europe in May 1968, when he was attacked for being too pessimistic in his belief that the workers would never revolt. The importance of Marcuse is that he analyses the sense of repression and frustration that the students already feel; many of his observations are very obvious and romantic – how you can't get away from advertising, how making love in the hay is more exciting than doing it in a car. He reflects a basic simplicity in the students' rebellion, in the tradition of the Romantics, which many of the leaders have stressed. 'I would like to know what is so complex about this society,' said Dr. Krippendorf, the Berlin student leader. 'There are certain basic simple truths which we still have to face, which we have to bring out, and it's a typical sort of concealing strategy of the ruling classes and of the public media to say: "Today the situation is more complex than it was fifty years ago." '[1]

There are, of course, large cross-purposes across frontiers.

1. BBC TV: 'Students in Revolt', 13th June, 1968.

The students from Spain are up against something much
more serious than 'repressive tolerance'; they are demon-
strating for the right to demonstrate, and risk their lives in
doing so. Students from eastern Europe have little sympathy
with the western complaints about consumer society, or the
attitude to elections that they 'are like choosing between
two kinds of toothpaste': they are desperately concerned
with practical politics. The Czech students knew that
Dubcek wasn't perfect but they knew the alternative: their
predicament now makes the western complaints look rather
unreal. The rebels in East Germany are not much impressed
by the horrors of the Springer monopoly. Their press (as one
of them said) 'is one big Springer'. But the two sides of
Europe find common ground in their hatred of the Establishment and the bureaucracies, in their search for truth in the
early writings of Marx, and in their contempt for the hypocrisy of their parents' generation.

The difference of generations in the west stands out in
their view of Europe; men in their thirties and men in their
early twenties, talking about the continent, seem to have
different maps. The young generation in the west accept all
the inheritance from the 'Europeans' – the open frontiers,
the reconciliation, the prosperity, the free trade. Ignoring
boundaries, popping between France and Germany, speaking three languages, assuming a common European consciousness, they might be a living advertisement for the
achievement of the earlier generation, and particularly for
the Franco-German exchange. But they are bored or even
hostile to the language of Monnet and the federalists: they
detest the assumption that Europe is divided; they have little
faith in institutions or supranational bureaucracies.
Monnet's notion of the '*engrenage*' or meshing of the
common market smacks too much of industrial 'manipulation' to attract them. (De Gaulle used '*engrenage*' in the
derogatory sense of men being meshed into a world of inhuman machines.) Some students (like Cohn-Bendit) see the
common market as an American colony; others (like Wolff)
accept it as the beginnings of a far bigger market, embracing
eastern Europe; but the technicalities of making Europe do
not much interest them. They are far more interested in
changing societies than in abolishing frontiers. As one of
them said: 'We're not making Europe. We're living it.'

The students are both more national and more international than their forebears. They are more national, in the sense that they are concerned with their own societies, with changing national structures and local institutions; they do not (like some Europeans) think that local problems can be by-passed or dissolved in the bigger context. They are more international, in that they assume that other societies must be the same, and that all students have the same interest. When the French communist paper *L'Humanité* insisted on always referring to Cohn-Bendit as a German anarchist, the Paris students sang in procession 'we are all German Jews'.

It is not always easy to know how seriously to take the students' statements. They talk with apparent conviction about the rout of the bourgeoisie, about 'making Vietnams in Europe', about the defeat of capitalism. But when faced with the question 'what would you put in its place', they usually decline to answer. To many of the previous generation, particularly to those who once believed in the communist system, this vagueness seems absurd, if not dangerous; but to others it comes as a relief that the new generation have no such total illusions. A few students no doubt would like to bring down the whole capitalist system in ruins: others enjoy a bit of violence. But most of them know well enough that the iron industrial structure, the web of bureaucracies and technocracies, will not be brought down by a few riots. The French students never thought that they would achieve a general strike. The most they would hope for would be to make pockets of resistance, to contest every assumption of their society and to dent the uniformity and authority. Some of their methods may be dangerous. But it has to be faced that if a group wants to put its ideas across effectively (particularly where there is no proper opposition) then some shock tactics are called for. The element of lethal violence has been much exaggerated; in Germany, in spite of the provocations of the killing of Ohnesorg, and the attempts on Dutschke, there were only three deaths; and in all the two months of the French crisis only five deaths at the most could be proved to be due to the revolt – including a policeman in Lyons and a schoolboy at Flins who was drowned. There were thousands of injuries, including very nasty ones; but during the month of the French strikes fewer people were killed than in any week since the war – no petrol, no cars, no road deaths. One of the students' slogans boasted: 'a single non-revolutionary weekend is infinitely more bloody than a month of permanent revolution'. To have so many casualties, and so few fatal ones, suggests a ritual element in the battles; it is this which distinguished the 1968 revolt from 1848 or 1871, when tens of thousands were killed. The absence of deaths suggest that one should not take quite literally the talk about 'Vietnams in Europe', or the French slogan that 'humanity cannot be free until the last capitalist has been hung with the intestines of the last bureaucrat'.

The decisive element in the ritual, of course, is the police; and however brutally they have behaved; their role is unenviable. The ritual requires them to represent a whole host of enemies – Repressive Tolerance, Mass Media, Consumer Society, Parents or the Violence of the State. Whatever their first purpose they are seen as soon as they appear in this symbolic role. (The French CRS, with their extraordinary medieval shields, their visors and shiny black coats, look heavily symbolic.) The confrontation takes on the character of a violent joust, a reliving of ancient battles. In Germany the long lines of police and students converge on each other, as if by previous arrangement, with recognized weapons. In Paris, police watch the barricades going up, which they later must charge; cobblestones, iron grids, black and red flags, all serve their traditional role. In Britain, with no real mythology of street-fighting, the ritual is more humdrum; police ride on horseback at the head of the procession, as if it was theirs, while black vans hide in back streets. Only when national traditions get muddled is the ritual likely to be upset – as when German students arrived in Grosvenor Square, prepared for a German-type attack. Sometimes there develops a friendship between students and police which upsets the whole ritual. In Berlin in June 1968, when students had occupied the Rector's house, and were battling with the police, they suddenly became friendly with the police chief, called Textor, sat down over beer and sandwiches, and coined the slogan 'Textor for Rektor'. Whatever the country, the police are the essential element in the students' battles, and as the pressure grows, this will demand a new and subtler kind of police force. After twenty-three years without war, some type of war-substitute is likely to be needed.

How far one regards the student revolt and its methods as desirable depends on what kind of Europe one wishes to see. For those who see the present consensus of technocrats and bankers as the only possible system, and bloody revolution as the horrible alternative, then the students are either silly or dangerous. But the issue that is emerging may be of a different kind from the issues which dominated the last few decades, between world systems of government. Behind the students' revolts and other revolts – in Scotland, in Brittany, in the Renault factories in Paris – there is an older issue, which can be described on the one hand as anarchism or on the other as decentralization. Europe is in the process of acquiring a technological system which, however benign, sents a much greater threat to local autonomy than any absolute monarch. It would not be surprising if Europeans were to assert themselves against this old threat in a new form; it would be much more worrying if they did not. I believe myself (as I will try to show in the last chapter) that this movement – if properly understood – is more likely to revitalize Europe than to wreck it.

Chapter Twenty-two

New Europeans

If people are too well off, they are apt to become unmanageable.

Richelieu

Following the trails that run through this book, it is difficult
to see one that leads towards a United Europe. The path is
full of dead ends. In all the ups and downs of the European
movement over the past twenty years, the present point
looks like the nadir, and it is not surprising that Monnet
should for the first time have become pessimistic. The
nations have not given up any of their real powers to a
federal centre. The common market, castrated of its political
ideals, is stuck at the stage of an uneasy customs union, and
may not even survive as that; the men who a few years ago
talked as Europeans now talk once again as Germans,
Frenchmen or Belgians. After the twenty-year peace of
NATO, the nations seem to be reasserting themselves, each
one with its own ineffectual foreign policy, its comic army
and touchy pride. If the fear of Russia recedes, thus the
older fear of Germany becomes uppermost again.

Germany remains, as it was twenty-three years ago, the
unsolved problem of Europe; and the problem is perpetuated by its division – which Europe alone cannot solve.
The rebuilding of Europe, which engrossed the post-war
generation, cannot satisfy the young Europeans, and the
war, with its aftermath of guilt and exhaustion, has faded
into history. The fruits of prosperity and the consumer
society are going sour, and at the end of those two decades,
there is a sense of coming back to the beginning – like an
unhappy family, who, after moving into a new house and
thinking it will all be better now, find themselves still stuck
with each other.

Industry and trade, which so many had hoped could by-
pass or dissolve these barriers, have all run into the political

obstacles, the obstacles of distrust. The old industries, including farming, still lean on the nation as their only reliable support – the nation which needs their votes, and thus has to look after them. Steel, coal and all forms of power take on a national colouring, with the worry about national security still lurking in the background. The new technological industries, it is true, have a much more stateless character, and many of them, including the defence industries, are too big and expensive to be developed by one European nation. As a result, they are developed by America. There is little sign that the American industrial challenge, though now glaringly obvious and passionately discussed, is forcing Europe to unite against it; on the contrary, the challenge seems more likely to divide Europe further, for most big companies would prefer an American ally to a neighbouring European one. For all the talk about multinational or geocentric companies, most of the giant European industries are still bound up with patriotism, like armies or football teams. The schemes for European technology, European computers or European aircraft are all difficult to believe in, because Europe does not show the will to assert herself emphatically enough to overcome national rivalries and suspicions. She does not fear America enough to want to be independent of her, and she shows no sign of being prepared to defend herself, by herself, against Russia or China – mainly because the only credible defence includes nuclear weapons, with which other countries would not trust Germany. The industrial trail thus ends up, too, in the dead end of the German problem.

The confident hopes of the forties, that nationalism had become discredited, now sound very hollow. It is not (it seems to me) credible to blame De Gaulle as the main agent for this upsurge. The nation was always a more formidable structure than many of the Europeans made out, for it was not only an instrument of aggression and war; it was the repository of the welfare state, the framework for political ideals, and a source of inspiration and leadership which could animate people in good causes as well as bad. All new endeavours, whether sailing alone round the world or transplanting hearts, still take the form of national competition. And since the war the nation has become, much more than ever before, the central hub of administration, industry and planning, equipped with a huge bureaucracy whose main purpose, in the end, is the defence of the national welfare and the national interest; the more they believe in that (like De Gaulle's highly motivated technocrats) the more effective they are likely to be. De Gaulle's special and disagreeable contribution was to restore to nationhood an older, nastier edge of ruthlessly selfish diplomacy, which has certainly helped to provoke reactions in other countries, particularly Germany; yet who can seriously imagine that, even without De Gaulle, Germany would not become impatient with her predicament – divided, patronized and caught between the super-powers?

It would be surprising if, after the long peace, Europe were not showing signs of her old restlessness and aggressiveness. The idea of Europe uniting for its own sake, or for the sake of prosperity, peace or human happiness, has always seemed rather out of character. In the first years of the cold war there was the challenging motive, to unite against the fear of Russia; when that fear subsided, a new motive was proposed, to unite against American industry; but that is not a sufficient incentive. The belief that Europe should unite to become a third force, to have her own say in world affairs, can still animate those who remember the old days of the *Belle Époque*, when the chancelleries of Paris, Berlin or London had a decisive influence on the world; but I doubt how far it inspires a new generation. It is quite possible, of course, that in the years to come western Europe will find a new threat or challenge which will give her a new purpose, and perhaps a new unity. Russian aggressiveness may become more alarming, in Czechoslovakia or elsewhere, and America may become still more preoccupied with commitments outside Europe, so that western Europe is forced to work out its own defence. Or it is possible that the emergence of China or the racial explosion in Africa, will give a real substance to revolutionaries, and bring the problems of the third world into the heart of European politics. But as it is, western Europe, shorn of overseas commitments and empires and protected by the American umbrella, is a continent without a cause; and in this situation, its components are very likely to reassert themselves.

Yet the status of the nations is not quite the same, for there is a restlessness inside them which may prove in the end to be more important to the future shape of Europe. It can take the shape of regionalism, or a general clamour for decentralization, or autonomy or anarchism. The Regional movement of its very nature is different in each place – that is the point of it. There is no real common cause between the regionalists in Brittany, Flanders, Scotland or the Basque country, except the common anger with the distant bureaucracy of the capital, administering them without knowledge of their problems or respect for their culture. Many of these resentments are centuries old, rooted in cultures, languages and traditions that pre-date the nation states. In the past, their complaints have been subdued or beaten down during wars or preparation for wars – for wars are always great centralizers. But since 1945 there has been no such common incentive to hold together, while the provinces have been provoked by a massive new movement of power towards the capitals. Rome, Paris and London have become more emphatically the centres not only of government, but of industry, planning and welfare; and the new machinery of centralized technology and management threatens the provinces with an embrace more suffocating than any Napoleonic system. It is an old problem, the same basic problem that obsessed De Tocqueville in the 1830s, and ran through his writing about America and Britain. But now, provoked by peace and technology, it is taking on an angrier aspect.

It is difficult to compare or classify the regional movements, because the ethnic divisions do not necessarily correspond at all with the functional divisions. No two European countries have the same structure, and the definition of decentralization is full of pitfalls and paradoxes. Britain has some of the most fiery regional movements, nourished by their own languages and history, which may yet succeed in getting their own parliaments; yet Britain also has a system of local government and a tradition of democratic administration which has been the envy of others, and specially French reformers. Italy, where the city-states were independent until a century ago, has the most obvious diversity and contrasts; but the Roman bureaucracy, favourite butt of the provinces, has accumulated a stifling power. (The Italian constitution of 1948, which stipulated a large measure of autonomy for the twenty regions, is now at last being implemented and passed through parliament. It will be expensive and wasteful, but it will reduce the power and corruption at the centre.)

France and Germany, as we have seen in their bureaucracies, television and newspapers, are at opposite extremes. France has always been the classic case of the centralized state; the phenomenon went back to the *ancien régime*, but it was massively strengthened by Napoleon, and his network of prefects who still govern the ninety-one French departments as if they were colonies. Since the war there have been new attempts to bring life to the 'French desert' of the provinces, and to plan their prosperity. Twenty-one new *régions* were proclaimed (on top of the departments), which were of a more sensible size for economic planning; regional development became the rage, and (much more than in Britain) became a passionate concern of the technocrats. Nearly everyone in France nowadays professes to be some kind of regionalist. Writers and intellectuals are cultivating the old languages of Provence or Brittany. Even De Gaulle, speaking in Lyons in March 1968, explained that 'the effort of centralization over the centuries, which was necessary to France for a long time, to achieve and maintain her unity, is no longer compelling. On the contrary, it is the regional activities which appear as the springs of her economic power tomorrow.' But the development was planned from the centre, and Paris still kept its hold: the *Inspecteurs des Finances* still ran the country from two small districts of Paris. The power of the prefects, the rigid control of the universities, the patriarchal bosses of industry, all played their part in provoking the surge of resentment in 1968. In July, writing in his magazine *Courrier de la République*, Pierre Mendès-France wrote: 'The project for decentralization must be, in this perspective, the first war-cry of the left, who must get rid of their Jacobin reflexes once for all.'

Germany has the opposite problem; it was largely the French who insisted, after the war, on such a drastic splitting-up, to weaken the centre. The German federation of *Länder*, with its eleven parliaments and eleven prime ministers, is looked at with envy by some other regionalists. It has many attractions. Each capital has its own intense pride, and boasts its own independence; Bavaria proclaims itself with big blue signs on its frontiers 'FREISTAAT BAYERN'; Hamburg looks back to its Hanseatic past, before Germany was invented, and calls itself FREIE UND HANSESTADT HAMBURG. Prime ministers entertain each other with some pomp. The parliaments provide small pools for big fishes, who can then move (like Kiesinger) to the bigger pool in Bonn. The German federation gives a scope for localized ambitions and rivalries that Scots or Bretons might dream of. But the regions have not really provided a substitute for nationalism. The federal structure is increasingly resented as an obstacle to major reforms, particularly in education; and the resentment is aggravated by the division of the country, which leaves it without a proper capital, to provide the ultimate forum for politics and culture.

The most extreme regionalist movement is in Belgium, where the young nation, which was proclaimed in 1830, has never really welded the two parts. The linguistic war between Flanders, speaking Flemish, and Wallonia, speaking French, can be seen on the slogans and crossed-out roadsigns all over the country. It came to a climax in the battle over Louvain University in Flanders, which brought down the government.

All these regionalists have very mixed motives. Many of them, being concerned with preserving cultures and languages, are essentially conservative, and regard the interference of the central state as a socialist monstrosity. In France since the Revolution, as also in Britain, centralization has been regarded as the weapon of the left; the champions of Free Brittany, and other French separatists, are predominantly from the right. Whereas in Italy it is the communists who protest most fiercely against the corruption of the central bureaucracy, and who set themselves up as the guardians of regional rights. There are also cross-purposes between the rooted regionalists, whose protests are atavistic and often crude, and the newer arrivals, who may themselves be refugees from London, Paris or Rome, who want to establish a modern community to compete with the capital. There is still a crackpot element in most regional movements, often with reactionary overtones: the most visible manifestations of regionalism, like the assassinations in the Basque country of Spain, or the bombs in Wales are not very attractive.

The new student rebels are not concerned with anything as

specific as regionalism; when discussing structures, most of them go no further than their own university, or a factory or two: they insist that the workers themselves must choose. What they have in common with the regionalists is simply the attack against centralized authority – *das Establishment*, *les technocrates* or just *them*. They have the simple but ferocious desire to establish their identity and dignity in the face of an industrial machine which is too big, too inhuman and too distant. Their cry for autonomy is as much on the psychological level as on the political level: they feel their independence of mind and their creative spirit threatened by the competitive new society, whether in education, management, computers or advertising, and are impelled to assert themselves against it.

To some of the older Europeans, it seems that Europe is now not merely reverting to nationalism, but disintegrating still further; that demagogy is breaking out all over, the Flemish against the Walloons, the Scots against the English, even the German-Swiss against the French-Swiss. 'What chance has Europe of being united,' said one veteran Belgian liberal, 'if we can't even unite our two halves?'

EUROPE OF REGIONS?

Centralization is the death-blow of public freedom

Disraeli

But does the retreat to the regions really make the unification of Europe still more difficult? If the Europe of Nations has reached deadlock because the capitals refuse to give up their powers, cannot this block be by-passed by establishing a Europe of Regions – a Europe which had its roots before nation-states were invented?

The idea has many attractions, and there are some federalists[1] who see it as a possible solution. There are strong arguments: the more the regions want to break away from their national capital, the more they will look towards a larger entity to protect them. Already the Scots and the Irish look towards the common market (as the Scots have so often looked towards France) as allies against England. The

1. For an exposition of recent theories, see *Naissance de L'Europe des Régions*, Centre Européen de la Culture, Geneva, Winter 1967–8.

Bretons look towards England as an ally against Paris. The two parts of Belgium each look to the common market as a protector against the other: when the new prime minister of Belgium, Gaston Eyskens, took over in 1968, he insisted that 'this new Belgium must be at one and the same time more regional and European'. The two trends are not necessarily contradictory, and some of the best internationalists (Lloyd George, Smuts, Gandhi) have been men with strong parochial roots. It was a weakness of some of the post-war Europeans that they too readily rejected the need for those roots.

For so many modern purposes, the nation is either too big or too small. For technological industries, for defence, for transport, for energy, it is too small. For welfare, for cultural loyalties, or for any real sense of belonging, it is too big. The conflicts, which will multiply in the future, between the great geocentric corporations and the interests of local communities are much more relevant to the region than to the nation. Since the capitals can less and less confer the technological benefits, but merely act as the go-betweens, why cannot the regions go direct to the real masters of technology, in America, Geneva or Brussels? And as Europe is more threatened by the uniformity of mass industries – whether cars, supermarkets, fish fingers or films – so the insistence on cultural diversity will become stronger; the diversity belongs much more obviously to the regions than the nations (as any gastronome will testify, eating his way, not from country to country, but from *Boeuf Bourguignon* to *Salde Niçoise* to *Risotto alla Milanese* to *Saltimbocca alla Romana*).

Even the new communications may encourage the region rather than the nation. The railways were powerful centralizers, spreading like spiders' webs from the capitals; the British and French networks, converging on London and Paris, still get in the way of the flow between regions. But cars and roads (as we noticed in the development of Italian tourism) are potentially decentralizers, and motorways may be able to revive the provinces – whether Northern France, South Wales or Calabria – without necessarily binding them closer to the capitals. Cars, which are so much more mobile than trains, show up the absurdities of national frontiers (a town like Lille, which suffers from being on the edge of

France, can now think of itself as being in the middle of
northern Europe). The role of airports is ambivalent; the
vast dependence of executives on Heathrow or Orly has encouraged companies to move their headquarters to London
or Paris. But airports can also dramatically revive distant
provinces, and airlines can (particularly in tourism) by-pass
the capitals with their international routes (Manchester-
Nice, Dublin-Düsseldorf, Lyons-Milan). Television can stir
up regional spirit, if the capitals allow it: the range of a TV
transmitter roughly defines the average region, and the development of regional programmes in Germany and in
Britain has given a new conviction to dubious entities like
Wessex or Baden-Württemberg. Perhaps most important,
the new universities that are springing up through Europe
can act as a real focus for regional culture.

All these trends could urge on the retreat from the nation.
It is a dream of many Europeans that the continent may be
reverting to a medieval pattern. A common language (probably American-English) in place of Latin; a common
scientific culture in place of the common theology; the mass
proletariat and trade unions splitting up into more specialized skills, like medieval guilds; the universities acquiring
again the democratic structure, and the universal learning,
of thirteenth-century Bologna. A Europe of the Regions
would be the climax of that trend: the map of the continent
would begin to look like a map which hangs in my hall, of
Europe 'between Ancient and Modern Geography', with
WEST SEXIA, AQUITANIA and LOMBARDIA in big
letters, and BRITANNIA, FRANCIA and ITALIA lying
across them. The map opposite shows the contemporary
French and Italian regions, the German *Länder*, and the
system of British regions proposed by the Liberal Party.

Or the map might look like America's. The fifty states of
America, with an average population of four million, are
much closer in populations to the regions than to nations:
even the biggest, California and New York (with 18 million
people each), are no more populous than the biggest
German Land, North Rhine-Westphalia. The division of
functions between the states and Washington may not be
perfect, and the smaller states (like Alaska with only a quarter of a million population) are hardly viable as units. But
the states are small enough to evoke real regional pride,

while the federation is big enough to protect and enrich them.

The parallels are tempting, but the contradictions facing any real Europe of Regions are still huge. The contexts and characters of the regions in different countries are incompatible. While Belgium seems already to be breaking up, in France it is hard to see how the regions could achieve real autonomy without some kind of revolution. The traditional motive for regionalism, to retain or restore local culture and privilege, is at odds with the whole aim of an expansive federal Europe, which would want to develop and plan its economy from the centre. And in most regional movements there is a contingent of sheer absurdity which will need a lot of shaking down. The Scottish Nationalists, for instance, will insist on their own navy and army; at a time when NATO is desperately trying to unite and standardize Europe's armies, the prospect of an army of kilts and claymores and a navy of ramshackle trawlers suddenly bearing down out of the northern mists might be more than the most tolerant Eurocrats could stand.

Moreover, the nation-states will not take the regional revolts lying down. The political parties, the bureaucracies, and the whole apparatus of modern government have grown up round the capitals, and the concentration of power is still in some fields mounting; national car industries, national airlines, national chemicals, national computers – these engines of industry will not be easily deflected by emotional movements from Brittany or the Highlands. Any suggestion of a plot between the Eurocrats and the regionalists wil soon be pounced on by the national politicians, who will if necessary offer more money and jobs to the provinces to buy off discontent, while hanging on to the established power in the capital.

REBELS AND TECHNOCRATS

I am sorry for anyone who has not been an anarchist at twenty.

Clemenceau

In spite of such counterattacks, I believe that the battles against the capitals will grow all over Europe, with an inexorable force. They will take many different forms, from regionalism to anarchism to sheer eccentricity. At this stage, to plan them from the centre, with notions of participation or a new federalism, would be hopeless; for they must each fight for their rights in their own way. Aggressiveness is an essential part of them, and their leaders will have to prove themselves and to find themselves in quite violent battles. The process will be a long and untidy one. But the new powers of the regions may in the end make the real unification of Europe more possible, for they can provide a much more realistic context for both practical and emotional needs. While outflanking the outdated confrontation of the nations, they can make a more sensible basis on which to build planning, technology and industry on the continental scale.

In any of the recent glimpses of the future that we have been offered, there is something altogether intolerable. Whether the study of the 'year 2000', by Herman Kahn of the 'think tank'[1] portraying a nightmare world of alienation and purposeless leisure; or in Professor Perlmutter's prediction of the three hundred giant companies dominating world industry; or in the prediction of IBM that computers will become the third biggest industry; or in the plan for Paris in the year 2000, with its row of eight satellite cities, to hold sixteen million people – all these visions are incredible, because they do not allow for the human reaction, the necessity for self-expression. The bankers are always leaving that out; Anthony Rothschild was predicting the dissolving of nationalism in 1866 in the warm glow of industrial prosperity.[2] *The Economist* in May 1968 was explaining that the French economy still expects a new surge of growth, partly because of the high proportion of young people. The calculation that gets left out is whether the young people will stand for it. The new student generation will be only fifty by the year 2000: a new nightmare of technocracy is imminent, and they seem unlikely to stand for it.

The new characteristics of Europe in the late sixties – the long peace, the isolation from the rest of the world, the rush of computers and new technologies, the sudden students' revolts – all seem to point to a new period of questioning of

1. Herman Kahn and Anthony Wiener: *The Year 2000*, Macmillan, 1968.
2. See p. 158.

society. The assumptions over the last twenty years that the
ideologies were dying, and that the western countries were
all gravitating towards the same kind of 'post-industrial
society', now seem much less convincing. The problem that is
ambiguously described as 'alienation' is likely to grow much
faster, and it will not easily be solved by formulae for 'participation' from above. It may be (as some sociologists suggest) that alienation will become accepted as an incurable
malaise among young intellectuals, who will inhabit their
own dream world, pretending to be proletarian revolutionaries and acting out rituals, while the rest of Europe goes on
undeterred, galloping ahead into the bigger and better consumer society. But it seems to me unlikely. The students
have already shown how their disaffection can spread, and it
is not only in France that workers are becoming restless. The
old European interest in anarchy has never quite died down,
and as the web of machinery spreads, the movement for
anarchy provides the most obvious unrest-cure.

Underneath the revolutionary fantasies of the students,
their most serious and promising contribution, I believe, is
their attack on the nature of modern bureaucracy; and here
they may in the end be able to bring about a real change in
the structure of society – if only because many of them are
destined to become bureaucrats themselves. How far can the
modern infrastructure of industry survive a measure of anarchy, without breaking down into chaos? How great, to use
the engineering term, is the margin of tolerance? At the
moment both sides – the technocrats and the revolutionaries
– talk as if the two are irreconcilable; the managers insist
that modern technology is so complex, so delicate, so disciplined, that only they can control it, and that any inter-
ruption will wreck it. The anarchists insist that they want to
bring down the whole system, and substitute some undefined
alternative. I doubt if either are quite honest. Any new technology, once established, becomes relatively easy and could
survive a measure of indiscipline; while the rebels would
probably be satisfied to have pockets of resistance and
periodic contestation, without wanting to wreck the productive machine on which their own comfort depends. The
element of ritual protest which showed itself so strongly in
1968 may succeed in challenging the individual routine,
without seriously damaging it. The question of anarchy may

acquire a new meaning in the coming computer age, and perhaps the two sides may reach some accommodation (it is worth recalling that many early anarchists saw machines, not as their enemy, but as the means of freedom and international amity).

BRITAIN AND EUROPE

De Tocqueville: Do you not think that the present tendency of this country is towards centralization?
John Stuart Mill: Yes.
De Tocqueville: Are you afraid of this tendency?
Mill: No, because I hope that it will not lead us on too far. Up to now centralization has been the thing most foreign to the English temperament.

De Tocqueville's Journey to England, 1835

Whatever the shape of it Europe is evidently now facing a period of unrest, of a new kind. There are many consolations. There is not much sign of the 'European civil war' of 1914–45 breaking out again. There is no major frontier dispute, except over Germany's eastern border. The Franco-German reconciliation still stands as the real achievement of post-war diplomacy. The new disturbance is likely to be more within nations than between them. The question of 'making Europe' may well take second place to the question of 'what kind of Europe'. The growth of international industry (that is, mainly American industry) will continue, bringing about an international consumer society, and an integration of a kind. But the political energy of young Europeans seems likely to turn back towards the problem of how to make the new society tolerable, inside each country, and how to reconcile the new wealth with individual freedom and fair distribution. This need not make the prospect of European unity more distant; the new generation, both of technocrats and rebels, is likely to think in a much more European context than their elders, because so many of their problems are the same.

On this score, the question of bringing Britain into Europe will, I believe, become more central. Not so much for the reason currently advocated, that Britain holds the keys to European big business and technology (though this is a powerful reason), as for the older and more lasting reason, that Britain still has a stability and continuity of a kind quite different from that of the continent. It is absurd, it seems to me, to pretend that Britain is part of the continent. In nearly every field – in every chapter of this book – the contrast stands out; in the strength and bloody-mindedness of her trade unions, in the muddle of her car industry, in the outspokenness of her television, in the range of her newspapers, in her two-party system, in the autonomy of her universities – in all these departments Britain sticks out as the odd-man-out of Europe, as clearly as in driving on the left. In most fields there are the same marks of conservatism, complacency, continuity, which have held back Britain's industrial performance. It would certainly be dangerous to try to justify the complacency and to underrate the damage that Britain's bankruptcy has done to her reputation on the continent (I remember, in Germany the day after devaluation, having the feeling of being regarded as fifteen per cent less important). That complacency can best be cured, I believe, by Britain's joining the Continent. But there remains the other side of the coin. The conservatism and slowness is linked with the old pattern of decentralization and local autonomy, of opposition to authority which, however exasperating, is the basis of Britain's stability and way of life. The difference is as organic as that between a beech tree and a pine: the beech, with its scattered roots, is slow to grow but stands up to high winds, while the pine, with its deep concentrated roots, grows faster and falls more easily. Of course the political structure at Westminster is dangerously antiquated and out of touch, and will probably provoke more violent protests, particularly in the regions. But the most ferocious and justified of the continental students' complaints – against the university system, the Springer monopoly, the French technocrats or the Italian professors – are not really translatable into English terms. The British autocrats, whether Cecil King or Lord Beeching, are always liable to disappear through a trap door. The technocrats are contantly being frustrated, whether over motorways, airports or telephone books. The trade unions are constantly playing with spells of anarchy – guerilla or wildcat strikes whose very names convey their underlying defiance. Looking at the big continental corporations – particularly car companies – after seeing British ones, I have each time been struck by their fundamental difference in character. In Renault or Fiat there is no real doubt where the power lies; orders are passed down from above without worry that they will be carried out; in any conversation between French or Italian managers you can notice the underlying assumption of authority. Few British bosses can have the same confidence: either the unions, or the board, or some stroppy manager will get in the way. How many times have I heard chairmen say (and not necessarily with false modesty): 'Of course, I'm only the chairman.' However many other and less honourable causes may lie behind this corporate bloody-mindedness, and however much it may earn the contempt of Swiss bankers or German industrialists, it is also important to remember that the main cause is still the British insistence on decentralization and self-determination, which has always marked it out from the continent.

It is precisely because Britain is so un-European that her membership of Europe is more necessary than ever. The economic question has never really been the decisive one: the French revolt of 1968 has reminded everyone how misleading the bankers' view of Europe can be, and how suddenly a political upsurge can upset the economic applecart. Now that the first preoccupation with growth is beginning to spend itself, and the honeymoon with affluence is over, the predicament of Europe is not so different from what it was twenty years ago. Germany remains the main problem, and Britain remains the most effective counterweight; without that balance, it will be very difficult to build much on top. It may be, in the new uncertainty of Europe, that Britain may again have the chance to join the continent. It will be tragic if (underestimating her strength and stability) she takes fright again.

Index

476INDEX